D1085182

Women Entrepreneurs and the Global Environment for Growth

Women Entrepreneurs and the Global Environment for Growth

A Research Perspective

Edited by

Candida G. Brush

Babson College, USA

Anne de Bruin

Massey University, New Zealand

Elizabeth J. Gatewood

Wake Forest University, USA

and

Colette Henry

University of London, UK

Edward Elgar

Cheltenham, UK • Northampton, MA, USA

Published by
Edward Elgar Publishing Limited
The Lypiatts
15 Lansdown Road
Cheltenham
Glos GL50 2JA
UK

Edward Elgar Publishing, Inc.
William Pratt House
9 Dewey Court
Northampton
Massachusetts 01060
USA

A catalogue record for this book
is available from the British Library

Library of Congress Control Number: 2010922122

MIX
Paper from
responsible sources
FSC® C018575

ISBN 978 1 84720 914 6

Printed and bound by MPG Books Group, UK

Contents

PART II　GROWTH STRATEGIES AND ENABLERS

Contributors

Haya Al-Dajani, PhD, is Lecturer in Entrepreneurship and Small Business Management at the Norwich Business School, University of East Anglia, England, UK. Her research focuses on gender, entrepreneurship and empowerment with emphasis on women in the Middle East region, displaced and migrant women.

Gry Agnete Alsos, PhD, is Managing Director of Nordland Research Institute in Bodø, Norway. Her interests include entrepreneurial experience, habitual entrepreneurs, business start-up process, entrepreneurship policy and gender perspectives on entrepreneurship.

Yvonne Brunetto, PhD, is Associate Professor of Human Resource Management at Southern Cross University, Australia. Her research interests include entrepreneurial idea generation through network behaviour, public policy development and implementation, women's entrepreneurship and the retention of skilled older workers.

Candida G. Brush is Professor of Entrepreneurship, holder of the Paul T. Babson Chair in Entrepreneurship, and Chair of the Entrepreneurship Division at Babson College, USA. She is a Visiting Adjunct Professor to the Norwegian School of Engineering and Technology in Trondheim, Norway. Dr Brush is a founding member of the Diana Project International, and received the 2007 FSF NUTEK Award for Outstanding Contributions to Entrepreneurship Research. Her research investigates women's growth businesses and resource acquisition strategies in emerging ventures.

Michelle Budig, PhD, is an Associate Professor of Sociology at the University of Massachusetts-Amherst, USA. She has been awarded the 2009 World Bank-Luxembourg Income Study Gender Research Award and the 2003 Rosabeth Moss Kanter Research Award for Excellence in Family Research. Her research interests include gender, work, family policy, self-employment, and wage penalties for motherhood.

Sara Carter, PhD, is Professor of Entrepreneurship and Head of Department at the Hunter Centre for Entrepreneurship, University of Strathclyde Business School, Scotland, UK. Her research interests include entrepreneurial incomes, wealth and economic well-being, entrepreneurial households, rural and agricultural entrepreneurship and women entrepreneurs.

Marc Cowling, PhD, is Principal Economist at the Institute for Employment Studies and Visiting Professor at Exeter University Business School, England, UK. His research interests include the job generation process and potential of small businesses, the dynamics of productivity growth over time, and the financing of small business.

Anne de Bruin, PhD, is Professor of Economics in the School of Economics and Finance (Albany), Massey University, New Zealand. Her research interests include entrepreneurship in the creative industries, women entrepreneurs, new conceptualizations of entrepreneurship, franchising, social innovation, sustainable employment and regional development.

Rodney Farr-Wharton, PhD, is Senior Lecturer and Program Leader in Innovation and Entrepreneurship at the University of the Sunshine Coast, Australia. His research interests include the innovation behaviour of entrepreneurs, the behaviour of networks of entrepreneurs in the generation of ideas, sustainable development of micro-enterprises, women's entrepreneurship and the retention of skilled older workers as affected by management practice.

Elizabeth J. Gatewood, PhD, is the Director of the National Science Foundation Partners for Innovation Program at Wake Forest University, Winston-Salem, North Carolina, USA. She is a founding member of the Diana Project International and won the 2007 FSF Nutek Award for Outstanding Contributions to Entrepreneurship Research. Her research interests include the factors influencing the success of women entrepreneurs, entrepreneurial cognition, and entrepreneurial development in developing economies.

Mark D. Griffiths, PhD, is the Jack Anderson Professor of Finance at the Farmer School of Business at Miami University, USA. He has authored numerous journal articles and several books, and conducts research on issues related to transactional impediments to entrepreneurship as well as issues in the US and international money markets.

Lisa K. Gundry, PhD, is Professor of Management in the Kellstadt Graduate School of Business, and Director of the Center for Creativity and Innovation at DePaul University, USA. Her research interests include innovation processes in organizations, creativity and entrepreneurship, and entrepreneurial growth strategies.

Richard T. Harrison is Professor of Management and Director of the Queen's University Management School, Belfast, Northern Ireland, UK. His research interests include entrepreneurial finance, entrepreneurial learning and leadership, academic entrepreneurship and technology transfer, gender issues in entrepreneurship, entrepreneurship in emerging economies and the analysis of public policy interventions. He is also founding editor of *Venture Capital: An International Journal of Entrepreneurial Finance* (Routledge).

Colette Henry, PhD, is the Norbrook Professor of Business and Enterprise at The Royal Veterinary College, University of London, England, UK. Her research interests include entrepreneurship education and training, programme effectiveness, women's entrepreneurship, incubation and creative industries enterprise. She is also the founding editor of the *International Journal of Gender and Entrepreneurship.*

Frances M. Hill, PhD, is Director of the Executive MBA programme at the Queen's University Management School, Belfast, Northern Ireland, UK. Her research interests encompass various aspects of new venture creation and business growth including gender and access to business finance, gender and business growth, entrepreneurial networks and networking behaviours, social enterprise, organizational learning and qualitative research methodology.

Karen D. Hughes, PhD, is Professor in the Department of Strategic Management and Organization (School of Business) and the Department of Sociology (Faculty of Arts) at the University of Alberta, Canada. Her research examines women's role in entrepreneurship, non-traditional employment, and corporate governance. She is author of *Female Enterprise in the New Economy*.

Tatiana Iakovleva is an associate professor at the Social Science Faculty, Business Administration Department at Stavanger University, Norway. Her research interests include personal and organizational antecedents leading to innovation and superior entrepreneurial performance, female entrepreneurship, social entrepreneurship, as well as factors affecting entrepreneurial intentions.

P. Devereaux Jennings, PhD, is Professor of Strategy and Organization Theory at the University of Alberta's School of Business in Edmonton, Alberta, Canada. His research interests include institutional entrepreneurship, the use of narratives in new venture creation, and co-entrepreneurs in family businesses.

Jennifer E. Jennings, PhD, is an Associate Professor in the Department of Strategic Management and Organization at the University of Alberta School of Business, Canada. Her current research interests focus on the influence of gender, family, discourse and effects on entrepreneurial processes and outcomes.

Ragnhild Steen Jensen, PhD, is a senior researcher at the Institute for Social Research, Oslo, Norway. Her research interests include gender aspects of business ownership and family businesses, as well as employment and regional development.

Jill Kickul, PhD, is the Director of the Stuart Satter Program in Social Entrepreneurship in the Berkley Center for Entrepreneurship and Innovation at New York University Stern School of Business, USA. Her current research interests include innovation strategies for new and emerging business as well as the evaluation and measurement of the impact of social ventures.

Kim Klyver, PhD, is a Professor at the University of Southern Denmark, although this work was completed during his position as a postdoctoral scholar at Stanford University, USA in 2009. His main research interests include nascent entrepreneurship, growth, social networks, entrepreneurship policy and women's entrepreneurship.

Annu Kotiranta, PhD candidate, is an analyst at Ramboll Management Consulting. In her prior position she worked as a researcher at ETLA, the Research Institute of the Finnish Economy (Helsinki, Finland). Her research interests concentrate on globalization and innovation.

Anne Kovalainen, PhD, is the Minna Canth Academy Professor at the Academy of Finland and Professor at the School of Economics, University of Turku, Finland. Her research interests include gender, entrepreneurship, restructuration of welfare states, labour markets and careers, innovation, Science and Technology Studies (STS), sociological theory and methodology. She has published widely in books and leading academic journals.

Wing Lam, PhD, is a Senior Lecturer in Entrepreneurship and Course Leader for the Business Enterprise Programme at the University of Central Lancashire, England, UK. Her primary research interests focus on female entrepreneurship, family business, ethnic entrepreneurship and entrepreneurship education.

Joanne Leck, MBA, PhD is the Associate Dean, Research at the University of Ottawa Telfer School of Management, Canada. Her research interests include managing diversity, mentoring, employment equity and violence in the workplace. Current research also focuses on how mentorship programmes can be better designed to foster the advancement of women in the workplace.

Claire M. Leitch, DPhil, is a Senior Lecturer and Director of Education (Postgraduate and Executive Education) at the Queens' University Management School, Queen's University, Belfast, Northern Ireland, UK. Her research interests are in entrepreneurial leadership, entrepreneurial learning, women entrepreneurs, technology transfer and the role of research universities in the commercialization process and regional development.

Elisabet Ljunggren, PhD, is a senior researcher at Nordland Research Institute, Bodø, Norway. Her research interests include gender aspects of entrepreneurship, entrepreneurship within farming and rural entrepreneurship, the household dimensions of entrepreneurship, the industry experience and innovation and policies to enhance entrepreneurship and innovation.

Susan Marlow, PhD, is Professor of Entrepreneurship at De Montfort University, Leicester, England, UK and Co-editor of the *International Small Business Journal*. Her research interests include the influence of gender upon entrepreneurship, women and business incubation and managing labour in small firms.

Maura McAdam, PhD, is a Lecturer in Management at Queen's University Belfast, Northern Ireland, UK. Her research explores female entrepreneurship, high-technology based enterprises and support mechanisms such as incubators and science parks. She is particularly interested in the growth patterns of female-owned high-technology firms and the role of incubators in supporting growth. She has a broad practical foundation from her work in industry which she gained prior to entering academia.

Barbara Orser, MBA, PhD, is the Deloitte Professor in the Management of Growth Enterprises at the University of Ottawa Telfer School of Management, Canada. Her research interests include women entrepreneurs, examining the influences of gender on organizational performance, entrepreneurship and small business policy.

Miroslav Rebernik, PhD, is a Professor of Business Economics and Entrepreneurship, Head of the Department for Entrepreneurship and Business Economics, and Director of the Institute for Entrepreneurship and Small Business Management at the Faculty of Economics and Business, University of Maribor, Slovenia. His research interests include entrepreneurship policy, growth, women entrepreneurship, innovation and development. He is currently leading the Global Entrepreneurship Monitor for Slovenia.

Petri Rouvinen, PhD, is Research Director at ETLA, the Research Institute of the Finnish Economy (Helsinki, Finland). His research interests include entrepreneurship, globalization and innovation. He has contributed to volumes by Oxford University Press and Stanford University Press and has published in *Information Economics and Policy*, *Labour Economics* and *Telecommunications Policy*.

Eleanor Shaw, PhD is a Reader in Marketing at Strathclyde Business School, Scotland, UK. She is also Principal Investigator of an Economic and Social Research Council (ESRC) funded research project which is exploring contemporary entrepreneurial philanthropy. Her research interests include entrepreneurial capital, social entrepreneurship and women's entrepreneurship.

Karin Širec, PhD, is an Assistant Professor of Business Economics and Entrepreneurship in the Department for Entrepreneurship and Business Economics at the Faculty of Economics and Business, University of Maribor, Slovenia. Her research interests include general entrepreneurship, growth, women's entrepreneurship and entrepreneurship policy.

David Smallbone is Professor of Small Business and Entrepreneurship, and Associate Director of the Small Business Research Centre at Kingston University, England, UK. His research interests include entrepreneurship in transition and emerging market economies, rural enterprise, ethnic minority and immigrant entrepreneurship, entrepreneurship and small and medium-size enterprise (SME) policy and regional development.

Robert Strohmeyer, Dipl.-Soziologe, is Senior Research Fellow at the Institute for SME Research at the University of Mannheim, Germany. He was awarded the 2006 Academy of Management's Best Paper Award (Entrepreneurship Division). His research interests include women's entrepreneurship, ethnic entrepreneurship, corruption and entrepreneurship, biotechnology entrepreneurship, and evaluation of firms' publicly funded research and development (R&D) activities.

Siri Terjesen, PhD, is an assistant professor of Management and Entrepreneurship in the Kelley School of Business at Indiana University, USA. Her main research interests include international entrepreneurship, strategy and female entrepreneurship.

Polona Tominc, PhD, is a full-time Professor of Statistics and Quantitative Methods in Entrepreneurial Research in the Department of Quantitative

Economic Analysis at the Faculty of Economics and Business, University of Maribor, Slovenia. Her research is focused on statistical methods in economics, especially in the field of entrepreneurship and gender differences.

Vartuhí Tonoyan is Assistant Professor of Management at the Business School of the University of Mannheim and Head of the Entrepreneurship Division at Mannheim's Institute for SME Research, Germany. She is a visiting research fellow at the Graduate School of Business at Stanford University, USA. She has been awarded the 2006 Academy of Management's Best Paper Award (Entrepreneurship Division) as well as the Best Reviewer Award (International Management Division). Her research interests include corruption, business ethics, women's entrepreneurship, innovation, strategy and high-tech entrepreneurship.

Lorna Treanor is Research Manager at the Centre for Entrepreneurship Research at Dundalk Institute of Technology, Ireland. Her research interests include women's entrepreneurship, social entrepreneurship, incubation and entrepreneurship education and training.

Friederike Welter is Professor of Entrepreneurship at Jönköping International Business School (JIBS), Sweden and holds the TeliaSonera Professorship for Entrepreneurship at Stockholm of Economics in Riga. Her research interests include women's entrepreneurship and SME development, as well as entrepreneurship in different contexts, including public policies.

1. Introduction: women entrepreneurs and growth

Candida G. Brush, Anne de Bruin, Elizabeth J. Gatewood and Colette Henry

Women-owned businesses are one of the fastest growing entrepreneurial populations in the world. They make significant contributions to innovation, employment and wealth creation in all economies (Brush et al., 2006). Statistics from the Global Entrepreneurship Monitor (GEM) indicate that women entrepreneurs create and run businesses across all of the broad industrial sectors of extraction, transformation, business services and consumer-oriented products. Women in developed economies are more likely to start businesses out of opportunity motivation while those in less developed economies are motivated by necessity. Latin America and Asia have higher rates of entrepreneurial activity for women than Europe and the US. However, women entrepreneurs make significant contributions to economies in terms of jobs, innovations and gross national product (Allen et al., 2007).

Despite the growing importance of women entrepreneurs, they are understudied and the paucity of research on the phenomenon of women's entrepreneurship is well documented (Baker et al., 1997; de Bruin et al., 2006, 2007). Recent literature reviews suggest that studies about women entrepreneurs comprise less than 10 per cent of all research in the field. The result is that we know comparatively little about women entrepreneurs even though they contribute positively to gross national product (GNP), jobs, innovations and societal welfare globally. For the past 10 years, the Diana Project has worked to resolve this disparity.

THE DIANA PROJECT

Early research on women's entrepreneurship focused on factors influencing the start-up of ventures (Gatewood et al., 2003). Notably absent was an understanding of factors affecting growth. In 1999, Candida Brush, Nancy Carter, Elizabeth Gatewood, Patricia Greene and Myra Hart launched the Diana Project to study the phenomenon of women's entre-preneurship in the United States. Historically, women-led ventures were smaller than those led by men, whether measured by size of revenues gen-erated or the number of people employed. The overarching question was, 'Why do women-owned businesses remain smaller than those of their male counterparts?' A multi-method research effort was undertaken to examine supply of and demand for growth capital relative to women entrepreneurs. United States research showed that women entrepreneurs seldom acquired sufficient funds to grow their businesses aggressively and to reach their full potential. This raised a new question, 'Do women face unique challenges in acquiring growth capital?'

While the collective research documents the demand by women entre-preneurs for equity capital, there was and still is a mismatch between the women, their ventures and sources of growth funding (Brush, et al., 2001b, 2004b). The Diana Project findings prompted great interest amongst the media, policy-makers, practitioners and educators wanting to learn more about ways to increase women entrepreneurs' receipt of growth capital by providing a better infrastructure of programmes and curricula for women who wished to grow larger businesses (see, for example: Hart, 2003; Henry, 2002; Hoover, 2002; Montandon, 2002). All these audiences shared the objective of facilitating the growth of new businesses that could produce innovation and wealth for the benefit of individual entrepreneurs, their families and ultimately their communities.

Simultaneous to the Diana Project research, interest in women entrepre-neurs and growth of their ventures was rising in most countries around the world. To capture and leverage that interest, the Diana Project team, in partnership with ESBRI (Entrepreneurship and Small Business Research Institute, Sweden), convened an international gathering of scholars in 2003 to develop a shared research agenda. The goal was to exchange ideas and learn from each other about the current state of research on creation and support for new women-led businesses, and particularly, support and development of growth-oriented businesses. The purpose of creating the Diana International collaborative was twofold:

- To provide a platform from which to develop, conduct and share a global research agenda.
- To create an international community of scholars dedicated to answering the questions about women entrepreneurs and growth-oriented businesses.

The product of the first Diana International Conference in 2003 was a report discussing the importance of growth-oriented women-led businesses and summarizing the state of knowledge about these businesses in the initial countries involved. This report was released in spring of 2005 and provided a summary of the presentations about the state of women's entrepreneurship by country. For the second conference in 2004, participants presented working papers. Following the event, papers were peer reviewed, revised and finally submitted for consideration for an edited volume entitled *Growth-Oriented Women Entrepreneurs and their Businesses* (Brush et al., 2006). The book is the product of the second Diana International Conference which represents the hard work and dedication of an expanded community of scholars passionate about understanding the growth of women's entrepreneurship.

Since 2004, research conferences were held in Stockholm (2005, 2006), Madrid (2007), and Belfast (2008). The Belfast conference was attended by more than 100 international scholars. Several special issues of journals have published refereed work specifically on the topic of women's entrepreneurship, notably: *Entrepreneurship Theory and Practice* (2 volumes), *Venture Capital Journal, Entrepreneurship and Regional Development*, the *Journal of Enterprising Culture, International Journal of Entrepreneurial Behaviour and Research* and *International Small Business Journal*. In addition, a new journal, the *International Journal of Gender and Entrepreneurship* was launched in 2008 and has published its first volume. In 2007 the founders of the Diana Project were awarded the prestigious Global Award for Entrepreneurship Research sponsored by the Swedish Entrepreneurship Forum, the Swedish Agency for Economic and Regional Growth and the Research Institute of Industrial Economics. Collectively, these efforts demonstrate significant progress in building a global research agenda and a growing community of scholars that can address the deficit in our knowledge of women entrepreneurs.

A FRAMEWORK FOR GROWTH

Growth-Oriented Women Entrepreneurs and their Businesses (Brush et al., 2006) introduced a framework to examine the factors influencing the growth of individual women-led businesses. This framework discussed four main constructs: the individual, venture concept, firm resources and institutional financial resources. Additionally, the framework showed that the potential for growth was influenced by both the business sector and the country context.

In this second volume, for continuity and consistency, we utilize these same framework elements but modify its portrayal to highlight that the individual is nested within the family. Figure 1.1 thus shows the individual

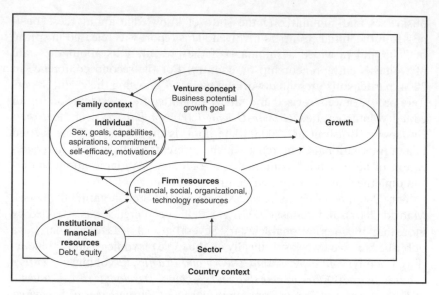

Source: Adapted from Brush et al. (2004a).

Figure 1.1 Research framework for women and growth businesses

enveloped within an outer circle of the family. Our interpretation of the framework also differs since we place greater emphasis on the need for contextualizing women's entrepreneurship at various levels including family and other institutional contexts.

The foundation for any new venture is the *individual* and the initial package of capabilities and resources that the entrepreneur and her team bring to the table. Not only does the entrepreneur's level of formal education and on-the-job experience and training have a positive relation to success, but so does women's self-assessment of having adequate skills and knowledge (Langowitz and Minniti, 2007). Male and female entrepreneurs also tend to differ in their aspirations and strategic choices, with some women intentionally preferring to keep their businesses smaller (Cliff, 1998; Orser and Hogarth-Scott, 2002). Other individual-level factors such as personal traits and the motivation for starting the business can vary widely (Buttner and Moore, 1997). While the entrepreneur's human capital, characteristics, motivations and aspirations form the base for the venture, entrepreneurs are not atomistic actors. They are embedded within their household and *family context* which usually has a larger impact on women than men in the entrepreneurial process (Brush et al., 2009).

The *venture concept* is what the business does or the product or service it provides (Bhide, 2000). It starts from an idea, innovation or a problem and is transformed into a concept which forms the basis of the organization. Breakthrough ideas, a solution to an important problem, or the creation of a product with low substitutes which will cater to a large market instead of a low-value niche, will spawn organizations with a high growth potential. Such business concepts are also likely to have a higher probability of attracting external funding for growth (Timmons and Bygrave, 1997).

Firm resources are used to convert the concept into reality and take the goods and services to market (Penrose, 1954). Resources fall into several categories: social, financial, organizational, physical and technical (Brush et al., 2001a). Social capital is a form of non-economic knowledge and emerges from norms, relationships and social structures in an individual's life (Coleman, 1988). This includes the network of contacts and reputation, as well as the skills and expertise that help entrepreneurs and their teams acquire the resources of the emerging organization (Aldrich, 1999). Other resources include organizational resources which are those relationships, structures, routines and information of the new venture (Dollinger, 1995). Physical resources include tangible and intangible assets needed for the operations of the business (Dollinger, 1995). These also may include technology and equipment as well as materials and other physical assets of the business. Financial resources are the cash and money assets of the business (Bygrave, 1992). Often personal savings of the entrepreneur and team are the first financial resources available to the firm.

The *business sector* or industry in which the venture operates also has implications for growth (Carter et al., 1997). Women are concentrated in sectors such as retailing, personal care services, catering and restaurants, which are characterized by ease of entry and low start-up financial capital. These sectors are intensely competitive and overcrowded and this limits growth potential (Brush et al., 2004a; Marlow et al., 2008).

Institutional financial resources comprise external funding sources outside the venture. The availability of and access to external financial capital from private sector financial institutions and equity providers, including venture capitalists and angels, is usually a prerequisite for business growth. There continues to be differences in external funding patterns between male and female-owned businesses (Brush et al., 2001b; Greene et al., 1999; Haines et al., 1999). In contrast to the earlier discussion, we seek here to explore some explanations for these differences, by highlighting how in Figure 1.1 this element intersects both the sector and the country context. With regard to the former, studies suggest that structural factors including sector-related factors can account for sex differences in external funding (for example, Haines et al., 1999). Other studies, however, suggest there is an unexplained gender residual (for example, Verheul and

Thurik, 2000). Consideration of other institutional factors, as indicated by the intersection with country context in Figure 1.1, may thus provide fertile ground for investigation. For us it also serves to emphasize that country contexts could explain how the role of women is socially constructed. Gender stereotyping also prevails and could impact powerfully in the entrepreneurship arena where in many countries entrepreneurs are perceived to have predominantly masculine characteristics (Gupta et al., 2009). As Carter et al. (2007: 440) point out in relation to external funding of ventures by banks, 'gender remains an important but often hidden variable'.

Our framework provides the basis for dividing the chapters into two broad sections. Part I comprises chapters that highlight how contextual factors, and especially the social and family embeddedness of entrepreneurs, have a differential impact on men and women. Chapters in Part II examine strategies, constraints and enablers of growth and performance, considering a wide variety of topics, including self-efficacy, mentors, networks, socio-political and technology sector factors.

CONTEXTUAL FACTORS

This section opens with a chapter that seeks in depth understanding of differences in gender entrepreneurship rates and job creation and the reasons for these differences. Using European Union (EU) survey data on wages and self-employment, Marc Cowling (Chapter 2) considers several questions related to the likelihood of women becoming entrepreneurs and creating jobs as compared to men, across different countries in Europe. He finds that gender differences in both cases were large, with men being significantly more likely to choose self-employment over waged employment and to be job creating self-employed. However, econometric investigation shows that the basic reason for the observed difference in self-employment rates between men and women were easily explained by differences in the nature of jobs they enter and the sectors they work in. Further investigation of the data shows that childcare and eldercare responsibilities actually increase the probability that women will choose self-employment and create jobs in self-employment. The chapter concludes with implications for policy.

Gry Alsos, Ragnhild Steen Jensen and Elisabet Ljunggren (Chapter 3) discuss the possible cultural, historical, social and economic reasons for what they termed 'the women entrepreneurship paradox'. Despite Norway pioneering gender equality, providing childcare and other social services, and a high rate of women in the labour force, the share of women entrepreneurs remains relatively low. According to the authors, the gendered construction of entrepreneurship is rooted in historical paths and reinforced through contemporary practices, such as the gendered division of labour, the tendency for women to work part-time and family-friendly policies strengthening the connotation of family and domestic tasks as female. These practices influence the likelihood of women becoming entrepreneurs and business owners. Interestingly, the authors argue that entrepreneurship is an important part of the capitalistic system, and capitalism is fundamentally gendered.

Annu Kotiranta, Anne Kovalainen and Petri Rouvinen (Chapter 4) identify the same 'paradox' in Finland. Despite labour force participation, political activity and gender-specific legislation, women's participation in the highest level of management and decision-making in Finland is very low. They contend that encouraging greater women's participation at this level is important for economic and competitive reasons. The authors examine the positive and significant correlation between female leadership and company profitability to posit possible reasons for this correlation. Their findings are consistent with the explanation that women go through a tougher 'screening' process and, therefore, the average leadership abilities of women in top management may be better than those of their male counterparts. They offer a possible explanation: that female leadership may be tied to the culture of organizations where advancement and appointments in these organizations are based on competence and merits rather than traditions and established conventions. Although not able to prove causality for their results, they suggest that a company may gain competitive advantage by identifying and eliminating the obstacles to women's advancement to top management.

The chapter by Lorna Treanor and Colette Henry (Chapter 5) compares influences on women's entrepreneurship in the Republic of Ireland and the Czech Republic. The study compares and contrasts the experiences, motivations, characteristics and influences on Irish and Czech women entrepreneurs in relation to business start-up and growth. The data were drawn from one sample in each country, of participants in a European Community Initiative under the EQUAL programme – the 'Supporting Unusual Entry Entrepreneurs' project, which sought to enhance social inclusion through entrepreneurship by providing supports to aspiring entrepreneurs in under-represented groups, in this case, women. Grounded in the literature on gender and entrepreneurship, the authors employ a highly qualitative methodology to explore how typical or atypical these women entrepreneurs are in comparison to the currently held female entrepreneurial 'norm' depicted in the literature. Key similarities were identified with respect to the women's business and personal profiles and the sectors in which they operated (mainly services, particularly retail). Major differences related to business growth and size. Their findings lend support to recent literature from institutional theory and suggest a number of interesting future research directions.

Friederike Welter and David Smallbone (Chapter 6) focus on the transition economies of Belarus, Moldova, Ukraine and Uzbekistan. They apply an institutional theory perspective to women's entrepreneurship in these countries and explore different levels of embeddedness and the impact of change. During Soviet times, women experienced different institutional 'realities', and these had significant implications for their opportunities to engage in entrepreneurial activities once transition started. The chapter conceptualizes the different layers of institutional embeddedness with respect to women's entrepreneurship, and links this to Soviet and post-Soviet experiences. Despite the contradictory attitudes of post-Soviet societies towards working women, the transition has contributed to the emergence of women entrepreneurs in the former Soviet Republics. Women's entrepreneurship plays an important role in modernizing these societies and in contributing to changing public attitudes towards women. The evidence presented by the authors demonstrates the contribution of women entrepreneurs to social change and to alleviating some of the negative effects of transformation through offering job possibilities for other women (as well as men) and providing positive role models.

Home-based producers in Jordan are the focus of the study by Haya Al-Dajani and Sara Carter (Chapter 7). The chapter identifies the processes through which women entrepreneurs empower home-based women producers and considers best practices for women's empowerment. The authors argue that an increase in popularity of home-based production among women in the Middle East will lead to increased economic significance beyond the informal work sector. Consequently, the direct effects on women's empowerment need to be addressed by researchers and policy-makers, especially in light of the gender segregated market phenomenon that has recently materialized within the region. The experiences discussed in this chapter illustrate the ways in which women-owned small and medium-sized enterprises (SMEs) contribute to the empowerment of home-based producers. By providing the home-based producers with market access, higher financial rewards and benefits than those provided in other sectors, as well as role models, independence and mobility beyond the local community, women entrepreneurs display a stronger understanding of home-based production than non-profit organizations, aid agencies and local policy-makers in the Middle East. The results from this particular study suggest that occupational gender segregation may, inadvertently, offer a potential route to women's empowerment.

The final chapter in this section highlights that both the family embeddedness of women and the particular institutional country context have an influence on the pathways of women entrepreneurs. Vartuhí Tonoyan, Michelle Budig and Robert Strohmeyer (Chapter 8) examine the impact of family structure (motherhood and partner's occupational status) and family policies (such as publicly funded childcare, maternity leave length) on entry into professional and non-professional entrepreneurship in the US and Europe. They test a series of hypotheses across 23 countries using data from the European Labor Force Survey and the National Longitudinal Survey of Youth for American data. Results show significant heterogeneity in women's self-employment. In contrast to motherhood, which is only a predictor for women's entry into non-professional self-employment, spousal self-employment is strongly positively associated with both professional and non-professional self-employment. Their findings suggest that institutional variations between welfare states are responsible for cross-country variations of the occupational status of women's self-employment. This study has many implications for policy and future research.

GROWTH STRATEGIES AND ENABLERS

Prompted by the need for new approaches to explain why women-led businesses 'underperform' relative to businesses led by men, Jennifer Jennings, Karen Hughes and Devereaux Jennings (Chapter 9) adopt a family embeddedness perspective by examining claims that there are significant differences in how female and male entrepreneurs manage the work–family interface (WFI). They build on the theoretical work of Jennings and McDougald (2007) and utilize survey data from 163 businesses in Alberta, Canada, to provide one of the first empirical examinations of the WFI strategies used by male and female business owners. Their analysis focuses on growth-constraining and growth-facilitating WFI strategies at both the individual and couple level. Contrary to expectations, they observe very few gender differences overall. Testing for gender differences within the three distinct industry sectors in which their sample firms operated – manufacturing; retail, wholesale and general services; and professional services – revealed that while there was little gender difference in the manufacturing sector, far more gender differences were evident in the other two sectors, and the pattern of differences was not identical. These findings highlight the importance of considering context more explicitly within women's entrepreneurship theory and research.

The chapter by Eleanor Shaw, Sara Carter and Wing Lam (Chapter

10) recognizes that the financing of entrepreneurial ventures is a complex process influenced by a range of economic, personal and societal factors. Using data from 30 matched pairs of male- and female-owned businesses in Scotland, they adopt an entrepreneurial capital perspective to explore the interplay between gender, finance and business ownership. Findings show the impact of non-financial capital on women entrepreneurs' possession of and access to finance. Their discussion contributes to the discourse on the gender, business ownership and finance nexus in a number of ways. First, the theoretical and methodological framework developed reveals the subtle, complex relationship between gender and entrepreneurial capital. Secondly, the chapter provides women business owners with deeper insights into the sources of some of the challenges they could face when financing their ventures, and may help women understand their own role in enacting these challenges. Thirdly, the insight into the interrelationship and implications between social structure and entrepreneurship could usefully be considered when developing policy directed to encourage more women into business ownership.

Frances Hill, Claire Leitch and Richard Harrison (Chapter 11) examine a small sample of high-technology businesses in Northern Ireland, focusing on a number of issues related to business growth. The matched samples of men and women business owners/managers were selected on the basis of firm characteristics (high-technology, business to business, less than 15 years old) and personal characteristics relating to human and social capital. The authors reported more similarities than differences among the women and men in the sample, confirming past findings. However, the authors found a few noteworthy differences. In general men and women had the same growth aspirations but women were less confident about exporting, which could limit future growth. Women and men were active networkers, however, women reported fewer benefits from networking and were less likely to belong to informal networks. One finding, which contradicts past research, is that men had greater reservations about seeking external funding than women. Although women showed a greater propensity to fund growth from external sources, women were unhappy with the amount of funding they received.

Kim Klyver and Siri Terjesen (Chapter 12) use data from entrepreneurs in Denmark to explore gender differences in the composition of social networks at four distinct phases of the new venture process. Consistent with prior research, they find that when compared with male entrepreneurs, female entrepreneurs have significantly lower proportions of males in their social networks. However, females' proportion of males in their networks increases in later venture development stages, suggesting that female entrepreneurs, who are able to persist in the new venture process, end up developing networks similar to those of their male counterparts. They find that female entrepreneurs report larger networks than their male counterparts, however, there are no gender differences in terms of density or composition with respect to the proportion of business, family or emotional support relations.

Rodney Farr-Wharton and Yvonne Brunetto (Chapter 13) focus on the importance of internal employee networks within the SME sector. They examine data on how 58 female and 64 male entrepreneurs located in Australia search for new business opportunities. In particular, using a learning organization lens, their findings provide reinforcing evidence that a majority of entrepreneurs do not actively seek new business opportunities from their interactions with employees. A networking and social capital lens is also used to provide interesting insights. They find evidence that the quality of social capital is far more important for female entrepreneurs compared with male entrepreneurs in embedding relationship-based management. Female entrepreneurs were more likely to use a relational management approach, which means that they were fostering the development of social capital and reciprocity of positive behaviour such as information sharing, resources and respect. Such behaviour becomes evident in the socializing processes in meetings and conversations that some of the female entrepreneurs promoted. These appeared to generate ideal conditions for learning about and acknowledging new business opportunities from internal employee networks.

Maura McAdam and Susan Marlow (Chapter 14) explore the incubator environment as a resource for women entrepreneurs using a case study of a woman entrepreneur with a business operating in the Science, Engineering and Technology (SET) sector. Although the number of women SET graduates has increased dramatically in Ireland, evidence exists that they are vertically integrated in lower positions and exit SET careers early. Entrepreneurial careers would appear to be a strategy for SET women to deal with the negative impacts of occupational segregation, however, women remain under-represented as business owners. The authors found that the business incubator model is appropriate for providing infrastructure, business and professional support, networks, and credibility to SET women entrepreneurs. However, the authors also found that the incubator culture remains highly gendered. They call for incubators to have greater recognition and value for women's operating preferences.

The chapter by Barbara Orser and Joanne Leck (Chapter 15) examines the evolution of a 'for women and by women' public health care centre in Canada, to discuss the gendered nature of the venture creation process. Specifically, they seek to understand the ways in which gender is embedded in opportunity recognition, resource acquisition and organizational form. Building on entrepreneurship and feminist theory, they present a gender-based typology of new venture organizations and the construct of 'feminist entrepreneur'. Feminist entrepreneurs are defined as change agents who seek to improve women's quality of life and well-being through innovative services, products and processes. The motives of these entrepreneurs are explicitly, although not exclusively, focused on enhancing women's life conditions. Orser and Leck use participant-observation and content analysis to document how gender is enacted in an entrepreneurial health care venture. Their study also provides insights on the 'silencing' of women's entrepreneurship in the sector. Observations call for executive leadership and tools to institutionalize integrated health care. Implications for health care and entrepreneurship research are considered.

While a plethora of studies has been carried out to explain the success of women-owned SMEs in advanced countries, research on entrepreneurship in transition economies is less developed. Jill Kickul, Mark Griffiths, Lisa Gundry and Tatiana Iakovleva (Chapter 16) add new theoretical and empirical insights to factors influencing the success of small firms owned and operated by women in the Russian transition economy. They consider the role of mentoring and self-efficacy on the performance of women-led firms. The sample on which the study is based comprised 555 Russian women entrepreneurs, and the results indicate that mentoring is an important developmental relationship that facilitates self-efficacy and influences the sustainability of firm performance. By understanding how mentors and role models support women in these tenuous environments, we are better able to create the support systems to nurture and support women's entrepreneurial efforts. Implications for women entrepreneurs in emerging and transitioning economies are presented.

The chapter on Slovenian entrepreneurs authored by Karin Širec, Polona Tominc and Miroslav Rebernik (Chapter 17) deals with the perceived differences in growth aspirations among female and male entrepreneurs. As the authors explain, although not all entrepreneurs' expectations materialize, growth aspirations have been shown to be a good predictor of eventual growth, and technology orientation may also play a part. Their findings reveal that current growth potential among entrepreneurs in Slovenia differs according to gender. In addition, a significant positive relationship between the intensity of applied new technologies and growth aspirations among Slovenian SMEs is confirmed. There are particular gender differences in growth aspirations. Males aspire to increase sales revenue, whereas women aspire to grow their company assets. However, neither men nor women aspire to promote employment growth. Increasing our understanding of these aspects of growth can help strengthen the empirical micro-level basis of theories of entrepreneurship and innovation.

ADVANCING THE GLOBAL RESEARCH AGENDA

During the decade since the launch of the Diana Project in 1999, women's entrepreneurship research and understanding of factors affecting the growth of women-owned business have advanced significantly. There is also heightened awareness that 'the landscape of women's entrepreneurship is gendered terrain' (Brush et al., 2009: 18). The contributions in this volume aptly demonstrate that a well-focused gender lens is necessary to delve further into explaining the phenomenon of women's entrepreneurship.

Many of the chapters in this volume have heeded the suggestion of de Bruin et al. (2007: 323) that 'a separate theory on women's entrepreneurship may not be required. Rather, existing theoretical concepts should be expanded to incorporate explanations for the distinctiveness of women's entrepreneurship, and current theoretical approaches, which are normally used in trying to explain women's entrepreneurship, should be broadened'. For instance an institutional analysis is used in the chapters by Tonoyan et al. and Welter and Smallbone. The latter chapter also explores variants of the embeddedness notion that institutional theory acknowledges and suggests the concept of mixed embeddedness as a potentially useful overarching conceptual framework for analysing women's entrepreneurship in transition conditions. Other examples, among several, of building on existing theoretical explanations are the chapter by Jennings et al., which builds on the family embeddedness approach in entrepreneurship research, and Orser and Leck, who utilize entrepreneurship and feminist theory to advance the construct of 'feminist entrepreneur'.

Moving forward, we believe it is important to build a holistic community whereby research about women's entrepreneurship not only continues to explore and develop theory but also examines questions and disseminates findings so as to inform policy and practice. In other words, the virtuous cycle of research should feed into policies and practice which should inform teaching and educational approaches. An exciting example is the Women's International Centre for Economic Development (WICED) located in Liverpool, UK. This organization focuses on helping women to start and grow their own businesses, and creating the conditions and infrastructure that will help achieve this. This world-leading concept now taking shape in Liverpool will, both through the physical form and intellectually, provide a beacon by which to raise all our aspirations for women's economic development. By bringing together the elements of research, gendered business incubation and high-quality business support, WICED hopes to achieve the aim of more women's businesses, creating more wealth and prosperity. The Diana International Project and all the scholars contributing to this volume are providing research that provides a foundation for expanding the work and vision of WICED.

It is our hope that this second volume contributes to existing knowledge about women's entrepreneurship and growth, raises new questions and inspires more research especially about women in emerging and less developed economies.

REFERENCES

Aldrich, H. (1999), *Organizations Evolving*, Thousand Oaks, CA: Sage Publications.
Allen, E., Elam, E., Langowitz, N. and Dean, M. (2007), *The GEM Women's Report.* Wellesley, MA: Babson College, Center for Women's Leadership.
Baker, T., Aldrich, H. and Liou, N. (1997), 'Invisible entrepreneurs: the neglect of women business owners by mass media and scholarly journals in the USA', *Entrepreneurship and Regional Development*, **9** (2), 221–38.
Bhide, A. (2000), *The Origin and Evolution of New Businesses*, New York: Oxford University Press.
Brush, C., Carter, N.M., Gatewood, E.J., Greene, P.G. and Hart, M.M. (2006), 'Introduction: the Diana Project International', in C. Brush, N.M. Carter, E.J. Gatewood, P.G. Greene and M.M. Hart, *Growth-Oriented Women Entrepreneurs and their Businesses*, Cheltenham, UK and Northampton, MA, USA: Edward Elgar.
Brush, C., Carter, N., Gatewood, E., Greene, P. and Hart. M. (2004a), *Clearing the Hurdles: Women Building High-Growth Businesses*, Upper Saddle River, NJ: Financial Times Prentice Hall Books.
Brush, C., Carter, N., Gatewood, E., Greene, P. & Hart, M. (2004b), *The Diana Project. Gatekeepers of Venture Growth: The Role and Participation of Women in the Venture Capital Industry*, Report 2, Kansas City, MO: Ewing Marion Kauffman Foundation.
Brush, C., Carter, N., Greene, P., Gatewood, E. and Hart, M. (2001b), 'An investigation of women-led firms and venture capital investment', report prepared for the U.S. Small Business Administration Office of Advocacy and the National Women's Business Council.
Brush, C., de Bruin, A. and Welter, F. (2009), 'A gender-aware framework for women's entrepreneurship', *International Journal of Gender and Entrepreneurship*, **1**, 8–24.
Brush, C.G., Greene, P.G. and Hart, M.M. (2001a), 'From initial idea to unique advantage: the entrepreneurial challenge of constructing a resource base', *Academy of Management Executive*, **15** (1), 64–80.
Buttner, E.H. and Moore, D.P. (1997), 'Women's organizational exodus to entrepreneurship: self-reported motivations and correlates with success', *Journal of Small Business Management*, **35** (1), 34–46.
Bygrave, W.D. (1992), 'Venture capital returns in the 1980s', in D.L. Sexton and J. Kasarda (eds), *The State of the Art of Entrepreneurship*, Boston, MA: PWS Kent.

Carter, N.M., Williams, M. and Reynolds, P.D. (1997), 'Discontinuance among new firms in retail: the influence of initial resources, strategy, and gender', *Journal of Business Venturing*, **12**, 125–45.

Carter, S., Shaw, E., Wilson, F. and Lam, W. (2007), 'Gender, entrepreneurship and bank lending', *Entrepreneurship Theory and Practice*, **31**(3), 427–44.

Cliff, J.E. (1998), 'Does one size fit all? Exploring the relationship between attitudes between growth, gender and business size', *Journal of Business Venturing*, **13** (6), 523–42.

Coleman, J. (1988), 'Social capital in the creation of human capital', *American Journal of Sociology*, **94**, S95–S120.

De Bruin, A., Brush, C. and Welter, F. (2007), 'Advancing a framework for coherent research on women's entrepreneurship', *Entrepreneurship Theory and Practice*, **31** (3), 323–39.

De Bruin, A., Brush, C. and Welter, F. (2006), 'Introduction to the special issue: towards building cumulative knowledge on women's entrepreneurship', *Entrepreneurship Theory and Practice*, **30** (5), 585–94.

Dollinger, M. (1995), *Entrepreneurship: Strategies and Resources*, Boston, MA: Irwin.

Gatewood, E.G., Carter, N.M., Brush, C.G., Greene, P.G. and Hart, M.M. (2003), *Women Entrepreneurs, their Ventures, and the Venture Capital Industry: An Annotated Bibliography*, Stockholm: ESBRI.

Greene, P., Brush, C., Hart, M. and Saparito, P. (1999), 'An exploration of the venture capital industry: is gender an issue?', in P.D. Reynolds, W. Bygrave, S. Manigart, C. Mason, G.D. Meyer, H. Sapienza and K.G. Shaver (eds), *Frontiers of Entrepreneurship Research*, Wellesley, MA: Babson College.

Gupta, V.K., Turban, D.B., Wasti, S.A. and Sikdar, A. (2009), 'The role of gender stereotypes in perceptions of entrepreneurs and intentions to become an entrepreneur', *Entrepreneurship Theory and Practice*, **33** (2), 397–417.

Haines, G.H., Orser, B.J. and Riding, A.L. (1999), 'Myths and realities: an empirical study of banks and the gender of small business clients', *Canadian Journal of Administrative Sciences*, **16** (4), 291–307.

Hart, D. (ed.) (2003), *The Emergence of Entrepreneurship Policy: Governance Start-ups and Growth in the U.S. Knowledge Economy*, Cambridge: Cambridge University Press.

Henry, S. (2002), 'Women Fighting for Venture Capital Study: Study Cites Entrepreneur Networks', *Washington Post*, 13 February, p. E05.

Hoover, K. (2002), 'Women entrepreneurs push for greater access to venture capital', *Washington D.C. Business Journal*, 22 February.

Jennings, J.E. and McDougald, M.S. (2007), 'Work–family interface experiences and strategies: consequences for entrepreneurship research and practice', *Academy of Management Review*, **32**, 747–60.

Langowitz, N. and Minniti, M. (2007) 'The entrepreneurial propensity of women', *Entrepreneurship Theory and Practice*, **31** (3), 341–64.

Marlow, S., Carter, S. and Shaw, E. (2008), 'Constructing female entrepreneurship policy in the UK: is the US a relevant benchmark?', *Environment and Planning C: Government and Policy*, **26** (2), 335–51.

Montandon, M. (2002), 'The ol' gal money hunt', *Fortune Small Business*, available at: http://www.fortune.com/indexw.jhtml?channel=artcol.jhtml&doc_id=207032 (accessed April 2002).

Orser, B. and Hogarth-Scott, S. (2002), 'Opting for growth: gender dimensions of choosing enterprise development', *Canadian Journal of Administrative Sciences*, **19** (3), 284–300.

Penrose, E. (1954), *Theory of Growth of the Firm*, New York: John Wiley.

Timmons, J. and Bygrave, W. (1997), 'Venture capital: reflections and projections', in D.L. Sexton and R. Smilor (eds), *Entrepreneurship 2000*, Chicago, IL: Upstart, pp. 29–46.

Verheul, I. and Thurik, R. (2000), *Start-up Capital: Differences between Male and Female Entrepreneurs. Does Gender Matter?* EIM Research Report 9910/E, Rotterdam: Erasmus University.

PART I

Contextual Factors

2. Entrepreneurship, gender and job creation: European dynamics

Marc Cowling

INTRODUCTION

Since the seminal Birch (1979) job generation study researchers have become interested in quantifying the numbers of jobs created by smaller firms and the nature of entrepreneurs who create these jobs. Early empirical papers focused explicitly on relative shares of net new jobs (see, for example, Davidsson et al. 1998; Davis et al., 1996), while others (Westhead and Cowling, 1995) focused on the relative impact of new technology-based versus more conventional small firms. A related strand of research focused explicitly on identifying the characteristics that differentiated job-creating entrepreneurs from lifestyle-oriented businesses (Burke et al., 2001; Carroll et al., 1996; Cowling et al., 2004).

Researchers have also become increasingly interested in two potentially related issues, that of gender differences in the propensity to become an entrepreneur (Brush, 1999; de Bruin et al., 2007), and potential gender impacts on business performance (see Kalleberg and Leicht, 1991, for an early seminal work). On the former the evidence is fairly consistent across countries and time, and broadly finds that males have a higher basic propensity to start their own business. Yet even this has been shown not to hold across all countries (Cowling, 2000, 2003), with Finland identified as a notable exception.

Marlow et al. (2008) also point out the important influences of history and culture in determining the relative prevalence of female entrepreneurship across countries. Yet Cowling and Bygrave (2007) find that differences in institutional arrangements and welfare systems have little impact on necessity (or pushed) entrepreneurship rates across countries. However, as the broader body of cross-country and even inter-regional work highlights substantive differences between male and female self-employment, it is an area that merits consideration.

On the role and breadth of human capital relevant to entrepreneurship, Lazear (2005) finds strong evidence to suggest that entrepreneurs differ from specialists (employees) in that they have a comparative disadvantage in a single skill but have more balanced talents that span a number of different skills. Colombo et al. (2004), using Italian data, find that informal, industry-specific human capital is a far more important determinant of start-up size than formal human capital or general work experience. Thus, we might expect that different allocations of human capital, and the nature of it, may be important in explaining gender differences in entrepreneurship.

Research examining performance outcomes of women entrepreneurs shows significant differences between men and women. Empirical evidence on female underperformance is provided by Brush (1992), Cowling and Taylor (2001), Watson and Robinson (2003) and Rosa et al. (1996). Du Rietz and Henrekson (2000) find evidence to the contrary. So what does previous research tell us about observed differences between male and female entrepreneurs and the reasons for any observed female underperformance? Early work tended to focus on discrimination. Coates and Tennyson (1992), for example, argued that general labour market discrimination can spill over into markets relevant to entrepreneurs. Others (Moore, 1983; Sowell, 1981) argue that this labour market discrimination in the formal waged sector is precisely why females move into entrepreneurship. If discrimination is part of the explanation for gender differences in entrepreneurship, at both a quantity and quality level, we might expect that this would manifest itself in a time dimension (perhaps less discrimination now than historically) and at a cross-country level (some countries may be inherently more discriminatory than others for historical and/or cultural reasons).

Research has also focused explicitly on the effect of family roles and time allocation between home and market production (Dolton and Makepeace, 1987), and argued that women with childcare responsibilities actively seek out employment that complements these roles. This is supported by Georgellis and Wall (2005) who argued that women and men have different strategies and desires for non-standard work and that self-employment can reduce the costs of childcare. Jennings and McDougald (2007) find that work–family interface experiences can explain much of the persistence in underperformance by male- and female-run businesses. Finally, Parker (2008) explores a relatively new avenue of investigation by considering how household relationships impact on the propensity of women to run their own businesses. Using US data, he finds that knowledge transfer between husbands and wives increases the probability that the spouse will also become an entrepreneur. Thus it is important for us to explore how family make-up and responsibilities, as well as informal learning and support, shape the entrepreneurial decision for women.

On the entrepreneurial propensity of women there is a strong body of work rooted in psychology that adds to our understanding. For example,

Langowitz and Minniti (2007) argue that subjective perceptual variables have a crucial influence on women, as they perceive themselves and the environment in a less favourable light. This is supported by Wagner (2007), who shows that fear of failure deters women from pursuing an entrepreneurial career. In contrast, Verheul et al. (2006), find that, for the most part, female and male entrepreneurs are influenced by the same factors. Morris et al. (2006) contend that the growth choice for female entrepreneurs is a much more serious and deliberate decision and is associated with women who value wealth more highly. Watson and Robinson (2003) argue that lower growth among female businesses reflects an unwillingness to tolerate high risk in the form of income and profit variability. Georgellis and Wall (2005) also find that money is a greater motivation for male entrepreneurs. Other researchers, notably Gatewood et al. (2009) and Manolova et al. (2007), have explored the role of informal networks in this context and found that the growth decision for women is supported by formal and informal networks that give them access to financial capital and, further, that for women growth is dependent upon prior experience of self rather than advice from peers in one's networks.

Thus the evidence broadly shows that entrepreneurs are important agents in the process of job creation and that there are many potential explanations for women to be less likely to (a) enter entrepreneurial activity and (b) underperform relative to men. In the remainder of this chapter we econometrically explore six questions:

1. Are men more likely to become entrepreneurs than women?
2. Does rate of entrepreneurship vary by gender cross-nationally?
3. Are male and female entrepreneurs different?
4. Are male entrepreneurs more likely to create jobs than women?
5. Are male and female job-creating entrepreneurs different?
6. Do the answers to these questions depend on what country you live in?

All these questions are set in the context of the potential for observed differences to explicitly or implicitly relate to different histories, cultures and institutional arrangements, to differences in the depth and breadth of human capital, potential discrimination, family roles and time allocation, and different psychological traits.

METHODOLOGY

The data used to investigate these research questions are derived from three European Union (EU)-wide surveys of the working populations (waged +

self-employed) across each member state. For consistency across the three surveys we focus on the core EU-15 countries and exclude the accession states. The surveys were carried out in 1995, 2000 and 2005 and involved face-to-face interviews with working adults. The minimum requirement for each country survey was 1000 working adults, with the exception of Luxembourg which has a very small population. We have data, for each individual, on personal demographics and job characteristics.

Each country-level survey is weighted to ensure that it is representative of the working population within each country and at the relevant point in time. We choose to focus the core econometric investigation on the 2000 data-set as it contains larger samples and also more detailed demographic data. But for comparative purposes, and to explore how gender effects play out over time, we also estimate similar sets of equations using the 1995 and 2005 data-sets but suppress the reporting of other findings unrelated to gender.

In terms of our methodological approach, we initially present the basic descriptive statistics of interest, namely entrepreneurial propensity and type by gender and country. We then proceed to estimate a series of probit models for each research question of interest. This reflects the binary nature of our responses to our key variables (for example, are you working in the waged or self-employed sector? Are you a job-creating entrepreneur?). In each case we estimate a full model with gender included as an explanatory variable in the right-hand-side of our equation and then estimate separate equations for men and women. The basic models can be written thus:

$$Pr\ (Y) = f\ (gender, age, marital\ status, children, occupation, sector, country)$$

For ease of interpretation, we report the marginal effects. This allows us to say, for example, that women are 3.1 per cent less likely to be self-employed than waged employed, holding other factors constant.

BASIC COUNTRY DIFFERENCES IN ENTREPRENEURIAL PROPENSITY

Here we discuss base data relating to the proportions of men and women in each of our 15 EU countries who (a) are engaged in entrepreneurial activity and (b) are job-creating. We note that the propensity to become an entrepreneur is highest in Southern European countries. For example, in Greece 45.94 per cent of the working population are self-employed, in

Italy 26.54 per cent and in Spain 24.66 per cent. Self-employment rates are low in Holland (5.70 per cent), Denmark (6.36 per cent) and Sweden (8.99 per cent). Thus, we observe tremendous variation in self-employment rates across Europe. It is also apparent that the majority of self-employed do not create any additional employment (individual self-employment – ISE). So which countries have relatively high (low) levels of job-creating (JC) self-employment in absolute terms? Countries with relatively high absolute rates of job-creating self-employment include Greece (8.18 per cent), Spain (7.10 per cent), Italy (6.67 per cent) and Ireland (6.18 per cent).

Further, we also note that with regard to the share of job-creating self-employment out of total self-employment, the EU-15 average is 28.73 per cent. Countries where entrepreneurs have a relatively high propensity to create jobs include Denmark and Germany, Austria, Holland and Luxembourg. By contrast, entrepreneurs in Greece, Finland and Italy are significantly less likely to create additional jobs. Thus, there appears to be some sort of trade-off between simple quantity of entrepreneurs and quality of the entrepreneurial stock within a country. This feature is consistent with previous empirical evidence at the EU level (Cowling, 2003), and with gender-based issues raised by Verheul et al. (2006) in their multi-country study, who argued that policy-makers need to be clear about whether they want more female entrepreneurs per se, a greater share of entrepreneurial activity accounted for by women, or better performance from female entrepreneurs regardless of the quantity. We explicitly address these questions in relation to gender in the following section.

BASIC GENDER DIFFERENCES IN ENTREPRENEURIAL PROPENSITY

We further observe, as illustrated in Figure 2.1, that the ISE rate is higher for women in Belgium, Luxembourg and Portugal, while the actual rate per se is highest for women in Greece, Spain and Italy (Southern European countries).

In other countries, notably Spain, France and Holland, male and female ISE rates are fairly similar. In contrast, male ISE rates are significantly higher in Denmark, Ireland and the UK. The data suggests that there is little relationship between the absolute country rate of ISE and the relative share of female ISE. Focusing on job-creating self-employment, we note that no one country has a higher share of female JC self-employment than male. And there appears to be a more striking separation between male and female self-employed at the JC level. Job-creating self-employment is more male-dominated than individual self-employment. We explore this

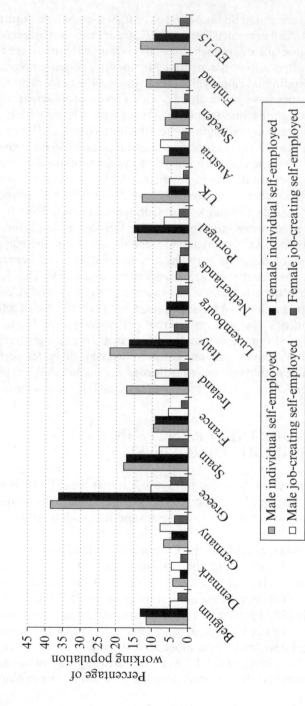

Figure 2.1 Individual and job-creating self-employment by country and gender

Percentage of working population

■ Male individual self-employed
□ Male job-creating self-employed
■ Female individual self-employed
■ Female job-creating self-employed

Belgium Denmark Germany Greece Spain France Ireland Italy Luxembourg Netherlands Portugal UK Austria Sweden Finland EU-15 below by considering, within gender, what proportion of total male and female self-employment is accounted for by job-creating men and women entrepreneurs.

From Figure 2.2 we note that the EU-15 average share of job-creating self-employment is 32.4 per cent for men and 21.4 per cent for women. For men, JC shares are particularly high in Denmark (52.3 per cent), Germany (53.7 per cent), Austria (53.2 per cent) and Sweden (43.3 per cent). In Denmark (48.3 per cent), Germany (45.5 per cent) and Holland (42.8 per cent) JC shares are also very high for women entrepreneurs. The disparity in job-creating potential across EU countries appears large when we consider that only 21.1 per cent of Greek male entrepreneurs, 25.2 per cent of Finnish male entrepreneurs, 11.7 per cent of Greek female entrepreneurs and 15.0 per cent of Portuguese female entrepreneurs create jobs. What is clear so far is that simply having lots of entrepreneurs in the labour force does not easily translate into additional job creation. In short, there appears to be a trade-off between quantity and quality of the entrepreneurial stock in a country.

ECONOMETRIC MODELLING OF SELF-EMPLOYMENT

We now present our econometric evidence using the binary probit (with marginal effects calculated) estimation procedure. The models to be esti-mated are:

- self-employed (1,0) full model
- self-employed (1,0) separately for men and women
- job-creating self-employed (1,0) full model conditional on being self-employed at all
- job-creating self-employed (1,0) separately for men and women con-ditional on being self-employed at all.

See Table 2.1.

WHO IS SELF-EMPLOYED?

In this section we directly tackle two key questions posed in our introduc-tion, considering differences by country:

- Are men more likely to become entrepreneurs than women?
- Are male and female entrepreneurs different?

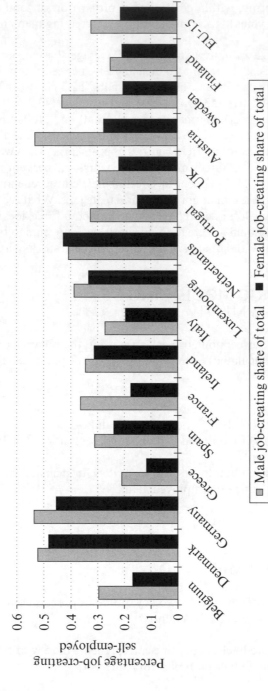

Figure 2.2 Job-creating shares of self-employment by country and gender

Table 2.1 The self-employed

Variable	Model 1: The self-employed-waged employed decision: full model		Model 2: The self-employed-waged employed decision: males		Model 3: The self-employed-waged employed decision: females		Model 4: ISE-Job-creator determination: full model		Model 5: ISE-Job-creator determination: males		Model 6: ISE-Job-creator determination: females	
	dF/dx	P>|z|	dF/dx	P>|z|	dF/dx	P>|z|	dF/dx	P>|z|	dF/dx	P>|z|	dF/dx	P>|z|
Male	0.03	0.00					0.11	0.00				
Age												
25–39	0.11	0.00	0.13	0.00	0.07	0.00	0.02	0.64	−0.01	0.84	0.21	0.08
40–54	0.16	0.00	0.18	0.00	0.13	0.00	0.02	0.73	−0.03	0.63	0.21	0.06
55+	0.30	0.00	0.33	0.00	0.25	0.00	−0.03	0.51	−0.07	0.27	0.16	0.24
Marital status												
Married	0.02	0.01	0.01	0.17	0.02	0.01	0.07	0.01	0.07	0.03	0.05	0.20
Unmarried	0.01	0.11	0.02	0.27	0.02	0.18	0.02	0.53	0.02	0.70	0.03	0.58
Divorced	0.01	0.42	0.04	0.04	−0.01	0.68	0.05	0.29	0.12	0.05	−0.05	0.43
Separated	0.00	0.90	0.03	0.25	−0.02	0.25	−0.13	0.03	−0.11	0.17	−0.16	0.07
Widowed	0.03	0.09	0.04	0.33	0.02	0.24	0.03	0.68	0.04	0.72	0.02	0.41
Children	0.01	0.06	0.01	0.18	0.01	0.02	0.02	0.18	0.03	0.22	0.05	0.20
Occupation												
Senior manager	0.44	0.00	0.45	0.00	0.50	0.00	0.36	0.00	0.37	0.00	0.32	0.00
Professional	0.14	0.00	0.22	0.00	0.08	0.00	0.19	0.00	0.19	0.01	0.15	0.09
Technician	0.13	0.00	0.19	0.00	0.07	0.00	0.18	0.00	0.17	0.02	0.16	0.07
Clerical	−0.03	0.01	−0.02	0.28	−0.02	0.10	0.13	0.05	0.10	0.30	0.11	0.22
Sales	0.04	0.00	0.09	0.00	0.02	0.05	0.15	0.01	0.19	0.01	0.09	0.26

Table 2.1 (continued)

Variable	Model 1: The self-employed-waged employed decision: full model		Model 2: The self-employed-waged employed decision: males		Model 3: The self-employed-waged employed decision: females		Model 4: ISE-Job-creator determination: full model		Model 5: ISE-Job-creator determination: males		Model 6: ISE-Job-creator determination: females	
	dF/dx	P>|z|	dF/dx	P>|z|	dF/dx	P>|z|	dF/dx	P>|z|	dF/dx	P>|z|	dF/dx	P>|z|
Skilled manual	0.49	0.00	0.56	0.00	0.37	0.00	−0.02	0.83	−0.10	0.35	0.17	0.27
Craft	0.10	0.00	0.11	0.00	0.17	0.00	0.14	0.01	0.15	0.03	0.09	0.33
Operative	0.02	0.11	0.04	0.05	0.02	0.50	0.07	0.34	0.08	0.34	0.00	0.98
Sector												
Agriculture	0.14	0.04	0.12	0.00	0.21	0.00	0.10	0.23	0.20	0.06	−0.07	0.54
Manufacturing	−0.02	0.17	−0.03	0.01	−0.02	0.13	0.18	0.00	0.23	0.00	0.09	0.13
Utilities	−0.06	0.01	−0.08	0.01	−0.02	0.61	0.02	0.86	0.11	0.49	0.47	0.01
Construction	0.07	0.07	0.09	0.00	0.03	0.35	0.13	0.00	0.15	0.00	−0.04	0.24
Retailing	0.14	0.17	0.17	0.00	0.09	0.00	−0.01	0.67	0.02	0.66	0.17	0.00
Hotels and catering	0.11	0.05	0.11	0.00	0.08	0.00	0.15	0.00	0.13	0.02	0.16	0.21
Transport and comms	0.02	0.07	0.03	0.10	−0.01	0.56	−0.02	0.65	−0.03	0.57	0.01	0.88
Finance	0.02	0.03	0.04	0.11	0.00	0.95	0.12	0.03	0.17	0.01	−0.07	0.11
Real estate	0.11	0.07	0.10	0.00	0.09	0.00	0.02	0.59	0.08	0.08	0.13	0.42
Public admin	−0.11	0.07	−0.15	0.00	−0.07	0.00	0.09	0.41	0.09	0.55	−0.07	0.54

Country												
Denmark	-0.08	0.00	-0.09	0.00	-0.06	0.00	0.31	0.00	0.31	0.00	0.31	0.00
Germany	-0.04	0.00	-0.03	0.04	-0.04	0.00	0.32	0.00	0.30	0.00	0.37	0.00
Greece	0.17	0.00	0.25	0.00	0.06	0.00	-0.04	0.23	-0.03	0.51	-0.05	0.30
Spain	0.08	0.00	0.09	0.00	0.07	0.00	0.08	0.07	0.06	0.25	0.12	0.07
France	-0.04	0.00	-0.04	0.02	-0.03	0.00	0.07	0.14	0.13	0.04	-0.01	0.87
Ireland	0.00	0.70	0.06	0.00	-0.05	0.00	0.17	0.00	0.17	0.00	0.21	0.02
Italy	0.11	0.00	0.15	0.00	0.06	0.00	0.08	0.07	0.07	0.22	0.12	0.09
Luxembourg	-0.05	0.00	-0.06	0.02	-0.03	0.14	0.20	0.04	0.15	0.24	0.30	0.04
Holland	-0.08	0.00	-0.11	0.00	-0.06	0.00	0.21	0.04	0.14	0.10	0.29	0.00
Portugal	0.01	0.21	0.01	0.57	0.01	0.60	0.02	0.71	0.04	0.46	0.00	0.94
UK	-0.02	0.03	0.02	0.39	-0.05	0.00	0.08	0.08	0.07	0.24	0.16	0.06
Austria	-0.04	0.00	-0.02	0.38	-0.04	0.00	0.27	0.00	0.31	0.00	0.16	0.04
Sweden	-0.05	0.00	-0.05	0.00	-0.05	0.00	0.18	0.00	0.23	0.00	0.10	0.23
Finland	-0.04	0.00	-0.03	0.12	-0.04	0.00	0.02	0.66	-0.01	0.91	0.06	0.36
Other	0.01	0.65	0.04	0.23	-0.01	0.52	0.02	0.80	0.02	0.84	0.00	0.98

Our motivation here is to move beyond the raw data that show a larger, and more substantive, difference between male and female entrepreneurial propensity and seek to draw out 'true' differences in gender entrepreneurship rates and the reasons for these differences. And equally interesting is to establish what we can explain using core demographic information and what remains unexplained. This is important for identifying and shaping future work in this area.

The main point of interest in the context of this chapter is that women are 3.11 per cent less likely to be self-employed than men in Europe. This is much less than the absolute difference in self-employment rates between men and women which is 7.64 per cent. This implies that 59.3 per cent of the observed gender variation in self-employment rates in Europe can be easily explained by differences in key personal, occupational and country characteristics. Of course, this also implies that there is a really interesting 40.7 per cent variation that is unexplained by basic demographic factors.

Aside from this identifiable gender difference, our model also shows that the probability to become self-employed increases in age of individual and is highest among the over-45s. We also find that married people are more likely to be self-employed, as well as widowers. The presence of children in the family also increases the probability of self-employment by around 1 per cent. This might suggest that the relative flexibility of self-employment hours is attractive to those with childcare responsibilities. Occupational status was found to be a very important determinant of self-employment with skilled manual workers being the most likely to become self-employed and clerical workers the least likely. Sector also had an effect on self-employment, although its influence was generally not as strong as occupation or age. At the country level, we find that Greece, Italy and Spain all had much higher self-employment probabilities, although the differences here were much smaller than the raw differences. Countries with low probabilities of self-employment include Denmark and Holland.

We now focus our attention on which types of men and women become self-employed by estimating separate models for men and women. This will help us answer the question of whether male and female entrepreneurs are fundamentally different. The first point of interest is that the positive age effect on the propensity to become self-employed is much stronger for men than for women. Turning this around, age is less important in the determination of self-employment for women, although it still matters. On marital status we find some key differences between male and females. For men, we find that divorce increases the probability of self-employment by 4.1 per cent. For women, we find that being married increases the probability of self-employment by 2.3 per cent. While we do not explicitly observe the timing of these events, our evidence might suggest different motivations for self-employment. It is also the case that the presence of children increases the probability of self-employment for women by 1.4 per cent, but had no effect on men. Again this is suggestive of different motivations for men and women.

With regard to occupation we generally find that the same occupations are more (less) associated with self-employment for men and women. However, the strength of these effects is quite different. For example, professional males have a 22.1 per cent higher probability of self-employment compared to only 7.8 per cent for women. Further, male skilled manual workers have a 55.6 per cent higher probability of self-employment while for female skilled manual workers this was only 36.6 per cent. Thus we might conclude that occupation is a key determinant of self-employment and that it is more important for men than women. In terms of sector effects, we find that there is much more variation in self-employment probabilities for men than women. For women we find that agriculture was associated with a 21.5 per cent increase in the probability of self-employment compared to only an 11.6 per cent difference for men. We also observe that female self-employment is concentrated in retailing, hotels and catering sectors, albeit to a lesser degree than was the case for men.

Finally, we note that there are significant country differences in the propensity for self-employment. But the cross-country variation is significantly lower (with a maximum difference of only 6.6 per cent) for women than men. Taking all this gender evidence together we might suggest that similar characteristics influence the male and female probability of self-employment, but the strength of these effects are typically larger for men, with the notable exceptions of having young children and being married which impact on the female decision but not the male decision.

Thus far we have presented econometric models of the general labour market status decision and the male and female decision separately. To answer our three research questions:

- Are men more likely to become entrepreneurs than women? Yes, men are more likely to become entrepreneurs than women. But much of this observed difference can be easily explained by occupational differences and other basic characteristics. The true difference in propensities is only 3.1 per cent.
- Are male and female entrepreneurs different? Not as different as some commentators have implied, although the presence of young children is a key defining characteristic for women.

- Do the answers to all these questions depend on what country you live in? Yes, countries with a high propensity to self-employment include Greece and Italy, and those with a low propensity include Denmark and Holland. Also, country effects are greater for men than women.

WHICH ENTREPRENEURS CREATE JOBS?

Here we focus solely on the self-employed and provide evidence relating to a further two questions posed earlier in this chapter:

- Are male entrepreneurs more likely to create jobs than women?
- Are male and female job-creating entrepreneurs different?

In response to the first question, we find that male entrepreneurs have an 11.1 per cent higher probability of being a job-creator. This is much larger than the raw absolute difference which is 3.8 per cent. This implies that most of the observed differences in probabilities of being a job-creating entrepreneur are easily explained by core personal and job characteristics, and differences in these between men and women entrepreneurs.

We also observe that age is no barrier to job-creating self-employment. But we also find that married people are 6.9 per cent more likely to be job-creators, whereas individuals who have undergone a marital separation are 13.3 per cent less likely to be JCs. Here again we also find occupation matters with senior management staff, professionals, technicians and sales staff having particularly high probabilities of being job-creators. At the sector level, we note that manufacturing, hotels and catering, construction and financial services all have higher probabilities of job-creating self-employment. Interestingly we find that the relative contributions of sector and occupation are much closer than for total self-employment. At the country level we also observe tremendous variation. Countries with much higher probabilities of JC self-employment include, Denmark (+30.6 per cent), Austria (+26.6 per cent), Germany (+32.3 per cent), and Holland (+21.4 per cent).

As to differences between male and female job-creators (JCs) compared to their respective ISE counterparts, we note firstly that male JCs are equally likely to be found across all age groups. For women, our evidence shows that the 25–54 years age range is when the probability of being a JC is highest. Again we observe that marital status is important but acts in different ways for males and females. For males, we note that married men have a 7.1 per cent higher probability of being a JC, and divorced men have an 11.7 per cent higher probability. For females, we find that marital separation gives them a 16.2 per cent lower probability of being a JC.

With regard to occupation, we find that the three occupations with the highest probability of being JCs are senior managers, professionals and technicians. But the strength of these effects is larger for men than women. Further, additional occupations such as skilled manual and craft related also increase the JC probability for men but not women. The same was true for sectors, with men and women in construction and hotels and catering both being more likely to be JCs, although here the female effect was more than three times as strong for women than men. Again we find that more sectors differentiated between male ISEs and JCs than was the case for women, including financial services and real estate.

For country effects, we also observe substantial gender differences. For men we find that JC probabilities are particularly high in Denmark (+30.5 per cent), Germany (+30.3 per cent), and Austria (+31.4 per cent), and high in France, Ireland, Holland and Sweden. For women we note that JC probabilities are also highest in Germany and Denmark at +37.3 per cent and +31.0 per cent respectively, and higher than was the case for their male peers. Other countries with high JC probabilities for women entrepreneurs include Luxembourg (+29.8 per cent), Holland (+29.3 per cent), and Ireland (+20.5 per cent). Thus country-level effects are very large for men and women in terms of the determination of job-creating self-employment and, importantly, are generally more important for women entrepreneurs.

UNEXPLAINED DIFFERENCES BETWEEN MEN AND WOMEN

We found that the presence of children and marital status tended to be more influential on the female labour market decision, suggesting that socio-economic variables and time allocation might be the key to understanding more about the female labour market decision.

So how can we explore these issues further to enhance our understanding of what is driving the self-employment decision for women? The econometric method we adopt is to save the residuals (the unexplained variation) from our base models and then estimate new models a set of time-allocation variables on the right-hand-side.

From our residual estimation, we find that women with childcare or eldercare responsibilities have a higher propensity to become self-employed than accept waged employment. This is fairly strong evidence that flexibility in employment patterns, particularly time allocation is important in the female decision to choose self-employment.

In terms of job-creating self-employment, the key time-allocation variables childcare and eldercare both act in a positive way on the probability of being a job-creating entrepreneur. And, importantly, these effects are four times stronger in the determination of being a job-creator, as opposed to a single self-employed, than simply choosing self-employment over waged employment. Taken together, these two findings might suggest that women who choose self-employment over a waged job appreciate the time flexibility that this form of working gives them but also have a desire to build their businesses at the same time and make a success of them. These findings are consistent with Dolton and Makepeace (1987) who argue that self-employment can complement childcare responsibilities, with Jennings and McDougald (2007) who stress the importance of the work–family interface, and with Morris et al. (2006) who suggest that only those women that choose self-employment as a positive career decision are orientated towards growing their businesses.

CHANGES IN MALE AND FEMALE SELF-EMPLOYMENT AND JOB CREATION OVER TIME

In this penultimate section, we present our evidence covering the three survey periods from 1995, 2000 and 2005. Figure 2.3 shows the estimated 'true' differences in the probabilities of women and men becoming (a) self-employed and (b) job-creating self-employed once they have entered self-employment.

From Figure 2.3 the evidence is striking. In 1995, the probability of a male being a self-employed job-creator was 14.85 per cent higher for men than women. By 2000, this differential had fallen to 11.1 per cent, and by 2005 it had fallen again to only 9.51 per cent. Over just a decade, this narrowing of the 'true' gender differential is a remarkable labour market dynamic. And a similar pattern was also found for self-employment per se. Here we find that in 1995, males were 3.37 per cent more likely to become self-employed. By 2000, this 'gap' had fallen to only 3.11 per cent, and by 2005 the 'gap' had narrowed again to only 1.53 per cent. If this latter dynamic, in particular, continued over the next decade, we might expect that the 'true' gender gap might all but disappear.

SUMMARY

We used EU data to explore six basic questions relating to gender differences in the propensity to become self-employed, and once self-employed

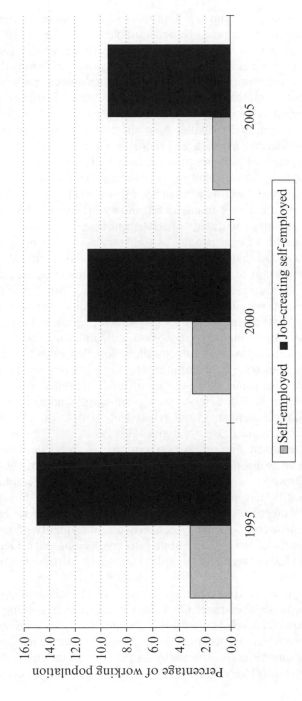

Figure 2.3   Gender dynamics in self-employment, 1995–2005

to create additional jobs. The raw data showed that gender differences in both cases were large, with men being significantly more likely to choose self-employment over waged employment, and to be job-creating self-employed. But on further econometric investigation we found that the basic reason for the observed difference in self-employment rates between men and women were easily explained by differences in the nature of jobs they enter and the sectors they work in. This means that the 'true' difference was substantially smaller than the raw difference. In terms of job-creating self-employment, again there is a gender gap, and this is virtually all explained by occupational choice, sector of employment and country-level effects. So we might easily conclude that historical legacy (in terms of what jobs and sectors women are more (less) represented in) and differences in culture across countries tell most of the story about gender differences in quantity and quality of self-employment.

But other strands of evidence tell us the story is much more complex. For example, we find that the presence of children and marital status are much more important in the female decision. Having children increases the propensity for women to become self-employed. Further, childcare and eldercare responsibilities increase the probability that women will choose self-employment and create jobs in self-employment. This suggests that women seeking to manage the work–family interface value the time flexibility that self-employment affords them and that once this decision has been made, they have the commitment and ability to grow their businesses. This implies some self-selection of goal-orientated women with familial responsibilities into job-creating self-employment, as opposed to women with children at school who tend to opt for lifestyle self-employment for the time flexibility it gives them.

We also questioned how important country of domicile was in the self-employment decision. We find that it is very important, but more so for men. However, when we looked at job-creating self-employment this was reversed. Here we found that country effects were much more important for women, hinting that cultural and historical differences were important. If we were particularly concerned about quality of women's self-employment, defined as their ability to create jobs, then Germany, Denmark and Holland stand as exemplars and merit further investigation in future research.

Finally, we posed the question as to whether gender differences persist, increase or diminish over time. On this our evidence is striking. On a quantity and quality level, and within a decade, the 'true' gender gap in terms of the propensity to become self-employed and to create jobs, subsequently, has diminished substantially in the European Union. If these dynamics persist, it is likely that the only remaining gender differences we will observe in self-employment rates will relate to differences in the occupational distribution of women. For those interested in promoting female self-employment, our evidence strongly suggests that activity should focus on growth not start-up or entry. Broader policies aimed at increasing women's participation in non-traditional sectors and occupations will naturally close this gender gap.

POLICY CONCLUSIONS AND RESEARCH IMPLICATIONS

Our work suggests that changes have occurred in the labour market that have substantially reduced the quantitative and qualitative imbalance between male and female self-employment over the past decade in Europe. The most significant, albeit very much reduced, imbalance that remains is in terms of quality of self-employment across genders. If we were to draw any policy conclusions we would suggest that promoting STEM (science, technology, engineering and mathematics) subjects amongst young women while they are still in the education system might play a major role in enhancing women's human capital in key areas relevant to self-employment. Once in the labour market, female entry into non-service sector employment would naturally raise the relevance of informal entrepreneurial human capital. Once in self-employment, policy initiatives aimed at promoting awareness of growth potential, opportunity identification and how to take advantage of these opportunities among women entrepreneurs would directly tackle this diminishing quality imbalance.

In terms of potential and fruitful avenues of future research, we have two strong recommendations. First, we need to know more about why countries such as Germany, Holland and Denmark have such high-quality female entrepreneurship and, equally, why countries such as France, Greece and Portugal have too much low-quality female entrepreneurship. Thus detailed individual country research would be helpful. Also, research that has a time dimension would be useful so we can learn more about how patterns in entrepreneurship and entrepreneurial quality are changing over time, possibly at different rates across countries and the reasons for this. Second, in terms of where we might best focus our efforts, it is clear that (in Europe at least) labour markets have changed and there may be less merit in hunting for discriminatory explanations for gender differences. If our broad evidence is correct, female entrepreneurship has blossomed in Europe within a single decade, and this is likely to continue. So we feel that research that focused on issues such as time allocation, work–family interface (including the under-researched area of eldercare), and particularly links between desired working hours, flexibility over the determination of hours and positive motivations for becoming an entrepreneur such as the desire for independence, and money, would tell us so much more that we need to know and understand.

ACKNOWLEDGEMENT

The author would like to thank all participants at the DIANA seminar in Belfast, December 2008, and particularly the editors of this book and an anonymous referee for genuinely helpful advice and guidance.

REFERENCES

Birch, D. (1979), *The Job Generation Process*, Cambridge, MA: MIT Press.
Brush, C. (1992), 'Research on women business owners: Past trends, a new perspective and future directions', *Entrepreneurship, Theory and Practice*, Summer, 5–30.
Brush, C. (1999), 'Women entrepreneurs: moving beyond the glass ceiling', *Academy of Management Review*, **24** (3), 586–9.
Burke, A., Fitzroy, F. and Nolan, M. (2001), 'When less is more: distinguishing between entrepreneurial choice and performance', *Oxford Bulletin of Economics and Statistics*, **62** (5), 565–87.
Carroll, R., Holtz-Eakin, D., Rider, M. and Rosen, H. (1996), 'Income taxes and entrepreneurs use of labour', Centre for Economic Policy Studies, Working Paper No. 32.
Coates, S. and Tennyson, S. (1992), 'Labour market discrimination, imperfect information and self-employment', *Oxford Economic Papers*, **44**, 272–88.
Colombo, M., Delmastra, M. and Grilli, L. (2004), 'Entrepreneurs' human capital and the start-up size of NTBFs', *International Journal of Industrial Organisation*, **22**, 1183–211.
Cowling, M. (2000), 'Are entrepreneurs different across countries?', *Applied Economics Letters*, **7** (12), 785–9.
Cowling, M. (2003), 'The employment contribution of the self-employed in the EU. Small Business Service Research report URN 03/539', London, available at: www.sbs.gov.uk/research/ and http://berr.gov.uk /files/file38300.pdf (accessed March 2003).
Cowling, M. and Taylor, M. (2001), 'Entrepreneurial women and men: two different species?', *Small Business Economics*, **6** (3), 167–75.
Cowling, M. and Bygrave, W. (2007), 'Entrepreneurship, welfare provision and unemployment', *Comparative Labor Law and Policy Journal*, **28** (4), 617–36.
Cowling, M., Taylor, M. and Mitchell, P. (2004), 'Job creators', *Manchester School*, **72** (5), 601–17.
Davidsson, P., Lindmark, L. and Oloffson, C. (1998), 'The extent of overestimation of small firm job creation – an empirical examination of the regression bias', *Small Business Economics*, **11**, 87–100.
Davis, S., Haltiwanger, J. and Shuh, S. (1996), 'Small business job creation:

dissecting the myth and reassessing the facts', *Small Business Economics*, **8**, 297–315.

De Bruin, A., Brush, C. and Welter, F. (2007), 'Advancing a framework for coherent research on women's entrepreneurship', *Entrepreneurship, Theory and Practice*, **31** (3), 323–39.

Dolton, P. and Makepeace, G. (1987), 'Marital status, child rearing and earnings differentials in the graduate labour market', *The Economic Journal*, **97**, 897–921.

Du Rietz, A. and Henrekson, M. (2000), 'Testing the female under-performance hypothesis', *Small Business Economics*, **14**, 1–10.

Gatewood, E., Brusch, C., Carter, N., Greene, P. and Hart, M. (2009), 'Diana: a symbol of women entrepreneurs' hunt for knowledge, money, and the rewards of entrepreneurship', *Small Business Economics*, **32** (2), 129–44.

Georgellis, Y. and Wall, H. (2005), 'Gender differences in self-employment', *International Review of Applied Economics*, **19** (3), 321–42.

Jennings, J. and McDougald, M. (2007), 'Work–family interface experiences and coping strategies: Implications for entrepreneurship research and practice', *Academy of Management Review*, **32** (3), 747–60.

Kalleberg, A. and Leicht, K. (1991), 'Gender and organisational performance: determinants of small business survival and success', *Academy of Management Journal*, **34** (1), 136–61.

Langowitz, N. and Minniti, M. (2007), 'The entrepreneurial propensity of women', *Entrepreneurship, Theory and Practice*, **31** (3), 341–64.

Lazear, E. (2005), 'Entrepreneurship', *Journal of Labor Economics*, **23** (4), 649–80.

Manolova, T., Carter, N., Manev, I. and Gyoshev, B. (2007), 'The differential effect of men and women entrepreneurs' human capital and networking on growth experiences in Bulgaria', *Entrepreneurship, Theory and Practice*, **31** (3), 407–26.

Marlow, S., Carter, S. and Shaw, E. (2008), 'Constructing female entrepreneurship in the UK: is the US a relevant benchmark?', *Environment and Planning C*, **26** (2), 335–51.

Moore, I. (1983), 'Employer discrimination: evidence from self-employed workers', *The Review of Economics and Statistics*, **65**, 570–79.

Morris, M., Miyasaki, N., Watters, C. and Coombes, S. (2006), 'The dilemma of growth: understanding venture size choices of women entrepreneurs', *Journal of Small Business Management*, **44** (2), 221–44.

Parker, S. (2008), 'Entrepreneurship among married couples in the US', *Labour Economics*, **15** (3), 459–81.

Rosa, P., Carter, S. and Hamilton, D. (1996), 'Gender as a determinant of small business performance', *Small Business Economics*, **8**, 463–78.

Sowell, I. (1981), *Markets and Minorities*, New York: Basic Books.

Verheul, I., Van Stel, A. and Thurik, R. (2006), 'Explaining female and male entrepreneurship at the country level', *Entrepreneurship and Regional Development*, **18** (2), 151–83.

Wagner, J. (2007), 'What a difference a Y makes: female and male nascent entrepreneurs in Germany', *Small Business Economics*, **28** (1), 1–21.

Watson, J. and Robinson, S. (2003), 'Adjusting for risk in comparing the performance of male and female controlled SMEs', *Journal of Business Venturing*, **18** (6), 773–88.

Westhead, P. and Cowling, M. (1995), 'Employment change in independent owner managed high technology firms in great Britain', *Small Business Economics*, **7** (2), 111–40.

3. Gender and entrepreneurship: revealing constructions and underlying processes – the case of Norway

Gry Agnete Alsos, Ragnhild Steen Jensen and Elisabet Ljunggren

INTRODUCTION

In spite of the increase in women's engagement in entrepreneurial activities, entrepreneurship and business ownership are still male-dominated activities. This is particularly true in Western countries, otherwise expected to have reached quite far when it comes to gender equality in society. Results from the Global Entrepreneurship Monitor (GEM) indicate that a significant gender gap exists for both early stage entrepreneurial participation and established business ownership, and that this gender gap is significantly greater in high-income countries (Allen et al., 2007). The proportion of women engaging in entrepreneurial activities lags behind that in the labour force (Verheul et al., 2006). This is particularly true in the Nordic countries, where the share of women in the labour force is very high, but the proportion of female entrepreneurs remains relatively low. These countries have put forward several efforts to increase entrepreneurship among women with varying results. In this chapter we argue that the relationship between gender and entrepreneurial activity is far more complex than these policy measures often assume. The construction of entrepreneurship as a masculine phenomenon has long historical roots, sustained by cultural, social and economic processes. To understand how the gender gap emerges, we must develop greater understanding of how entrepreneurship and a gendered understanding of entrepreneurship are embedded in societal constructions (Elam, 2008).

In this chapter the Norwegian case is used to discuss possible cultural, historical, social and economic reasons for what may be termed 'the women entrepreneurship paradox', that is, the relatively low level of women entrepreneurs in a society often portrayed as a pioneer of gender equality. In Norway there is a well-developed welfare state with childcare and other social services, which makes it easier to combine career and family. This in combination with a relatively strong focus on equality issues has contributed to a high rate of women in the labour force. Gradually the principle of gender balance in positions of power and decision-making, particularly at the political level, has taken root in Norway. The proportion of women in Parliament and in the Cabinet has been high since 1986. Nevertheless the share of women in the business sector, entrepreneurs, business managers and board members, is relatively low. It has been seen as a paradox that this relatively gender-equal country has not been able to present a higher proportion of women in positions of power in the business sector (Foss and Ljunggren, 2006).

This chapter discusses the main processes creating and re-creating the business sector as predominantly masculine. We argue that the lack of progress in women's participation in entrepreneurial activity and business ownership indicate that the processes related to women in the business sector is deeply rooted in how this sector is socially constructed and gendered. We suggest that this is why policy measures often fall short. In particular we focus on how capitalism itself is gendered and how gendered perceptions of competence are related to women's participation in entrepreneurial activities.

In the following sections we present a theoretical point of departure that proposes how one can understand capital and competence as gendered constructions. Next we further elaborate the Norwegian case and analyse it with the proposed theoretical framework. We explain how historical roots, as well as contemporary policies, create and enforce masculine constructions of the business sector. Consequently, the efforts put forward to increase women's entrepreneurship struggle against strong forces working against change.

ENTREPRENEURSHIP AS GENDERED PHENOMENON

In studies of entrepreneurship across countries, there is an obvious similarity in the gender division both in business start-ups and, consequently, in business ownership. Figures from the GEM study are consistent; fewer women than men start up businesses regardless of national context (Allen et al., 2007). The gender gap is even larger in high-income countries and is particularly related to opportunity-based entrepreneurship. A plausible interpretation of these GEM findings is that women are less engaged in entrepreneurship in contexts where entrepreneurship is one among several options – where participation in entrepreneurial activities is solely a result of desire.

The phenomenon of entrepreneurship has to a growing extent become acknowledged as gendered (see, for example, Elam, 2008; Gatewood et al., 2003; Ljunggren, 2003). During the 1980s the early studies on gender and entrepreneurship began to appear. In the early period the understanding of gender applied to entrepreneurship was 'gender as a variable' (Ahl, 2002; Harding, 1987; Ljunggren, 2003). These studies revealed the gender imbalance in entrepreneurship and gave us some information on frequency and characteristics of men and women entrepreneurs. However the explanations for the imbalance remained unclear. More recent studies have applied a theoretical perspective on gender as socially constructed (Ahl, 2002; Berg, 1997). 'Doing gender' and 'doing business' are both perceived as social practices (Bruni et al., 2004). The inclusions of several theoretical standpoints have contributed to a more diversified knowledge of the phenomenon. As a result the discussion of gender and entrepreneurship has become broader, including elements such as human and social capital, access to financial capital, attitudes and social support. Also, female entrepreneurs have increasingly been seen as a heterogeneous group (Bruni et al., 2004; Lewis, 2006).

Adopting feminist perspectives to study entrepreneurship has allowed researchers to see beyond the simple division of entrepreneurs into women and men (Bird and Brush, 2002). As a result, studies are beginning to reveal how entrepreneurship as a phenomenon is highly gendered, not only in the share of women and men engaged, but also in our norms, attitudes and understanding of the concept, for instance, as shown in how media presents entrepreneurs (Baker et al., 1997; Ljunggren and Alsos, 2007), or even, in how researchers discuss gender and entrepreneurship (Ahl, 2002). When entrepreneurship is depicted in society, the entrepreneur has a masculine image (Ljunggren and Alsos, 2007). Entrepreneurs are connected with masculinity; the lonely hero, the patriarch, the adventurous, the venturesome, the daring (Bruni et al., 2004; Chell et al., 1991). However, this knowledge has scarcely been used to understand how entrepreneurship is constructed and reconstructed as masculine, and how these processes are influencing the actual distribution of women and men as business founders and business owners.

By analysing the Norwegian case, we will show that the gendered construction of entrepreneurship and the business sector is deeply rooted in historical paths and reinforced through contemporary practices, and further how these paths and practices directly influence the likelihood of women and men becoming entrepreneurs and business owners. Entrepreneurship is an important part of capitalism and the capitalistic system, as the capitalist system is among the basic premises of entrepreneurship. We argue that the root of the gendered construction of entrepreneurship lies in how capitalism itself is fundamentally gendered.[1]

CAPITALISM AS GENDERED[2]

Gender is not a limited social phenomenon but a general cultural principle of categorization that has large societal implications. The gendered constructions of entrepreneurship and business ownership are not isolated processes but must be seen as a part of the general gender division in society. Solheim (2007) sees 'modernity' as a part of the societal construction based on an assumption of the two genders as diametrical opposites. This fundamental assumption is also among the basics of capitalism. The gendered division is totally integrated and inseparable in modern society; the economic, political and cultural parts of society are structured around this gender division (Solheim, 2007).

To Marx the capitalist has one motive, namely, the desire for capital accumulation (Yanagisako, 2002). However Yanagisako argues that capitalist action is culturally produced and, therefore, always filled with cultural meaning and value. She proposes an alternative theory of capitalist motivation in which meaning operates as a force of production that initiates different types of capitalist practices. Economic relationships 'carry' cultural meaning and, as for all symbolic expressions, they are anchored in the material. Economy is a symbolic organized construction of reality; economy is culture. Polanyi (2001) saw modern capitalism (along with other economic systems) as institutionalized processes where economic life is embedded in social relationships and cultural conventions (Swedberg and Granovetter, 2001). As a central part of capitalism, entrepreneurship is also a cultural phenomenon (Bruni et al., 2004), and thus embedded in social relationships and cultural conventions.

Modern gender relationship is funded on two demarcations: (1) the demarcation between family and labour life (that is, the division between the household and the market) and (2) the demarcation between private and public life (that is, the intimate sphere and the public sphere) (Solheim, 2007). Women belong to the intimate sphere (childbirth, reproduction work), while men belong to the public sphere (markets, trading, production work, politics). This leads to a gendered division between household and market (females belong to the household, males to the market), a pattern still vibrant today. Bruni et al. (2004: 409) argue that: 'A sharp distinction between home and work is taken for granted, with value placed on the unique and rational nature of work, while the emotional component necessary to manage interpersonal relations is ignored.' Capitalism as an economic system has its starting point in the family as economic unit in the early capitalistic area (Solheim, 2007). In historical terms the role of the bourgeois is central in developing these demarcations. The bourgeois is closely connected both to the development of the market economy and capitalistic production. Consequently, capitalism itself contributes to the re-creation of the gender division embedded in the model from which society is organized.

The phenomenon of entrepreneurship clearly belongs to the public sphere and the market, that is, the male sphere. Women in starting a business are entering the market or the public sphere and breaking with the rules and norms dominating the household and the intimate sphere. Consequently, women entering entrepreneurship are crossing the border from the female to the male sphere. Crossing gender borders is not easy, as it breaks with social and cultural conventions. Further, women often cannot leave the intimate sphere. Instead, women entrepreneurs end up struggling to be able to fulfil the obligations of both spheres, generally known as the dual work burden. Many household-based firms can be described as an arena where the household and the market sphere meet (Wheelock and Mariussen, 1997).

When women enter the entrepreneurship field they need to comply with as well as challenge existing expectations about entrepreneurship: the characteristics of an entrepreneur, the actions of entrepreneurs and the image of entrepreneurship. The need to comply with existing arrangements reflects the need for women to follow the rules composed by the institutions, norms and structures. They have to convince current field inhabitants that their practices conform to what is generally perceived as entrepreneurial practices to gain legitimacy (cf. Bourdieu, 1990). Women will need to convince customers, investors and other stakeholders that they are viable entrepreneurs in line with existing expectations about what is perceived as acceptable in the marketplace (Aldrich, 1999).

However, the fact that they are women leads to expectations among field stakeholders that challenge the existing institutions, norms and structure. They are noticed as women entrepreneurs, who are generally perceived as something slightly different than 'ordinary' entrepreneurs. Consequently, women entrepreneurs need to not only attract acceptance for their products or ventures as 'real entrepreneurs' but also are expected to enrich their entrepreneurial ventures with an appeal that relates to the fact that they are women. This is important not only to their entrepreneurial endeavours but also to confirm their femininity; they are not only entrepreneurs, they are also women.

ENTREPRENEURIAL AND OWNERSHIP COMPETENCE AS GENDERED

Being accepted as 'viable' entrepreneurs is strongly related to being considered to possess the relevant competence for entrepreneurial activity. Competence can be viewed as the most central translation mechanism putting value on gender in capitalist societies. Competence, defined as skills, knowledge and qualifications of a person, is the main asset women and men bring to the entrepreneurial process, and it constitutes the most important basis for gendered categorization and hierarchy (Solheim, 2002).

Lack of competence is an often used argument for why women are not recruited to management positions, board positions and to entrepreneurial activity. However, what is seldom discussed is that competence and gender are interconnected concepts. Competence and knowledge cannot be treated as independent variables but should be discussed in relation to the social field in which they are embedded (Solbrække, 2002). Solbrække argues that competence must be understood as a dynamic and historically created phenomenon, that is, as a result of cultural processes of definition. This means that different forms of competence, such as entrepreneurial competence, cannot be discussed as if they were universal or gender neutral.

The gendering of entrepreneurial competence takes form in at least two principal ways. First, the definition of entrepreneurial competence is in itself gendered. As entrepreneurship and business ownership historically belong to the male sphere, the norm of what entrepreneurship is and what competence is needed has been shaped by men. The dynamic and historical creation of entrepreneurial competence is not only based on experiences of the competences needed, but also on a description of the competence held by the norm, that is, the male entrepreneur. The historical descriptions of the entrepreneur, including the entrepreneur's activities as masculine, are still accepted as general (Bird and Brush, 2002). The development of entrepreneurial competence as a concept is tightly connected to how the entrepreneur is described or characterized, that is, by masculine connotations. Consequently, the understanding of entrepreneurial competence is formed by the competence the male entrepreneur is presupposed to have, much more than related to the competence actually needed to become an entrepreneur. It might be that women entrepreneurs possess slightly different forms of entrepreneurial competence, in the same way as it has been found that women manage their businesses differently (Carter et al., 1997).

Second, gendered understandings of competence also influence the actual competence men and women are perceived to have. The gendered division of labour is disseminated through a concept of competence that allocates specific tasks as women's or men's domain based on cultural conceptions on what suitable characteristics women and men have (Solheim, 2002). Women possess competence from the intimate and household sphere, while men possess competence from the public and market sphere. Specific types of competence, such as entrepreneurial competence, constitute a symbolic connection of meaning and appear as gendered characteristics through associations with women and men. In this way entrepreneurial competence has strong masculine associations resulting in a general understanding of this competence as something men, but not women, possess.

THE CASE OF NORWAY

Norway is a small and sparsely populated country in Scandinavia; it has 4.7 million inhabitants. It is not a member of the European Union (EU). The Norwegian economy is strong, as it is based on the export of oil, gas and farmed fish. The country has a strong welfare state orientation built in the post-Second World War period. Along with the other Nordic countries, Norway has a relative large public sector.

Norway has reasonably good scores on international statistics on gender equality. Women's participation in the labour market is high; 74.8 per cent of women compared to 81.4 period of men (Statistics Norway, 2008). In comparison the USA numbers are 69.3 per cent for women and 81.9 per cent for men, and the UK numbers are 70.3 per cent for women and 83.2 per cent for men. Yet Norway hits rock bottom when it comes to women's participation in the business sector, including entrepreneurship, ownership, management and board positions.

The GEM studies show that women's early stage entrepreneurial participation in Norway is 4.28 per cent, accounting for about one-third of total Norwegian participation. The comparable numbers for the UK and the USA are 3.60 per cent and 7.25 per cent respectively (Allen et al., 2007). Even though the proportion of women participating in entrepreneurial activities lags behind the participation in the labour force in many countries (Verheul et al., 2006), this is particularly true for Norway. A high proportion of Norwegian women have higher education, and Norway, together with Sweden, is considered to be one of the most gender-equal countries in the world. It has been considered a paradox that the level of female entrepreneurship is still relatively low (Foss and Ljunggren, 2006). This paradox has, to some extent, been shared with other Scandinavian countries and has partly been explained by the gender division of the labour market (vertically and horizontally) in these countries, which all have a large public sector. Figures from Nordic Statistics (Nordic Statistical Yearbook, 2007) show, for example, that construction and building firms have 11 per cent men employees and 1 per cent women employees, while the service industry firms have 55 per cent women employees and 21 per cent men employees.

Sole proprietorship is the most usual legal form for all businesses, and especially more women use this legal form. This form sets no lower limit of equity capital or other resources to start a business and has less formal requirements than other legal forms. It is therefore considered to be an easier way to start a small business. On the other hand, self-employed women have fewer rights in the welfare system when it comes to maternity leave, sickness allowance, and so on. Policies have been changed to make up for this, including, amongst other things, full coverage for maternity leave for self-employed women.

A deducted consequence of the labour division of education and occupation is the gendered structure of entrepreneurship and business ownership. In addition to the relatively low percentage of women among business founders and owners, industries are highly gender segregated (Statistics Norway, 2007).

When looking at overall motives to start businesses, both women and men, and particularly women, maintain that they conduct their businesses in order to realize an idea, achieve job satisfaction and independence, and to support themselves and their families, and that profit is not the main goal (Ljunggren, 2003). However there are differences in terms of growth motivation between men and women, where women have lower growth ambitions than men (Delmar and Holmquist, 2004). These results are stable across industries and over time.

ENTREPRENEURSHIP POLICY – TO INCREASE ENTREPRENEURSHIP AMONG WOMEN

Several policy measures have been put forward to increase women's participation in the business sector as entrepreneurs, managers and board members. Policies and measures were implemented to encourage women's entrepreneurship and business ownership as a part of the regional policies in the 1980s. The aim was to get women to start their own businesses and create their own employment and, by this, avoid depopulation and demographic imbalance as many women moved to urban areas for education and work (Pettersen et al., 1999). Encouraging women is currently integrated as one important goal of the Norwegian industry and entrepreneurship support organization (Innovation Norway) at national and regional levels, and is included in most support schemes directed towards entrepreneurs in Norway. Support schemes are mainly financial (grants and loans), but these are also combined with 'soft support' including network programmes and advisory services. Supporting female entrepreneurs has become a more integrated general goal of central support schemes for entrepreneurs (Alsos et al., 2006). For some schemes clear objectives on the share of women beneficiaries have been put forward such as an objective of 40 per cent of the entrepreneurial grants allocated to women. In recent years, women in management and board positions have received the largest attention in the debate on women in the business sector. A new law introduced on 1 January 2006 requires boards in all public limited companies in the private sector to have a minimum of 40 per cent representation of each gender. By February 2008, 39 per cent of the representatives in public limited companies were women; 93 per cent of the 459 public limited companies fulfilled the requirements on representations of both genders.

While the other policy measures implemented seem to have advanced women's positions as wage earners, politicians and cabinet members, the results when it comes to entrepreneurs and business ownership have been much more disappointing. The idea that women can own and run a business has become more accepted, but as we have shown, women business owners are still few. Ownership of a business and entrepreneurship still has the flavour of 'being different', and entrepreneurship is still viewed as a male domain. The view of entrepreneurship as predominantly a male domain means that men shape the norm, whereas women entrepreneurs are seen as deviations from that norm.

In the remaining parts of this chapter we discuss the reasons for the women entrepreneurship paradox. We start with the historical paths forming the cultural and structural gender division we see today. Following on from this, we discuss how contemporary practices re-create this structure and serve as mechanisms counteracting the gender-equality means and policies put forward to fill the gender gap in the business sector.

HISTORICAL PATHS OF A GENDERED BUSINESS SECTOR

Property structures in present capitalist society are based on historical paths of how inheritance and ownership structures used to be organized. This influences how property, capital and profit are conceived and valued in society today, and consequently forms the gendered structure of business ownership.

In the nineteenth century the juridical doctrine in Norway was that the husband had the experience and insight into economic life and, therefore, had to hold authority over the family economy (Sandvik, 2005). It was presumed that wives had too little understanding of economic matters to make right choices and their economic insight was too limited to have authority in the family economy.

During this period, the economy was regarded as something compli-cated to which men rather than women had insight. A dimension of risk-taking was also added to the qualities of economic actor, and there was a clear notion of a public male sphere and a private female sphere. A study of a big family firm in Trondheim reveals that while women through the eighteenth century took part in the firm, they turned to homemaking in the nineteenth century (Bull, 1998). The cultural tradition that places women and men in different social positions with gender-based definitions of work and home responsibilities plays a large part in keeping women invisible in business life. Historically women's work responsibilities outside the home were secondary to their obligations to organize the domestic, emotional and social life of the family. Men, on the other hand, have organized their lives in accordance with the demands of their work. Both in the bourgeois and the farm sector, work in the household sphere (milking, housekeeping) and work outside on the fields and in the forest were highly gendered. With the mechanizing of dairy farming, milking also became a male activity.

Although liberal legal reforms gave unmarried women legal majority (1845), equal inheritance (1854) and access to higher education (1884), the new matrimonial law of 1888 ensured once again that husbands had author-ity over the joint estate. It was not until 1927 that the husband's authority in marriage was repealed. Also the law that gave sons and daughters equal inheritance was opposed by conservatives; they presumed that the husband should govern the joint estate 'because he knew what economy was about' (Sandvik, 2005: 116). There was also an exception in the law for farms. According to the Allodial Rights Act (*Odelsloven*) of 1821, the first-born son in the family had first option to take over the family farm and its forest. This law was restricted to farms, but patrilinear inheritance of family busi-ness has been a common practice. The norm within family businesses has traditionally been of transferring ownership from father to first-born son. Daughters have inherited other values or smaller parts of the firm. As firm owners, daughters have often been invisible successors. This invisibility is part of traditional family business configurations, which have focused on the male founder and his heirs. The strength of traditional family roles, both within society and within individual families, kept women's business contributions from being acknowledged (Dumas, 1998). After the revision in 1974 the first-born child (born after 1965) regardless of sex, was allowed the first priority to allodial possession. But, it is still most common that sons take over both farms and family businesses.

In contemporary Norway we still see traces of this, for example, in the Allodial Rights Act. Even though it was changed in 1974, the tradition of sons inheriting farms (and firms) is still strong. The reason why women work part-time is that they have reproduction and care obligations, that is, taking care of children and being responsible for other reproductive activities such as cooking and cleaning. Women or young girls choosing specific sectors for education and occupation could also be interpreted as the commoditization of household and intimate sphere activities (Wheelock, 1992). Female sphere activities are continued in the market part of the economy. These business opportunities are understood as more eligible to women, as women then adapt the activities within the female sphere to business activities. In this sense they comply with both the entrepreneurship field and the female field, and also live up to the expectations to bring in something new when they enter the entrepreneurship field. However in Norway the occupations many women are educated for (for example, care) have not offered many opportunities for women to become self-employed as these services are organized within the public sector.

GENDERED DIVISION OF EDUCATION AND LABOUR

As we have shown, the labour force participation for women is high in Norway, and the gap between women and men's participation is small compared with other countries. However, more women than men work part-time; in 2004, 43 per cent of women and 13 per cent of men worked part-time. In particular, women with more than one child under the age of 16 more frequently work part-time. For men, part-time work is more common in combination with studies or at the end of their career.

As mentioned, there is a strong gender division of the labour market when it comes to industries. Despite the increase in the educational level, particularly for young women, male and female career paths are still quite traditional. Young women tend to choose education for work in the public sector, while young men are educated for work in the private sector. This implies that, for instance, nurses, teachers, cleaners and secretaries are female-dominated occupations while joiners, plumbers, drivers and engineers are male-dominated occupations. During the past decades the public sector has experienced strong growth, primarily in health, social care and education. Today approximately one-third of all employed people work in the public sector, 53 per cent of women compared with 21 per cent of men

(Statistics Norway, 2006). Consequently, the Norwegian labour market is strongly gender segregated, that is, that women are predominantly found in female-dominated occupations and industries.

The labour market is not only horizontally segregated, it is also vertically segregated – men and women are on different hierarchical levels. In the whole Norwegian economy approximately one in six organizations is led by a woman (Jensen and Schøne, 2007). According to figures from Statistics Norway, in 2004 approximately 29 per cent of the managers were women, respectively 44 per cent in the public sector and 25 per cent in the private sector (Statistics Norway, 2006). This horizontal and vertical segregation may be one important explanation of why there are few women entrepreneurs in Norway. Some types of education and work experience may provide more competences which are helpful when starting and running a business. As we have seen, women and men's competences differ. Women have less experience from the private sector and less management experience than men, and this may be one explanation of why there are so few women entrepreneurs in Norway. This is in accordance with Delmar and Holmquist's (2004) argument that if the labour market is segregated, then ownership will also be segregated. Women and men will mostly engage in entrepreneurial activities where they have some previous experience and knowledge.

One of the arguments presented for the relatively low incidence of women entrepreneurs in Norway is that women lack the competences and networks needed to be able to identify new business opportunities and to start new firms. Many of the government's support initiatives build on this presumption of a competency barrier (Alsos and Ljunggren, 1998). Entrepreneurial training or networking activities are offered women entrepreneurs, along with financial support for this type of activities. The competency barrier can, among other things, be connected to the gender division of education and labour mentioned earlier. Women lack experience in the private sector and consequently may have less experience of how businesses are run and fewer network contacts among entrepreneurs or the business sector.

FAMILY-FRIENDLY POLICIES

One of the main reasons that Norway receives attention as a country with a high degree of gender equality is its family-friendly policies. The basic assumption is that family-friendly policies have a positive effect on women's employment and entrepreneurship, because it allows women to more freely manage their time and still have a career. However, patterns of family policy related to women entering the labour market and subsequently entering entrepreneurship is far from straightforward. Many of these policies are related to the political system in general. For example, countries that are low in women's entrepreneurship, such as Norway and Sweden, provide universal provisions for public supported childcare and maternity leave, whereas the USA and the UK, countries experiencing relatively high and increasing levels of women's entrepreneurship, neither provide government paid leave nor have adopted policies that guarantee access to childcare. So while higher levels of childcare provision as in the Nordic welfare states often are accompanied by high levels of women's employment, it does not seem to follow high levels of women's entrepreneurship and business ownership.

Also the gender-equality policies in these countries have had divergent foci: the USA has implemented a powerful policy of equal opportunities within the labour market but regarded family issues as private matters. The Norwegians have a long-term political goal of gender equality in all areas of society, compromising work–family linkages with a strong emphasis on arrangements allowing parents to combine work and family life. In combination with traditional gender roles, these arrangements have been utilized to a much higher degree by women then by men. This may be conceptualized as though Norway has been less successful in implementing a powerful policy of equal opportunities within the labour market and, in particular, within the private sector (Birkelund and Sandnes, 2003). Thus one conclusion could be that the Norwegian family policy and gender policy have been family-friendly, which is favourable for the family but, when utilized by women, not favourable for their career opportunities in the labour market or for their (potential) entrepreneurial career.

CONCLUSIONS AND IMPLICATIONS

Historical paths have identified entrepreneurship and business ownership as something connected to men in the Norwegian society. When gender equality has been gradually implemented in society and resulted in remarkable progress when it comes to women's engagement in the labour market and representation in political systems, one could expect the strong masculine connotations related to entrepreneurship and business ownership to fade. Nevertheless it seems that the masculine constructions are also reinforced by contemporary processes. These are, for instance, related to the gendered division of labour, including horizontal and vertical gender segregation, as well as the tendency for women to work part-time. Further, the family-friendly policies, which have a positive effect on women's employment, may also strengthen the connotation of family and domestic tasks as female. The Nordic welfare model has provided good opportunities for women to take part in the economic sphere without removing opportunities to build and take care of a family. Secure employment possibilities in the public sector and the dual model, where women can be good mothers and build a career simultaneously, have made the business sector and a career as an entrepreneur or manager less attractive for women. The discourse of the good mother and what it means to be a woman, as well as the social creation of large parts of the business sector as masculine, contributes to gendered understandings of what women and men can and should do. These processes influence women's career choices.

A number of measures have been put forward to increase women's entrance into the business sectors as entrepreneurs and business owners. However, when looking at the results it is apparent that the policy initiatives implemented so far have not been as successful as expected. The measures implemented have largely been based on an assumption that the lack of women as entrepreneurs and business owners are due to women's lack of resources. Consequently, resources have been provided to increase women's engagement in entrepreneurial activities, including financial competence and network support to increase financial, human and social capital. However, the gender gap in entrepreneurship is more deeply embedded in wider societal processes. These measures have therefore just scratched the surface of the gender gap, to some extent mended the symptoms, but not been able to change the fundamentally gendered aspects of the business sector.

Enhancing women's entrepreneurship would require coordination of different policy areas. Family policies need to promote men's equality and bring men into the intimate sphere to take domestic responsibilities at the same level as women. Education policies should find mechanisms to encourage girls and boys to make choices that are not bound only by tradition. Policies encouraging equality need to encompass the business sector and more attention needs to be paid to encouraging the business sector to work together with other sectors in equality issues. We also see the need to set both a short- and long-term horizon on aims and work. Long term means reallocating financial resources – on an aggregated level – to enhance human, social, symbolic and cultural capital.

This chapter has discussed gendered aspects of entrepreneurship and business ownership in Norway. It is important to take national circumstances into account when explaining gender diversity. Important factors include size and composition of the economy, management styles, education level, labour force participation, welfare systems and politics that directly or indirectly affect gender diversity. This also means that research results from one country cannot necessarily be transferred to a geographical setting that is considerably different. However, lessons can be learned about the mechanisms advancing and hampering women's participation in the business sector. Norway is an interesting case for the study of these mechanisms, as many of the basic conditions for gender equality are in place while the proportions of women as entrepreneurs, managers and board members are still relatively low. Thus the focus should be turned to the mechanisms causing gender imbalance in positions of power in the business sector, rather than viewed as embedded in a relatively gender equal context. While many aspects are particular for the Norwegian context, we believe that the processes described here are fundamental and can be found in other contexts as well, although in different forms.

NOTES

1. It seems though that the research field on capitalism and gender in the present literature often deals with economic development in so-called under-developed countries (for example, Boserup, 2007), not saying that 'developed' countries have nothing to learn from this.
2. This subsection is largely based on the work of anthropologist Jorunn Solheim, particularly as discussed in her book *Gender and Modernity* (2007).

REFERENCES

Ahl, H.J. (2002), *The Making of the Female Entrepreneur: A Discourse Analysis of Research Texts on Women's Entrepreneurship*, JIBS Dissertation Series No. 015, Jönköping: Jönköping University.

Aldrich, H.E. (1999), *Organizations Evolving*, London: Sage Publications.

Allen, I.E., Elam, A., Langowitz, N. and Dean, M. (2007), *Global Entrepreneurship Monitor. 2007 Report on Women and Entrepreneurship*, Wellesley, MA: Babson College.

Alsos, G.A., and Ljunggren, E. (1998), 'Does the business start-up process differ by gender? A longitudinal study of nascent entrepreneurs', *Journal of Enterprising Culture*, 6 (4), 347–67.

Alsos, G.A., Brastad, B., Iakovleva, T. and Ljunggren, E. (2006), *Flere og bedre bedriftsetableringer? Evaluering av Innovasjon Norges stipendordninger 1999–2005*, Bodø: Nordlandsforskning.

Baker, T., Aldrich, H.E. and Liou, N. (1997), 'Invisible entrepreneurs: the neglect of women business owners by mass media and scholarly journals in the USA', *Entrepreneurship & Regional Development*, 9 (3), 221–38.

Berg, N.G. (1997), 'Gender, place and entrepreneurship', *Entrepreneurship & Regional Development*, 9 (3), 259–68.

Bird, B. and Brush, C. (2002), 'A gendered perspective on organizational creation', *Entrepreneurship Theory and Practice*, 26 (3), 41–65.

Birkelund, G.E. and Sandnes, T. (2003), 'Paradoxes of welfare states and equal opportunities: gender and managerial power in Norway and the USA', *Comparative Social Research*, **21**, 201–41.
Boserup, E. (2007) *Woman's Role in Economic Development*, London: Earthscan.
Bourdieu, P. (1990), *The Logic of Practice*, Stanford, CA: Stanford University Press.
Bruni, A., Gherardi, S. and Poggio, B. (2004), 'Doing gender, doing entrepreneurship: an ethnographic account of intertwined practices', *Gender, Work and Organization*, **11** (4), 406–29.
Bull, I. (1998), *De trondhjemske handelshusene på 1700-tallet. Slekt, hushold og forretning*, vol. 26, Trondheim: NTNU.
Carter, N.M., Williams, M. and Reynolds, P.D. (1997), 'Discontinuance among new firms in retail: the influence of initial resources, strategy, and gender', *Journal of Business Venturing*, **12** (2), 125–45.
Chell, E., Haworth, J. and Brearely, S. (1991), *The Entrepreneurial Personality: Concepts, Cases and Categories*, London: Routledge.
Delmar, F. and Holmquist, C. (2004), *Women's Entrepreneurship: Issues and Policies*, Istanbul: OECD.
Dumas, C. (1998), 'Women's pathways to participation and leadership in the family-owned firm', *Family Business Review*, **11** (3), 219–29.
Elam, A.B. (2008), *Gender and Entrepreneurship. A Multilevel Theory and Analysis*, Cheltenham, UK and Northampton, MA, USA: Edward Elgar.
Foss, L. and Ljunggren, E. (2006), 'Women's entrepreneurship in Norway: recent trends and future challenges', in P.G. Greene, C.G. Brush, N.M. Carter, E.J. Gatewood and M.M. Hart (eds), *Growth Oriented Women Entrepreneurs and their Business – a Global Research Perspective*, Cheltenham, UK and Northampton, MA, USA: Edward Elgar.
Gatewood, E.J., Carter, N.M., Brush, C.G., Greene, P.G. and Hart, M.M. (eds) (2003), *Women Entrepreneurs, their Ventures, and their Venture Capital Industry. An Annotated Bibliography*, Stockholm: ESBRI.
Harding, S. (1987), *Feminism and Methodology*, Milton Keynes: Open University Press.
Jensen, R.S. and Schøne, P. (2007), 'Kvinneledede virksomheter – gjør det noen forskjell for bedrifters familievennlighet?', *Sosiologisk tidsskrift* (3).
Lewis, P. (2006), 'The quest for invisibility: female entrepreneurs and the masculine norm of entrepreneurship', *Gender, Work and Organization*, **15** (5): 453–69.
Ljunggren, E. (2003), 'Entreprenørskap og kjønn. En kunnskapsreise mellom to perspektiver: fra individ til relasjon', PhD-thesis, Umeå University.
Ljunggren, E. and Alsos, G.A. (2007), 'Media expressions of entrepreneurs: presentations and discourses of male and female entrepreneurs in Norway', in N.M. Carter, C. Henry, B.Ó. Cinnéide and K. Johnston (eds), *Female Entrepreneurship: Implications for Education, Training and Policy*, London: Routledge, pp. 88–109.
Nordic Statistical Yearbook (2007), *Nordic Statistical Yearbook*, ed. U. Agerskov, Nord 2007:1, Copenhagen: Statistics Denmark.
Pettersen, L.T., Alsos, G.A., Anvik, C.H., Gjertsen, A. and Ljunggren, E. (1999), *Blir det arbeidsplasser av dette da, jenter? Evaluering av kvinnesatsingen i distriktspolitikken*, Bodø: Nordland Research Institute.
Polanyi, K. (2001), *The Great Transformation: The Political and Economic Origins of our Time*, Boston, MA: Beacon Press.

Sandvik, H. (2005), 'Decision-making on marital property in Norway, 1500–1800', in M. Ågren and A.L. Ericsson (eds), *The Martial Economy in Scandinavia and Britain 1400–1900*, Aldershot: Ashgate.

Solbrække, K.N. (2002), 'Synlig bransje – usynlig makt: kjønn som implisitt maktstruktur i reklamebransjen', in A.L. Ellingsæter and J. Solheim (eds), *Den usynlige hånd? Kjønnsmakt og moderne arbeidsliv*, Oslo: Gyldendal akademisk, pp. 360–90.

Solheim, J. (2002), 'Kjønn, kompetanse og hegemonisk makt', in A.L. Ellingsæter and J. Solheim (eds), *Den usynlige hånd? Kjønnsmakt og moderne arbeidsliv*, Oslo: Gyldendal akademisk, pp. 110–40.

Solheim, J. (2007), *Kjønn og modernitet (Gender and Modernity)*, Oslo: Pax.

Statistics Norway (2006), *Mot maktens tinder*, Oslo: Statistics Norway.

Statistics Norway (2007), http://statbank.ssb.no/statistikkbanken/Default_FR.asp?PXSid=0&nvl=true&PLanguage=0&tilside=selectvarval/define.asp&Tabellid=05188 (accessed 20 October 2008).

Statistics Norway (2008), *Personer i arbeidsstyrken, etter Kjønn. Utvalgte Land. 2006 (Persons in Workforce, by Gender. Selected Countries. 2006)*, available at: http://www.ssb.no/aarbok/2008/tab/tab-210.html (accessed 20 October 2008).

Swedberg, R. and Granovetter, M.S. (2001), *The Sociology of Economic Life*, Boulder, CO: Westview Press.

Verheul, I., Van Stel, A. and Thurik, R. (2006), 'Explaining female and male entrepreneurship at the country level', *Entrepreneurship & Regional Development*, **18**, 151–83.

Wheelock, J. (1992), 'The household in the total economy', in P. Ekins and M. Max-Neef (eds), *Real Life Economics – Understanding Wealth Creation*, New York: Routledge.

Wheelock, J. and Mariussen, Å. (eds) (1997), *Household, Work and Economic Change: A Comparative Perspective*, Boston, MA, Dordrecht and London: Kluwer Academic.

Yanagisako, S.J. (2002), *Producing Culture and Capital: Family Firms in Italy*, Princeton, NJ: Princeton University Press.

4. Female leadership and company profitability

Annu Kotiranta, Anne Kovalainen and Petri Rouvinen

INTRODUCTION

There is a great amount of statistical evidence that shows that women are important drivers of growth in many of the world's economies (Arenius and Kovalainen, 2006; Minniti et al., 2005), especially in small business and new business creation. However, the position of women in top management is less convincing (Carter et al., 2003; Eurostat, 2007; Kotiranta et al., 2007). The percentage of women is lower than men at all levels of managerial hierarchy. This is especially the case in the highest managerial levels in corporations. Even today the number of women in the highest ranks of corporate management and decision-making positions is still less than 10 per cent in most industrialized countries (Eurostat, 2007). Likewise an average of only 10–11 per cent of members of the highest decision-making bodies in the top 50 companies in Europe are women (European Commission database on women and men in decision-making), and the development towards gender equality has been slow. In particular the presence and share of women in the top positions of corporate governance has been highlighted as being important not only with respect to corporate values but also due to the importance of the diversity of boards and firm value (Carter et al., 2003). Corporations themselves have started to argue that the board of directors signals good managerial patterns, diversity in values and the dynamics within corporation culture. The argument in much of the literature on corporate governance is that gender diversity plays a specific role in the company's value and profitability (Bilimoria, 2006; Burke, 2000), and this has been verified through empirical evidence (Carter et al., 2003; Smith et al., 2006).

Given the positive relationship stated in some of the literature, gender should be considered in top corporate appointments, taking into consideration the relationship to the general company structure and, more importantly, to societal structure. The scarcity of women in the top positions of large companies and corporations worldwide can also be seen as a hindrance to the competitiveness of European companies in terms of the best use of available human resources.

The Nordic countries, Finland being one of them, have taken a leadership position for Europe and globally in questions of public and private gender equality and women's labor force participation, political activity and representation, and even in the development of gender-specific legislation. The enabling structures and other measures of gender activity in the economy and in society are in place for formal and informal equality between women and men (for example, gender equality legislation, childcare support, women's activity in the labor market, in local and state government and in politics). As an example, publicly available, universal day care, irrespective of family form, family income or women's employment relationship is a prerequisite for women's high labor force participation. The existence of childcare systems and other possible family support systems thus facilitates women's employment and high educational patterns. Even if women's participation in the labor force is high, and in fact their educational qualifications are even higher than for men, the gender gap persists among women and men in management positions. According to the Global Gender Gap index Finland shows equality in educational attainment and health indexes but does not show the same equality in economic participation and opportunities (Hausmann et al., 2007). Which leads us to wonder why women do not make it to top management in otherwise gender equal countries such as Finland?

Less than a tenth of the chief executive officers (CEOs) of Finnish firms and less than a fourth of corporate board members in Finnish corporations are women. From a social standpoint more women are wanted in top management, the possibilities for recruitment among the highly skilled female labor force exist, but one of the questions remains, should company owners and those representing their business interests be concerned with the role of women in top management? Scientific research methods have been applied in this study to try to find an answer to this question.

Our results indicate that a company led by a female CEO is on average slightly higher than one percentage point – in practice about 10 per cent – more profitable than a corresponding company led by a male CEO. This observation holds true even after taking into account size differences and a number of other factors that could affect profitability. The percentage share of female board members also has a similar positive impact. These findings are significant and important not only from a statistical and research perspective, but also from a business standpoint.

But why does female leadership contribute to a company's bottom line?

Several suggestions are consistent with our findings, even though – due to data constraints – we were unable to evaluate their respective merits empirically. Simply put, women may be better leaders than men, or it is possible (and even likely) that due to the tougher selection process, female business leaders constitute a more exclusive – and thus a more competent – group than their male peers. Female leadership may also be associated with a company's overall cultural diversity and multidimensionality as well as good governance and management practices.

WHY DO GENDER, BOARD DIVERSITY AND COMPANY PROFITABILITY MATTER?

The European Commission (2005) found that on average in 2004 only 10 per cent of the highest decision-making body (board) of the 50 largest publicly listed companies were women. The comparison covered the EU-25 and five non-EU countries. Furthermore the share of women in corporate board rooms in the USA is also relatively low despite the high share of female managers in general. Women held only 15 per cent of all the Fortune 500 board seats in 2005 (Catalyst, 2006). The Catalyst report concludes that the rate of progress for gender equality on corporate boards has been slow (Catalyst, 2006).

Finland has in general achieved high gender equality when compared with many nations – except when it comes to business leadership and ownership. Less than a tenth of company CEOs and chairmen of the board are women; less than a fourth of company board members are women.[1] The corresponding shares for large multinational corporations in Finland are even lower. For women's entrepreneurship the participation of women is slightly higher; including self-employment approximately 27–30 per cent of companies and businesses are owned by women. Of the employed population 48.3 per cent are women. In politics, women received the right to vote in 1906 and became eligible to stand as candidates in general elections that same year – a first in Europe. The first women in the Parliament were elected in 1907. Today the Finnish Parliament has 82 out of 200 total members (41 per cent). Twelve out of 20 of Ministers are women in 2009 (60 per cent).

For the purpose of this research we will focus only on business ownership of limited companies, their management and profitability. We estimate that approximately one-fourth of these companies have been established by women, according to their relative share of all entrepreneurship in Finland.

According to a Finnish proverb, 'War does not long for one man'. But is business leadership in need of additional women? From a social stand-point the answer is obviously 'yes'. It would appear right and fair that women and men should have equal opportunities for success in business.

Another and more challenging question can be raised: is it worthwhile for business owners and those representing their interests to be concerned about the role of women in top management? From a corporate social responsibility perspective, the answer is again 'yes'. But does this hold true in the light of cold accounting figures? From an equality perspective, the answer is also 'yes'.

Many politicians have stated that Finland cannot afford not to utilize women's knowledge on the board of directors of listed companies. Vladimír Špidla, European Union (EU) Commissioner for Employment, Social Affairs and Equal Opportunities, has claimed that appointing women to leadership positions is profitable for businesses. Despite this political support the attitude of the research and business communities has been more reserved due to the scarcity of hard facts on the matter.

Several studies can be found in international academic literature focusing on the connection between female leadership and the financial success of a business (see discussion to follow). The research topic is not an easy one and the findings are often strongly contradictory. Small and skewed data-sets often limit the credibility of the studies. The shares of women in top executive and management positions are often so small that even in samples of thousands of companies there might only be a few female leaders. Nevertheless the literature indicates that there might be a positive correlation between female leadership and financial success.

PREVIOUS EVIDENCE ON GENDER AND COMPANY PERFORMANCE: HIERARCHICAL DIVISION OF LABOR, CORPORATE DIVERSITY, MANAGERIAL PRESSURES OR BETTER MANAGEMENT?

Research strongly suggests that corporate board diversity and manage-rial recruitment are positively correlated with several aspects of company activities, that is, companies that recruit, develop and advance diverse employees, including women, make better decisions, produce more mar-ketable products and retain several key business advantages over more homogeneous companies (for example, Bradshaw and Wicks, 2000; Carter et al., 2003; Robinson and Dechant, 1997). Board diversity is often related to the number of outsider directors relative to inside directors on the board. Less empirical research can be found on the gender composi-tion of the board and its relationship to shareholder value creation, as measured by profitability. The lack of evidence for or against the matter in question might be due to the lack of generalizable, large data-sets and/or studies based on longitudinal data-sets.

This short review will not cover the entire variety of types of literature on women's leadership and all performance measures used in business. Much of the literature in general focuses on middle management, which may have only limited direct influence on the performance of the company. We are specifically interested in looking at the activities of boards of directors. We specifically did not focus on firms' internal boards or executive boards, boards of management, managing boards, management boards or similar groups, which are most often a group of people responsible for the every-day management and administration of a company and the implementation of plans, and which are accountable to the board of directors (or the supervisory board). It is worth noting, however, that the composition, role and importance of the board of directors (or the supervisory board) in terms of the actual leading of the company varies from one country and corporate governance system to another, and thus organizational solutions can influence companies' results in a variety of ways. Even if our results are not necessarily country specific, the context where research is conducted has an important role for the settings. In the following we begin by briefly describing some features of the Finnish labor market. We then move on to discuss the research results of the possible connections between lower and middle management and company productivity, and in the final part of the literature review focus more specifically to the board and CEO levels and their relation to firms' productivity.

GENDER IN THE FINNISH WORKFORCE

In Finland women's employment grew rapidly with the modernization of Finnish society and with the development of its societal structure and economy from an agricultural society into a postindustrial service society with high-technology telecommunications corporations such as Nokia and more traditional, yet high-technology, corporations such as global forest product companies. But at least as strongly as telecommunications mirror the present-day Finland, so also does the image of the strong Nordic welfare state: one key part of the public image of Finland comes from the strong and universal welfare state service sector, which employs a large share of women. The strong and salient segregation prevailing in the labor markets is at least partly offset by the strong public sector participation of women (Kovalainen, 2003: 190). The Act on Equality between Women and Men has been in force since 1987. In public sector activities (formal committees, political life) the quota system for minority sex at 40 per cent was introduced in 1995. It is worthwhile to note that the corporate governance code under preparation does not include quotas.

Women have an active role in the labor markets in Finland. Employment rates of women and men are very similar, 69 per cent for women and 70 per cent for men (2008), and even unemployment rates at the labor-force level resemble each other. Employment, however, is highly segregated according to gender. The horizontal segregation is most visible in the division of labor between public and private sector. Of women 58 per cent are employed at the private sector, 36 per cent by local public governments and 6 per cent by the central government. Of men 83 per cent are employed in the private sector, 10 per cent by local governments and 7 per cent by the central government (Kovalainen, 2003: 193). Vertical segregation is also apparent. Even if the state has a substantial role in promoting formal equality in education and politics and strong support for the comprehensive social welfare system, the family policy system has not directly fostered women's managerial careers (Arenius and Kovalainen, 2006; Aaltio and Kovalainen, 2003). Partly as a consequence of high segregation in education and in working life, vertical segregation is high as fewer than 2–3 per cent of top managers in companies are women.

GENDER, MIDDLE MANAGEMENT POSITIONS AND FIRM PERFORMANCE

Even if it is argued that traditional career paths are no longer viable and a better understanding of careers is needed (for example, Woodd, 2000), patterns of career promotions and hierarchies and segregation in organizations do matter both for individuals and for companies. But to what extent and how careers and gender are related to company profitability is a complex question and has several contingent factors. The analyses of the impact of cultural diversity of personnel (in addition to gender cultural diversity also includes ethnic background) and organizational structure on company performance and profitability in the US banking sector have shown that the gender division of employees is not related to profitability (Richard et al., 2006). According to Richard et al.'s (2006) results the share of female workers was not connected with company profitability, however, in top-heavy and hierarchical organizations (a high number of managers as a proportion of the total employees) a positive relationship can nevertheless be found. In mature and rigid organizations the relationship may even be negative. However, the results of this study may have limited generalizability because the respondents were from only 79 companies in the banking sector, representing a 16 per cent response rate (Richard et al., 2006: 2096).

The diversity of boards, in terms of its members representing different societal groups, has become a major issue within corporate governance. A number of studies have sought to explore the impact of diversity on firm performance. The debate focuses on whether a corporation's board should reflect the variety of the firm's stakeholders or be more in line with society in general. The relationship between gender structure of corporate boards and business performance can be analysed using diversity measurements (see Rose, 2007; Terjesen et al., 2009). According to Rose (2007) the gender diversity of the board does not affect performance. In Rose's study the data was from slightly over 100 listed companies from 1998–2001. Tobin's Q was the only indicator of stock market success used in Rose's study. (Tobin's Q is the ratio of the market value of a firm's assets and the replacement cost of the firm's assets.) There is some question as to what indicates company success. Therefore, several indicators are usually used. Tobin's Q, as the only measure of performance, is not used as often as different rates of return (Lindenberg and Ross, 1981; Smirlock et al., 1984; Wolfe and Sauaia, 2003).

GENDER, BOARD MEMBERS, CEOS AND FIRM PERFORMANCE

If gender is to have measurable effect on company performance it can be assumed to take place at the highest management level. The positions of CEO and the board of directors, because of their strategic and managerial roles, are assumed to directly affect business performance, even if the question of gender and firm profitability is complex. One of the extensive studies analysing the relationship between the gender structure of company management and business performance is a study of 2500 Danish companies from 1993–2001. Smith et al. (2006) found that the share of female board members and female CEOs was positively correlated with company profitability. In particular, highly educated female CEOs improved the profitability of the company. The positive effects of women in top management on performance strongly depended on the qualifications of the particular female managers. According to Smith et al. (2006: 570) this effect was largely due to female managers having the best educational qualifications. With respect to female board members and company performance, it appears that female board members who represent the staff have a positive impact on company performance. However, the effect often disappears when controlling for unobserved company-specific factors.

A major labor market and work organization literature on gender and work has found evidence of a 'glass ceiling', whereby women are under-represented among senior management. One of the key questions is the extent to which this reflects unobserved differences in productivity, preferences, prejudice or systematically biased beliefs about the ability of female managers.

It has been argued that one of the areas where gender inequality is strongly rooted is in the financial markets which continuously provide a variety of measures of the market's perception of the value of firms. These measures should take account of the beliefs of market participants about the abilities of men and women in senior management (for example, Mohan and Chen, 2004; Wolfers, 2006). Therefore financial data is potentially valuable when providing insight into the dynamics of discrimination, gender inequality and specifically the persistence of biased beliefs about abilities of women and men.

Wolfers (2006) investigated possible discrimination against women as CEOs by examining whether expected earnings of companies led by female CEOs were systematically underestimated by stock market analysts and found they were not. The indicators used were expected and realized returns from holding the stock. The Execucomp database used for the study traced 1500 S&P firms from 1992 to 2004. This 15-year database identified only 14 female CEOs and 4175 male CEOs during this period. Wolfers remarked that in the 15-year sample 1.3 per cent of all CEO-years were worked by women. However, the results may say more about the weakness of the data than about the market's underestimation of the profit-making ability of female CEOs.[2]

Carter et al. (2003) analysed the share of women on boards and stock exchange success of companies. They found, interestingly, that there was a positive correlation between a high share of women on boards and the high market value of shares. However, Rose (2007) did not find any statistical correlation between the share of women on boards and stock exchange success.

Finally, Krishnan and Park (2005) found that ethnic and gender diversity of boards influences the values of shares, as well as ways of leading, networking and managing within the company, which have been found with positive correlation to profitability.

It seems that the literature comes to different conclusions about gender equality and firm performance, depending on the analysis performed and the data used. Therefore the previous results should be interpreted with caution, and hypotheses building from this research is suspect. Our general argument is that business decisions do not respect the logic of democracy or the aim to achieve gender equality. There is evidence that gender diversity on corporate boards contributes to more effective corporate governance through a variety of processes, some of which do not show up as a direct influence on the firm's bottom line (Terjesen et al., 2009). Business owners and those representing their interests are of course concerned about the issue in the name of corporate social responsibility. While gender equality might be listed among corporate values, ultimately only its connection to financial success ensures the interest of owners. Therefore we find it important to analyse the gender-equality performance link in order to come to an informed decision.

FEMALE LEADERSHIP PAYS OFF: MATERIALS, METHODS AND RESULTS

Data

The results presented here are based on accurate and comprehensive data and appropriate research methods. The research question has been approached as 'objectively' as possible. Our target population – compiled by Statistics Finland – comprised Finnish limited companies employing at least 10 persons in 2003. We have removed from the data-set all companies not in operation in the time period. The sample covers 91 per cent of the target population.[3] The average sizes of firms with male and female CEOs were 71 and 56 employees, respectively. The average size of companies with male-dominated boards (over half) was over 80 employees, while the corresponding figure for companies with female-dominated boards (at least half) was under 30 employees. Our sample was the most internationally extensive and nationally representative company-level data to have been used in gender research.

Since we analyse data on limited companies we do not know the origins of the companies in terms of their entrepreneurial ownership, that is, whether it was owned by a man or a woman. However, we consider that the information derived from the analysis of our data is informative with respect to women's entrepreneurship.

Of the sample businesses, 7.6 per cent have female CEOs and 7.1 per cent have a female chairman of the board. On average 22.3 per cent of the board members were female. Because the gender of the board's chairmanship does not, according to our empirical analysis, have a significant effect, we focused on female CEOs and on the share of women on corporate boards. Several indicators of business profitability were examined in our study: return on assets (the primary indicator), return on investments and the operating margin.[4]

Analysis and Results: Is Female Leadership Correlated with Financial Success?

Description

A simple comparison of respective (unconditional) means revealed that businesses managed by women and men were different in several respects. The average profitability of firms in the sample was 12.3 per cent. The average profitability of firms with a male CEO was 12.2 per cent and with a female CEO was 14.0 per cent. The difference (1.8 percentage points) was statistically very significant (.01). The average profitability of companies where at least half of the board members were female was 14.7 per cent. The difference (3.1 percentage points) with respect to the 11.5 per cent of other companies was statistically very significant (.01). When comparing direct (unconditional) means, companies led by women were two to three percentage points (from slightly over 10 per cent to well over 20 per cent) more profitable than companies led by men. This in itself was not a solid basis for drawing conclusions, as companies led by men and women also differed in several other respects. In all of the examined dimensions companies with female leadership had less export activity, they were less likely to be a part of a business group and they were less capital intensive. We also observed statistically significant differences in a number of other variables, although the degree varied according to the leadership dimension considered. Furthermore female leadership varied by industry and region as well as by company size and age. For example, female leadership was most common in education, health and social services, as well as in hotels and restaurants. Female leadership was more common in smaller firms. The average sizes of firms with male and female CEOs were 71 and 56 employees, respectively. The average size of companies with a male-dominated board (over half) was over 80 employees, while the corresponding figure for companies with a female-dominated board (at least half) was under 30 employees.

Modeling

In order to isolate the effect of female leadership, multidimensional regression analysis was carried out to control for other factors possibly affecting company profitability. The dependent variable in our models was profitability. A total of 24 different regressions were carried out that included 44 or 46 dependent variables. In addition to six dependent profitability variables and the basic independent variables, there were four different alternatives for female variables – three separate indicators, all three together and the heteroskedasticity-consistent least squares method.

Of the independent variables the most interesting were naturally the gender of the CEO and the share of women on the board. The literature gives several indications for the importance of the gender balance of the board. The other independent variables were the age of the company's CEO, the size of the board, the average age of the board members, the age difference between the youngest and oldest board member (a proxy for heterogeneity), whether the CEO was also the chairman of the board, the company's export activity, capital intensity, foreign ownership, group relationship, credit rating, auditor's statement (unconditionally approved), gearing ratio, as well as the industry of the company, its geographical location (the headquarters), size (in terms of personnel) and age.

Our model controls for all of the factors referred to. In other words, our findings are not attributable to, for example, industry or size differences, but rather the findings drawn from the regression analysis were conditional on all of the above factors, that is, the effects have already been taken into account in the remaining partial correlation between female leadership and company profitability (see Table 4.1).

Discussion

The findings of this study empirically support the notion that women corporate directors and top management gender diversity are positively related to company profitability. The findings provide support for previous

Table 4.1   *Female leadership and company profitability analysis*

	Return on assets (ROA)	Return on investments (ROI)	Return on sales (ROS)
(1) Least square analysis (whole data, 46 explaining variables)			
Female CEO	1.31	4.63*	−0.92
Female chair in board	−0.03	−0.99	7.14***
Women's share at board	2.20***	3.94*	9.39***
(2) Least square analysis (whole data, 46 explaining variables)			
Female CEO	1.18**	2.975***	0.07
Female chair at board	−0.50	−1.122	−0.08
Women's share of board	1.53***	1.278	1.41***
(3) Least square analysis (whole data, no extreme cases, 46 explaining variables)			
Female CEO	1.27**	3.73***	−0.01
Female chair of board	−0.64	−1.06	−0.46**
Women's share of board	1.40**	1.65	0.00
(4) Estimate less sensitive to extreme cases (whole data, 46 variables)			
Female CEO	0.77*	1.00	0.11
Female chair of board	−0.47	−1.01	−0.45*
Women's share of board	1.57***	1.90***	0.52**

Note: *** $p < .001$; ** $p < .01$; * $p < .05$.

research findings of profitability and management gender. The observed positive and statistically significant correlation between female leadership and profitability is an interesting and important finding for both the academic and business communities. Unfortunately we cannot shed light on any causal relationships underlying our findings. Data permitting a wide range of personal and sociocultural factors should be considered in order to shed more light on the relationships. Even so, several conclusions from the empirical results can be drawn. The possible explanations for the positive correlation between female leadership and company profitability fall into one or more of the following four categories:

1. Generally speaking, women may be better leaders than men (adjusted for the executive compensations of the respective groups).
2. To advance to top management women may face a tougher selection process (due to, for example, discrimination), making them a more exclusive and thus, on average, a more capable group as compared to men in top management.
3. Women may seek management positions in or may be hired to lead more profitable businesses that practice gender diversity oriented recruitment policies.
4. Both female leadership and profitability is connected to some third (unobserved) factor.

In the first two categories women achieve better business performance through their qualities and actions; in the third category, the causality runs from better performance to female leadership; in the fourth category, unobserved factor(s) mislead research efforts.

Are women, generally speaking, better leaders?   Although our findings are consistent with the argument that women are better leaders than men, they do not actually prove this. Indications that the leadership style of women might be better suited to modern-day requirements has been raised, for example, in the literature on psychology (Bilimoria, 2006; Singh and Vinnicombe, 2003; Terjesen et al., 2009). In a study by Smith et al. (2006) the causality issue was explored by employing instrumental variable methods. The study found that in Denmark female leadership seemed to have a causal effect on the company's better profitability.

Because our data did not include information on CEOs' wages we could not explicitly study their effect. Information gathered from other sources and our preliminary calculations suggest, however, that the (possibly) lower wages of female CEOs were of only minor significance to the observed correlation.

Are female leaders more exclusive and thus, on average, a better group than their male counterparts? Provided that the leadership qualities of men and women are somewhat similar and that those best suited for business management are in fact selected, the present imbalance between genders in business management indicates the existence of a 'glass ceiling' obstructing the advancement of women. Thus, because women go through a tougher 'screening' process, the average leadership abilities of women who have ended up in top management may be better than those of their male counterparts. The findings of our study are consistent with this positive selection of women, although they do not, as such, prove it.

Do women end up in more profitable companies? The causality of profit-ability stemming from female leadership is not among the most plausible explanations for the observed correlation, even if it is nevertheless a pos-sible one. If it were true in the broad sense, female leaders would, more often than men, seek to be employed by more profitable companies (or companies that become so due to exogenous reasons), or more profitable companies would be more eager to employ women leaders than similar firms that are (exogenously) less profitable. In addition, the similarities in educational qualifications, the pressures and challenges of top manage-ment work, corporation socialization and the long pipeline before reach-ing managerial top positions would not separate women and men from each other to the extent that women would gain a leading edge in this matter.

Does some third factor account for both female leadership and company profitability? Unobserved factors relating to female leaders and their companies could explain the observed correlation. As discussed in the literature female leadership might be more broadly connected to the cul-tural diversity and multidimensionality of a business (Carter et al. 2003). Indeed our further (preliminary) analysis suggests that a balanced gender composition on corporate boards might have the highest correlation with company profitability.

The connection between a firm's multidimensionality and its profitabil-ity is a complex one. It seems likely that only a sufficiently tolerant and flexible organization is able to utilize the competitive advantage brought about by multidimensionality. If an organization is rigid and unable to question old ideas and welcome new it may perform more poorly.

Female leadership may also be connected to good corporate govern-ance and management practices. The existence of women at the top of the corporate hierarchy may indicate that advancement and appointments in these organizations are based on competence and merits, not on traditions and established conventions. Furthermore, it seems only logical that the compositions of top management and corporate boards should reflect the diversity of the company's employment and customer base also in terms of gender.

It is plausible that several factors, from so-called natural differences in values, choices and preferences of men and women to educational segregation, lead to some sort of gender imbalance in business leadership, which is not to be conflated to women and men in leadership positions, but culture prevailing, to several processes of culture.

CONCLUSIONS

Business decisions do not respect the logic of democracy or the altruistic striving for gender equality. Business owners and those representing their interests are, of course, concerned about the issue in the name of corporate social responsibility. Gender equality might be listed among corporate values, but ultimately only its connection to financial success ensures the interest of owners. Our findings reveal a positive and significant correlation between female leadership and company profitability. Even if we have not been able to prove causality, our findings have several important implications. Our findings suggest that a company may gain competitive advantage over its competitors by identifying and eliminating the obstacles to women's advancement to top management. While there is on average a positive correlation between female leadership and profitability, it would be too straightforward and the wrong conclusion to state that male leaders should be replaced by women to improve company profitability. The focus should rather be on the numerous and often difficult-to-observe processes, mechanisms and networks that favour men or hinder women from climbing the executive ladder. Gender-neutral career opportunities are – besides being fair – also in the best interest of companies. According to research results, if and when Finland seeks to increase the share of women in top management, these endeavors should not be hindered because of concerns about the profitability of private companies – quite the contrary in fact.

NOTES

1. By the term 'board' we refer here to the board of directors (or board of supervisors, supervisory board), which is the group of people who monitor the interests of shareholders and officially administer a company. We are not referring to the board of executives (or executive board, board of management, managing board, management board), which is the group of people responsible for the everyday management and administration of

a company and for putting plans into practical effect and which is accountable to the board of directors (or the supervisory board). It is worth noting, however, that the composition, role and importance of the board of directors (or the supervisory board) in terms of the actual leading of the company varies from one country and corporate governance system to another.

2. For the sake of simplicity, we will not describe the literature on the following concepts but just refer to their existence and importance in general when explaining the position of women in economic activities:

    Glass ceiling. The opportunities for women to move up in an organization above a certain hierarchical level are hindered by sex discrimination. 'Glass' refers to the notion that this is an unofficial and difficult-to-observe phenomenon. 'Ceiling' refers to the idea that climbing up the corporate ladder is prevented. The glass ceiling does not refer to discriminatory practices that take the form of official rules (such as the fact that until recently women could not join the Finnish army) or other barriers to promotion (for example, the lack of necessary skills or experience).

    Glass wall. Their gender might limit women's possibilities to move within the organization from one job or business division to another.

    Glass door. Owing to their gender, women have fewer opportunities to get their foot in the door of an organization. In the recruitment stage, for example, they might be less likely to be asked for interviews than men with similar qualifications.

3. The supplementary financial statement and other information have been obtained from Asiakastieto Ltd. The sample (12 738 firms) used in our analysis covers over 90 per cent of the target population as defined by Statistics Finland.

4. Strictly speaking there were six indicators used, since the three profitability indicators referred to were assessed as given and as adjusted figures where the extreme values had been eliminated. This is because there was no consensus on the best indicator or measurement practice. In this analysis, profitability refers to the adjusted (winsored ±2.5 per cent) return on assets (ROA), which we regard as the best indicator and which gives results that are fairly uniform compared with the other alternatives.

REFERENCES

Aaltio, I. and Kovalainen, A. (2003), 'Using gender in exploring organizations, management and change', in B. Czarniawska and G. Sevón (eds), *The Northern Lights – Organization Theory in Scandinavia*, Copenhagen: Copenhagen Business School Press, pp. 175–81.

Arenius, P. and Kovalainen, A. (2006), 'Similarities and differences across the factors associated with women's self-employment preference in the nordic countries', *International Small Business Journal*, **24** (1), 31–59.

Bilimoria, D. (2006), 'The relationship between women corporate directors and women corporate officers', *Journal of Managerial Issues*, **38** (1), 47–61.

Bradshaw, P. and Wicks, D. (2000), 'The experiences of white women on corporate boards in Canada: compliance and non-compliance to hegemonic masculinity', in R.J. Burke and M.C. Mathis (eds), *Women on Corporate Boards of Directors: International Challenges and Opportunities*, Dordrecht: Kluwer Academic, pp. 197–212.

Burke, R.J. (2000), 'Women on Canadian corporate boards of directors: still a long way to go', in R.J. Burke and M.C. Mathis (eds), *Women on Corporate Boards of Directors: International Challenges and Opportunities*, Dordrecht: Kluwer Academic, pp. 97–109.

Carter, D.A., Simkins, B.J., and Simpson, G.W. (2003), 'Corporate governance, board diversity, and firm value', *The Financial Review*, **38**, 33–53.

Catalyst (2006), *2005 Catalyst Census of Women Corporate Officers and Top Earners of the Fortune 500*, New York: Catalyst.

European Commission (2005), *Report from the Commission on Equality between Women and Men, 2005*, Brussels: European Commission.

Eurostat (2007), *The Life of Men and Women in Europe: A Statistical Portrait*, Luxembourg: Office for Official Publications of the European Communities.

Hausmann, R., Tyson, L.D. and Zahidi, S. (2007), *The Global Gender Gap Report 2007*, Geneva: World Economic Forum.

Kotiranta, A., Kovalainen, A. and Rouvinen, P. (2007), 'Female leadership and firm profitability. EVA analysis', unpublished report, EVA.

Kovalainen, A. (2003), 'Case Finland', in L. Greenwood (ed.). *The Greenwood Encyclopedia of Women's Issues Worldwide. Europe*, London: Greenwood Press, pp. 189–204.

Krishnan, H.A. and Park, D. (2005), 'A few good women: on top management teams', *Journal of Business Research*, **52** (12), 1712–20.

Lindenberg, E.B. and Ross, S.A. (1981), 'Tobin's q ratio and industrial organization', *Journal of Business*, **15**, 159–70.

Minniti, M., Arenius, P. and Langowitz, N. (2005), *2004 Global Entrepreneurship Monitor Special Topic Report: Women and Entrepreneurship*, Babson Park, MA: Centre for Women's Leadership at Babson College.

Mohan, N. and Chen, C. (2004) 'Are IPOs priced differently based on gender?', *Journal of Behavioral Finance*, **5** (1), 57–65.

Richard, O.C., Ford, D. and Ismail, K. (2006), 'Exploring the performance effects of visible attribute diversity: the moderating role of span of control and organizational life cycle', *International Journal of Human Resource Management*, **17** (12), 2091–109.

Robinson, G. and Dechant, K. (1997), 'Building a business case for diversity', *Academy of Management Executive*, **11** (3), 21–31.

Rose, C. (2007), 'Does female board representation influence firm performance? The Danish evidence', *Corporate Governance: An International Review*, **15** (2), 404–13.

Singh, V. and Vinnicombe, S. (2003), 'The 2002 Female FTSE Index and women directors', *Women in Management Review*, **18** (7), 349–58.

Smirlock, M., Gilligan, T. and Marshall, W. (1984), 'Tobin's q and the structure–performance relationship', *American Economic Review*, **74**, 1051–60.

Smith, N., Smith, V. and Verner, M. (2006), 'Do women in top management affect firm performance? A panel study of 2500 Danish firms', *International Journal of Productivity and Performance Management*, **55** (7), 569–93.

Terjesen, S., Sealy, R. and Singh, V. (2009), 'Women directors on corporate boards: a review and research agenda', *Corporate Governance: An International Review*, **17** (3), 320–37.

Wolfe, J. and Sauaia, A.C.A. (2003), 'The Tobin q as a company performance indicator', *Developments in Business Simulation and Experiential Learning*, **30**, 155–9.

Wolfers, J. (2006), 'Diagnosing discrimination: stock returns and CEO gender', *Journal of the European Economic Association*, **4** (2/3), 531–41.

Woodd, M. (2000), 'The psychology of career theory – a new perspective?', *Career Development International*, **5** (6), 273–78.

5. Influences on women's entrepreneurship in Ireland and the Czech Republic

Lorna Treanor and Colette Henry

INTRODUCTION

While the United States is an entrepreneurial role-model for many European countries, within Europe accession countries like the Czech Republic look to smaller European nations such as Ireland as exemplary of how European Community membership can positively impact on a national economy. In 2003, Ireland's gross domestic product (GDP) had increased more than fourfold from its accession level of 1973, and gross national product (GNP) increased more than threefold during the same period (CSO, 2004). Prior to the current global economic downturn, the Celtic Tiger era witnessed increasing rates of foreign direct investment and indigenous new venture creation, resulting in high employment levels and economic prosperity.

However, women's participation in new venture creation in Ireland lags behind the US and other EU countries. Irish academics have explored social, cultural and historical factors to explain the lower entrepreneurial rates among Irish women compared with their male counterparts (Henry and Kennedy, 2003; Hisrich and Ó Cinnéide, 1985). That being said, smaller transition economies such as the Czech Republic still look toward Ireland as an example of the economic potential they have yet to realize.

To date, there is limited research on entrepreneurship in emerging economies, with available literature suggesting that findings from Western developed economies may not be readily applicable in this context. Hence, Bruton et al. (2008) contend that there is a need to develop our understanding of entrepreneurship in emerging economies. Save for a few notable exceptions, there is a particular lack of research examining the nature of female entrepreneurship in emerging economic contexts (Wells et al., 2003; Welter et al., 2003; Zapalska, 1997), hence the motivation for this study.

The objective of this chapter is to compare and contrast the experiences, motivations, characteristics and influences on Irish and Czech women entrepreneurs in relation to business start-up and growth. The data for our exploratory study were drawn from two samples of female entrepreneurs, one in Ireland and one in the Czech Republic; both groups of women had participated in a European Community Initiative under the EQUAL[1] programme. The project – Supporting Unusual Entry Entrepreneurs – sought to enhance social inclusion through entrepreneurship by providing supports to aspiring entrepreneurs in under-represented groups, in this case, women. This chapter draws on a body of international literature relating to entrepreneurship, and uses empirical, highly qualitative data to explore how typical or 'atypical' these women entrepreneurs are in comparison to the currently held female entrepreneurial 'norm' depicted in the literature.

First, we provide an overview of the economic and entrepreneurship contexts of both Ireland and the Czech Republic followed by a review of the extant literature, our detailed findings and, finally, we discuss our conclusions in the context of neo-institutional theory literature.

ECONOMIC AND ENTREPRENEURSHIP CONTEXT

It has been almost two decades since the commanded economies and communist governments of Central and Eastern Europe (CEE) gave way to the demands for political and economic freedom. The Czech Republic is one of the most stable and prosperous of the emerging CEE democracies, largely due to its relatively developed industrialized economy. When it joined the European Union (EU) in 2004, its principal industries (steel, textiles, ceramics and brewing) required investment. However, EU membership also brought economic opportunities that saw the national GDP per capita rate in 2007 reflect a 52 per cent increase on the accession rate, while inflation remained largely static and controlled.

That growth was supported by exports to the EU, primarily to Germany, and a strong recovery of foreign and domestic investment. Domestic demand played an ever more important role in underpinning growth as interest rates dropped and the availability of credit cards and mortgages increased. The current account deficit declined to around 3 per cent of GDP as demand for Czech products in the European Union increased. Recent accession to the EU gives further impetus and direction to structural reform. Intensified restructuring among large enterprises, improvements in the financial sector and effective use of available EU funds were expected to strengthen output growth. The transition to a market economy undoubtedly brought economic and social difficulties, not least for women in Czech society. The current global recession has also been reported as impacting upon women more adversely than men in all countries and has undoubtedly increased the difficulties faced by women in the Czech Republic.

In contrast, the Irish economy is open and mostly export based. Ireland experienced an unprecedented growth during the latter half of the 1990s, which was expected to continue at least for the first decade of the twenty-first century. Ireland's economy is heavily dependent on trade, with export of goods and services amounting to over 96.8 per cent of GDP (1999 figure). Membership of the European Union and access to the Single Market has allowed Ireland to diversify its trade patterns. Although Britain has always been Ireland's largest single trading partner, almost half of all Irish exports now go to the other EU member states (Irish Government website, 2007). The global recession has, however, impacted upon the currency exchange rate. Irish goods are now almost 40 per cent more expensive for British customers while Irish consumerism is increasing in the UK, adding to Irish national budgetary woes.

According to the Global Entrepreneurship Monitor report (Bosma and Harding, 2006), prior to the current recession the Czech Republic outperformed Ireland in terms of early stage entrepreneurial activity (7.9 per cent versus 7.4 per cent) and was also reported to exhibit higher rates of nascent entrepreneurial activity (6.4 per cent as opposed to 4.5 per cent in Ireland). Ireland had, as would be expected, significantly higher rates of established business owners (7.8 per cent versus 5.4 per cent).

In 2008 Ireland was ranked as the fifth easiest place to start a business, taking an average of 13 days at a cost of 0.3 per cent of gross national income (GNI). By way of contrast, the Czech Republic was ranked ninety-first, taking an average of 17 days at a cost of 10.6 per cent of GNI[2] (World Bank, 2008).

WOMEN'S ENTREPRENEURSHIP POLICIES

Until recently, most EU countries had no specific policy pertaining to the promotion of female entrepreneurship. It was not until 2000 that the European Union's Multi-Annual Programme for Enterprise and Entrepreneurship 2001–2005 highlighted the promotion of entrepreneurship among women as one of its key actions (EC, 2000). While some countries such as Ireland do not yet have a specific policy on women's entrepreneurship, the effort to increase women's participation in enterprise is now being addressed by economic development agencies worldwide (Henry, 2008).

Support for women entrepreneurs in the Czech Republic has become apparent in recent years. Small and medium-sized enterprise (SME) support programmes, open to both genders, from the Ministry of Industry and Trade made 2584 grants to women entrepreneurs, that is, 17.1 per cent of the total grants awarded. This represented financial aid of €9 million to Czech business women, that is, 5.7 per cent of the total financial support available. The development of female entrepreneurship specifically has received attention in areas where unemployment rates were high. Thus, special support was administered to women entrepreneurs within the SME ADVICE programme, an initiative focusing on advice services and educational projects.

The Women in Enterprise support programme was set up by the Social Democratic Party in 2004. Its goals were to support consultancy services, educational activities, workshops and conferences dealing with problems faced by women in industry. Despite the initiative being hailed a success by both female entrepreneurs and the Ministry of Trade and Industry itself, a change in government saw the loss of 1.5 million crowns (approximately €60 000) for supporting female entrepreneurship. As a result, there currently exists no specific targeted support or policy.

Ireland's history, culture and former enterprise policies have all had an impact on women's current level of entrepreneurial activity. The traditional role of women in Irish society was that of homemaker, and women often had sole responsibility for children and other family dependants. In the past, Ireland was one of the poorest countries in the EU with high inflation, high emigration, slow growth rates and alarming unemployment. There was no enterprise tradition or culture and there appeared to be limited economic opportunities for the creation of indigenous entrepreneurship overall (Henry and Kennedy, 2003). Furthermore, Ireland's economic policies had deliberately focused on inward foreign direct investment, typically in the high-technology sectors. Most support programmes relating to women's entrepreneurship in Ireland are initiated at regional rather than national levels. Currently, there is no women's entrepreneurship support program or initiative offered by central government, and this has resulted in an ad hoc, 'patchwork' of funding-dependent support offerings. Despite an apparent willingness to develop dedicated women's entrepreneurship programs at the national level, a definitive policy lead is still awaited. That said, GEM (Bosma and Harding, 2006) indicates that the number of women in Ireland setting up new ventures is beginning to increase.

THEORETICAL FOUNDATION

Institutional Theory

Institutional theory is widely employed in comparing entrepreneurial activity and experiences within and between emerging and developed economies. Formal institutions comprise the formal laws and regulations in existence within a given society, that is, the regulatory pillar of the institutional framework. Informal institutions can be either normative, such as the informal trade conventions and standards in operation, or cognitive, that is, the belief system held in relation to expected standards of behavior within a particular culture. The nature and rates of entrepreneurial activity in any country are significantly determined by the dominant influence of the institutional environment within that country; the inhibitive nature of institutions is particularly apparent in Central and Eastern European countries (Ahlstrom and Bruton, 2002; Manolova et al., 2008: 203; Smallbone and Welter, 2001, 2006).

A review of the literature might lead us to expect that the formal institutional environment in the Czech Republic may pose a macro-level barrier to entrepreneurial activity as it may be a 'predominantly vertically oriented, state-centered institutional environment . . . wherein a legacy of central planning . . . permeates the business . . . environment through excessive regulation' (Manolova and Yan, 2002: 177). In contrast, pre-recession, the developed economy of Ireland was expected to be less bureaucratic and more conducive to entrepreneurship, especially given the World Bank rankings outlined above.

The normative dimension would be expected to be markedly different between both countries given the legacy of socialist ideology in the Czech Republic where personal wealth creation was considered a result of the exploitation of fellow citizens, as opposed to Ireland where a market economy was the norm and personal wealth creation was an aspiration. In terms of the cognitive dimension of the institutional environment, the prior education and work experience of Czech individuals would not have been focused on efficiency in free market enterprises, and so, the entrepreneurial skill set may be lacking (Lyles et al., 2004; Smallbone and Welter, 2006).

Characteristics and Motivations of Female Entrepreneurs

While entrepreneurs, regardless of gender, share a number of common characteristics such as drive, enthusiasm, commitment, creativity, problem-solving ability and innovative flair, women entrepreneurs also display

some unique characteristics that distinguish them from their male counterparts. For example, women differ widely across individual dimensions
related to skills, education, work experience, approach to venture creation or acquisition, business goals, problems and performance, and also
experience different opportunities and barriers to their male counterparts
(Carter, 2000b; CEEDR, 2001; Henry, 2008).

A particularly significant differential in the extant literature relates to
entrepreneurial motivation. While some earlier literature suggests that
women may be less motivated by profit than their male counterparts,
Carter and Bennett (2006) counter this finding. That said, women are
more likely to cite as a motivation for entrepreneurship such factors as a
pursuit of independence, a sense of self-fulfilment, and a quest for work–
life balance that suits their particular personal and family situation (Henry
and Treanor, 2007; Marlow, 1997).

Self-employment is often viewed by women as a more flexible working
option when compared with traditional employment, providing more free
time and facilitating childcare responsibilities. In practice, however, this
does not always prove to be the case, as most entrepreneurs, regardless of
gender, tend to spend considerably more time getting their business off the
ground than they had originally anticipated. Furthermore, it has also been
suggested that women start a business as a result of restricted progression
opportunities in the workplace – the so-called 'glass ceiling' effect (Carter
et al., 2001). Similarly, in Poland, Mroczkowski (1997) had reported that
poor employment opportunities was a motivating factor for 46 per cent of
the women surveyed in 1995, approximately twice that cited by men (Bliss
and Garratt, 2001).

When compared with men, it would appear that most women enter self-
employment with less management experience, fewer financial assets and
relatively under-resourced in terms of human capital (Carter et al., 2006;
Deakins, 1996; Storey, 1994). It has also been suggested that women entrepreneurs have less confidence in their entrepreneurial abilities. Such lack
of confidence is often attributed to women often having fewer resources at
the start-up stage, their lack of senior management experience where decisions on resources are made, their unfamiliarity with business language,
and the traditional view of women as mothers and carers rather than as
entrepreneurs and risk-takers (Henry, 2008).

It has also been noted that, in terms of new venture creation, women
tend to be more attracted to industry sectors that have traditionally provided high levels of female employment, that is, the services and retail
sectors (Carter et al., 2001; Schreier, 1973). Some of the earlier literature
(for example, Watkins and Watkins, 1984) also suggested that women's
choice of business sector was largely determined by a consideration of

which areas posed least obstacles to success due to lower technical and financial barriers to market entry. Furthermore, the literature has indicated that women-led businesses have a tendency to be smaller-scale ventures with fewer core staff and less growth potential than male-owned enterprises (Rosa et al., 1996).

Barriers

A study by Hisrich and Fulop (1994) explored the unique barriers facing women entrepreneurs in transition economies. The three most commonly cited difficulties encountered in starting a business were obtaining credit, having a weak collateral position and trying to meet the demands of the company on family life (Bliss and Garratt, 2001: 339). In contrast, in Poland, Zapalska (1997) and Mroczkowski (1997) cited a lack of information and insufficient training opportunities as barriers to starting a business that may impact women more than men. They found the most common response to the question of 'what makes it difficult for women to start and run a company' was coping with family and work (as cited in Bliss and Garratt, 2001: 339).

According to Bruni et al. (2004), women entrepreneurs are said to face three main types of start-up barriers. These include sociocultural barriers, barriers relating to networks of information and access to assistance, and access to finance and investment funds. Adopting Bruni et al.'s framework, the particular start-up barriers faced by women entrepreneurs in Ireland and the Czech Republic are discussed below.

Sociocultural Barriers to Women's Entrepreneurship

Ireland
Historically Ireland did not have an enterprise tradition or culture (Garavan et al., 1997). The traditional role of women was as homemakers. While women began to enter the workforce throughout mainland Europe in the 1940s, women in Ireland were disadvantaged by legislation as recently as 1973. It was then that the 'Marriage Bar' – a law requiring women to retire from employment in the civil service upon marriage (Civil Service Regulations Act, 1956) was abolished. The 1990s then saw Irish women joining the workforce at four times the rate of the two previous decades, and a 1998 survey revealed that women accounted for 38 per cent of the total workforce (Fás, 1998). Against this background, Henry and Kennedy (2003) highlight that it is unsurprising that Ireland did not capitalize on the potential for female entrepreneurship – an area still awaiting a policy lead today.

Czech Republic

Following the socialist transformation, in 1950 the Czech Republic introduced a law on family which legislated that men and women had equal rights and responsibilities. While similar laws were not introduced in the West until the 1970s, this should not be mistaken to represent the introduction of greater female equality within the socialist society. True (2003: 39) argues that, contrary to the state policy of emancipating women through collective labour, the socialist regime reinforced traditional roles of women within families and society at large: 'As a result, less visible but greater gender inequalities than in some capitalist countries developed under socialism (for instance, in work time and remuneration).' This occurred through pro-natalist policies introduced in the 1960s that encouraged women to reproduce while maintaining their 'primary' contributions in the labour force. These policies worked; the lowest ever birth rate of 1968 was followed by steady growth towards the highest birth rate, at that time, in 1975. This, however, undermined equality as employers treated women's labour as less effective than men's.

Unlike the large-scale withdrawal of women from the labour force that occurred in other transition economies (Bliss and Garratt, 2001), Czech women remained in the workforce during this period. However, Czech women have and still do face gender discrimination in the labour force. Despite the legislation introduced as part of the harmonizing process in 2004, the European Foundation for the Improvement of Living and Working Conditions (EFILWC, 2004) found that ignorance of the law surrounding discrimination, and the difficult and protracted enforcement process, often means that discrimination based on gender is not uncommon in the Czech Republic.

Access to Finance

According to Marlow and Patton (2005: 717): 'Barriers or impediments to accessing appropriate levels or sources of funding will have an enduring and negative impact upon the performance of affected firms.' Access to finance and investment funds is a particularly significant barrier for women, and under-capitalization during new venture creation and development stages has also been found to result in underperformance during the life of the business (Carter and Marlow, 2003). While other constraints relating to work–life balance (women's restricted access to career advancement opportunities, the gender pay gap) still exist, the issue of finance remains one of the most significant barriers for women entrepreneurs (EC, 2000). Furthermore, some studies have also found discrimination on the part of finance providers (CEEDR, 2001) with a US study suggesting that women were impeded by myths associated with their gender (Brush et al., 2001). Others contend that lending officers are being prudent in their decision-making and that it is the background of the typical female applicant that militates against her (Fay and Williams, 1993: 365). As an example, women have been found to be less likely to have generated a credit history to indicate formal credit worthiness to lenders than their male counterparts (Shaw et al., 2001).

In particular, women still face problems when accessing equity finance, which is often needed to facilitate rapid growth. They also tend to encounter a number of problems in raising funding at key stages in developing and growing their business (Brush, 1997), and there is some evidence to indicate that accessing bank loans is more problematic for women business owners than it is for men. The difficulty accessing growth capital, often due to women's difficulty in penetrating informal financial networks, underlines the importance of building appropriate business networks from an early stage.

Difficulties in accessing start-up capital often lead many women to start businesses that are under-resourced, and this initial under-capitalization affects long-term growth in terms of turnover and employee numbers.

METHODOLOGY

Sample Selection

The samples of women involved in this study were those involved in the EQUAL-funded Sustaining Unconventional-entry Entrepreneurs project. This covered the geographic sub-regions of Southern Moravia in the Czech Republic and County Longford in Ireland. In both regions, women were considered to be 'unconventional', 'disadvantaged' or 'atypical' entrepreneurs by the partner organizations due to the gender-specific barriers they experienced and the relatively low rates of female entrepreneurial activity. We randomly surveyed samples of the women EQUAL participants, as contained in the partner databases.

The methodology adopted for the study included an electronic questionnaire and case examples. These tools were designed to explore the nature of women's entrepreneurship in Ireland and the Czech Republic and to gather data on a number of key issues relating to start-up and early-stage female entrepreneurship experiences. We included research areas that were identified in the literature as important in the context of women's entrepreneurship: the women's business profile; their personal profile; their particular start-up experiences and how they financed their business. With these issues in mind, we developed the following research questions:

1. What is the typical business and personal profile of women entrepreneurs in Ireland and the Czech Republic?
2. What were the particular start-up experiences of these women and did they differ significantly from those contained in the extant literature?
3. How did these women finance their businesses and what were their particular experiences when attempting to access start-up and growth finance?
4. What 'soft supports' were available to these women?

The questionnaire was structured in four sections, covering the key research questions, and contained 41 questions. The survey was designed and pilot-tested prior to electronic administration during mid-late 2006. Owing to the rural nature of Longford and potential difficulties with technological access in the Czech Republic, the survey was also administered by post. Six in-depth, interview-based case studies comprising three paired samples of women entrepreneurs in each of the survey regions were also constructed. These cases yielded additional rich insights into the women's actual start-up experiences.

In total, the survey was administered to 330 women. Responses were received from 242 women entrepreneurs, representing an overall response rate of 73 per cent (80 per cent response rate, n = 202 in the Czech Republic sample, and 50 per cent response rate, n = 40, in the Irish sample). It must be noted, however, that the South Moravian region of the Czech Republic is much larger and more populated than the area under investigation in Ireland. Based on Organisation for Economic Corporation and Development (OECD) data,[3] it is estimated that our sample corresponds to *circa* 5 per cent of the total population of female entrepreneurs in the South Moravia region, and *circa* 10 per cent of the population of female entrepreneurs in the County Longford region.

FINDINGS

Business Profiles

Almost all of the businesses (95.5 per cent) in the Irish sample were in the services sector, as compared with 90 per cent in the Czech sample. As Table 5.1 illustrates, the types of businesses in both samples ranged from professional services through personal services to retail enterprises.

Interestingly, the predominant business type in both the Irish and the Czech studies was retail, followed by training and consulting services. The GEM 2006 study (Bosma and Harding, 2006) indicated that 24 per

Table 5.1 Business type

Business type	% response: Czech sample	% response: Irish Sample
Retail	21	17.5
Training and consulting	20	18
Hair/beauty	15	11
Gastronomy and catering service	15	6.5
Manufacture/production	10	4.5
Fitness	10	2.5
Language teaching	9	
Childcare providers	—	5.5
Book-keeping and accountancy	—	5.5
Other professional services	—	5
Other services[1]	—	24

Note: [1] Dog grooming, wedding stationery design, Irish dancing teaching, clothing alterations, property management, garden centre and photographer.

cent of Irish women entrepreneurs were engaged in Retail Trade, Hotel and Restaurants; a similar proportion of established enterprises in these sectors was apparent in this study. Interestingly, 36 per cent of the Czech sample was engaged in these sectors. This may be considered surprising given that the Czech Republic is a lower-income country where citizens would arguably have less disposable income than in Ireland, even post Celtic Tiger. However, Bosma and Harding (2006) also indicated that early-stage entrepreneurs in high-income countries such as Ireland were much more likely to be found in the business services sector than those in middle-income countries such as the Czech Republic (25 per cent to 9 per cent). The engagement of Czech women in business services in this study is significantly higher than this estimate (28.5 per cent versus 20 per cent). While this could be excused as a peculiarity of the Irish sample, the representative nature of the Czech sample means this is a somewhat surprising finding.

In the Irish sample, almost 37 per cent of the respondents indicated that they were the sole employees of the business, compared to 60 per cent of the Czech respondents. Only a very small percentage of the Irish women (7.9 per cent) employed more than five staff, which compared poorly with the Czech study, where some 20 per cent of the women had reached these employment levels.

Turnover levels were also low, with only 20 per cent of the Czech women registering a turnover in excess of €50 000, compared with 43 per cent of the Irish women. Indeed, in the Czech sample, the largest category of business owners (26 per cent) had a turnover of less than €10 000. The comparative figure in the Irish sample was 10 per cent. However, the findings were more aligned in terms of the women's growth plans. In both samples, the majority of women (55 per cent in the Czech sample and 58 per cent in the Irish sample) indicated that they had no long-term growth plans for their business, and this possibly reflected their low turnover levels. In both samples, the women who indicated that they had long-term growth plans for the business revealed vague plans, referring to increasing product lines, sales and profits, but with no clear targets or timescales. The turnover, employment levels and growth prospects of these enterprises in both regions would appear to be consistent with the literature, that is, given the choice of sector within which the majority of enterprises were started, that is, low entry barrier, crowded sectors with low growth potential.

In terms of ownership and source of income, there were clear similarities between the findings of the Irish and Czech studies. In both studies, around 85 per cent of the women respondents were the sole owners of their business; their business was their main source of income and, for around 34 per cent of the women who participated in the study in Ireland and the Czech Republic, this was the only source of income for their family.

Personal Profiles

Most of the women responding to the survey were in the 36–45-year age bracket (40 per cent Czech, 48 per cent Irish). Only a very small percentage of the women (3.5 per cent Czech, 5.7 per cent Irish) were 25 years or under. Despite the similarities in terms of age profile, there was a noticeable difference in the level of education between the two samples, with over half of the Irish women entrepreneurs having a qualification at diploma, degree or postgraduate level, compared to only 37 per cent of the Czech women entrepreneurs. The majority of the women surveyed in both Ireland and the Czech Republic had work experience of ten years or more prior to starting up their business, although this was not always directly related to their chosen business sector.

The Global Entrepreneurship Monitor report (Bosma and Harding, 2006) suggests that early stage entrepreneurial activity was relatively low in high-income countries; furthermore, the comparative rates for necessity and opportunity entrepreneurship in both countries would suggest that necessity entrepreneurship is more prevalent in the Czech Republic than in Ireland. Given that citizens in Ireland, pre-recession, could achieve higher incomes from paid employment, enjoyed lower rates of long-term unemployment and benefited from the existence of a welfare state, it is perhaps not surprising that the Irish infrastructure was not as conducive to necessity entrepreneurship as that of the Czech Republic.

When asked if the driving force in their decision to become an entrepreneur was necessity- or opportunity-driven, the overwhelming response from both samples in this study was the identification of an opportunity in the marketplace, with over 58 per cent of the Irish women and over 56 per cent of the Czech women choosing this response option. However, respondents were also offered the opportunity to identify their main reason for starting a business in a *free* response format. Whereas 56 per cent of Czech women who answered the previous question had identified themselves as being opportunity-driven entrepreneurs, 30 per cent said the desire for independence and/or to be their own boss was their main motivation. Furthermore, 20 per cent reported their main motivation was an inability to get a suitable job/unemployment, 16 per cent reported personal development or interest in the business idea, and 6 per cent cited financial reward. This more detailed analysis of Czech women entrepreneurs' motivations would tend to correspond with other findings (Acs et al., 2004; Manolova et al., 2008) that long-term unemployment and relatively lower income rates had resulted in predominantly necessity-based entrepreneurship in developing economies. This is perhaps what may be expected of a sample of women who were supported by this particular EQUAL project.

When Irish women responded freely to this question, their answers identified a greater tendency to pursue new venture creation due to opportunity identification (37 per cent). The other main responses included: personal development/fulfilment (15 per cent), flexibility with regard to caring commitments (15 per cent), the desire for independence (12 per cent), financial reward (9 per cent) and the loss of employment/dissatisfaction with employment opportunities (9 per cent).

Start-up Experiences

Respondents were asked to rank a list of barriers, according to their own personal experience, on a scale from 1 to 5 where 1 represented 'not significant' and 5 was 'very significant'. Table 5.2 contains the barriers presented to respondents and outlines the percentage of respondents in each sample that rated the given barrier as a '4' or '5' on the scale.

A key barrier identified by the women in both samples was access to finance, with family responsibilities also attracting high ratings from both groups.

Table 5.2   Barriers encountered at the start-up stage

Barriers	% of respondents rating this as 4* or higher in terms of significance (Czech sample)	% of respondents rating this as 4* or higher in terms of significance (Irish sample)
Credibility as a business owner	12	24
Access to finance	43	39
Access to business networks	14	27
Cultural and social attitudes	7	18
Confidence	13	31
Family responsibilities	23	45
Work Experience & education	11	28
Isolation	14	28
Finding suitable premises	19	19

Note: * Where 1 = Not Significant at all and 5 = very significant.

Sociocultural Barriers

Ireland
Arguably the sociocultural factors discussed earlier are still very evident in parts of Ireland today. In this study, Irish women found their family responsibilities to represent a much more significant barrier to entrepreneurship than their Czech counterparts (15 per cent in comparison to 6 per cent). The traditional role attached to women in Ireland in terms of caring for home and family seems to remain a strong influence on Longford women today with 34 per cent of women of working age recorded as 'Looking after home/family', in comparison with a national 'stay at home' rate of 22 per cent for women (Central Statistics Office, 2004). Irish women are aware of the sociocultural pressures they face with 18 per cent of Irish women identifying cultural and social attitudes as being a highly significant barrier experienced in relation to their entrepreneurial activity.

These figures, taken in conjunction with barriers relating to 'isolation' and 'accessing business networks', directly impact the potential of a woman in Ireland to become an entrepreneur, suggesting that starting and developing a successful business in more rural Ireland may be more difficult than is currently recognized. These findings contrast with recent analysis undertaken in the UK where GEM, in conjunction with Prowess, identified that rural women in England are almost twice more likely to be entrepreneurs than urban-based women. Interestingly, only a small proportion of Irish women identified dissatisfaction with available employment opportunities as a motivator, but reference was made to the 'glass ceiling' effect in the Irish workplace.

Czech Republic

The sociocultural barriers to women's entrepreneurship are strongly felt by many women in South Moravia and its environs today. The issue of gender inequality in the workplace is recognized in society and acknowledged at government level. For example, the Ministry of Industry and Trade participated in an EU Phare project, which ran from September 2003 to July 2005, entitled 'The role of equal opportunity in the prosperity of businesses'. This project undertook sociological research mapping the methods of coping with gender issues in companies, explored the representation of women in management positions in the Czech Republic and examined management initiatives within companies to facilitate work–life balance. The project also incorporated a Best Company with Equal Opportunities for Women and Men competition. However, the fact remains that 16 per cent of Czech women in this study were motivated to start their own business because they could not find suitable employment, with some respondents referring to negative experiences within the workplace. This was also mentioned as a factor in the related motivation of personal fulfilment (9 per cent), with one respondent citing gender discrimination as the motivating factor for starting her own business. Thirty per cent of respondents sought independence and an opportunity to be their own boss. Only 6 per cent of women in this sample specifically indicated flexibility, to facilitate balancing their home and family commitments, as a motivating factor for entering self-employment.

These findings would strongly suggest that the sociocultural barriers experienced by Czech women relate more to gender discrimination issues in the workplace and wider society than the traditional domestic role issues that still encumber Irish women. Yet, somewhat surprisingly, only 7 per cent cited cultural and social attitudes as a significant or very significant barrier to starting a business. This should not understate the effect of the traditional roles that Czech women are expected to perform. As mentioned earlier, Czech women undertake most of the domestic chores associated with home and family. The domestic roles are a lesser symptom of the widespread gender inequality that pervades Czech society, with gaining employment, progressing in a chosen career, accessing finance to create a new venture and the bureaucracy surrounding new venture creation all appearing as much more significant issues in the Czech context.

Access to Finance

Just over half (52 per cent) of the Irish women surveyed indicated that they had sought funding from their local bank, with almost 45 per cent stating that they used their own personal savings. Around a third of the women sought grant funding. However, the actual amounts of funding secured by the Irish women entrepreneurs at the start-up stage were low, with around a third of the women (who responded to this question) securing between €2000 and €5000, and only another third securing more than €20000. At the growth stage of the business, only a very small number (n = 3) of the women had managed to secure funds. Again, these were very small amounts, ranging from a €3000 grant to a €15000 loan. Where the women were refused a loan or grant, this appeared to be due to either the ineligibility of their business, that is, there were no grants for local non-export oriented service businesses, or the potential displacement impact.

By way of contrast, almost 95 per cent of the women surveyed in the Czech study had not managed to obtain a grant or loan to either start or expand their business. The reasons for this appeared to relate to the lack of information provided by the women or the feeling that they did not have the confidence to ask for the necessary financing. The fact that many of the women did not have a regular source of income prior to applying for a loan also had an impact. This meant that start-up was slower than expected and the growth potential was significantly limited from the outset. Interestingly, while over half of the Czech women (58 per cent) felt that their business did not have sufficient capital at the start-up stage, over 80 per cent of the Irish women felt that they had sufficient start-up capital.

Both the Irish and the Czech women entrepreneurs indicated that they had experienced a negative attitude from financial providers, particularly the banks, explaining that one particular funder 'gave no encouragement, was extremely pessimistic and had a very cynical attitude' (Irish sample). This was further evidenced by the fact that, when applications for funding had been rejected, most of the women had not been given an opportunity to resubmit (75 per cent of the Czech women and 100 per cent of the Irish women). Indeed, in the Irish survey, a small number of the women (n = 6) identified particular organizations from which they would not seek support in the future. These included banks, government sources and their local County Enterprise Board. In the Czech survey, 30 of the women respondents identified particular organizations they would not approach, and these included banks, private capital providers, their employment office and Chambers of Commerce.

Funding gaps identified by the women related to the amount of time for grant applications to be processed and the delays in monies being received, the excessive paperwork involved in applying for supports and the overemphasis on collateral (Irish sample). Access to finance, the negative attitudes of the banks and the overall lack of information and supports in general were identified as key gaps in the Czech sample. In both samples, there was a clear sense that current start-up support is completely inadequate for women entrepreneurs, particularly with regard to finance provision.

Soft Supports

Information was also sought regarding the types of business training the women had received in preparation for self-employment. In contrast to the strong similarities highlighted above between the two samples, a number of stark contrasts became evident.

In the Czech sample, almost three-quarters of the women surveyed had not attended any specialized business training or had not received any form of support for starting their business, despite approaching a range of support organizations. The lack of support they received at the critical start-up stage was seen as a clear disadvantage.

By comparison, almost half of the women in the Irish sample had attended some sort of start-your-own-business training programme and had approached a number of support organizations. Although not always in a position to offer financial support due to the nature of the women's businesses, the County Enterprise Board was mostly rated as 'extremely helpful' by the women.

DISCUSSION AND CONCLUSIONS

The objective of this chapter was to compare and contrast the motivations, characteristics, experiences and influences on Irish and Czech women entrepreneurs in relation to business start-up and growth. While our study revealed clear differences between the two samples in relation to business and personal profiles, it also appears that women entrepreneurs in Ireland and the Czech Republic experience the same types of difficulties reported by women globally when seeking to establish or grow a business, that is, difficulty accessing finance coupled with a range of sociocultural constraints, as discussed in the extant literature.

Key similarities with respect to the women's business and personal profiles related to the sector in which they operated (mainly services, particularly retail); their lack of growth plans (and the absence of specific targets); the ownership of the business (most of the women were the sole owners of their business; it was their first venture and their main source of income); their level of work experience (most had over ten years' work experience prior to start-up), and their age profile (predominantly 36–45 years).

Major differences between the Irish and Czech samples related to the number of employees (significantly more Czech than Irish women were the sole employee of their business, with Czech women being almost three times as likely to have more than five employees); turnover levels (twice as many Irish women entrepreneurs had a turnover of €50 000 or more), and qualifications (significantly fewer Czech women entrepreneurs had a diploma or higher qualification).

Our findings would also appear to lend support to recent literature that has examined and contrasted Western and emerging economies from an institutional theory perspective (Baughn et al., 2006; Spencer and Gómez, 2004; Welter and Smallbone, 2003). According to the literature, the institutional framework of a society comprises the fundamental political, social and economic incentives, and thereby limits the scope of the strategic choices available to individuals and organizations (DiMaggio and Powell, 1983). Whereas many CEE countries have been criticized for not introducing formal institutions to support the transition to a free market economy (Ireland et al., 2008; True, 2003), the Czechs implemented a programme of macroeconomic reform that was heavily supported by the World Bank and International Monetary Fund. They also introduced a new labour market policy to reduce the workforce by incentivizing women and older workers to leave (True, 2003).

Despite joining the European Union in 2004, there remains significant progress to be made in the Czech Republic in relation to harmonizing the regulatory dimension of the institutional environment with the laws, rules and practices established within the developed market economies of Western Europe. Our findings suggest the regulatory dimension in the Czech Republic produces necessity-driven, low-growth entrepreneurship for Czech women.

Smallbone and Welter (2006) suggest that entrepreneurs in societies with a socialist history may possess higher educational attainments but lower levels of entrepreneurial knowledge and skills due to the longstanding suppression of entrepreneurialism. Other commentators argue that employment positions under the communist regime would not have equipped individuals with the necessary business and management skills available in Western societies in private and quasi-private, market-centred organizations (Lyles et al., 2004). It is considered that these propositions are not mutually exclusive; rather, they contribute to a fuller understanding of the informal institutional factors that interplay in emerging economies, often with the impact of inhibiting women's entrepreneurship.

In this case, the lack (and removal) of formal institutional supports for women in the Czech Republic is a cause for concern. To date, it seems that women entrepreneurs in the Czech Republic face significant formal institutional barriers, particularly in relation to the economic, legal and bureaucratic barriers to accessing finance and starting a business. However, Czech women may be less aware of the informal institutional barriers that influence their entrepreneurial activities, particularly the cognitive aspects, societal norms and role expectations. The widespread recognition of gender inequality and discrimination against women in the Czech workforce, coupled with their domestic and family responsibilities, can only mean that Czech women also face the informal institutional barriers of which women in the Irish sample complain; the difference is that, in terms of scale and significance, these are less recognized by Czech women due to the scale and primacy of the formal barriers. What was perhaps unexpected and somewhat surprising in the findings was that, despite these greater institutional barriers experienced, Czech women-owned businesses were more likely than Irish women-owned enterprises to employ a staff of five persons or more.

In contrast, despite the absence of formal government-driven female entrepreneurship policies, Irish women enjoy a more supportive and encouraging institutional environment, with start-up training and finance widely available from County Enterprise Boards and a business start process that is relatively non-bureaucratic. However, the main informal institutional barriers experienced by Irish women entrepreneurs emanate from cognitive beliefs and social norms surrounding the traditional role of women in society and the home.

In the case of the Czech Republic, the cognitive aspects permeate, with the formal institutional barriers serving to exacerbate the difficulties experienced by Czech women entrepreneurs. That said, an interesting finding emerging from the Irish study is that the significant economic progress made following EU accession has not produced a society devoid of gender inequalities; rather, it has made female entrepreneurship less likely through the removal of *necessity* motivation and the ongoing expectation that women will undertake their historical roles in addition to any paid labour in which they choose to engage, either on an employed or self-employed basis.

While this study has acknowledged limitations and reflects only the institutional environment at the time the study was completed, the authors fully appreciate that their study and the literature to which they refer relates to a pre-global recession period. That being said, it does lend itself to recommendations for policy-makers. In the Czech Republic and Ireland, policy-makers need to devise enterprise and entrepreneurship policies that specifically acknowledge the contribution of women entrepreneurs within the national and European economies and aim to promote women's entrepreneurship nationally. In order for such policies to be effective, they must recognize the gender-related barriers in existence and the impact of the formal and informal institutional environments.

NOTES

1. EQUAL is a Community Initiative promoted by the European Commission and funded through the European Social Fund. Its mission is to promote a more inclusive work life through fighting discrimination and exclusion based on sex, racial or ethnic origin, religion or belief, disability, age or sexual orientation.
2. This figure was calculated pre-recession and may have changed as a result of the economic downturn.
3. OECD statistics extracts accessed 25 January 2008.

REFERENCES

Acs, Z.J., Arenius, P., Hay, M. and Minniti, M. (2004), *Global Entrepreneurship Monitor: 2004 Executive Report*, Babson Park, MA: Babson College and London: London Business School.

Ahlstrom, D. and Bruton, G.D. (2002), 'An institutional perspective on the role of culture in shaping strategic actions by technology-focused entrepreneurial firms in China', *Entrepreneurship Theory and Practice*, **26** (4), 53–70.

Baughn, C., Bee-Leng, C. and Neupert, K.E. (2006), 'The normative context for women's participation in entrepreneurship: a multicountry study', *Entrepreneurship Theory and Practice*, **30** (5), 687–708.

Bliss, R. and Garratt, N. (2001), 'Supporting women entrepreneurs in transitioning economies', *Journal of Small Business Management*, **39** (4), 336–44.

Bosma, N. and Harding, R. (2006), *Global Entrepreneurship Monitor – 2006 – Global Report*, Wellesley, MA: Babson College and London Business School.

Bruni, A., Gherardi, S. and Poggio, B. (2004), 'Entrepreneur-mentality, gender and the study of women entrepreneurs', *Organizational Change Management*, **17** (3), 256–68.

Brush, C. (1997), 'Women owned businesses: obstacles and opportunities', *Journal of Developmental Entrepreneurship*, **2** (1), 1–25.

Brush, C., Carter, N., Gatewood, E., Green, P. and Hart, M. (2001), *The Diana Project, Women Business Owners and Equity Capital: The Myths Dispelled*, Insight Report, Kansas City, MO: Kauffman Center for Entrepreneurial Leadership.

Bruton, G., Ahlstrom, D. and Obloj, K. (2008), 'Entrepreneurship in emerging economies: where are we today and where should the research go in future', *Entrepreneurship Theory and Practice*, **32** (1), 1–14.

Carter, N.M., Henry, C., Ó Cinnéide, B. and Johnson, K. (2006), *Female Entrepreneurship: Implications for Education, Training & Policy*, London: Routledge.

Carter, S. (2000a), 'Gender and enterprise', in S. Carter, and D. Jones-Evans (eds), *Enterprise and Small Business: Principles, Practice and Policy*, London: Prentice Hall.

Carter, S. (2000b), 'Improving the numbers and performance of women-owned businesses: some implications for training and advisory services', *Journal of Education and Training*, **42** (4/5), 326–34.

Carter, S. and Bennett, D. (2006), 'Gender and entrepreneurship', in S. Carter and D. Jones-Evans (eds), *Enterprise and Small Business Principles, Practice and Policy*, 2nd edn, London: Prentice Hall.

Carter, S. and Marlow, S. (2003), 'Professional attainment as a challenge to gender disadvantage in entrepreneurship', paper presented at the 48th International Small Business Conference, June, Belfast.

Carter, S., Anderson, S. and Shaw, E. (2001), 'Women's business ownership: a review of the academic, popular and internet literature', report to the Small Business Service, RR002/01.

Central Statistics Office (CSO) (2004), 'Ireland and the EU 1973–2003: economic and social change', available at: http://eumatters.ie/getmedia/a6fbe03e-a168-4ac7-a6f9-f0903845761f/CSO-Ireland-and-EU-Doc.aspx.

Centre for Enterprise and Economic Development Research (CEEDR) (2001), 'Young, women, ethnic minority and co-entrepreneurs – final report', Middlesex University Business School.

Deakins, D. (1996), *Entrepreneurship and Small Firms*, London: McGraw-Hill.

DiMaggio, P.J. and Powell, W. (1983), 'The iron cage revisited: institutional isomorphism and collective rationality in organizational fields', *American Sociological Review*, **48** (2), 147–60.

European Commission (EC) (2000), Staff working document, 'Benchmarking enterprise policy, first results from the scoreboard', Brussels.

European Commission (EC) (2004), 'Third report on economic and social cohesion', February, p. 155.

European Foundation for the Improvement of Living and Working Conditions (EFILWC) (2004), *Quality of Life in Europe: First European Quality of Life Survey 2003*, Luxembourg: Office for Official Publications of the European Communities.

Fás (1998), *Women in the Irish Labour Force*, Dublin: Department of Enterprise and Employment.

Fay, M. and Williams, L. (1993), 'Gender bias and the availability of business loans', *Journal of Business Venturing*, **8** (4), 363–76.

Garavan, T., Ó Cinnéide, B. and Fleming, P. (1997), *Enterprise and Business Start-Ups in Ireland, Volume 1: An Overview*, Dublin: Oak Tree Press.

Henry, C. (2008), 'Women entrepreneurs', in C. Wankel (ed.), *Handbook of 21st Century Management*, Thousand Oaks, CA: Sage Publications.

Henry, C. and Kennedy, S. (2003), 'In search of a new Celtic Tiger – female entrepreneurship in Ireland', in J. Butler (ed.), *New Perspectives on Women Entrepreneurs*, vol. 3, Greenwich, CT: Information Age Publishing, pp. 203–24.

Henry, C. and Treanor, L. (2007), 'A business-growth training programme for women entrepreneurs', report to the Gender Equality Unit of the Department of Justice, Equality and Law Reform, Ireland.

Hisrich, R.D and Fulop, G. (1994), 'The role of women in Hungary's transition economy', *International Studies of Management and Organisation*, **24** (4), 100–118.

Hisrich, R.D. and Ó Cinnéide, B. (1985), 'The Irish entrepreneur: characteristics, problems and future success', working paper, University of Tulsa.

Ireland, R.D., Tihanyi, L.and Webb, J. (2008), 'A tale of two politico-economic systems: implications for entrepreneurship in Central and Eastern Europe', *Entrepreneurship Theory and Practice*, **32** (1), 107–30.

Irish Government (2007), Irish Government website, http://www.gov.ie.

Lyles, M.A., Saxton, T. and Watson, K. (2004), 'Venture survival in a transitional economy', *Journal of Management*, **30** (3), 351–75.

Manolova, T.S., Eunni, R.V. and Gyoshev, B.S. (2008), 'Institutional environments for entrepreneurship: evidence from emerging economics in Eastern Europe', *Entrepreneurship Theory and Practice*, **32** (1), 203–18.

Manolova, T.S. and Yan, A. (2002), 'Institutional constraints and entrepreneurial responses in a transforming economy: the case of Bulgaria', *International Small Business Journal*, **20** (2), 163–84.

Marlow, S. (1997), 'Self-employed women – new opportunities, old challenges?', *Entrepreneurship and Regional Development*, **9**, 199–210.

Marlow, S. and Patton, D. (2005), 'All credit to men? Entrepreneurship, finance and gender', *Entrepreneurship Theory and Practice*, **29** (6), 717–35.

Mroczkowski, T. (1997), 'Women as employees and entrepreneurs in the Polish transformation', *Industrial Relations Journal*, **28** (2), 83–91.

Rosa, P., Carter, S. and Hamilton, D. (1996), 'Gender as a determinant of small business performance: insights from a British study', *Small Business Economics*, **8**, 463–78.

Schreier, J. (1973), *The Female Entrepreneur: A Pilot Study*, Milwaukee, WI: Center for Venture Management.

Shaw, E., Carter, S. and Brierton, J. (2001), *Unequal Entrepreneurs: Why Female Enterprise is an Uphill Business*, London: The Industrial Society.

Smallbone, D. and Welter, F. (2001), 'The distinctiveness of entrepreneurship in transition economies', *Small Business Economics*, **16** (4), 249–62.

Smallbone, D. and Welter, F. (2006), 'Conceptualising entrepreneurship in a transition context', *International Journal of Entrepreneurship and Small Business*, **3** (2), 190–206.

Spencer, J.W. and Gómez, C. (2004), 'The relationship among national institutional structures, economic factors, and domestic entrepreneurial activity: a multi-country study', *Journal of Business Research*, **57** (10), 1098–107.

Storey, D.J. (1994), *Understanding the Small Business Sector*, London: Routledge.

True, J. (2003), *Gender, Globalisation and Post-socialism: The Czech Republic after Communism*, New York: Columbia University Press.

Watkins, J. and Watkins, D. (1984), 'The female entrepreneur: background and determinants of business choice – some British data', *International Small Business Journal*, **2** (4), 21–31.

Wells, B., Pfantz, T. and Bryne, J. (2003), 'Russian women business owners: evidence of entrepreneurship in a transition economy', *Journal of Developmental Entrepreneurship*, **8** (1), 59–71.

Welter, F. and Smallbone, D. (2003), 'Entrepreneurship and enterprise strategies in transition economies: an institutional perspective', in D. Kirby and A. Watson (eds), *Small Firms and Economic Development in Developed and Transition Economies*, Aldershot: Ashgate.

Welter, F., Smallbone, D., Aculai, E., Isakova, N. and Schakirova, N. (2003), 'Female entrepreneurship in post-Soviet countries', in J. Butler (ed.), *New*

Perspectives on Women Entrepreneurs, Greenwich, CT: Information Age Publishing, pp. 243–69.

World Bank (2008), 'Doing business' report, Washington DC, June.

Zapalska, A. (1997), 'A profile of woman entrepreneurs and enterprises in Poland', *Journal of Small Business Management*, **35** (4), 76–83.

6. The embeddedness of women's entrepreneurship in a transition context

Friederike Welter and David Smallbone

INTRODUCTION

There is growing recognition in entrepreneurship research that economic behaviour can only be understood within the context of its social relations (for example, Davidsson, 2003; Katz and Steyaert, 2004). This chapter applies an institutional theory perspective to women's entrepreneurship in transition economies, exploring the different levels of embeddedness as well as the impact of change. During Soviet times, women experienced different institutional 'realities' (Ashwin, 2000; Kandiyoti and Azimova, 2004; Kiblitskaya, 2000, Zhurzhenko, 2001), with implications for their opportunities to engage in entrepreneurial activities once transition started. This includes the officially propagated gender equality fostering women's labour market participation, as well as the Soviet model of 'worker-mothers'. This contributed to an ongoing double burden for women and the 'renaissance of patriarchy' (Zhurzhenko, 1999: 246) that both European and Central Asian societies experienced after transition had started. This is not surprising in Central Asian countries, where cultural values emphasizing patriarchal family relations survived throughout the Soviet period. However, there is a similar trend in European countries, such as Belarus, Ukraine and Moldova, reflected in 'widely held public assumptions that business is a masculine occupation' (Zhurzhenko, 1999: 246).

With regard to (women's) entrepreneurship, the variety of institutional contexts can either be a liability or an asset. Thus, an institutional analysis of women's entrepreneurship in a transition context needs to take into account gender roles as supported by Soviet governments as well as pre-Soviet legacies. The chapter begins by conceptualizing the different layers of institutional embeddedness with respect to women's entrepreneurship, with particular emphasis on linking this to Soviet and post-Soviet experiences. It proceeds with some background information about the empirical studies conducted in Belarus, Moldova, Ukraine and Uzbekistan, on which the chapter draws, before discussing the embeddedness of women's entrepreneurship in a transition context. The chapter concludes by suggesting some implications for entrepreneurship theory and research.

THE EMBEDDEDNESS OF WOMEN'S ENTREPRENEURSHIP

Institutional theory acknowledges different levels of embeddedness in which economic actions take place: political embeddedness, which emphasize the sources and means of economic action (North, 1990; Zukin and DiMaggio, 1990), cultural embeddedness, as collective understanding of a society which forms the basis for economic behaviour (Denzau and North, 1994; North, 1990; Zukin and DiMaggio, 1990), social embeddedness, as reflected in networks of interpersonal relations (Granovetter, 1985, 2005), and cognitive embeddedness as 'ways in which the structured regularities of mental processes limit the exercise of economic reasoning' (Zukin and DiMaggio, 1990: 15–16; similarly, Denzau and North, 1994).

The concept of mixed embeddedness, which has been developed in relation to analyses of ethnic minority entrepreneurship in mature market economies (Kloosterman et al., 1999), contains characteristics that make it potentially useful as an overarching conceptual framework for analysing women's entrepreneurship in transition conditions. This is because the concept embraces the interplay between social, economic and politico-institutional contexts, as well as between structure and agency. The opportunity structure is a key element in mixed embeddedness. Business opportunities are understood as shaped by a combination of market trends and conditions, which themselves are embedded in a broader institutional framework. Decisions about going into business can also be influenced by the wider structure of alternative opportunities for earning a living. Unlike approaches which narrowly focus on agency and/or cultural mores, a mixed embeddedness perspective recognizes the politico-institutional environment in which human agency is embedded. As such, it would appear to represent a potentially useful frame of reference for analysing societal, economic and institutional influences on women entrepreneurs, because of the differentiated nature of the impact of many of these processes on men and women. Moreover, a combination of its emphasis on interaction between structure and agency, together with the broader institutional context makes it particularly relevant in a transition context. In these countries, the development of women's entrepreneurship since 1990 is, theoretically, located at the intersection of changes in sociocultural frameworks, on the one hand, and transformation processes and the institutional framework on the other.

The Political and Cultural Embeddedness of Women (Entrepreneurs)

Political embeddedness refers to the political and economic boundaries for individual action, in this case for entrepreneurship. Examples of gender-specific formal institutions include the overall constitution ensuring equal opportunities for women and men; labour market rules giving equal access to employment positions; family policies, such as specific tax regulations and the overall infrastructure for childcare; and property rights allowing for female ownership of land.

Soviet politics officially fostered gender equality. Family policies encouraged women to enter the workforce, while at the same time acknowledging their role as mothers by guaranteeing maternity leave. Many women were highly educated, providing a substantial share of professionals and scientific workers. Their workforce participation was among the highest in the world, with 90 per cent of working-age women being employed or in education (Kuehnast and Nechemias, 2004). However, this never translated into leading positions in the Soviet economy, as less than 6 per cent of Soviet managers were women. Moreover, Soviet women were invisible in key decision-making institutions and few women were able to gain access to high party positions beyond 'show' institutions (Kuehnast and Nechemias, 2004: 4). During the transition period, institutional change removed or lowered barriers to market entry and market exit, thus creating opportunity fields for entrepreneurs. This included the introduction of private property rights at the beginning of the transformation process, which generally boosted entrepreneurship for men and women. However, institutional change also had a negative impact on women specifically, as family policies changed and subsidies for state enterprise kindergartens, for example, were reduced, resulting in a lack of public childcare facilities.

Institutions, particularly informal ones such as values and societal norms, are path-dependent and changing slowly. This is of particular relevance for women's entrepreneurship, drawing attention to the impact of culture as well as spatial and political influences (Anderson, 2000). Soviet ideology fostered a widespread emancipation of women, which had positive implications for the (working) lives of women, particularly in the Central Asian Soviet republics. Nevertheless, the emerging worker-mother role model of Soviet societies still left women with a dual responsibility for performing the roles of successful worker and successful mother. In Central Asian Soviet republics, this was reinforced by persisting traditional values. During the transformation period, most societies shifted from the Soviet notion of women as worker (-mothers) to a more traditional role where women stay at home with their families, which went hand in hand with redefining motherhood as a private responsibility (Ashwin, 2000: 2). Zhurzenko (2004: 28) explains the surge of 'neofamiliasm' as an inevitable reaction to the modernization processes in Soviet society: 'The process of searching for new patterns and ways of continuing modernization is accompanied by nostalgia for the "traditional family".' In order to legitimize themselves, governments also reinvented Soviet institutions as 'traditional' ones, which often further restricted women's scope for action (Jones Luong, 2004). In Uzbekistan, for example, this involves drawing on Islam ideology as well as traditional patriarchal values in prescribing housebound roles for women (Welter and Smallbone, 2008), but it also refers to merging village soviets with local neighbourhood committees (*mahallas*) which socially control women (Jones Luong, 2004; Kamp, 2004; Kandiyoti and Azimova, 2004; Werner, 2004).

These social changes have implications for the nature and extent of women's entrepreneurship as well as for the strategies they (may) pursue in developing their ventures. For example, Mirchandani (1999) draws attention to the effect of the location of a business on its survival and development, with home-based ventures experiencing difficulties in gaining legitimacy with clients and creditors because they are frequently seen as leisure activities with limited growth potential. Additionally, she points to a gendered effect of industry which often accompanies the socio-spatial embeddedness of women entrepreneurs because they prefer (or are forced to accept) industries they can operate from home. Thus, for women, the new gender roles could restrict their access to resources needed for entrepreneurship and limit possibilities for venture development.

The Social Embeddedness of Women's Entrepreneurship

In this context, social contacts and family resources gain importance. Research has shown networks to be an important resource for starting and developing a business in general (for example, Brüderl and Preisendörfer, 1998; Dubini and Aldrich, 1991; Liao and Welsch, 2005), for women entrepreneurs specifically (for example, Aldrich, 1989; Allen, 2000; Caputo and Dolinsky, 1998), and particularly for entrepreneurs in hostile and turbulent environments, such as former Soviet countries (Manolova and Yan, 2002; Smallbone and Welter, 2001). In a turbulent environment, networks can substitute for deficiencies in the institutional environment. Furthermore, network contacts, often inherited from the Soviet period, are essential resources when entering entrepreneurship and also subsequently in developing a business. Moreover, emphasizing that opportunities are enacted and socially constructed (Fletcher, 2006), social networks can be important for opportunity recognition and exploitation (de Koning, 2003; Jack and Anderson, 2002).

However, as few women were found in high-level positions during the Soviet period, they also had restricted possibilities to build networks beyond those they acquired when queuing for shortage products and bartering in everyday life. As a result, once transition started, women seldom entered entrepreneurship through privatizing and/or selling state-owned enterprises, with the exception of small-scale privatization of retail trade and services. Moreover, they had little access to 'old' enterprise networks of reciprocity, which forced some to recur to bribery as a means of gaining access to local administrations (Humphrey, 2002).

Another means of accessing resources and identifying business opportunities is linked to the household and family contexts. In this regard, Aldrich and Cliff (2003) suggest a family embeddedness perspective on entrepreneurship, showing how the wider family can influence opportunity emergence and recognition, the decision to set up a new venture, and access to resources (cf. also Jennings and McDougall, 2007). The family embeddedness perspective is also emphasized by Oughton and Wheelock (1996) who argue that in microenterprises the most appropriate unit of investigation is not the individual but the household, as far as both consumption and labour supply decisions are concerned. This emphasizes the social setting, as well as the need to recognize the contributions of different members of a household, in a microenterprise. The role of women in entrepreneurship often goes beyond what may be formally recognized in terms of ownership, including co-ownership. With regard to a transition context, some research draws attention to the 'multiple economies' in which households partake (Pavlovskaya, 2004; Smith, 2002), which has an impact on their access to resources and consequently on business development. All this has implications for women's entrepreneurship, since it emphasizes the potential roles of men and women in a household context, together with access to resources, as possible influences on women's ventures.

The Cognitive Embeddedness of Women's Entrepreneurship

Cognitive embeddedness, as suggested by Zukin and DiMaggio (1990), refers to the bounded rationality of human actions, thus restricting economic behaviour. Dequech (2003) recognized additional cognitive functions of institutions, namely, information that institutions provide on the actions of others and the way that individuals perceive and process information. Moreover, cognitive and cultural embeddedness are closely linked, as cognitive structures are also culturally acquired, resulting from social interaction (Dequech, 2003). In relation to women entrepreneurs it can thus be suggested that cognitive embeddedness influences the strategies they utilize and the actions they take in entering and developing businesses.

From an institutional theory viewpoint, Oliver (1991) suggests a typology of strategic responses to institutions and institutional change, namely, acquiescence, compromise, avoidance, defiance and manipulation. Acquiescence and compromising strategies signal that entrepreneurs have recognized the changed institutional framework and adapted their behaviour accordingly. Avoidance, defiance and manipulation strategies constitute the other end of institutional responses. Peng (2000) developed a threefold typology, which integrates elements of Oliver's framework, while simultaneously paying attention to a transition context. He identifies prospecting, networking and boundary-blurring as distinctive strategies for new and small enterprises in transition environments. The term 'prospector' characterizes firms which operate in a changing market context, focus on innovation and change and consist of a flexible organization structure. While prospecting might paint a rather idealized picture, given the circumstances in which most entrepreneurs in transition economies work, networking typically takes on particular importance in such environments, facilitating economic exchanges. 'Boundary-blurring' resembles Oliver's avoidance and defiance patterns, with entrepreneurs working both illegally and legally because deficiencies in the institutional framework make it difficult for them to operate while remaining completely within the law. Neither of the authors, however, takes into account the impact of the distinctive institutional embeddedness of women on their entrepreneurial behaviour.

As shown by Bruno (1997), in the case of Russian businesswomen, Soviet legacies resulted in distinctive behaviour patterns of women entrepreneurs during transition because of their Soviet experiences in organizing their daily life and household consumption, which left them with experience of managing shortages through a complicated system of bartering goods and favours and cultivating informal knowledge and information networks. At one level, the networks of these women entrepreneurs may be viewed as a potential asset to support business development, while at another they may be viewed more negatively compared with men who often had higher-level connections. In the later Soviet period, women's roles as providers for the household 'could afford them a cover for involvement in the underground supply of consumer goods and informal trading' (Heyat, 2002: 23). This provided them with direct entrepreneurial experiences, although these may have fostered a tendency during transition to (overly) rely on avoidance and defiance strategies.

Cultural and cognitive embeddedness are closely linked, since social ideals concerning gender roles may govern an individual's behaviour. This contributes to regulating both the nature and extent of women's entrepreneurship, as gender roles contain information about 'typical' and 'wanted' behaviour for a woman, as well as the behaviour of an entrepreneur (Ogbor, 2000: 621). With the return of traditional gender roles, post-Soviet societies also re-established the 'concept of male guardianship' (Akiner, 1997: 285) in both public and private life. This is a trend with enormous potential consequences for women's entrepreneurship. For example, research has shown that in the Newly Independent States (NIS), female entrepreneurs were more likely to pursue a business with their husband/friend or father as partners or guardians, while in Central European countries it was apparently easier for women to act as entrepreneurs on their own (Roberts and Tholen, 1999). In a post-Soviet context, business is typically considered a predominantly male territory, requiring so-called male qualities, such as strength and assertiveness. Consequently, in such circumstances, women's entrepreneurship would imply 'breaking out of the norms' (Berg, 1997: 265) of female behaviour. Interestingly, women entrepreneurs have used the predominant male image to construct an alternative ideology for their entrepreneurial activities, emphasizing 'their "natural" feminine attitudes when engaging in business and turning them into the central principle behind their work activities' (Bruno, 1997: 63–4).

EMPIRICAL EVIDENCE

This section presents findings from an empirical investigation of some facets of institutional contexts for women's entrepreneurship. The main empirical data come from two international research projects (financed by INTAS – the International Association for the promotion of cooperation with scientists from the New Independent States of the former Soviet Union, projects 00-0843 and 04-79-6991). The chapter draws mainly on the case studies undertaken as part of these projects. All interview reports were analysed using a computer programme designed for qualitative data analysis, allowing a systematic exploration of patterns.

Description of the Samples

The first project (INTAS 00-0843) focused on women's entrepreneurship in Moldova, Ukraine and Uzbekistan. A survey was conducted in each country in 2002. In Ukraine, a total of 297 females together with a control group of 81 male entrepreneurs were surveyed; in Uzbekistan, the sample consisted of 200 females and 60 males; and in Moldova, 218 and 63, respectively. Case studies with up to 30 women and 5 men entrepreneurs were also carried out in each country in spring 2003. Interviewees were selected from the survey sample, to represent, as far as possible, different enterprise ages, sizes and sectors, roughly in survey proportions. The samples had an approximately even distribution between core and periphery regions. However, both the survey and case samples mainly included older entrepreneurs, which might have been influenced by the databases used to identify the entrepreneurs, but also reflect a generally lower rate of younger entrepreneurs. Most of the women entrepreneurs interviewed were between 30 and 49 years old and were married. Few women entrepreneurs were below 30 years of age, despite high levels of youth unemployment. In Uzbekistan, this appears to reflect traditional role models, which attribute a housebound role to young girls. In comparison with men (20 per cent), only 6 per cent of the Uzbek women were below 30 years of age.

The second project (INTAS 04-79-6991) was concerned with the involvement of households, enterprises and institutions in Belarus, Moldova and Ukraine in cross border entrepreneurial activities. Case studies were carried out in 2006 in three regions in Belarus and Ukraine respectively, and two in Moldova, involving a total of 20 enterprises, 10 households and 10 institutions in each region. Interviews were conducted on a semi-structured basis, using a topic guide. Household respondents were identified by researchers at random, through observation of petty trading activities at markets on both sides of the border and/or railway stations at border crossing points. Enterprises were purposively identified with assistance from institutions, such as Chambers of Commerce and business support agencies, since no comprehensive database existed that would enable enterprises involved in cross border cooperation to be identified. Enterprises were selected to represent different sizes, sectors and age groups.

Economy, Society and Women's Entrepreneurship: Exploring Political and Cultural Embeddedness

Our evidence demonstrates the *political and cultural embeddedness* of women's entrepreneurship during transition, both positively in that political and economic change created new opportunities, and negatively in that Soviet legacies and renewed cultural traditions impeded women wanting to enter entrepreneurship or seeking to develop their businesses. In all project countries, institutional change allowed private entrepreneurship to exist, sometimes even creating opportunities for entrepreneurship. In creating their businesses, some of the interviewed women had benefited from privatization where, for example, they were either able to privatize their own workplace, buy machinery and/or rent premises. Examples include a woman in Moldova renting equipment and premises from her previous employer, who ran a former state-owned company manufacturing television sets; another Moldovan entrepreneur who privatized her former workplace, a restaurant; an entrepreneur in Tashkent, Uzbekistan, who, together with colleagues, privatized a large retail store; and an Uzbek entrepreneur who had worked in a state optical company as manager and consequently privatized this company. In all cases, the women had extensive professional connections in the industry which they used to access state resources.

Economic influences, in particular the necessity to earn an income, was one of the main drivers for the interviewed women to enter entrepreneurship, as well as influencing the choice of activities and the growth potential of the enterprises that were established. With privatization, many women entrepreneurs lost their jobs in (state) enterprises, forcing them to search for income opportunities, which they found in building their own ventures. In addition, older and retired women entrepreneurs frequently mentioned a need to top up their pensions. Some women took over an enterprise after their husband's or father's death. In such cases, entrepreneurial behaviour is often restricted to low-income activities, conducted partly or entirely informally, with few, if any, possibilities for (legal) enterprise development. However, even in these cases, women demonstrated entrepreneurial qualities in identifying possibilities to provide an income for themselves and their families. At the same time, few of the women entered entrepreneurship solely to earn additional income. This applies to women whose spouses provided the main income, and to younger female respondents, who often combine waged employment with entrepreneurial activities.

Many women also mentioned dissatisfaction with their previous employment as a trigger for entrepreneurship. This may be illustrated by a 28-year-old entrepreneur from Moldova, who, together with her husband, started a firm producing sewn toys in 2000. At the time of the interview in 2003, they already employed 12 workers.

One recurrent theme in the interviews linked the need to earn incomes to the women's ambitions to develop their own businesses. In the surveys from Moldova, Ukraine and Uzbekistan, more than half of respondents named growth as their most important objective when asked for their business objectives during the 12 months prior to the interviews in 2001. The survival goal was ranked second (22 per cent), followed by a desire to increase income. This suggests that in transition conditions, business growth, survival and increased family income can be intertwined as

---

BOX 6.1 INSTITUTIONAL 'LOOPHOLES' AND ENTERPRISE DEVELOPMENT

This Moldovan entrepreneur started a minibus route between Strasheni in the Central region and Chisinau, the capital of Moldova. She recounted her difficulties in setting up the business: it took her more than two months to register and obtain the licence and for each document she brought, clerks asked for payment or presents, sometimes having established fixed sums per document. Once up and running, she needed to continue bribing the police, the State Traffic Inspectorate and pay to her 'roof', which reflects a mafia-like structure offering protection to her business. The day before the interview, her driver had been stopped four times and paid a 'fine' to four different officials from the State Traffic Inspectorate.

---

business objectives, reflecting a specific interplay between entrepreneurial activity and the social context. This may be further illustrated by evidence from Moldova, the poorest country in Europe, where some growth is an important requirement to secure the survival of a business and thus maintain a living for a family. A typical statement in this regard was, 'I had a growth orientation in my business right from the beginning, because I needed the money for my family'.

Institutional deficiencies in the political and legal framework also impact on business development. Frequently, loopholes in laws and regulations impeded the financial sustainability of women's businesses. Many of our interviewees mentioned 'payments' to fire inspectors and local administrations for licences and registrations, and to customs and border officers in the case of shuttle traders. The example in Box 6.1 serves to illustrate the enormous impact this can have on business development, while simultaneously showing the perseverance of women entrepreneurs despite difficult circumstances. While such bribes are not specific to women entrepreneurs, there is evidence that women react differently to the need to pay them than men. In some cases, women can circumvent bribes by drawing on networking contacts, which they access through family, while in other instances they refuse to pay bribes, using their gender to embarrass the male officials who demand them.

Cultural influences on women's entrepreneurship are less obvious and visible at the society level, but much more so at the family level, which draws attention to the close links between cultural, social and cognitive embeddedness. One cultural pattern that may be illustrated with reference to empirical evidence from Moldova in particular shows that many women apparently had been socialized to conform to a 'typical' stereotype by demonstrating attributes such as shyness and indecisiveness, which they themselves identified as a hindrance once they had started their businesses. At the same time, our case study evidence demonstrates the learning experiences of women entrepreneurs since setting up their businesses, encouraging them to become more self-confident, with rising aspirations for their business over time.

In Uzbekistan, the specific local environment plays an additional role in enabling (or constraining) female entrepreneurs, and this is associated with a resurgence of traditional and Islamic values in the post-Socialist period. Examples include both supportive attitudes from the local governing council where *mahalla* representatives assisted women in the registration process, as well as negative reactions in the form of envy from neighbours: 'they don't send their girls to my sewing school, but take them to another district'. Some women entrepreneurs also support their community by training local girls, setting up businesses in response to local needs or problems (one example is a kindergarten for paralysed children) and/or offering reduced prices for local community members. Both instances demonstrate recognition of social responsibility by these women entrepreneurs that extends beyond their businesses, fostering institutional change within their local communities. This attitude is also apparent in many of the women-owned ventures studied in Belarus, Moldova and Ukraine, although it is sometimes the family and household that profit most, followed by local communities. In those cases, norms of reciprocity allow women entrepreneurs to access social capital at the community level, thereby illustrating one aspect of the social embeddedness of women entrepreneurs at the local level.

Women's Entrepreneurship from a Family Perspective: Exploring Social Embeddedness

Empirical evidence from both projects demonstrates the need to interpret women's entrepreneurship from household and family perspectives, particularly in transition conditions (cf. also Pavlovskaya, 2004). Survey data from the project on women entrepreneurs show that non-material assistance (such as advice and emotional support) is by far the most common type of assistance provided by both family and spouses, regardless of sex, followed by a labour input into the business itself (Table 6.1). The greater insight allowed by case evidence shows that sometimes another family member identified the business opportunity, as in the case of a Moldovan

Table 6.1   Support of family and spouse for women and men entrepreneurs in Ukraine, Uzbekistan and Moldova

Type of support provided	Women		Men	
	Family	Spouse	Family	Spouse
Capital	16.6%	33.4%	3.8%	8.3%
Working in the business	25.5%	39.1%	20.2%	28.9%
Providing advice	21.5%	65.9%	25.7%	62.8%
Emotional support	25.2%	66.9%	31.1%	77.8%
Other ways	0.5%	3.2%	4.9%	2.8%
No	10.8%	14.2%	14.2%	14.4%
No. of respondents	651	532	183	180

Note: The table summarizes answers to two questions: does your family (spouse) support your business? If so, how? Each respondent was able to give up to three types of support.

Source: Authors' own survey data.

entrepreneur whose husband suggested that she could get involved in trading goods. He prepared all the documentation and even accompanied her on her first business trips to Poland in order to help her build up contacts. Our case study evidence also demonstrates the importance of family assistance in coping with institutional change. For example, in Ukraine, women with young children would not be able to combine running a business and raising children without external help from the family, because of the demise of state-run crèche facilities following the collapse of the former Soviet Union.

One notable difference between the male and female entrepreneurs we studied concerns access to financial resources, with women more likely than men to draw on their family, particularly their spouses, for financial help (Table 6.1). Disapproval, where it occurs, appears to be more common with respect to certain business activities such as trade, and/or microenterprise activities and/or when spouses generally disapprove of their wife being involved in business.

In several cases across all four countries studied, family involvement leads to the creation of family businesses (Box 6.2, example A), in which women are sometimes the driving forces in setting up the businesses (Box 6.2, example B). In some cases, family help can extend across borders, as in the case of shuttle traders (Box 6.2, example C), although this cross-border element of family support is not confined to women entrepreneurs.

Family can also assist more indirectly with entrepreneurial activity, by

BOX 6.2   EXAMPLES OF FAMILY INVOLVEMENT
IN WOMEN'S ENTREPRENEURSHIP

Family businesses

Example A   The company in Ukraine, manufacturing plastic
packets, was set up in 1999 and currently employs 48 people,
which is a considerable size in the Ukrainian context. The woman
owner, who is in her late fifties, had previously worked in a knit-
ting factory as a 'journeyman' for 20 years, followed by nine
years of retail trading at a market. She is responsible for financial
management and, according to her, for all main decisions at the
firm, while her husband and younger son are responsible for production and equipment. The older son is managing the import of
material and dealing with customs.

Example B   This Uzbek woman has run a private drugstore
in Chartak, a rural region in Uzbekistan, since 2001. She is
56 years of age and has worked 35 years as midwife in a
maternity ward. Her husband is a pharmacist. She had tried to
persuade him to open his own business for a long time, as they
needed the money to support their five children and 15 grand-
children.

Example C: A cross-border family business   One typical example
is a 65-year-old woman, from Vitebsk in Belarus, bordering
Lithuania, Latvia and Russia. The respondent's sister is married
and living in Vilnius in Lithuania, while the respondent herself
and her daughter live on the Belarusian side of the border with
Lithuania. The respondent trades in medicines and clothes. As
the daughter works in a chemicals firm in the Grodno region (near
Vilnius, Lithuania), she has access to cheap traditional medicines
from Russia, Ukraine and Belarus, which are popular with elder
people in Lithuania, but not legally importable in most cases. On
her way to Lithuania, where she regularly travels to visit relatives,
the respondent visits her daughter in order to buy a stock of medicines, using a medicinal import certificate (obtained with the help
of her daughter). Once in Vilnius, her sister helps her to sell the
medicine through pensioners, who they both know. Occasionally,
she has to sell on the Vilnius market, if her personal network of

> contacts do not purchase all the medicines she has brought for sale. On her return to Belarus, she brings clothes for sale, which she buys in second-hand stores, assisted by the girlfriend of her niece who works in such a store in Vilnius.

providing contacts, another recurrent pattern reported in many of the interviews. 'My husband helped me with his personal contacts', 'my father knew someone' and 'my husband knew exactly where to go and who to address' are all typical statements. When interpreted in context, such comments show how other members of a household provide the required inputs, which may help a woman overcome her lack of high-level networks. This also indicates the role of the family context (broadly defined) as potentially important for fostering business development.

It must also be recognized that family might hinder business development, suggesting that this type of embeddedness can have a negative as well as a positive impact on women's entrepreneurship. This is particularly the case in situations where women have to cope with a family or household environment where traditional gender roles and attitudes towards their potential entrepreneurial activities dominate and the implications of this for their entrepreneurial behaviour.

Women's Entrepreneurial Behaviour: Coping with or Breaking out of Norms?

This section explores the cognitive embeddedness of women's entrepreneurship by looking at how women entrepreneurs deal with institutional norms, taking up Berg's assumption (1997) that entrepreneurship might enable (or force) women to break out of norms governing their behaviour. The evidence illustrates two distinctive patterns of entrepreneurial behaviour of women towards norms, which may be interpreted as forms of cognitive embeddedness. One pattern refers to women breaking out of societal norms ascribing traditional gender roles, either in relation to sector choices or related to their role as housewives. The second pattern includes women's behaviour in relation to the dominating norm of entrepreneurship in post-Soviet societies, where women combine defying and conforming actions. Educational levels, together with previous professional experience might be of importance in cases where women voluntarily defy traditional gender roles and values. The majority of women (and men) interviewed in both projects had university-level education, with secondary vocational education the next most common highest educational

---

BOX 6.3   ESCAPING TRADITIONAL GENDER NORMS

Sector norms This Ukrainian woman entrepreneur described how, when she started her construction business, many of her male competitors were waiting for her to fail. She continued her story by complaining about men not taking women in construction seriously, even though she owned a business employing 25 people at the time of the interview.

Housebound roles
This young Ukrainian woman started to work as a tailor, initially at home because she did not like her job in a state-owned company, involved in a similar line of business. Her husband was irritated by the mess her business created at home, complaining also of her customers coming and going. As a result, he forced her to rent premises, while continuing to voice his discontent with her activities, wanting her to stay at home and care for their child.

Another example refers to a young woman in rural Uzbekistan, who had to go into business after her father's death, and who had previously been the sole breadwinner for the family. She set up in a traditional activity, namely, gold embroidery and sewing because this was one of the few vocational training opportunities available to her. Similar to her, two of her three sisters set up home-based traditional business activities in carpet weaving and cookery. All three became involved in training unemployed girls in these activities.

---

achievement for women. While this reflects the paucity of opportunities for educated people to find satisfying ways of earning a living in primitive transition conditions, it also might assist them in seeing new possibilities beyond the accepted societal gender roles.

One example of the first pattern of cognitive embeddedness, namely, women entrepreneurs who have broken out of norms, refers to the sectors of their business activities (Box 6.3). Several women own and operate businesses in the construction and manufacturing sectors, which in a Western context are still considered 'non-traditional' female sectors. This pattern is a result of the Soviet legacy supporting the participation of women in a non-discriminatory labour market, although transition has changed this.

Defying norms gains an additional dimension in relation to the family context, since entrepreneurship can apparently help to redefine traditional gender roles, despite the post-Soviet trend towards traditional roles for women. One pattern concerns the distribution of household responsibilities between wife and husband. Where women entrepreneurs are successful, or men earn considerably less from their jobs, men take over responsibilities in the household, thus allowing the respondent to pursue their entrepreneurial activity. At the same time, this implies a positive and supportive attitude of the family, which is not always the case.

In this regard, case evidence shows women entrepreneurs breaking norms in a family context, with a potentially high impact on societal change. In some instances, women used their entrepreneurial activities to gain greater independence from spouses and/or families, persisting despite family disapproval. Sometimes, women were also involuntarily pushed to overcome traditional gender roles because of their husband's or father's death. However, as examples from rural Uzbekistan demonstrate, women in such a situation are often restricted to home-based traditional business activities with low growth potential (Welter and Smallbone, 2008).

The second pattern of cognitive embeddedness is related to the prevailing attitudes and values towards entrepreneurship found in a transition context. Our evidence shows both defying and conforming behaviour, which can sometimes go hand in hand. Breaking out of norms in this context refers to overcoming the legacy of the attitudes of the Soviet state towards entrepreneurial activities. Previous research has shown that some entrepreneurs, especially market traders and those engaged in simple entrepreneurial activities, consider their business activities to be shameful, particularly in cases where they previously occupied a prominent public position during the socialist period (Kaneff, 2002). Similar feelings are visible in our empirical evidence, particularly for older women with long management experience in state-owned enterprises, who when interviewed were working in market trade and shuttle businesses. Their assessment of their current entrepreneurial activities as 'shameful' may partly result from their loss of professional identity but also from the low-growth and frequently partly illegal activities they (are forced to) pursue.

Women also defy cultural norms that ascribe them a feminine role, which they perceive as a hindrance for entrepreneurial activities. This is visible in those instances where women entrepreneurs describe their own learning experiences and growing self-confidence. It is also apparent in cases where women are willing to 'play' a role as prescribed in gender stereotypes in order to overcome difficulties they experience in developing their businesses. Our evidence shows women entrepreneurs applying different 'strategies'. There were a few cases where women appeared to accept society's attitude towards women's entrepreneurship, stating that 'Big business is for men, small business is for women', although this may simply be to gain acceptance in a male-dominated business world. A few women referred to advantages of male entrepreneurs, because 'it is sometimes easier for them to solve problems by drinking together or going to the sauna', which are activities that help in building trust and networks. Other women entrepreneurs see a need to adapt to perceived male entrepreneurial behaviour, as described in the words of one Ukrainian entrepreneur: 'I sometimes forget that I am a woman.' Similarly, a Russian woman owning a wholesale business in Uzbekistan felt that she had lost her femininity, as even her business partners had referred to her 'thinking like a man'. For her, being a successful businesswoman had resulted in personal conflicts, since her husband, an Uzbek Muslim, constantly reproached her for not taking care of the household. This evidence illustrates how women's entrepreneurship is assessed and justified by women entrepreneurs themselves, comparing it to male entrepreneurship, which they accept as the norm (Bruni et al., 2004). This may encourage some women to emphasize their similarities to the male norm, thus concealing their gender when doing business (Lewis, 2006).

Others are proud of their 'outsider' status, as voiced by one Ukrainian woman entrepreneur: 'If some people do not like female entrepreneurs, let them. We do not care. But female entrepreneurs do exist and you have to take account of the fact.' In this regard, women actively defy the male norm of entrepreneurship, as described by Bruno (1997) for Russian businesswomen. For example, several of our interviewees vividly described how they had used their identity as a woman to cope with administrative bodies: 'The tax inspector saw me as a weak woman and felt pity for me. He did not ask for bribes and sometimes even confined himself to minimal fines for my mistakes', a Ukrainian trader, importing and retailing women's clothes, explained. Similarly, an Uzbek entrepreneur described how she used her image as a weak and inexperienced woman in a man's world (that is, business) to get the tax inspectorate to lower her tax liability.

In this respect, several women entrepreneurs make an interesting distinction between bribes and gifts, indicating that offering bribes, in the form of monetary payments, is unacceptable to them, although gifts are an accepted and tolerated part of business behaviour. Gifts could include flowers or alcohol, but also services and materials provided from their respective businesses. In these situations, women conform to Soviet values, which are visible in the importance they place on networks of reciprocity, as constituted by their gifts. In contrast, offering bribes involves stepping out of their community into 'an asocial, monetized world' (Humphrey, 2002: 138). From an institutional theory perspective, such behaviour is an important signal of path-dependency, as the women continue to rely on the trust-based networks of mutual help which characterized Soviet life (Rehn and Taalas, 2004) and which continued during transition (Ledeneva, 1998, 2006). At the same time, many do not adapt to the norms and values of the emerging market economies, which forces them to behave in ways they consider unwomanly. By making this distinction, they also define part of their identity as a businesswoman. This draws attention to the complex relationship between individual actions, the overall institutional environment and the nature of women's entrepreneurship. It also suggests a potentially important role for the adaptations to societal and familial norms, visible in the examples of women entrepreneurs described above.

CONCLUSIONS AND IMPLICATIONS

This chapter aims to make a contribution to our conceptual understanding of women's entrepreneurship under 'early stage' transition conditions by researching the nature of its embeddedness in Belarus, Moldova, Ukraine and Uzbekistan. The empirical evidence demonstrates a contribution of women entrepreneurs to social change and to alleviating some of the negative effects of transformation through offering job possibilities for other women (as well as men). Even more importantly, they provide positive role models and add to a more positive image of (women's) private entrepreneurship. This is even more important in some post-Soviet societies where the revival of traditional values and attitudes restricts the nature of women's entrepreneurship.

Our evidence suggests that there is a need to draw on different layers of embeddedness and context, as women's entrepreneurship is highly dependent on the specific contexts in which it occurs. This includes the overall political and cultural context, as well as family and household contexts, but also how women entrepreneurs cope with and respond to these conditions. In this regard, it is argued that an institutional framework, as applied in this chapter, which acknowledges different layers of context, is an appropriate way to analyse the embeddedness of women's entrepreneurship, particularly when this is combined with an individual perspective that takes into account the adaptability and learning behaviour of (female) entrepreneurs.

Transition conditions provide additional dimensions to the concept of mixed embeddedness, of which path-dependency is one of the most prominent constraining and enabling factors. While political and economic institutional change has fostered entrepreneurship by both men and women, women face additional challenges associated with cultural embeddedness, reflected in the attitudes of post-Soviet societies towards women's entrepreneurship and the renewal of patriarchal orders in many post-Soviet republics. This aspect of transition forced women back into the traditional role of housewives and into the private sphere of the family. In this regard, the evidence shows that women entrepreneurs often start to break out of norms ascribing traditional gender roles and types of stereotypical behaviour. Examples of young Muslim women in mature market economies, such as the UK, who use involvement in entrepreneurship as a means of self-assertion rather than simply accepting a traditional gender role, are broadly comparable. Thus, women's entrepreneurship may foster institutional change, especially with regard to social norms and values, while institutional change is also needed for women's entrepreneurship to emerge.

Despite contradictory attitudes of post-Soviet societies towards working women, transition has also contributed to the emergence of women entrepreneurs in the former Soviet republics. Women's entrepreneurship has played, and continues to play, an important role in modernizing these societies and in contributing to changing public attitudes towards women, with possible benefits relating to the economic potential of female entrepreneurs. Assisting more women to start up businesses and supporting existing firms to grow can contribute to a more competitive economy and economic growth, as well as reducing social exclusion. However, there is also a need to avoid stereotyping women entrepreneurs across transition countries, such as characterizing all women entrepreneurs as 'necessity driven'. Faced with system collapse, while most women entrepreneurs may be driven by a need to raise family income at start-up, this does not necessarily determine their subsequent development path, or their evolving aims for the business. The latter may involve more 'opportunity recognition' and growth ambitions for their businesses, as external circumstances change and individuals grow in confidence, ambitions and competence, with the result that necessity may ultimately become a source of opportunity for women entrepreneurs.

REFERENCES

Akiner, S. (1997), 'Between tradition and modernity: the dilemma facing contemporary Central Asian women', in M Buckley (ed.), *Post-Soviet Women: From the Baltic to Central Asia*, Cambridge: Cambridge University Press, pp. 261–304.
Aldrich, H. (1989), 'Networking among women entrepreneurs', in O. Hagan, C. Rivchun and D.L. Sexton (eds), *Women-Owned Businesses*, New York: Praeger, pp. 103–32.
Aldrich, H. and Cliff, J. (2003), 'The pervasive effects of family on entrepreneurship:

toward a family embeddedness perspective', *Journal of Business Venturing*, **18**, 573–96.

Allen, W.D. (2000), 'Social networks and self-employment', *Journal of Socio-Economics*, **29**, 487–501.

Anderson, A. (2000), 'Paradox in the periphery: an entrepreneurial reconstruction?', *Entrepreneurship & Regional Development*, **12**, 91–109.

Ashwin, S. (2000), 'Introduction: gender, state and society in Soviet and post-Soviet Russia', in S. Ashwin (ed.), *Gender, State and Society in Soviet and Post-Soviet Russia*, London: Routledge, pp. 1–29.

Berg, N.G. (1997), 'Gender, place and entrepreneurship', *Entrepreneurship & Regional Development*, **9** (3), 259–68.

Brüderl, J. and Preisendörfer, P. (1998), 'Network support and the success of newly founded businesses', *Small Business Economics*, **10**, 213–25.

Bruni, A., Gherardi, S. and Poggio, B. (2004), 'Doing gender, doing entrepreneurship: an ethnographic account of intertwined practices', *Gender, Work and Organization*, **11** (4), 406–29.

Bruno, M. (1997), 'Women and the culture of entrepreneurship', in M. Buckley (ed.), *Post-Soviet Women: from Baltic to Central Asia*, Cambridge: Cambridge University Press, pp. 56–74.

Caputo R.K. and Dolinsky, A. (1998), 'Women's choice to pursue self-employment: the role of financial and human capital of household members', *Journal of Small Business Management*, **36** (3), 8–17.

Davidsson, P. (2003), 'The domain of entrepreneurship research: some suggestions', in J. Katz and D. Shepherd (eds), *Cognitive Approaches to Entrepreneurship Research*, vol. 6 of *Advances in Entrepreneurship, Firm Emergence and Growth*, Amsterdam: Elsevier/JAI Press, pp. 315–72.

De Koning, A. (2003), 'Opportunity development: a socio-cognitive perspective', in J. Katz and D. Shepherd (eds), *Cognitive Approaches to Entrepreneurship Research*, vol. 6 of *Advances in Entrepreneurship, Firm Emergence and Growth*, Amsterdam: Elsevier/JAI Press, pp. 265–314.

Denzau, A.T. and North, D.C. (1994), 'Shared mental models: ideologies and institutions', *Kyklos*, **47** (1), 3–31.

Dequech, D. (2003), 'Cognitive and cultural embeddedness: combining institutional economics and economic sociology', *Journal of Economic Issues*, **37** (2), 461–9.

Dubini, P. and Aldrich, H. (1991), 'Personal and extended networks are central to the entrepreneurial process', *Journal of Business Venturing*, **6**, 305–13.

Fletcher, D. (2006), 'Entrepreneurial processes and the social construction of opportunity', *Entrepreneurship & Regional Development*, **18** (5), 421–40.

Granovetter, M. (1985), 'Economic action and social structure: the problem of embeddedness', *American Journal of Sociology*, **91**, 481–510.

Granovetter, M. (2005), 'The impact of social structure on economic outcomes', *Journal of Economic Perspectives*, **19** (1), 33–50.

Heyat, F. (2002), 'Women and the culture of entrepreneurship in Soviet and post-Soviet Azerbaijan', in R. Mandel and C. Humphrey (eds), *Markets and Moralities: Ethnographies of Postsocialism*, Oxford and New York: Berg, pp. 19–31.

Humphrey, C. (2002), *The Unmaking of Soviet Life: Everyday Economies after Socialism*, Ithaca, NY, and London: Cornell University Press.

Jack, S. and Anderson, A. (2002), 'The effects of embeddedness on the entrepreneurial process', *Journal of Business Venturing*, **17**, 467–87.

Jennings, J. and McDougall, M.S. (2007), 'Work–family interface experiences and coping strategies: implications for entrepreneurship research and practice', *Academy of Management Review*, **32** (3), 747–60.

Jones Luong, P. (2004), 'Politics in the periphery: competing views of Central Asian states and societies', in P. Jones Luong (ed.), *The Transformation of Central Asia: States and Societies from Soviet Rule to Independence*, Ithaca, NY, and London: Cornell Press, pp. 1–26.

Kamp, M. (2004), 'Between women and the state: mahalla committees and social welfare in Uzbekistan', in P. Jones Luong (ed.), *The Transformation of Central Asia: States and Societies from Soviet Rule to Independence*, Ithaca, NY, and London: Cornell Press, pp. 29–58.

Kandiyoti, D. and Azimova, N. (2004), 'The communal and the sacred: women's worlds of ritual in Uzbekistan', *Journal of Royal Anthropological Institute*, New Series), **10**, 327–49.

Kaneff, D. (2002), 'The shame and pride of market activity: morality, identity and trading in post Socialist rural Bulgaria', in R. Mandel, and C. Humphrey (eds), *Markets and Moralities: Ethnographies of Postsocialism*, Oxford and New York: Berg, pp. 33–51.

Katz, J. and Steyaert, C. (2004), 'Entrepreneurship in society: exploring and theorizing new forms and practices of entrepreneurship', special issue of *Entrepreneurship & Regional Development*, **16** (3), 179–250.

Kiblitskaya, M. (2000), 'Russia's female breadwinners: the changing subjective experience', in S. Ashwin (ed.), *Gender, State and Society in Soviet and Post-Soviet Russia*, London: Routledge, pp. 55–70.

Kloosterman, R., van der Leun, J. and Rath, J. (1999), 'Mixed embeddedness: (in)formal economic activities and immigrant businesses in the Netherlands', *International Journal of Urban and Regional Research*, **23** (2), 253–77.

Kuehnast, K. and Nechemias, C. (2004), 'Introduction: women navigating change in post-Soviet currents', in K. Kuehnast and C. Nechemias (eds), *Post-Soviet Women Encountering Transition: Nation Building, Economic Survival and Civic Activism*, Washington, DC: Johns Hopkins University Press, pp. 1–20.

Ledeneva, A.V. (1998), *Russia's Economy of Favours: Blat, Networking and Informal Exchange*, Cambridge: Cambridge University Press.

Ledeneva, A.V. (2006), *How Russia Really Works: The Informal Practices that Shaped Post-Soviet Politics and Business*, New York: Cornell University Press.

Lewis, P. (2006), 'The quest for invisibility: female entrepreneurs and the masculine norm of entrepreneurship', *Gender, Work and Organization*, **13** (5), 453–69.

Liao, J. and Welsch, H. (2005), 'Roles of social capital in venture creation: key dimensions and research implications', *Journal of Small Business Management*, **43** (4), 345–62.

Manolova, T. and Yan, A. (2002), 'Institutional constraints and entrepreneurial responses in a transforming economy', *International Small Business Journal*, **20**, 163–84.

Mirchandani, K. (1999), 'Feminist insight on gendered work: new directions in research on women and entrepreneurship', *Gender, Work and Organization*, **6** (4), 224–35.

North, D.C. (1990) *Institutions, Institutional Change and Economic Performance*, Cambridge: University Press.

Ogbor, J.O. (2000), 'Mythicizing and reification in entrepreneurial discourse:

ideology-critique of entrepreneurial studies', *Journal of Management Studies*, **37** (5), 605–36.

Oliver, C. (1991), 'Strategic responses to institutional processes', *Academy of Management Review*, **16** (1), 145–79.

Oughton, E. and Wheelock, J. (1996), 'The household as a focus for research', *Journal of Economic Issues*, **30**, 143–59.

Pavlovskaya, M. (2004), 'Other transitions: multiple economies of Moscow households in the 1990s', *Annals of the Association of American Geographers*, **94** (2), 329–51.

Peng, M. (2000), *Business Strategies in Transition Economies*, Thousand Oaks, CA, London and New Delhi: Sage.

Rehn, A. and Taalas, S. (2004), '"Znakomstva i svyazi" (acquaintances and connections) – blat, the Soviet Union and mundane entrepreneurship', *Entrepreneurship & Regional Development*, **16** (3), 235–50.

Roberts, K. and Tholen, J. (1999), 'Junge Unternehmer in den neuen Marktgesellschaften Mittel- und Osteuropas', in D. Bögenhold (ed.), *Unternehmensgründungen und Dezentralität – Eine Renaissance der beruflichen Selbständigkeit?* Opladen: Westdeutscher Verlag, pp. 257–78.

Smallbone, D. and Welter, F. (2001), 'The distinctiveness of entrepreneurship in transition economies', *Small Business Economics*, **16** (4), 249–62.

Smith, A. (2002), 'Culture/economy and spaces of economic practice: positioning households in post-communism', *Transactions of the Institute of British Geographer*, New Series **27**, 232–50.

Welter, F. and Smallbone, D. (2008), 'Women's entrepreneurship from an institutional perspective: the case of Uzbekistan', *International Entrepreneurship and Management Journal*, **4**, 505–20.

Werner, C. (2004), 'Women, marriage, and the nation-state: the rise of nonconsensual bride kidnapping in post-Soviet Kazakhstan', in P. Jones Luong (ed.), *The Transformation of Central Asia: States and Societies from Soviet Rule to Independence*, Ithaca, NY, and London: Cornell Press, pp. 59–89.

Zhurzhenko, T. (1999), 'Gender and identity formation in post-Socialist Ukraine: the case of women in the shuttle business', in R. Bridgman, S. Cole and H. Howard-Bobiwash (eds), *Feminist Fields: Ethnographic Insights*, Ontario: Broadview Press, pp. 243–63.

Zhurzhenko, T. (2001), 'Free market ideology and new women's identities in post-socialist Ukraine', *The European Journal of Women's Studies*, **8** (1), 29–49.

Zhurzhenko, T. (2004), 'Strong women, weak state: family politics and nation building in post-Soviet Ukraine', in K. Kuehnast and C. Nechemias (eds), *Post-Soviet Women Encountering Transition: Nation Building, Economic Survival and Civic Activism*, Washington, DC: Johns Hopkins University Press, pp. 23–43.

Zukin, S. and DiMaggio, P. (1990), 'Introduction', in S. Zukin and P. DiMaggio (eds), *Structures of Capital: The Social Organization of the Economy*, Cambridge: Cambridge University Press, pp. 1–36.

7. Women empowering women: female entrepreneurs and home-based producers in Jordan

Haya Al-Dajani and Sara Carter

INTRODUCTION

While the social inequalities between men and women in the Arab Middle East region have been widely documented (Moghadam, 2004), the inequalities in economic participation and their resulting outcomes have not been as rigorously addressed (Al-Dajani, 2010; Metcalfe, 2007). This is partly due to the lack of available data about women's economic participation, although various international agencies have made some efforts to address this (CAWTAR, 2007; UNDP, 2006; World Bank, 2007). Data produced by the United Nations suggest that women's economic participation in the Arab Middle East region is gaining increased importance, increasing by 19 per cent between 1990 and 2003 compared with the world average increase of 3 per cent (UNDP, 2006). However, Arab women's economic participation remains the lowest in the world (UNDP, 2006). In 2005, an average of 33.3 per cent of women aged over 15 were defined as 'economically active' in this region, compared with the world average of 55.6 per cent. Furthermore, Arab women's participation as a percentage of male economic participation was also the lowest in the world (UNDP, 2006).

While the increase in women's economic participation in the Middle East region over the past 15 years is encouraging, and women's accomplishments have contributed to transforming the region's political economy and social demography, great challenges remain. For example, women's home-based work has acquired new momentum in the region but remains largely ignored (Tomei, 2000). In this regard, female self-employed producers in Jordan, typically engaging in traditional embroidery piecework and working from a home base, continue to be invisible. This situation is similar to other parts of the developing world (Maskiell, 2004; Wilkinson-Weber, 2004) and may be due to a lack of understanding and confusion regarding what constitutes home-based work (Al-Dajani, 2010). The home-based sector is understood to be unique in its fluidity, flexibility and proactive response to economic situations and trends (Tomei, 2000). Nevertheless, whether home-based work contributes to or alleviates the feminization of poverty is debatable.

Poverty risk theory (Chen et al., 2005) suggests that poverty risk is lowest among individuals engaged in formal wage employment and highest among industrial outworkers. According to this theory, women engaged in home-based self-employment within the informal work sector face a significant risk of poverty. Although regional data are scarce regarding the number of women engaged in this type of work, a survey by UNIFEM (2004) suggests that the majority of women in employment operate within the categories defined by Chen et al. (2005) as 'Informal Self Employment: Own Account' and 'Casual Informal Wage Employment and Domestic Work'. International agencies explain the rise in home-based self-employed women as an outcome of armed conflict leading to intra-regional migration and single-female headed households in some instances, coupled with rising unemployment and exaggerated increased prices for basic necessities including fuel, water, electricity, housing and staple food items (Fanek, 2005; UNIFEM, 2004).

Despite the growth in the number of home-based self-employed women, there have been few studies that have explored their particular experiences. Indeed, the feminist literature has acknowledged that women's experiences within their homes have been greatly neglected by both researchers and policy-makers (Walker and Webster, 2004). This has led to what some researchers have described as the invisibility of women and their work (Mosedale, 2005; WIEGO, 2003), and the view that theories explaining women's work have been framed using male experiences and perspectives on women's daily lives (Snyder, 1995). In response to these concerns, there have been several calls for research focused solely on women's experiences within the home and undertaken from a female perspective (Chen et al., 2005; Greer and Greene, 2003; ILO, 2002a; Walker and Webster, 2004).

Within the developed world, there has been a growth in the number of women-owned small and medium-sized enterprises (SMEs), and an accompanying increase in research seeking to explore this widespread phenomenon (Carter and Shaw, 2006; Chen et al., 2005). While it was acknowledged that women-owned SMEs make a substantial contribution to their local economies (Allen et al., 2007), their role as potential catalysts of women's empowerment and development has not, so far, been recognized either by researchers, international donors or policy-makers (Heyzer, 2006). Certainly, within developing countries, women-owned SMEs and their inter-relationships with home-based women producers continue to be invisible (Premchander, 2003). Cohen and Musson (2000) argued that research exploring the operations of women-owned SMEs is essential from a grassroots rather than a policy-maker's perspective, a theme which was similarly urged by Kantor (2005) and Chen et al., (2005) among others.

To enhance the grassroots perspective and to adhere to feminist research methodology principles, a study must include an empowerment focus. Since its definition in the early 1990s (Wallerstein, 1992), empowerment has been primarily concerned with the oppressed self gaining power to be recognized and valued as an independent entity (McNay, 2000). Al-Dajani (2007: 20) defined women's empowerment as 'a continuous, ongoing process entailing enhanced abilities to control choices, decisions and actions'. This approach reaffirms the individual's role in contributing to positive change and progress within her community (Mosedale, 2005) and is largely grounded in Longwe and Clarke's (1994) authoritative empowerment cycle (see Figure 7.1). This cycle includes five progressive levels: welfare, access, conscientization, participation and control. The cyclical approach argues that at the welfare level, women's and men's resources are not equally recognized and met. At the access level, women need to realize this inequality and confront it by taking action to gain access for resources. At the conscientization level, referred to in this chapter as concretization, women recognize that their inequalities to access resources and their general subordinate status are socially

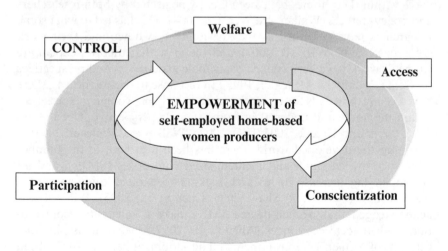

Source: Longwe and Clarke (1994: 178).

Figure 7.1   The women's empowerment cycle

constructed beliefs and phenomena. Therefore, at the participation level, women take action and participate in the decision-making processes within their households, communities and societies at large. Finally, at the control level, women's increased participation is used to achieve increased control over access to resources and distribution of benefits. This control increases women's power and respect within their households, communities and societies at large. Empowered individuals will have increased self-confidence, self-assertiveness, motivation, ambition and persistence to ensure that their welfare needs and access to resources are recognized and met.

The cyclic representation of the framework illustrates the process of women's empowerment whereby the pattern of growth and development is continuous (Mosedale, 2005) and suggests that women's empowerment is not simply about achieving control, but rather going beyond and using the control to increase welfare and access to resources.

The study presented in this chapter focuses on women embroiderers in Jordan as examples of home-based producers. Traditionally, embroidery as a craft-based industry in the Arab world has been bound to the female arena. Women undertake this handicraft within their homes, and sell their pieces through small retail outlets owned by women entrepreneurs (UNIFEM, 2004). The inter-relationships between the home-based women embroiderers and their respective women-owned SMEs are typical of the exchanges between home-based women producing handicrafts other than embroidery and their respective businesses. Although it is acknowledged that such inter-relationships exist between home-based women embroiderers and men-owned SMEs, men are excluded from this study to ensure that the focus on women is not diluted.

To a large extent, it has been accepted by policy-makers that the empowerment of highly impoverished women is best achieved by women-led charitable non-profit organizations (NPOs). This study challenges that assumption. By focusing on two groups of women entrepreneurs – self-employed home-based producers and women business owners who commission their embroidery work – and the inter-relationships between the two, this study sheds new light on current conventional wisdom regarding women's experiences of entrepreneurship within this region.

METHODOLOGY

Adrienne Rich stated 'when those who have the power to name and to socially construct reality choose not to see or hear you . . . there is a moment of psychic disequilibrium, as if you looked into a mirror and saw nothing' (Rich, 1980: 640). To address this, feminist scholars have adopted alternative approaches to social enquiry. As this study focused on women's experiences within their private (home-based women producers) and public (women-owned SMEs) domains, the adoption of a feminist methodological approach was most appropriate. Its five overarching principles are: a continuous focus on gender as a basic component of all social life; raising awareness; challenging the objectivity norm within social research; recognizing the exploitation of women in research; and emphasizing women's empowerment through research. As 'empowerment' was defined as a process rather than a goal, a longitudinal approach was most suited to explore this phenomenon. Thus, a feminist longitudinal approach was adopted in this study.

Following a pilot phase, the longitudinal study constituted three consecutive phases of data collection which took place in Amman, Jordan, and consisted of semi-structured individual in-depth interviews. The advantages of this approach were threefold. First, since women's empowerment is an ongoing process, using a longitudinal approach was appropriate. Second, qualitative methodologies are well suited to exploratory research (Miles and Huberman, 1994). Third, Arab culture is not only private but also verbal since locals prefer to talk rather than complete a questionnaire (Jabre et al., 1997). Hence, undertaking semi-structured interviews in all three phases of data collection constituted a practical choice. The use of semi-structured interviews has been successfully used in many cultures where the issue of women's empowerment has been investigated (see, for example, Jabre et al., 1997).

A theory-driven, multiple-case sampling framework was applied as the selection of participants was driven by 'a conceptual question, not by a concern for representativeness' (Miles and Huberman, 1994: 29). As such, the major concern was the understanding of the empowerment process for the individual and not the generalizations that can be made. The sample consisted of four women entrepreneurs and twenty home-based women producers. Each woman-owned SME was supplied by five of the participating twenty home-based producers.

THE WOMEN ENTREPRENEURS

To ensure comparability among the sample, the selection criteria for the sample of four women entrepreneurs were that they owned and managed a business that subcontracts home-based women producers. In addition, each business focuses on the sale of traditional Palestinian embroidered items, subcontracts women from the East Amman suburbs and has been

Table 7.1   Characteristics of the women entrepreneurs

SMEs	Year established	Owner/ manager	Age	Education level	Total number of home-based embroiderers
SME 1	1977	SME 1m	47	University	6
SME 2	1975	SME 2m	68	University	60
SME 3	1994	SME 3m	33	University	15
SME 4	1993	SME 4m	39	University	10

running for at least three years. Each business was locally established and run in Amman, Jordan, though this did not exclude it from having business partners or representatives abroad. The subcontracted home-based women embroiderers collect the required materials from the women-owned SME but implement all necessary work at home.

The four women entrepreneurs were typical of the women-owned SME sector specializing in Palestinian embroidery operating in Amman. Table 7.1 highlights some indicators related to the women entrepreneurs. SME 1, established in 1977, represented the exclusive sector of the market where embroidered dresses are considered designer works of art. It continues to be conveniently located on the ground floor of the owner's home. SME 2, established in 1975, was typical of the majority of traditional embroidery businesses in Amman, in as much as its customers are primarily tourists and affluent Jordanians. SME 3, established in 1994, and SME 4, established in 1993, were owned and managed by women entrepreneurs who were initially trained and employed as project managers in local women-led NPOs. Both businesses operated from home and catered for wholesale clients such as hotels, restaurants and the national airline carrier. Both firms represent the highly competitive wholesale stream of the traditional embroidery market in Jordan and the wider Middle East, and both also operated showrooms at home for individual customers. Their clients included middle-class and affluent Ammanis, Jordanian expatriates and foreign residents in Amman. Table 7.1 shows that three of the entrepreneurs subcontracted between 6 and 15 home-based women embroiderers, while SME 2m subcontracted 60 home-based women embroiderers. This illustrates the potential outreach that women entrepreneurs have in giving visibility to home-based women producers, a group often ignored by policy-makers in the Middle East region.

THE HOME-BASED PRODUCERS

To ensure comparability among the sample of home-based producers, the selection criteria for the 20 home-based women producers participating in this study were rigorous. First, the producers had to be embroiderers of Palestinian origin and carry '1967 refugee' status. This status provides the bearer with both privileges and hardships unique to this population. Second, the home-based women embroiderers resided in the East Amman region inhabited primarily by Palestinian refugees. This defines the population from which the embroiderer sample is drawn. Third, the home-based women embroiderers had to be married women aged between 16 and 60.[1] This permits a gendered perspective of empowerment to be examined, since the majority of the participants had dependent children and husbands who might be economically active. Thus, the double burden of work and family could be explored. Fourth, the home-based women embroiderers supply one of the participating businesses. The purpose of this was to examine the relationships between the home-based women producers and their respective 'organizational managers'. Fifth, the home-based women embroiderers undertook all paid work within the home. This continues to be the typical approach to women's embroidery production throughout the developing world, due to existing cultural norms that discourage women from participating in paid work beyond their homes.

Although the advantages and disadvantages of home-based work continue to be debated, women in developing countries tend to opt for this work style rather than full-time work outside the home (Tomei, 2000). Table 7.2 highlights some indicators related to the participating home-based women embroiderers, showing their average age (35 years) and educational level. The average number of children per participant was four, which reflects the average family size across the Middle East region (UNDP, 2006), and no participant was divorced, indicating the very low documented divorce rate in this region (UNIFEM, 2004). From a business perspective, the majority of participants engaged with multiple clients and had been operating their home-based embroidery production for an average of 17.4 years. The mean of 8.6 years for subcontracting with the current business illustrates the extent of loyalty and long-term commitment between the owner of the SME and the home-based women producers. The average monthly income from the one contractor resulted in a mean of US$154.60. For the participants engaging with multiple clients, the average monthly income shown in Table 7.2 does not indicate earning from other clients.

The sample was split into four comparative cases (Miles and Huberman, 1994), which comprised each of the women-owned SMEs and their respective home-based embroiderers. Cross-case analysis (Abbott, 1992; Ragin,

Table 7.2   *Indicators for the home-based women producers*

SME	Age	Education level	No. of children	Average monthly income US$	Years as home-based em-broiderer	Years sub-contracting with business	Multiple clients
SME 1.1	47	Primary	5	420	30	25	No
SME 1.2	26	Secondary	3	112	6	4	No
SME 1.3	31	Secondary	4	182	10	10	No
SME 1.4	28	Secondary	4	266	7	2	No
SME 1.5	29	Secondary	3	350	11	8	No
SME 2.1	45	Secondary	3	140	25	15	Yes
SME 2.2	41	University	4	182	23	15	No
SME 2.3	49	Secondary	5	154	30	10	Yes
SME 2.4	37	Secondary	3	175	20	12	Yes
SME 2.5	36	Secondary	3	227	18	16	Yes
SME 3.1	43	Primary	1	112	27	6	No
SME 3.2	48	Primary	6	98	32	6	No
SME 3.3	47	Primary	5	92	32	6	Yes
SME 3.4	28	Primary	6	87	14	6	Yes
SME 3.5	24	Primary	3	88	10	6	Yes
SME 4.1	27	Secondary	4	73	6	5	Yes
SME 4.2	39	Primary	6	102	18	7	Yes
SME 4.3	38	Primary	5	98	18	7	Yes
SME 4.4	23	Secondary	2	56	4	2	Yes
SME 4.5	25	Secondary	3	78	7	4	Yes
Mean value	35.5	Secondary	4	154.60	17.4	8.6	Yes

1987) utilizing all four comparative cases was undertaken to explore the processes and the best practices for women's empowerment. Within this analytical approach, variable-oriented analysis was employed. The categories of empowerment processes were identified from the four comparative cases' data. These were SME management approach, awareness and concretization, rewards and benefits, market access and, finally, creative control. To analyse the advantages and disadvantages of each empowerment process, a contrast table (Miles and Huberman, 1994) was developed whereby the six generated empowerment process categories were rated as high, low or negative empowerment by the participants of each comparative case. To determine the best practices for women's empowerment, content analytic summary tables (Miles and Huberman, 1994) were generated for exploring the extent to which each of the six outcomes of women's empowerment were positively influenced by each of the six categorized processes of women's empowerment. Following Al-Dajani (2007), the six outcomes of women's empowerment were: accountability and responsibility, making decisions and having choices, leadership, reduced poverty, self-identity and economic establishment. In addition, a contrast table outlining the perspectives of the four comparative cases on the extent to which the six empowerment process categories positively or negatively influenced the outcomes of empowerment was also generated.

THE STUDY AREA

The study was undertaken in Amman, Jordan, where the circumstances of Palestinian refugee women mirror those found in other Arab countries (UNIFEM, 2004). In common with other developing countries, Jordan has applied structural adjustment programmes to suit the New Policy Agenda as requested by the International Monetary Fund (Fanek, 2005). Such programmes have direct consequences on the poorest communities within any country (Moghadam, 1998). As in other parts of the Middle East, home-based work within the informal work sector in Jordan is associated with low-productivity activities, engaging principally non-organized labour in situations of over-exploitation and poverty (Chen et al., 2005). Here, women resort to home-based work due to economic necessity, family demands, and lack of education and training required for formal sector employment. Necessary skills for work are obtained through informal education and passed down from mothers to daughters. However, home-based work is increasingly emerging as a middle-class trend in the Arab Middle East, absorbing qualified labour with substantial bargaining power (Tomei, 2000). Al-Dajani (2007) found that within both the formal and informal work sectors in Amman, the majority of home-workers are women, often assisted by other female family members or friends. Furthermore, within the formal work sector, professionally qualified women resort to home-based enterprises due to a combination of independence, family demands, social pressures and gender discrimination within paid employment.

EMPOWERMENT PROCESSES AND BEST PRACTICES

Engaging in the production of embroidery products is welcomed by the home-based embroiderers' communities. Traditional embroidery provides a source of pride and legitimacy in Palestinian self-identity and is considered a means to empowerment by the overwhelming majority of participants, especially since it could be implemented within the home. For the majority of producers, home-based work is their only source of employment and, therefore, income.

Home-based work within the informal work sector has become a significant trend for women throughout the developing world (ILO, 2002a) although it lacks regulation and attention from policy-makers who choose to ignore its expansion and work conditions (ILO, 2002b). This will no longer be possible as the home-based work trend significantly increases within the formal work sector. For example, all the women entrepreneurs participating in this study ran home-based enterprises operating in the formal work sector and registered with the Jordanian Ministry of Trade and Industry. Their operational success is largely dependent on the socio-political environment in which they operate as well as the home-based embroiderers supplying the products. This interdependence between the owner-managers and the home-based embroiderers has resulted in a unique relationship considered to be highly empowering by those involved in it.

Five empowerment process categories adopted by the women-owned SMEs were found in this study. They are presented here in order of importance (most important to least important) from the home-based producers' perspectives, and to illustrate the extent to which they can be considered a 'best practice': market access; creative control of products; women-owned SME management approach; rewards and benefits; and awareness and concretization.

MARKET ACCESS

Market access refers to the degree of control placed on the home-based producers by their clients (women SME owners) and whether the producers have direct access to clients other than the women-owned SME they were supplying. Having such access is considered by the home-based embroiderers to be the most empowering process. Interestingly, only one of the women SME owner-managers (SME 1) controlled the number of clients the home-based embroiderers engaged with, and thus their market access. Perhaps this liberalized approach resulted from the women entrepreneurs themselves often functioning as home-based enterprises operating within the formal work sector. This characteristic provided the women SME owners with a realistic view of the existing market and the environment of interactions in which they operated. They realized that the embroidery subcontracted to the home-based embroiderers is irregular and seasonal and provided an inconsistent income. Market access addressed this as the home-based embroiderers could gain additional subcontracted work.

On the other hand, those home-based embroiderers supplying only one SME believed that market access had a negative effect on women's empowerment. However, with the ongoing developments and change occurring within the region, market access had become a necessity for the majority of participants during phase 3 of the data collection when participants reported the increasing number of home-based embroiderers opting for full-time employment beyond the home due to the financial security it provided vis-à-vis subcontracted home-based work.

Considering best practices, market access was, to a large extent, considered by the participants to positively influence all six outcomes of empowerment and thus is considered a best practice for women's empowerment.

CREATIVE CONTROL

While the majority of home-based embroiderers and all SME owner-managers agreed that providing the home-based embroiderers with 'creative control' would be highly empowering to them, no action was taken by SME owner-managers to address this. From the home-based embroiderers' perspective, limiting their control over their embroidery diminished their creativity, energy and interest. On the other hand, the SME owner-managers stated that limiting the producers' creative control resulted in uniformity of production, standardized quality and maintained order. Such limited control over their own creative handiwork led to frustration among the home-based embroiderers who believed that control over their own creative output would be highly empowering to them and would lead to a sense of apathy among those who complied with the instructions and directions provided. Creative control was considered a best practice by the majority of participants who stated that it positively influenced all outcomes of women's empowerment, even though it was neither practised nor encouraged by the majority of participating owner managers.

WOMEN ENTREPRENEURS' MANAGEMENT APPROACH

The management approach adopted by the women entrepreneurs was considered empowering by the majority of home-based embroiderers who claimed that the management approach they experienced at their respective women-owned SMEs was characterized by respect and appreciation rather than exploitation. The home-based embroiderers generally considered the owner-managers as role models and sought their advice and guidance on issues concerned with everyday life and unrelated to embroidery. As a best practice, the SME management approach was generally perceived to positively contribute to all empowerment outcomes except self-identity. Only the home-based embroiderers of SME 1 and SME 3 suggested that the SME management approach positively contributed to their self-identity. The home-based embroiderers of SME 1 did not engage with multiple clients, while in SME 3 the home-based embroiderers were involved in the establishment of the business from the start up stage and developed a sense of shared ownership of the business. The majority of home-based embroiderers subcontracted by SME 3 had direct access to the business's customers and clients.

REWARDS AND BENEFITS

Financial rewards such as salaries and bonuses were considered empowering as they helped to alleviate the households' financial burdens. The rewards and benefits were primarily financial returns and did not include specific services except for those subcontracted by SME 1 where transport and meals were provided. The home-based embroiderers often compared their rewards and benefits with those of their peers supplying women-led NPOs, who provided local services including a crèche, awareness programmes and medical facilities. However, there was a general agreement that supplying the women-owned SME sector provided much higher financial returns than the women-led NPOs, and the relationship was characterized by long-term commitments while also offering flexibility, networking and market access with the potential for additional earnings. In addition, SME 1 and SME 2 provided the home-based embroiderers with financial bonuses during peak periods, and all SME owner-managers offered their respective home-based embroiderers substantial financial bonuses during Ramadan (the Islamic month of fasting). The category of rewards and benefits was also considered to positively influence all six outcomes of empowerment and, therefore, is considered a best practice for women's empowerment.

AWARENESS AND CONCRETIZATION

The awareness and concretization programmes offered to the home-based embroiderers through the women-owned SMEs were considered to be empowering especially by home-based embroiderers aged over 40 and by those educated to primary level only. However, such programmes were only provided by SMEs 3 and 4, possibly as a result of the entrepreneurs' previous experience in the non-profit sector. For example, SME 3 introduced a new approach whereby she brought together the home-based embroiderers, customers and managers to voluntarily attend a presentation on a monthly basis. She assembled a list of topics of interest generated from the customers and home-based embroiderers and arranged monthly coffee mornings where professionals addressed these topics. The majority of home-based embroiderers and customers attended regularly. The incentives for the home-based embroiderers were social networking, as they were free to meet the customers, and personal space, as they exited their local communities independently of children and husbands. For the customers, the incentives were a 15 per cent discount on purchases made at the event and the social aspects of the gathering. From a best practice perspective, awareness and concretization were generally perceived to positively influence the outcomes of self-identity, making decisions and having choices, and accountability and responsibility by the home-based embroiderers supplying SMEs 3 and 4 only. However, awareness and concretization were also perceived to negatively influence the empowerment outcomes of leadership, reduced poverty and economic establishment.

EMPOWERMENT FRAMEWORK APPLICATION

The best practices for women's empowerment derived from this study enhance existing empowerment frameworks, such as Longwe and Clarke's empowerment cycle (1994), by considering processes which address the cycle's five stages. Although Longwe and Clarke's (1994) model defines the stages of the empowerment cycle, it does not address how these may be achieved in practice. The best practices outlined in this study suggest processes through which women entrepreneurs contribute to the empowerment of home-based women producers. For example, Table 7.3 shows that market access, considered most important by the home-based producers, can influence Longwe and Clarke's stages of access and participation whereby the networking involved in market access creates avenues for satisfying other welfare needs. Similarly, women's market access perpetuates their community participation and, therefore, increases awareness of their socio-political and economic environment. A further best practice was creative control, and this can impact Longwe and Clarke's stages of concretization and control. The home-based producers' consciousness of the limitations imposed on their creativity raised an important dialogue, reflecting their sense of control

Table 7.3   Best practices and Longwe and Clarke's (1994) empowerment cycle

Empowerment cycle stages	Welfare	Access	Conscientization	Participation	Control
Best practices	Rewards and benefits	Market access Management approach Rewards and benefits Awareness and conscientization	Creative control Management approach Awareness and conscientization	Market access Management approach Rewards and benefits Awareness and conscientization	Creative control Rewards and benefits

which can be transcended to other aspects of their daily lives. The best practice of the management approach could be influential on the stages of access, concretization and participation to the extent that it provides access to the home-based producers, opportunities that are unavailable within the local communities and increased participation in their widening social and professional networks. At the welfare stage, rewards and benefits may also influence the stages of access, participation and control (Longwe and Clarke, 1994). Finally, the best practice of awareness and concretization furthers the home-based producers' knowledge, provides increased access to previously unavailable services and enhances participation in the local communities beyond the home environment. Overall, this approach recognizes the extent to which empowerment can be collectively achieved through supportive mechanisms from employers, contractors and other social organizations operating within the local communities.

CONCLUSIONS

The chapter has identified the processes through which women entre-preneurs empower the home-based women producers and considers best practices for women's empowerment. As home-based production regains popularity among women in the Middle East, its economic significance beyond the informal work sector and its direct effects on women's empow-erment need to be addressed by researchers and policy-makers, especially in light of the gender-segregated market phenomenon that has recently materialized within the region.

The experiences discussed in this chapter illustrate the ways in which women-owned SMEs contribute to the empowerment of home-based producers. In providing the home-based producers with market access, substantially higher financial rewards and benefits than those provided in other sectors, role models, independence and mobility beyond the local community, women entrepreneurs display a stronger understanding of female home-based production than non-profit organizations, aid agencies and local policy-makers in the Middle East. However, their actions challenge the development agendas of international donors and local policy-makers who prefer to see more women engaged in employment beyond their homes (ILO, 2005).

Although the home-based embroiderers may never progress their self-employment into the formal work sector due to limited opportunities, resources and support, their employment within the informal work sector is orderly and controlled. The network of home-based embroiderers is well established and functioning. They share clients and workloads when necessary, assisting each other with tasks such as childcare, and lobby together to influence pay rates. Female organizing is a necessity within these communities, since the men spend an average of 12 hours a day away at work (also within the informal work sector). These examples indicate the extent to which the home-based embroiderers are active participants within their local communities and the extent to which they can be empowered individuals with influence within those communities.

As home-based production regains popularity among women in the Middle East its significance to local and national economies beyond the informal work sector needs to be addressed by academics and policy-makers, especially as a gender-segregated market phenomenon is materializing within the region. The inter-relationships between the women home-based producers and their women entrepreneur counterparts are an example of the gender-segregated marketplace that is growing within the Middle East region. The entire network of home-based producers and small businesses was exclusively operated by women.

Within the often gender-segregated communities of the Arab Middle East region, women entrepreneurs are flourishing. For example, female hairdressers, photographers, caterers, musicians and entertainers offering their services only to women are becoming commonplace. Similarly, women-only clinics, gyms, spas and swimming pools are proving to be successful businesses throughout the region, as are women-only colleges and universities. Gender-segregated schools have been a feature of this region for decades. In addition, women-only hospitals, bank branches (for example, the Saudi American Bank, a subsidiary of CitiBank and the Saudi British Bank, a subsidiary of HSBC), malls and restaurants, especially in Saudi Arabia and Sharjah, are on the increase (Al-Dajani, 2007). All such businesses employ only women and cater only to women. Whether or not this trend contributed to the marked increase of 19 per cent in women's economic participation in the Arab Middle East region (UNDP, 2006) is yet to be determined. While it is agreed that gender segregation may be the result of freely made choices by men and women on the basis of their skills or preferences, it may also result from constrained opportunities (World Bank, 2004). Various international agencies have argued that gender segregation is economically inefficient, leads to women's low labour participation (ILO, 2005) and artificially limits the pool of available talent. Chang (2000) claimed that gender-based occupational segregation perpetuates gender gaps in earnings, limits women's opportunities for job mobility and career advancement, and reduces women's possibilities for autonomy at work. However, the results from this study suggest that occupational gender segregation may, inadvertently, lead to women's empowerment.

Finally, research investigating female experiences of starting and running businesses suggests that, although their motivations are very similar to those of male entrepreneurs, many of the barriers and constraints they face are gender specific (Carter, 2000). Lerner et al. (1997) claimed that socio-cultural differences and their effects on women entrepreneurs outweigh the similarities. They argued that these differences have not been considered in relation to theories explaining performance of women-owned businesses. 'The extent to which existing theories are useful in the context of non-OECD countries is of increasing importance as women in these countries are assuming a greater role in enterprise creation and economic development as a result of radical geopolitical and economic changes worldwide' (Lerner et al., 1997: 315). To this extent, further research into the experiences of women-owned businesses in the Arab Middle East region, will contribute to the identified gaps in the literature.

FUTURE RESEARCH

A number of future research directions can be proposed. First, existing theoretical frameworks do not capture the entirety of women's empowerment experiences and do not accommodate the experience of displacement or exile, although this is a common experience among women in the developing world. Furthermore, current frameworks do not address the empowerment potential for women from establishing and engaging in home-based enterprises. A future theoretical research direction implies the incorporation of the themes of displacement, entrepreneurship in exile and home-based enterprise into women's empowerment frameworks.

In terms of addressing Palestinian women entrepreneurs, the Palestinian population displaced across cities in the Middle East since 1948 continues to face a similar existence to those in Amman. For a substantial proportion of this displaced population there is a significant dependence on the informal work sector for income generation. Within these communities, networking is a predominant survival tool, especially as home-based women producers engage in various economic activities including catering and tailoring. To this extent, there is scope to further analyse the effect of informal networks and organizing on the empowerment of home-based producers. Such analysis could indicate potential prospects and strategies for entrepreneurship among these communities. To date, there is no research available on women entrepreneurs emerging from these communities. Future research can be applied across industry sectors to capture the entrepreneurial experience of the Palestinian women operating in exile, bridging the gap in our understanding of their contributions to their host economies. Furthermore, future research could be extended to Iraqi and Lebanese exiled women entrepreneurs operating either within the Arab Middle East region or beyond. A detailed portrayal of Arab women entrepreneurs operating beyond their home communities may have significant policy implications within the Arab Middle East region.

With regard to empowerment processes, the extent to which creative control of products and market access were considered highly empowering by the home-based embroiderers presents a future research direction with significant theoretical and practical implications, especially since creative control was not encouraged by the women entrepreneurs and market access is not promoted within the conservative communities in which women's home-based enterprises are situated. Exploring the implications of creative control and market access across a variety of sectors in which women operate home-based enterprises will shed light on the extent to which women's social roles within Palestinian exiled communities are reflective of other entrepreneurial Arab women operating in the region.

These potential research directions offer immediate appeal as they are grounded in the theoretical developments of women's empowerment, policy implications and socio-political identity. Although policy-makers acknowledge that women entrepreneurs are rapidly expanding in the Middle East, the role of the home-based enterprise remains ignored and invisible. Further research on this sector is crucial in order to understand women's entrepreneurship in the Middle East region.

NOTE

1. Although girls aged under 16 engage in home-based work (especially during school holidays), they were excluded from the study as their employment and marriage are considered illegal in Jordan (UNIFEM, 2004).

REFERENCES

Abbott, A. (1992), 'What do cases do? Some notes on activity in sociological analysis', in C. Ragin and H. Becker (eds), *What Is a Case? Exploring the Foundations of Social Inquiry*, New York: Cambridge University Press.

Al-Dajani, H. (2007), 'Women's empowerment: a comparison between non-profit and for-profit approaches in empowering home based women producers', unpublished PhD Thesis, University of Strathclyde.

Al-Dajani, H. (2010), 'Diversity and inequality among women in employment in the Arab Middle East region: a new research agenda', in M. Özbilgin and J. Syed (eds), *Managing Gender Diversity in Asia*, Cheltenham UK and Northampton, MA, USA: Edward Elgar, Chapter 2.

Allen, E., Elam, A., Langowitz, N. and Dean, M. (2007), *Global Entrepreneurship Monitor: 2007 Report on Women and Entrepreneurship*, Wellesley, MA: Babson College.

Carter, S. (2000), 'Gender and enterprise', in S. Carter and D., Evans-Jones (eds) *Enterprise and Small Business: Principles, Practice and Policy*, London: Prentice Hall.

Carter, S. and Shaw, E. (2006), 'Women's business ownership: recent research and policy developments', DTI Small Business Service Research Report, November.

Centre of Arab Women for Training and Research (CAWTAR) (2007), *Women Entrepreneurs in the Middle East and North Africa: Characteristics, Contributions and Challenges*, Tunis: The Centre of Arab Women for Training and Research.

Chang, M.L. (2000), 'The evolution of sex segregation regimes', *American Journal of Sociology*, **105** (6), 1658–701.

Chen, M., Lund, F., Heintz, J., Jhabvala, R. and Bonner, C. (2005), *Progress of the World's Women 2005: Women, Work and Poverty*, New York: UNIFEM.

Cohen, L. and Musson, G. (2000), 'Entrepreneurial identities: reflections from two case studies', *Organization*, **7** (1), 31–49.

Fanek, F. (2005), *How Jordan Earned Foreign Aid*, Amman: Jordan Times.

Greer, M.J. and Greene, P.G. (2003), 'Feminist theory and the study of entepreneurship', in J. Butler (ed.), *New Perspectives on Women Entrepreneurs*, Greenwich, CT: Information Age Publishing.

Heyzer, N. (2006), *Poverty and Women's Work in the Informal Economy*, Washington, DC: World Bank.

International Labour Office (ILO) (2002a), *Women and Men in the Informal Economy: A Statistical Picture*, Geneva: ILO.

International Labour Office (ILO) (2002b), *On Measuring Place of Work*, Geneva: ILO.

International Labour Office (ILO) (2005), *Discrimination at Work in the Middle East and North Africa*, Geneva: International Labour Office.

Jabre, B., Underwood, C. and Goodsmith, L. (1997), *Arab Women Speak Out: Profiles of Self-Empowerment*, Baltimore, MA: Johns Hopkins Centre for Communication Programs.

Kantor, P. (2005), 'Determinants of women's microenterprise success in Ahmedabad, India: empowerment and economics', *Feminist Economics*, **11** (3), 63–83.

Lerner, M., Brush, C. and Hisrich, R. (1997), 'Israeli women entrepreneurs: an examination of factors affecting performance', *Journal of Business Venturing*, **12** (4), 315–39.

Longwe, S. and Clarke, R. (1994), 'Women in development, culture and youth', workshop preparatory readings, 1–3, April–December, Lusaka, Longwe Clarke Associates.

Maskiell, M. (2004), 'Embroidering the past: *Phulkari* textiles and gendered work as tradition and heritage', in S. Mann's (ed.), *Women and Gender Relations: Perspectives on Asia*, Ann Arbor, MI: Association for Asian Studies.

McNay, L. (2000), *Gender and Agency; Reconfiguring the Subject in Feminism and Social Theory*, Cambridge: Polity Press.

Metcalfe, B.D. (2007), 'Gender and human resource management in the Middle East', *International Journal of Human Resource Management*, **18** (1), 54–75.

Miles, M.B. and Huberman A.M. (1994), *Qualitative Data Analysis*, London: Sage.

Moghadam, V. (1998), *Women, Work and Economic Reform in the Middle East and North Africa*, London: Lynne Rienner.

Moghadam, V. (2004), 'Towards gender equality in the Arab Middle East region: Islam, culture and feminist activism', United Nations Development Programme, Human Development Report Office.

Mosedale, S. (2005), 'Assessing women's empowerment: towards a conceptual framework', *Journal of International Development*, **17** (2), 243–57.

Premchander, S. (2003), 'NGOs and local MFIs – how to increase poverty reduction through women's small and micro-enterprise', *Small Business Futures*, **35** (4), 297–421.

Ragin, C. (1987), *The Comparative Method: Moving Beyond Qualitative and Quantitative Strategies*, Berkeley, CA: University of California Press.

Rich, A. (1980), 'Compulsory heterosexuality and lesbian existence', *Signs: Journal of Women in Culture and Society*, **5** (4), 631–60.

Snyder, M. (1995), *Transforming Development: Women, Poverty and Politics*, London: Intermediate Technology Publications.

Tomei, M. (2000), *Home Work in Selected Latin American Countries: A Comparative View*, Geneva: IFP/SED – Job Creation and Enterprise Department, ILO.

United Nations Development Programme (UNDP) (2006), *Arab Human Development Report*, New York: United Nations.

United Nations Development Fund for Women (UNIFEM) (2004), *Progress of Arab Women 2004*, Amman: UNIFEM.

Walker, E. and Webster, B. (2004), 'Gender issues in home-based businesses', *Women in Management Review*, **19** (8), 404–12.

Wallerstein, N. (1992), 'Powerlessness, empowerment, and health: implications for health promotion programs', *American Journal of Health Promotion*, **6**, 197–205.

Wilkinson-Weber, C. (2004), 'Women, work and the imagination of craft in South Asia', *Contemporary South Asia*, **13** (3), 287–307.

Women in Informal Employment Globalizing and Organizing (WIEGO) (2003), 'The informal economy', available at: www.wiego.org/main/fact1.shtml (accessed 6 April 2010).

World Bank (2004), *Gender and Development in the Middle East and North Africa: Women in the Public Sphere*, Washington, DC: World Bank.

World Bank (2007), *Environment for Women's Entrepreneurship in the Middle East and North Africa Region*, Washington, DC: World Bank Group.

8. Exploring the heterogeneity of women's entrepreneurship: the impact of family structure and family policies in Europe and the US

Vartuhí Tonoyan, Michelle Budig and Robert Strohmeyer

INTRODUCTION

Recent work suggests that both self-employed women and men represent a heterogeneous group with regard to their occupational profile. For instance, in the US and Southern Europe, the majority of self-employed women are unskilled workers in the service sector (Arum, 1997; Arum and Müller, 2004; Budig, 2006; McManus, 2001). In contrast, the share of professional (female and male) and highly compensated self-employed (for example, lawyers, doctors, architects and engineers) is the highest in conservative and highly regulated corporatist welfare states in Western Europe (such as Germany, Austria and the Netherlands) (Arum and Müller, 2004; Lohmann, 2004). However, prior work did *not* systematically consider the heterogeneity of women's self-employment when examining the effects of individual determinants on women's entry into entrepreneurship. Rather, empirical studies usually pool all types of female self-employment together, without taking into account whether self-employed work is being performed in professional or non-professional/low-skilled occupations.

Against this background, our study makes three new contributions. First, we explore whether determinants predicting women's entrepreneurship *vary* by the type of occupation entered. We disaggregate entrepreneurship into professional (high-skilled) and non-professional (low-skilled and unskilled) occupations. Our primary focus is to understand whether *family structure* (motherhood and partner's occupational status; see Budig, 2006) has a differential impact on the qualification profile of self-employed women. We analyse the pathways into different forms of entrepreneurship across 23 countries to understand how country-specific *institutional environments* may influence women's entry into high-skill entrepreneurship versus low-skill entrepreneurship. Specifically, we seek to examine how family policies (such as publicly funded childcare, maternity leave length) might affect self-employed women's occupational profile.

Next, we elaborate on the theoretical arguments and develop hypotheses. We then provide a description of the sources of data for Europe and the US, as well as variables, methods, and findings. Finally, we conclude with a discussion of our results and limitations and offer implications for future research and public policy.

THEORETICAL BACKGROUND AND HYPOTHESES

In the US, non-professional wage work (compared to professional occupations) is more likely to lack employer-sponsored childcare, to pay wages too low to fund private daycare, and to entail closely supervised and inflexible schedules. Recent research demonstrates that workers with lower wages and occupational status are less likely to have access to family-friendly benefits (Budig, 2006). In addition, women in non-professional jobs are less likely to be in control of the pace and timing of their work, factors which are positively associated with reduced work and family conflict (Thomas and Ganster, 1995). Considering this, self-employment may offer female non-professional wage workers more autonomy and greater flexibility in setting the time and place of work. Past research partially substantiates this argument (see, for example, Presser, 1995). Given this, we expect that motherhood and thus women's responsibilities for childcare should predict engagement in non-professional self-employment more strongly than in professional self-employment.

However, women's self-employment is often low-earning and does not provide paid leave for caregiving (Carr, 1996). Self-employed women may thus require a financial safety cushion that might be provided by their husband's earnings. If this is the case, being married or cohabitating should positively affect women's likelihood of self-employment, and this effect should be stronger for women in lower-paying non-professional self-employment activities. Second, marriage/cohabitation might positively affect women's self-employment if women are more likely to join their partner's business. Recent research finds that having a self-employed husband dramatically increases the likelihood of becoming self-employed for a woman (see, for example, Arum and Müller, 2004; Budig, 2006; Firkin et al., 2003; Greene, 2000; Taniguchi, 2002). It seems more likely that a woman is likely to join the husband's self-employment activity to support her husband's career rather than to advance her own. We thus expect that having a self-employed spouse will affect the likelihood of non-professional self-employment the strongest. Yet, not all women may become self-employed to balance work and family demands. Single and childless women may not experience work and family conflict. Still others may become self-employed to earn a higher amount of money, advance their careers and/or socio-economic class positions (Budig, 2006). Since professional occupations are more likely to have good job characteristics, workers transitioning between wage and self-employed professional work may rather be 'pulled' by the attractiveness of self-employment than 'pushed' by the unattractiveness of wage employment. This second group of workers should be more likely to be professionals than non-professionals prior to entering professional self-employment. They should be more likely to enter self-employment from wage employment, rather than after a labor force absence (Budig, 2006). From these arguments, we derive our first two hypotheses:

Hypothesis 1a: Motherhood positively affects women's entry into non-professional self-employment (but not professional self-employment) as a solution to reconcile childcare and work.

Hypothesis 1b: The partner's occupational status (for example, self-employment) is a predictor for women's entry into non-professional self-employment (but not women's professional self-employment).

INSTITUTIONAL ENVIRONMENT OF WOMEN'S ENTREPRENEURSHIP

Little is known about the factors that are responsible for international variations in women's self-employment rates and their occupational profile. Past research on women's self-employment concentrates on differences in psychological characteristics (for example, risk preferences, fear of failure) (Koellinger et al., 2007; Langowitz and Minniti, 2007; Minniti and Nardone, 2007; Wagner, 2007) and resources (for example, human capital, financial capital and social capital) (Verheul and Thurik, 2001). However, variation in self-employment rates across countries indicates that country-level factors, such as institutional environments and policies, may matter.

While some recent work considers the institutional embeddedness of entrepreneurship and self-employment (see, for example, Bjornskov and Foss, 2008; Carree et al., 2002; Nyström, 2008; Wennekers et al., 2002), most prior work did not analyse the association between the country-specific institutions and women's entrepreneurship. Given the evidence that American women turn to self-employment to balance family and work responsibilities (Brush, 1992; Budig, 2006), cross-national variation in women's self-employment rates and occupational profile may be linked to welfare state policies that attempt to reconcile unpaid-care responsibilities and paid work.

We propose that policies that support women's employment and childcare are likely to influence their self-employment participation, particularly in non-professional occupations. Subsequently, the effect of children on women's entry into non-professional self-employment will differ among countries with different institutions regulating women's reconciliation of family and work duties. Welfare states differ in the supply of publicly supported measures (for example, childcare coverage, maternity entitlement, voluntary family leaves, flexible arrangements of working time and social tax policies) that influence women's participation in the labor market (Gornick et al., 1997; Korpi, 2000; OECD, 2001: 129–66; Sainsbury, 1994b). For example, liberal and laissez-faire welfare states such as the US or the UK maintain policies oriented to individual solutions. Public involvement in family policies is weak. Childcare facilities are provided on a private basis and no public support exists for the provision of childcare facilities and/or other family support orientated services, compared to other types of welfare regimes (Gustafsson and Wetzels, 1997). Moreover, parental leave is short, with very low income compensation (Esping-Andersen, 1990; Gustafsson and Wetzels, 1997). This constellation of policies differs markedly from conservative welfare states such as Germany, the Netherlands and Austria, which largely support a traditional male breadwinner model. In such regimes, priority is given to a general family support that reduces the family costs of caregiving, for example, cash child allowances, family tax benefits for minor children, and tax benefits for mothers of young children staying at home. Public daycare services exist predominantly for children above 3 years old, but not minor children (under 3 years old). Full-time childcare is rather limited in such countries. For example, in Germany only 9 per cent of children of kindergarten age attend all-day-institutions (Gustafsson and Wetzels, 1997; Lohmann and Luber, 2004; OECD, 2001). As a rule, such countries are characterized by a traditional division of labor, with men being responsible for earning incomes and women being responsible for childcare. Women's (especially young mothers') participation in the labor market is rather restricted, resulting in higher part-time rates of female employment.

Despite similarities among several countries in Continental Europe which follow the so-called 'conservative'/'corporatist' welfare state model, there are clear differences with regard to specific policy measures which influence women's compatibility of family and paid work. For instance, although Belgium, France and Italy are characterized as conservative welfare states, their policies actively support women's employment (Lohmann, 2004). Further, France is the best performer on policies for mothers with children under 6 and policies for mothers with children aged 3 to school-age among 14 investigated welfare states. This reflects the strong French commitment to nearly universal enrollment of children in *écoles maternelles* beginning at age 3. Moreover, France scores very well with regard to the policy support for infants (Gornick et al., 1997, Lohmann and Luber, 2004). Similarly, Belgium has highly developed packaging policies that support employment for mothers with children under age 6. This can be exemplified by the fact that 95 per cent of children in Belgium and France are in public daycare or preschools, compared to only 14 and 38 per cent of children in publicly funded childcare, for example, in the US and the UK, respectively, that is, countries which rank at the lowest end of the spectrum. By the same token, Italy scores well with regard to policies supporting employment for mothers with children under 6, and it provides generous maternity policies and widespread preschool coverage for children aged over 3, although it has only moderate support for mothers with infants (Gornick et al., 1997; OECD, 2001).

The preceding discussion leads us to predict that the impact of children on the entry into (non-professional) self-employment will differ among countries with different welfare state institutions that influence the compatibility of women's family and work duties. Thus, we develop the following hypotheses:

Hypothesis 2a: Children will positively influence low-qualified women's decision to become self-employed in liberal welfare states such as the UK and US. Moreover, the association between children and non-professional self-employment should be the strongest in the UK and US compared to any other type of welfare regimes of Western industrialized societies.

Hypothesis 2b: Children will positively influence low-qualified women's decision to become self-employed in most corporatist conservative welfare states of Western Europe but not France, Belgium and Italy. Given extended welfare state provisions for mothers in these countries, low-qualified women will not be pushed into self-employment to reconcile family and work duties.

Beyond these broad predictions for country differences, we also consider whether specific policies may be correlated with self-employment outcomes cross-nationally. Following prior work (Gornick et al., 1997; Korpi, 2000; Misra et al., 2007; OECD, 2001; Sainsbury, 1994a), institutions which may influence mothers' ability to combine family and work duties can be classified into three main groups, namely, (1) institutions which support women's uninterrupted labor force attachments around the time of childbirth ('leave policies'), (2) institutions which increase the supply or reduce the cost of non-maternal childcare ('childcare') and (3) institutions which provide childcare via public school schedules ('school scheduling') that are compatible with parental employment. Next, we derive hypotheses about the way these institutions may impact women's decision to work as self-employed as well as their choice of professional status of self-employment.

Leave Policies – Paid Maternity Leave

Theoretical predictions concerning the impact of maternity leave on women's attachment to the labor force are ambivalent. On the one hand, maternity leaves that allow women to return to the same job should increase their attachment to paid work. This should decrease the likelihood of self-employment, particularly in non-professional work, by making wage work more attractive. On the other hand, policies that allow for long leave periods may limit certain career-enhancing opportunities that require continuity at work (for example, opportunities for training and promotion) or result in human capital depreciation. The scarce empirical evidence on this topic is controversial (for a review see, for example, Gornick et al., 1997; Korpi, 2000).

Given women's lower endowments with resources in non-professional work to reconcile family and work duties, we expect that maternity leave policies will impact non-professional self-employment more strongly than professional self-employment. Specifically, we expect that the absence of maternity leave will push women out of the paid work force and into non-professional self-employment. But, given the higher earnings and potentially greater employment benefits garnered by women in professional work, we do not expect the same positive effect of children on self-employment in countries with no provisions for maternity leave. At the same time, very long leaves that negatively impact women's attachment to their employer might increase both non-professional and professional self-employment, as women seek these entrepreneurial activities as alternatives to being left out of the workforce following extended care leaves. We thus assume that there will be a positive association between the length of the country-specific policy measures that impact paid maternity leave and women's non-professional self-employment.

Hypothesis 3: Long length of maternity leave should increase women's share of self-employment overall, and women's share of non-professional self-employment. Additionally, high replacement wages should increase women's attachment to paid employment and lower the necessity of self-employment, particularly among less-skilled women.

Hypothesis 4: The higher the country-specific maternity leave wage replacement, the higher the opportunity costs of becoming self-employed relative to wage employment and thus the lower women's share of overall, professional, and non-professional self-employment.

Public School Schedules

From a labor supply perspective, it can be suggested that school schedules are highly likely to influence mothers' employment decisions, because public schools provide childcare for mothers of school-aged children. Improvements in public school schedules would imply having children enrolled in public school for longer hours per day and more weeks per year, as well as schedules that are more consistent with typical employment schedules (Gornick et al., 1997; Korpi, 2000; OECD, 2001). As a consequence, improvements in women's childcare options should be associated with increases in maternal labor supply.

However, is there a link between public school schedules and (the professional status of) women's self-employment? Assuming that low-qualified women primarily choose non-professional self-employment because the latter is compatible with self-provided childcare, the hypothesis can be put forward that longer school days would decrease low-qualified women's likelihood of becoming self-employed, since they would lower their need for childcare. This argument leads to the following hypothesis:

Hypothesis 5: The longer school-hours per week, the lower women's share of non-professional self-employment.

DATA, VARIABLES AND METHODS

This study draws on the European Labor Force Survey (ELFS, 2004–05) and the National Longitudinal Survey of Youth (NLSY) for American data. The ELFS includes 14645 female founders and 657909 female employees (the reference category) from 22 Western and Eastern European countries in 2004. The NLSY is a multi-stage stratified national probability sample that includes 6283 female respondents interviewed annually from 1979 to 1998, of which 1377 became self-employed during the 21-year period. The NLSY over-sampled various populations (that is, racial minority groups). Descriptive analyses use sample weights, but due to the spell structure of the event history data, sample weights are not used in regressions. In both sources of data, we analyse female respondents aged between 22 and 44 years.

Dependent Variable

For the ELFS data, we use the International Standard Classification of Occupations (ISCO-88) to capture the dependent variable, which measures women's entry into professional self-employment versus unskilled/low-skilled self-employment. The differentiation between professional and non-professional self-employment roughly resembles the collapsed EGP (Erikson, Goldthorpe and Portocarero) class scheme (Erikson and Goldthorpe, 1992). Category I, which describes 'professional self-employment', is comprised of professional, semi-professional, and higher managerial occupations (equivalent to EGP I and II). Category II, which describes 'low-skilled self-employment', consists of traditional skilled, petty bourgeois self-employment including shopkeepers and restaurant owners (mostly EGP IIIa, V and VI) as well as unskilled self-employment (EGP IIIb and VII). In the NLSY, we define the respondent as self-employed if she answered 'yes' to the survey question: 'Are you self-employed in this job?' Analyses distinguish between two subgroups of self-employment based on the three-digit Census codes for professional and managerial occupations. Professional and managerial occupations (coded 1–199) are classified as 'professional' occupations, while all other occupations are classified as 'non-professional' occupations.

We use a discrete time event history model, Cox's proportional hazards regression, to analyse the transition rates into self-employment for the US NLSY data. Only the first transition into self-employment is modeled. The competing risks model takes the form of a multinomial logistic regression model with three competing outcomes (for elaboration see Allison, 1984). The competing hazards model predicts self-employment in professional versus non-professional occupations. Event history analysis allows us to handle the ubiquitous problems of sample selectivity, non-random sorting, censoring, time-varying explanatory variables, and unobserved heterogeneity (Wooldridge, 2002). Cox proportional hazards model is designed to explain why some individuals are at greater risk to experience an event than others, and to estimate the effect of time-varying covariates (such as marital status and motherhood) on the change in the hazard of an event occurring (such as entry into self-employment).

If we do not account for the fact that female entrepreneurs are *not* a random sample of individuals, but have characteristics which made them select into the labor market in the first place, a simple regression model of women's choice of professional self-employment versus non-professional self-employment on a set of covariates can generate misleading estimations of the regression parameters. Ignoring the 'sample selection bias' would lead us to the overestimation of the predicted values (Heckman, 1979). To correct for the sample selection bias, we use the Heckman probit model with a sample selection equation in the ELFS. The Heckman correction has a two-stage structure. In the first stage, the selection equation is used as a basis for predicting women's labor market participation in the sample. In the selection equation, we introduce an 'extra' exogenous variable, which has an effect on the selection equation, predicting women's decision either to participate in the labor market or not, but not on the main equation, which determines women's choice of professional self-employment versus non-professional self-employment. In the second stage, transformed predictions are included as an additional variable into the main equation model. For technical details, see Greene (2003).

Independent Variables

We harmonized all available variables from the NLSY and ELFS that could be consistently measured. In the ELFS data, variables are measured in the year of observation. In the NLSY data, respondents who never become self-employed are treated as right-censored observations. Here, time-varying family characteristics include marital/cohabitation status, the partner's self-employment status and the number of children (within child age categories). Unpartnered women (neither married nor cohabitating) and those with either unemployed or retired partners are the reference category for the partner's status variable. We include two dummy variables indicating partner's status. The partner self-employed dummy variable is coded 1 if the woman has a partner who is self-employed. The partner employed dummy variable is coded 1 if the woman has a partner in the wage and salaried work. The reference category is defined as having no partner or an unemployed partner. We use three categorical variables to measure the number of children aged 0 to 4 years (preschoolers), the number of children aged 5 to 9 years, and the number of children aged 10 to 18 years.

Time-varying measures of human capital are education, age (proxy for experience) and employment status prior to self-employment. Given the high level of inconsistency in the coding of education across the countries in our analysis, we were only able to capture high education (post-secondary qualifications) versus low education with a dummy variable indicating high education. We use four age categories and include three dummy variables indicating that the respondent is aged 30 to 34 years, 35 to 40 years and 40 to 45 years (with 18 to 29 years as the reference category). Thus, we also control for employment status prior to becoming self-employed by using a dummy which is '1' if the respondent was not employed prior to founding her own business or becoming self-employed. Time-varying demographic characteristics include whether the respondent lives in a rural, suburban or urban area (rural being the reference category). We include these measures since self-employment opportunities may be greater in areas with higher population density.

Moreover, we utilize macro-level data on family policy indicators which revolve around (1) leave policies, (2) early childhood education and care, and (3) school scheduling for 22 countries. These data are provided by Misra et al. (2007).

FINDINGS

The share of women's professional self-employment has experienced an increase during 1992 and 2004 in most Western European countries (Germany, Sweden, the Netherlands, Belgium, the UK, Italy, France, Austria, Greece, Portugal and Spain). However, countries differ in the scope of the growth of women's professional self-employment. At the aggregated level, there is a clear indication for the impact of the country's institutional make-up on women's share of professional self-employment. More exactly, the probability of entering a low-skilled occupation is the highest in Central-Eastern Europe (Poland, Slovenia, Slovakia, Estonia, Hungary and Lithuania). In contrast, there is a positive association between the share of women's professional self-employment and highly regulated types of labor markets in Belgium, the Netherlands, Luxembourg, Germany, Austria and France. In the US, the proportion of women who are self-employed has grown in both professional and non-professional self-employment. However, the growth has been much larger for non-professional self-employment.

Demographic characteristics show that self-employed women are younger than their employed counterparts across all countries (with self-employed professionals being the youngest, on average), and more highly educated (again, with self-employed professionals having the highest average education). In terms of family structure, we find great heterogeneity among the self-employed, with a disproportionate number of non-professionals being mothers and partnered with men who are also self-employed. The majority of female professional founders have no children (59 per cent), compared to the share of female non-professional founders (43 per cent). Also, female professional founders live without a partner more often (50.5 per cent) than their non-professional counterparts (39.4 per cent). In contrast, couple entrepreneurs (that is, businesses which have been set up by couples) are more prevalent among female non-professionals (21 per cent) than female professionals (15.8 per cent).

Summing up, female non-professional founders seem to be much more strongly embedded in the family context than their professional founders in almost all investigated countries.[1] But, can the bivariate association between self-employment in professional/non-professional occupations and women's individual characteristics be reproduced in the multivariate estimations?

First, the effect of family composition on women's inclination to become self-employed differs substantially across professional and non-professional occupations. On the one hand, responsibilities for caring for children (up to 4 years old and 5–9 years old) positively affect women's decision to engage in non-professional occupations and strongly significantly across the majority of countries analysed (Austria, Germany, Ireland, the Netherlands, Luxembourg, Greece, Portugal, Spain, Hungary, Poland, the Czech Republic). This strongly supports hypotheses 1a and 2b that motherhood is a strong predictor for women's entry into non-professional self-employment in corporatist and conservative welfare states in Western Europe. Moreover, children are strongly positively associated with mothers' entry into non-professional self-employment in the US and the UK as liberal welfare states with missing childcare infrastructure. The results for the UK and US thus strongly confirm hypothesis 2a. Furthermore, looking at the regression coefficients for the impact of minor children (up to 4 years and 5–9 years old) on women's non-professional self-employment in the UK and the US, one finds that they are far stronger than the respective coefficients for other welfare states in Western Europe (for example, Austria or Germany). In contrast, children do *not* influence mothers' entry into non-professional self-employment in France, Belgium and Italy. This supports hypothesis 2b that low-qualified women in France, Belgium and Italy are not apparently pushed into self-employment to combine family and work duties, given extended welfare states provisions for mothers to reconcile family and work duties.

Furthermore, children either do not have any effect on the entry into professional self-employment or impact women's professional self-employment strongly negatively in most Western European countries, the US and some Eastern European countries (Latvia, Poland and Slovenia). This is clear evidence for hypothesis 1a, which states that balancing family

Table 8.1 Determinants of entry into professional and non-professional self-employment (Heckman probit regression)

	Austria		Belgium		Germany		France	
	Model 1 non-profess.	Model 2 profess.	Model 1 non-profess.	Model 2 profess.	Model 1 non-profess.	Model 2 profess.	Model 1 non-profess.	Model 2 profess.
Children								
Child up to 4 years	0.198** (0.068)	0.277** (0.077)	0.048 (0.071)	-0.11 (0.072)	0.054 (0.051)	0.062 (0.073)	0.055 (0.053)	-0.042 (0.059)
Child 5–9 years	0.158** (0.052)	0.174** (0.056)	0.146 (0.075)	-0.282** (0.104)	0.115** (0.033)	-0.049 (0.043)	0.069 (0.046)	-0.073 (0.061)
Child 10–19 years	0.149** (0.047)	-0.176** (0.065)	-0.062 (0.077)	-0.122 (0.088)	-0.018 (0.032)	-0.324** (0.047)	0.027 (0.046)	-0.358** (0.077)
Partner								
Partner self-empl.	0.240** (0.054)	0.165* (0.065)	0.319** (0.075)	0.155 (0.088)	0.207** (0.049)	0.097 (0.065)	0.473** (0.044)	0.256** (0.063)
Partner employee	-0.033 (0.041)	0.004 (0.049)	-0.140* (0.057)	-0.207** (0.064)	-0.175** (0.03)	-0.142** (0.038)	-0.226** (0.034)	-0.120** (0.042)

	Ireland		Luxembourg		Netherlands		Cyprus	
	Model 1 non-profess.	Model 2 profess.	Model 1 non-profess.	Model 2 profess.	Model 1 non-profess.	Model 2 profess.	Model 1 non-profess.	Model 2 profess.
Children								
Child up to 4 years	0.056 (0.055)	0.018 (0.075)	-0.156 (0.107)	-0.262 (0.152)	0.013 (0.038)	0.126* (0.057)	0.061 (0.083)	-0.276 (0.214)
Child 5–9 years	0.151** (0.046)	-0.153* (0.067)	-0.083 (0.102)	-0.404* (0.166)	0.122** (0.039)	0.049 (0.06)	-0.141 (0.104)	-0.269 (0.187)
Child 10–19 years	0.03 (0.047)	-0.127* (0.065)	-0.015 (0.106)	-4.964 (4191.535)	0.071 (0.041)	-0.113 (0.073)	-0.194* (0.094)	-0.564** (0.211)
Partner								
Partner self-empl.	0.491** (0.043)	0.390** (0.056)	1.152** (0.111)	0.440** (0.155)	0.600** (0.036)	0.193** (0.057)	0.099 (0.099)	0.058 (0.167)
Partner employee	0.079* (0.038)	0.148** (0.047)	0.173 (0.094)	0.051 (0.108)	-0.154** (0.032)	-0.216** (0.045)	0.143 (0.074)	-0.184 (0.139)

	Greece (1)	Greece (2)	Italy (1)	Italy (2)	Portugal (1)	Portugal (2)	Spain (1)	Spain (2)
Children								
Child up to 4 years	0.023 (0.038)	−0.009 (0.069)	−0.050* (0.021)	−0.041 (0.033)	0.122** (0.039)	−0.156 (0.086)	0.03 (0.023)	0.217** (0.038)
Child 5–9 years	0.111** (0.039)	−0.172* (0.076)	0.014 (0.023)	−0.097* (0.039)	0.107** (0.041)	−0.144 (0.092)	0.137** (0.023)	0.096* (0.041)
Child 10–19 years	0.175** (0.032)	−0.1 (0.068)	0.062** (0.019)	−0.128** (0.034)	−0.031 (0.04)	−0.058 (0.07)	0.149** (0.02)	0.014 (0.034)
Partner								
Partner self-empl.	−0.05 (0.034)	0.312** (0.059)	0.116** (0.022)	0.125** (0.034)	0.339** (0.04)	0.269** (0.089)	0.405** (0.027)	0.212** (0.038)
Partner employee	−0.284** (0.032)	0.1 (0.063)	−0.146** (0.018)	−0.05 (0.029)	−0.073* (0.032)	−0.003 (0.065)	−0.112** (0.018)	−0.071* (0.035)

	Czech Republic (1)	Czech Republic (2)	Estonia (1)	Estonia (2)	Hungary (1)	Hungary (2)	Latvia (1)	Latvia (2)
Children								
Child up to 4 years	0.421** (0.121)	0.784** (0.209)	0.148 (0.439)	1.137** (0.074)	0.546** (0.072)	0.847** (0.112)	0.164 (0.211)	−0.051 (0.136)
Child 5–9 years	0.164** (0.042)	−0.044 (0.068)	0.216 (0.148)	0.018 (0.049)	0.116** (0.04)	−0.137 (0.072)	−0.104 (0.207)	0.116 (0.125)
Child 10–19 years	−0.031 (0.04)	−0.268** (0.07)	0.226 (0.138)	0.013 (0.074)	0.078* (0.037)	−0.1 (0.058)	−0.743** (0.264)	0.067 (0.118)
Partner								
Partner self-empl.	0.322** (0.039)	0.205** (0.068)	−0.137 (0.195)	−0.114 (0.099)	0.333** (0.042)	0.187** (0.058)	0.602** (0.18)	0.713** (0.113)
Partner employee	−0.161** (0.033)	−0.041 (0.054)	−0.011 (0.1)	−0.114 (0.068)	−0.098** (0.031)	−0.245** (0.057)	−0.385* (0.182)	0.101 (0.084)

Table 8.1 (continued)

	Lithuania		Poland		Slovenia		Slovak Republic	
	Model 1 non-profess.	Model 2 profess.	Model 1 non-profess.	Model 2 profess.	Model 1 non-profess.	Model 2 profess.	Model 1 non-profess.	Model 2 profess.
Children								
Child up to 4 years	0.152 (0.312)	0.824** (0.04)	0.310** (0.071)	-0.018 (0.161)	0.148 (0.094)	0.275** (0.059)	-0.036 (0.128)	1.091** (0.044)
Child 5–9 years	0.14 (0.11)	0.011 (0.012)	0.216** (0.05)	-0.056 (0.109)	-0.163 (0.12)	0.043 (0.062)	0.082 (0.065)	0.017 (0.025)
Child 10–19 years	0.068 (0.096)	-0.018 (0.009)	0.067 (0.048)	-0.342** (0.12)	0.131 (0.083)	0.015 (0.057)	0.051 (0.059)	-0.024 (0.026)
Partner								
Partner self-empl.	0.028 (0.145)	0.036 (0.023)	0.425** (0.049)	0.330** (0.109)	0.067 (0.123)	-0.867 (32.955)	0.528** (0.066)	0.172** (0.042)
Partner employee	-0.15 (0.089)	-0.007 (0.021)	-0.125** (0.04)	-0.068 (0.088)	-0.118 (0.079)	-0.084* (0.042)	0.170** (0.053)	0.070** (0.025)

	UK		USA	
	Model 1 non-profess.	Model 2 profess.	Model 1 non-profess.	Model 2 profess.
Children				
Child up to 4 years	0.344** (0.047)	0.158 (0.088)	0.315** (0.067)	0.059 (0.184)
Child 5–9 years	0.125** (0.038)	-0.199** (0.059)	0.419** (0.087)	0.148 (0.251)
Child 10–19 years	-0.105* (0.041)	-0.289** (0.062)	0.420** (0.129)	-0.502 (0.480)
Partner				
Partner self-empl.	0.340** (0.039)	0.275** (0.058)	1.385** (0.109)	0.742* (0.304)
Partner employee	-0.075** (0.029)	-0.062 (0.041)	0.550** (0.061)	0.152 (0.169)

Notes: ** p < .01 , * p < 0.05, two-tailed tests. Heckman selectivity correction includes dummies for marital status, age categories, child up to 4 years and nationality. All models include control variables (age and education).

and work duties is not a motive to become self-employed for highly qualified women. Among Western industrialized states, the outliers from this pattern are Austria, the Netherlands and Spain. In these countries, women with children (up to 4 years) are highly likely to work as self-employed professionals – a pattern which is also surprisingly reproduced for most post-Socialist countries in Eastern Europe, namely, the Czech Republic, Estonia, Hungary, Lithuania, Slovenia and the Slovak Republic.

Besides, having a self-employed partner impacts the female founder's decision to work in non-professional occupations positively and highly significantly in Europe (but Belgium where the effect is only significant at a 10 per cent level) – a finding which is remarkably stable across 18 out of 22 investigated countries with different institutional regimes. This gives clear support for hypothesis 1b. But, spousal self-employment activity also influences women's professional self-employment likelihood positively and strongly significantly in most countries, supporting the contention that 'self-employment often comes in twos' (Arum and Müller, 2004: 446). Indeed, the pattern of cross-national variation in effects of the spousal self-employment on women's professional self-employment is largely similar to the variation found for the effect of spousal self-employment on women's non-professional self-employment. This contradicts hypothesis 1b. Summarizing, spousal self-employment is a positive and robust predictor (at a 1 per cent level) for the wife's entry into professional self-employment in 17 out of 22 European countries and the US. However, the mechanisms which underlie the positive relationship between spousal involvement in self-employment and women's non-professional and professional self-employment might be different. Low-qualified women entering non-professional self-employment may join their husband's self-employment activity to support their husband's business and career (Budig, 2006; Firkin et al., 2003). This can be the case for family-run businesses in craft, retail, catering and lodging. As indicated by prior work, the spouse of self-employed males usually performs ancillary roles, for example, she is doing accounts, administration, answering phones, and so on (Firkin et al., 2003). On the other hand, the positive association between spousal self-employment and high qualified women's choice of self-employment suggests that marriage, generally, is a valuable asset (Becker, 1965) that provides a suitable background for self-employment. Collectively, a married couple can put up more resources (financial capital, self-employment relevant know-how and skills, networks, and so on, and emotional support (Brüderl and Preisendörfer, 1998) for starting their own businesses. With the support of the self-employed husband, a married woman thus would be more willing to take the risk. Finally, self-employed husbands may also serve as 'role models' (Bandura, 1977), thus supporting the wife's perceived feasibility of becoming self-employed ('If he can do it, so can I') (Tonoyan et al., 2005). Indeed, having a self-employed partner in the US increases women's likelihood of non-professional self-employment significantly, more exactly, by a factor of 4. However, it has a far smaller effect on the likelihood of transition into professional self-employment.

On the other hand, we observe a strong negative association between the spousal involvement in dependent employment and women's entry into both professional and non-professional self-employment in almost all investigated European countries. Put differently, women with husbands in wage and salaried work are significantly less likely to become self-employed (both in professional and non-professional occupations) than their counterparts who either do not have partners/husbands or live with an unemployed partner/husband.

Next, we turn to a set of correlation analyses. We run correlations between family policy indicators and women's total share of self-employment, professional self-employment and non-professional self-employment. This analysis gives us a sense of how work–family policies may impact women's engagement in entrepreneurship.

First, we observe a positive correlation between paid maternity leave and women's non-professional self-employment (Pearson correlation being 0.40). This means that the longer the paid maternity leave, the longer women's detachment from the labor force. To the extent women's non-professional self-employment is a result of poor labor market characteristics, it seems to be intuitive that longer labor force detachments increase the probability of becoming self-employed for low-qualified women. This supports hypothesis 3. However, there is almost no correlation between paid maternity leave and women's professional self-employment. Second, we notice a negative relationship between maternity leave wage replacement rates and both women's non-professional and professional self-employment, although the correlation values are not high, namely −0.22 and 0.29, respectively. This holds true for both types of women's entrepreneurship and substantiates hypothesis 4.

Furthermore, one notices a negative relationship between the percentage of children aged 0–4 years in public childcare and women's share of non-professional self-employment. This gives support for the hypothesis 5 that the lower the country-specific publicly provided childcare, the higher women's share of non-professional self-employment. This may result from two factors. The first is that the demand for private childcare in these countries may create entrepreneurial opportunities for women to provide childcare and other household services in the non-professional sector. It may also result from the necessity of women in non-professional

Table 8.2   Correlation between family policy indicators and female entrepreneurship rates in 22 European countries

	Share of women's non-professional self-employment	Share of women's professional self-employment	Share of women's self-employment (total)	Number of countries
A: Leave policies				
1. Weeks of maternity leave	0.40	−0.09	0.28	22
2. Maternity leave wage replacement rate	−0.22	−0.29	−0.26	22
B: Early childhood education and care				
3. % of 0–2-year-old children in public childcare	−0.28	0.08	−0.20	20
4. % of 3–6-year-old children in public childcare	0.10	0.38	0.20	19
C: School scheduling				
5. School hours per week	−0.22	0.24	−0.11	18

Source: Misra et al. (2007).

employment to turn to self-employment when childcare is unavailable in order to balance work and family responsibilities.

At the same time, there is almost no relationship between the percentage of children aged 0–2 years in public childcare and women's share of professional self-employment. The positive association between the percentage of 3–6-year-old children and women's professional self-employment does not hold. Again, these results strongly support hypothesis 5.

Finally, we observe a negative association between school hours per week and women's share of non-professional self-employment (the correlation value being −0.22), and a positive relationship between school hours per week and women's share of professional self-employment (the correlation value being 0.24). While the former finding supports hypothesis 6, no theoretical justification can be given for the latter.

SUMMARY AND DISCUSSION

This study makes several contributions to prior research. First, we show profound heterogeneity in women's self-employment in a cross-national comparison among 23 European countries and the US. Second, we highlight differences in the individual determinants of women's entry into low-skilled versus high-skilled occupations in self-employment. Third, we examine the impact of country-specific institutions on women's entry into self-employment, showing the association between welfare state policies which regulate women's reconciliation of family and work and entry into (non-professional) self-employment.

Self-employed women represent a strongly heterogeneous group. Women working in low-skilled occupations seem to pursue self-employment to combine childcare and work responsibilities (we call them 'family-oriented' female self-employed). It could be shown that motherhood is a strong predictor for the entry into entrepreneurship for low qualified women – a result which is strikingly similar for almost all investigated countries. Albeit self-employment is a job solution for highly qualified but less 'family embedded' women who enter professional occupations, but they are not pushed into self-employment to reconcile family and work duties. Rather, they are pulled into it by the prospect of better earnings and career advancement, thus resembling the pattern found for self-employed men (Budig, 2006).

In contrast to motherhood, which is only a predictor for women's entry into non-professional self-employment, spousal self-employment is strongly positively associated with both professional and non-professional self-employment. Put differently, women's low-skilled and high-skilled entrepreneurship are embedded in matrimonial relationships, thus supporting the contention that 'self-employment often comes in twos' (Arum and Müller, 2004: 446). Still, the mechanisms which underlie the positive association between spousal self-employment and women's entry into non-professional versus professional self-employment may be different. For instance, less qualified women may join husbands' self-employment activity to support their husbands' work and career. This is usually the case for low-skilled or skilled self-employment in crafts, retail, catering, and lodging, that is, typical family-run businesses (cf. Aldrich and Cliff, 2003; Firkin et al., 2003). Also, they might draw on strong ties with own husbands to compensate for the shortage of financial and human capital (Brüderl and Preisendörfer, 1998). In contrast, the positive effect of the spousal self-employment on women's entry into high-skilled occupations could be traced back to other mechanisms, for example, self-employed husbands could play a role by serving as positive 'role models' for highly skilled women.

Moreover, our findings suggest that institutional variations between welfare states are responsible for cross-country variations of the occupational status of women's self-employment. This complements recent work on female entrepreneurship which recommends addressing the heterogeneity among female entrepreneurs when examining institutional environments in which the entrepreneur is embedded (De Bruin et al., 2007; Jennings and McDougald, 2007). As a general pattern, countries with a higher level of women's entrepreneurship usually have *lower* levels of women's professional self-employment. In contrast, the highest share of women's professional self-employment is found in highly regulated and conservative/corporatist welfare states of Western Europe.

Furthermore, the differences in welfare states regimes which regulate women's reconciliation of family and work duties moderate the effect of motherhood on women's entry into entrepreneurship. For instance, the effect of motherhood on becoming self-employed in non-professional occupations is the highest in liberal welfare states such as the UK and the US, where the publicly funded infrastructure for women's reconciliation of family and work is largely missing. On the aggregated level, the weaker public institutions supporting mother's employment are (for example, weak public childcare, school scheduling which do not support mothers' full-time employment), the higher the country's share of non-professional self-employed women. Besides, countries with longer paid maternity leave and thus women's longer detachment from the labor force seem to have higher share of women's non-professional self-employment. Finally, countries with higher maternity leave wage replacement (and thus higher opportunity costs of becoming self-employed) have lower rates of women's professional and non-professional self-employment.

CAVEATS AND IMPLICATIONS FOR PUBLIC POLICY AND RESEARCH

Several implications for future research can be derived from our analysis. First, we have discovered that some but *not* all post-Socialist countries in Central-Eastern Europe resemble the pattern found for the corporatist welfare states in Western Europe quite strongly. This calls for future research on the role of the institutional environments of Central-Eastern European countries for women's entrepreneurship, considering that research on this topic is still in infancy (De Bruin et al., 2007), despite some recent contributions on it (see, for example, Welter et al., 2006).

A limitation of our study is the use of different data sources and methods, namely, the panel data and survival analysis for the US sample and cross-sectional data and Heckman correction model for the European sample. While the most important results could be corroborated in both samples, it would be useful to employ panel data for the European sample too to account for unobserved heterogeneity.

Furthermore, it would also be rewarding to study country-specific informal institutions, that is, traditions, customs, societal norms, 'shared mental models', unwritten codes of conduct, ideologies and templates (Baumol, 1990; Denzau and North, 1994; North, 1990), and thus the cultural aspects of the environment in which (women's) entrepreneurship takes place (instead of only focusing on formal political and economic rules and regulations). If the society predominantly defines women through roles associated with family and household responsibilities (see, for example, Welter, 2006, for Germany), it will design formal rules and regulations which provide women with incentives to stay at home and care for their children (Pfau-Effinger, 2004), thus subsequently influencing the occupational character of self-employment work.

Fruitful research and policy agenda could also focus on examining working conditions and outcomes (for example, earnings, job stability) that result from professional versus non-professional self-employment. Supposing that highly skilled and well-compensated professions in self-employment provide higher returns to self-employment and have higher survival and growth chances (for the US evidence see Budig, 2006), it would probably be more rewarding to create institutional environments that are more favorable for women's entry into professional self-employment.

NOTE

1. The respective tables are available upon request.

REFERENCES

Aldrich, H.E. and Cliff, J. (2003), 'The pervasive effects of family on entrepreneurship: towards a family embeddedness perspective', *Journal of Business Venturing*, **18**, 573–96.
Allison, P. (1984), *Event History Analysis*, Newbury Park, CA: Sage.
Arum, R. (1997), 'Trends in male and female self-employment: growth in a new middle class or increasing marginalization of the labor force?', *Research in Stratification and Mobility*, **15**, 209–38.
Arum, R. and Müller, W. (2004), *The Reemergence of Self-Employment. A Comparative Study of Self-employment Dynamics and Social Inequality*, Princeton, NJ and Oxford: Princeton University Press.

Bandura, A. (1977), *Social Learning Theory*, Englewood Cliffs, NJ: Prentice Hall.

Baumol, W.J. (1990), 'Entrepreneurship: productive, unproductive, and destructive', *Journal of Political Economy*, **98** (5), 893–921.

Becker, G.S. (1965), 'A theory of the allocation of time', *Economic Journal*, **75**, 493–517.

Bjornskov, C. and Foss, N.J. (2008), 'Economic freedom and entrepreneurial activity: some cross-country evidence', *Public Choice*, **134** (3/4), 307–28.

Brüderl, J. and Preisendörfer, P. (1998), 'Network support and the success of newly founded businesses', *Small Business Economics*, **10** (3), 213–225.

Brush, C. (1992), 'Research on women business owners: past trends, a new perspective and future directions', *Entrepreneurship Theory and Practice*, **16** (4), 5–30.

Budig, M.J. (2006). 'Intersections on the road to self-employment: gender, family, and occupational class', *Social Forces*, **84** (4), 2223–39.

Carr, D. (1996), 'Two paths to self-employment? Women's and men's self-employment in the United States', *Work and Occupations*, **23**, 26–53.

Carree, M., van Stel, A., Thurik, R. and Wennekers, S. (2002), 'Economic development and business ownership: an analysis using data of 23 OECD countries in the period 1976–1996', *Small Business Economics*, **19**, 271–90.

De Bruin, A., Brush, C. and Welter, F. (2007), 'Advancing a framework for coherent research on women's entrepreneurship', *Entrepreneurship: Theory and Practice*, **5**, 323–39.

Denzau, A.T. and North, D.C. (1994), 'Shared mental models: ideologies and institutions', *Kyklos*, **47** (1), 3–31.

ELFS (2004–05), 'EUROSTAT LFS Users Guide: Labor Force Survey: anonymized data sets', European Commission EUROSTAT.

Erikson, R. and J.H. Goldthorpe (1972), *The Constant Flux*, Oxford: Clarendon.

Esping-Anderson, G. (1990), *The Three Worlds of Welfare Capitalism*, Cambridge: Polity Press.

Firkin, P., Dupuis, A. and De Bruin, A. (2003), 'Familial entrepreneurship', in P. Spoonley, A. Dupuis, and A. De Bruin (eds), *Work and Working in 21st Century New Zealand*, Palmerston North, New Zealand: Dunmore Press, pp. 154–79.

Gornick, J.C., Meyers, M.K. and Ross, K.E. (1997), 'Supporting the employment of mothers: policy variation across fourteen welfare states', *Journal of European Social Policy*, **7** (1), 45–70.

Greene, P. (2000), 'Self-employment as an economic behavior: an analysis of self-employed women's human and social capital', *National Journal of Sociology*, **12**, 1–55.

Greene, W.H. (2003), *Econometric Analysis*, Englewood Cliffs, NJ: Prentice Hall.

Gustafsson, S. and Wetzels, C. (1997), 'Family policies and women's labor force transitions in connection with childbirth', *Vierteljahreshefte zur Wirtschaftsforschung*, **3** (4), 118–24.

Heckman, J. (1979), 'Sample selection bias as a specification error', *Econometrica*, **47**, 153–61.

Jennings, J.E. and McDougald, M.S. (2007), 'Work–family interface experiences and coping strategies: implications for entrepreneurship research and practice', *Academy of Management Review*, **32**, 747–60.

Koellinger, P., Minniti, M. and Schade, C. (2007), 'I think I can, I think I can – overconfidence and entrepreneurial behavior', *Journal of Economic Psychology*, **28** (4), 502–07.

Korpi, W. (2000), 'Faces of inequality: gender, class, and patterns of inequalities in different types of welfare states', *Social Politics*, **7** (2), 127–91.

Langowitz, N. and Minniti, M. (2007), 'The entrepreneurial propensity of women', *Entrepreneurship Theory and Practice*, **31** (3), 341–64.

Lohmann, H. (2004), 'Berufliche Selbständigkeit von Frauen und Männern im internationalen Vergleich – welche Rolle spielt die Vereinbarkeit von Familie und Erwerbstätigkeit', in G. Schmid. M. Gangl and P. Kupka (eds), *Arbeitsmarktpolitik und Struktarwandel: Empirische Analysen*, BeitrAB 286, Nuremberg: Institute für Arbeitsmarkt- und Berufsforschung, pp. 205–26.

Lohmann, H. and Luber, S. (2004), 'Trends in self-employment in Germany: different types, different developments', in R. Arum and W. Müller (eds), *The Re-Emergence of Self-Employment Dynamics and Social Inequality*, Princeton, NJ: University Press, pp. 36–75.

McManus, P. (2001), 'Women's participation in self-employment in Western industrialized societies', *International Journal of Sociology*, **31**, 70–97.

Minniti, M. and Nardone, C. (2007), 'Being in someone else's shoes: the role of gender in nascent entrepreneurship', *Small Business Economics*, **28**, 223–38.

Misra, J., Moller, S. and Budig, M.J. (2007), 'Work–family policies and poverty for partnered and single women in Europe and North America', *Gender and Society*, **21** (6), 804–27.

North, D.C. (1990), *Institutions, Institutional Change and Economic Performance*, Cambridge: Cambridge University Press.

Nyström, K. (2008), 'The institutions of economic freedom and entrepreneurship: evidence from panel data', *Public Choice*, **136** (3), 269–82.

Organisation for Economic Co-operation and Development (OECD) (2001), 'Balancing work and family life: helping parents into paid employment', *Employment Outlook*, **1**, 129–66.

Pfau-Effinger, B. (2004), *Development of Culture, Welfare States and Women's Employment in Europe*, Hamburg: Ashgate.

Presser, H. (1995), 'Job, family, and gender: determinants of nonstandard work schedules among employed Americans in 1991', *Demography*, **32**, 577–98.

Sainsbury, D. (ed.). (1994a), *Gendering Welfare States*, London: Sage Publications.

Sainsbury D. (1994b), 'Women's and men's social rights: gendering dimensions of welfare states', in D. Sainsbury (ed.), *Gendering Welfare States*, London: Sage Publications, pp. 150–70.

Taniguchi, H. (2002), 'Determinants of women's entry into self-employment', *Social Science Quarterly*, **83**, 875–93.

Thomas, L. and Ganster, D. (1995), 'Impact of family-supportive work variables on Work–family conflict and strain', *Journal of Applied Psychology*, **80**, 6–15.

Tonoyan, V., Strohmeyer, R. and Wittmann, W.W. (2005), 'Gendered and cross-country differences in the perceived difficulty of becoming self-employed: the impact of individual resources and institutional restrictions', in *Frontiers of Entrepreneurship Research*, Wellesley, MA: Babson College, pp. 57–72.

Verheul, I. and Thurik, A.R. (2001), 'Start-up capital: does gender matter?', *Small Business Economics*, **16** (4), 329–45.

Wagner, J. (2007), 'What a difference a Y makes – female and male nascent entrepreneurs in Germany', *Small Business Economics*, **28** (1), 1–21.

Welter, F. (2006), 'Women's entrepreneurship in Germany: progress in a still traditional environment', in C.G. Brush, N. Carter, P.G. Greene and M. Hart (eds), *Growth Oriented Women Entrepreneurs and Their Businesses: A Global Research Perspective*, Cheltenham, UK and Northampton, MA, USA: Edward Elgar, pp. 128–53.

Welter, F., Smallbone, D. and Isakova, N. (eds) (2006), *Enterprising Women in Transition Economies*, Aldershot: Ashgate.

Wennekers, A.R.M., Noorderhaven, N.G., Hofstede, G. and Thurik, A.R. (2002), 'Cultural and economic determinants of business ownership across countries', *Frontiers of Entrepreneurship Research*, Babson Park, MA: Center for Entrepreneurial Studies, pp. 179–90.

Wooldridge, J.M. (2002), *Econometric Analysis of Cross-Section and Panel Data*, Cambridge, MA: MIT Press.

PART II

Growth Strategies and Enablers

9. The work–family interface strategies of male and female entrepreneurs: are there any differences?[1]

**Jennifer E. Jennings, Karen D. Hughes and
P. Devereaux Jennings**

INTRODUCTION

Three predominant perspectives are evident within existing work on the factors influencing the growth of female-led firms and the reasons why they tend to be smaller than those headed by men. The first focuses on individual-level characteristics, attributing the differential to gender differences in personality traits (e.g., Buttner and Moore, 1997; Sexton and Bowman-Upton, 1990) or human and social capital (e.g., Cooper et al., 1994; Davis and Aldrich, 2000; Fischer et al., 1993). The second draws attention to strategic choices, emphasizing that male and female entrepreneurs tend to differ with respect to the growth objectives established for their firms (e.g., Cliff, 1998; Orser and Hogarth-Scott, 2002) and/or the industries in which they operate (e.g., Carter et al., 1997; Hughes, 2005; Kalleberg and Leicht, 1991). The third considers the role played by broader external determinants, such as the existence of any discriminatory practices with respect to the provision of financial capital (e.g., Fabowale et al., 1995; Haines et al., 1999).

Although these predominant perspectives are wide-reaching, intuitively appealing and theoretically grounded, empirical investigations reveal that they account for only a modest amount of variation, at best, in the relative performance of male-headed and female-headed firms (see, for example, Fischer et al., 1993; Kalleberg and Leicht, 1991; Loscocco et al., 1991). As such, the field is in need of new approaches to the puzzling and socio-economically important questions of what factors might lead to differences between female and male-run businesses.

One such approach has recently emerged. Building on the family embeddedness approach to entrepreneurship research more generally

(Aldrich and Cliff, 2003; Dyer, 2003; Firkin et al., 2003; Heck and Trent, 1999), Jennings and McDougald (2007) proposed that the gender-based business size differential might stem from key differences in the way that male and female entrepreneurs experience and manage the interface between work and family. According to these authors, male entrepreneurs are particularly likely to enact work–family interface (WFI) strategies that facilitate business growth whereas female entrepreneurs are especially likely to enact those that constrain the growth of their enterprises. Although these ideas resonate with themes apparent within earlier conceptual or qualitative work on women entrepreneurs (for example, Allen and Truman, 1992, 1993; Brush, 1992; Goffee and Scase, 1985), they have not yet received systematic research attention.

To the best of our knowledge, this chapter offers the first empirical test of the claim that male and female business owners tend to enact very different strategies for managing the work–family interface. We do so by analysing data collected through a survey of 163 small business owners in Alberta, Canada. After testing for the existence of any gender differences, we explore whether and how these strategies were enacted differentially by male and female business owners within three very different environments: the manufacturing sector, the retail/wholesale/general services sector and the professional services sector.

THEORY AND HYPOTHESES

The Family Embeddedness Approach

The family embeddedness perspective (Aldrich and Cliff, 2003; see also Dyer, 2003; Firkin et al., 2003; Heck and Trent, 1999) emerged out of growing dissatisfaction with the manner in which researchers traditionally depicted entrepreneurs in general; that is, as atomistic actors who launch and operate businesses without consideration of the one social institution (the family) in which they are all embedded. Similarly, numerous scholars have criticized the literature on female entrepreneurs, in particular, for overlooking how the personal lives of these women influence – and are influenced by – their entrepreneurial pursuits (for example, Aldrich, 1989; Allen and Truman, 1992, 1993; Brush, 1992; Green and Cohen, 1995; Stevenson, 1986). As Ahl (2006: 604) notes in her wide-ranging review, existing studies of women's entrepreneurship commonly 'assume a division between work and family and between a public and a private sphere of life', thus failing to address the interconnections between work and family satisfactorily.

In our view, the family embeddedness perspective offers a means of responding to this critique. Within their conceptual framework, for example, Aldrich and Cliff (2003) elucidated a number of family system characteristics that can affect entrepreneurial processes and outcomes, drawing attention to the role played by transitions, resources, and norms, attitudes and values within the family sphere. The empirical work conducted to date provides illustrative support. With respect to entrepreneurial processes, several studies demonstrate how family-level factors can trigger the decision to launch a business venture or become self-employed (Boden, 1999; Cramton, 1993). Likewise, others demonstrate the role played by family in terms of providing critical resources at founding (for example, Aldrich and Langton, 1998; Ruef et al., 2003). With respect to entrepreneurial outcomes, further studies reveal how family involvement and/or ownership can influence a firm's organizational culture, structure and performance (for example, Anderson and Reeb, 2003; Klein et al., 2005; Miller and LeBreton-Miller, 2005).

Another promising line of entrepreneurship research consistent with the family embeddedness approach has focused on the interface between the domains of family and business – rather than on how factors within one sphere influence the other. Illustrative examples here include the work–family interface studies conducted by Foley and Powell (1997), Kim and Ling (2001), Loscocco and her colleagues (1991), Parasuraman et al. (1996) and Smith (2000). For the most part, these studies have focused upon the nature and consequences of an entrepreneur's experiences of the WFI, such as the degree and effects of actual or perceived work–family conflict. As emphasized by Jennings and McDougald (2007), however, an entrepreneur's strategies for managing the WFI are also likely to play an influential role in shaping entrepreneurial outcomes. We summarize those strategies below, explicating why and how they are likely to be enacted differentially by male and female entrepreneurs.

The WFI Strategies of Male and Female Entrepreneurs

Jennings and McDougald (2007) depicted the WFI strategies of entrepreneurs along two dimensions: (1) whether they facilitate versus constrain business growth; and (2) whether they tend to be enacted primarily at the individual versus couple level. Table 9.1 provides a visual overview of the four different combinations that result from this conceptualization. We discuss specific strategies consistent with each combination in the following subsections, deriving testable

Table 9.1   An adaptation of WFI strategies from Jennings and McDougald (2007)

Level/type	Growth facilitating	Growth constraining
Individual	Segmentation of work and family domains (e.g. suppressing family-related thoughts at work) Accommodation within family domain (e.g. 'scaling back' family commitments)	Integration of work and family domains (e.g. dealing with work and family tasks concurrently) Accommodation within work domain (e.g. reducing work hours to focus on family)
Couple	Prioritization of entrepreneur's career (e.g. entrepreneur's romantic partner takes 'stay-at-home' role) Postponement of major family transitions (e.g. delayed marriage, childbearing)	Prioritization of spouse's career (e.g. entrepreneur restricts work hours in order to care for family and support romantic partner's career) Postponement of major business transitions (e.g. delayed start-up, expansion)

hypotheses relevant to our interest in differences between male and female entrepreneurs.

Growth-facilitating strategies at the individual level
One individual-level WFI strategy enacted by entrepreneurs that is likely to facilitate the growth of their ventures is segmentation. As defined more broadly by Edwards and Rothbard (2000: 181), this strategy involves the conscious suppression of other-domain thoughts, feelings and behaviours while engaged within the focal domain. In the context of entrepreneurship, entrepreneurs enact such a strategy when they deliberately limit thoughts, feelings and behaviours related to the family sphere when performing tasks related to their role as business owners (including those that directly or indirectly impact the growth of their enterprises). A second growth-facilitating WFI strategy enacted at the individual level is that of accommodation within the family domain. As described by Lambert (1990: 246), this strategy involves 'scaling back', both behaviourally and psychologically, one's commitment to and involvement in the role of family

member. By reducing behavioural and psychological commitment to the family sphere, entrepreneurs can devote greater time and mental energy to growing their businesses.

Jennings and McDougald (2007) developed a compelling case to suggest that clear differences will be observable in the extent to which male and female business owners enact the above-noted WFI strategies. For instance, conceptual and descriptive work in the women's entrepreneurship literature (for example, Belcourt et al., 1991; Brush, 1992), combined with empirical findings for men and women in general (for example, Rothbard, 2001; Rothbard and Edwards, 2003; Rothbard et al., 2005; Williams and Alliger, 1994), suggests that female business owners will be especially unlikely to engage in segmentation. Likewise, findings from both the broader work–family literature (for example, Becker and Moen, 1999; Greenhaus and Parasuraman, 1999; Moen and Wethington, 1992; Moen and Yu, 2000) and the women's entrepreneurship literature (for example, Longstreth et al., 1987; Parasuraman et al., 1996; Smith, 2000) suggest that female entrepreneurs will also be less likely to scale back their family-domain commitments than their male counterparts. We thus derive the following hypothesis from Jennings and McDougald's (2007) work:

Hypothesis 1:   Female entrepreneurs will be less likely to enact growth-facilitating WFI strategies at the individual level than male entrepreneurs.

Growth-facilitating strategies at the couple level
At the couple level, Jennings and McDougald (2007) also elucidated two WFI strategies likely to facilitate business growth. The first involves the prioritization of the entrepreneur's career over that of his/her spouse (or significant other). Such a strategy is being enacted when the entrepreneur's romantic partner either: (1) commits full-time to the family sphere in the role of 'stay-at-home' spouse; or (2) agrees to take on 'just a job' instead of pursuing a more demanding career of their own. It can also be enacted, in the context of entrepreneurship, when the spouse (or significant other) provides more direct and instrumental support to the entrepreneur's business, such as through the provision of labour. The second growth-facilitating WFI strategy at the couple level involves the postponement of major transitions within the family sphere. One example is when a couple decides to delay having any children until the entrepreneur's business is sufficiently established. Another illustrative example is when a couple decides to postpone marriage or cohabitation for the same reason.

Jennings and McDougald (2007) provided theoretically grounded arguments and illustrative empirical evidence to argue that these couple-level growth-facilitating WFI strategies are also likely to be implemented differentially by male and female entrepreneurs. More specifically, work from a life course approach (for example, Becker and Moen, 1999; Martins et al., 2002; Milkie and Peltola, 1999; Moen and Yu, 2000; Tenbrunsel et al., 1995), combined with that on women entrepreneurs (Allen and Truman, 1992, 1993; Belcourt et al., 1991; Goffee and Scase, 1985; Jurik, 1998; Parasuraman et al., 1996), suggests that the strategies of prioritizing the entrepreneur's career and postponing major family transitions are less likely to be enacted by female business owners (and their spouses/ significant others) than by male business owners (and their spouses/ significant others). We thus examine the following additional hypothesis pertinent to WFI strategies that are likely to facilitate business growth:

Hypothesis 2:   Female entrepreneurs will be less likely to enact growth-facilitating WFI strategies at the couple level than male entrepreneurs.

Growth-constraining strategies at the individual level
In terms of WFI strategies enacted by entrepreneurs that can constrain the growth of their enterprises, Jennings and McDougald (2007) focused upon those of integration and accommodation within the work domain. Individuals enact the former approach to the work–family interface when they allow for fluidity between the two spheres, responding cognitively, emotionally and/or behaviourally to demands from one domain while fulfilling role obligations within the other (Kossek et al., 1999). Individuals enact the latter approach when they reduce their commitment to, and involvement in, the work domain – whether psychologically, through decreased identification with their work, or behaviourally, through a reduced amount of time devoted to work-related responsibilities (Lambert, 1990).

Drawing on theoretical concepts within the work–family literature, such as the notions of spillover and depletion (Edwards and Rothbard, 2000; Greenhaus and Beutell, 1985; Rothbard, 2001), Jennings and McDougald (2007) argued that the enactment of either strategy is likely to interfere with an entrepreneur's ability to grow his or her business. Citing studies from both the work–family and entrepreneurship literatures, these scholars further surmised that women business owners will be especially likely not only to exhibit a more integrative approach to the work–family interface – but also to make greater accommodations within the work domain in order to fulfil other-role commitments. Synthesizing the two claims, we examine the following hypothesis in this chapter:

Hypothesis 3:   Female entrepreneurs will be more likely to enact growth-constraining WFI strategies at the individual level than male entrepreneurs.

Growth-constraining strategies at the couple level

Turning to the couple level, Jennings and McDougald (2007) described two WFI strategies that are likely to detract from an entrepreneur's ability to expedite the growth of his or her enterprise. The first involves the prioritization of the spouse's (or significant other's) career over the business owner's career. An example here is when an entrepreneur chooses to restrict the firm's hours of operation because he or she has agreed to assume a disproportionate share of the domestic chores so that his or her spouse has more time available to pursue their career. Citing empirical work in the work–family literature (Becker and Moen, 1999; Kossek et al., 1999; Moen and Yu, 2000), which suggests that women in general are more likely to engage in such a strategy, Jennings and McDougald (2007) speculated that female entrepreneurs would be apt to do so as well.

The second WFI strategy enacted by couples that is likely to constrain business growth involves the postponement of major transitions in the business sphere until family or household demands have abated. Examples include putting any major expansion initiatives 'on hold', or even refraining from starting a business venture on a full-time basis, until the couple's children are older. Drawing once again on life course theory and research (Becker and Moen, 1999; Kossek et al., 1999; Moen and Yu, 2000), integrated with anecdotal evidence regarding the work–life decisions made by women entrepreneurs (for example, Goffee and Scase, 1985), Jennings and McDougald (2007) suggested that such a strategy is particularly likely to be followed by female rather than male entrepreneurs. We thus examine this final hypothesis, which combines the preceding arguments, in our empirical investigation:

Hypothesis 4:   Female entrepreneurs will be more likely to enact growth-constraining WFI strategies at the couple level than male entrepreneurs.

METHODS AND DESCRIPTIVE STATISTICS

Data Collection

In order to examine these hypotheses we collected data through a self-administered questionnaire mailed in the summer of 2004 to the owners of 600 businesses located in the province of Alberta, Canada. We used the Alberta Business Directory from InfoCanada[2] to create the sampling frame, selecting 200 businesses from each of the following three industry sectors: (1) manufacturing firms (for example, artisans, printers, durable goods producers); (2) retail, wholesale or general service firms (for example, furniture stores, electronics/computer dealers, caterers, cleaners); and (3) professional service firms (for example, accountants, attorneys, dentists, engineers, optometrists, veterinarians). Inclusion in the study was restricted to firms classified as non-franchised companies within the directory. For each of the three industry sectors, we selected all businesses headed by women and randomly chose 100 firms headed by men located within the province's two largest metropolitan districts of Edmonton and Calgary. Although the vast majority of the businesses (94 per cent) were located within these cities, in some cases it was necessary to include firms located in the surrounding bedroom communities in order to obtain the minimum number headed by women within each sector. We received completed questionnaires from the primary active owner-manager of 163 firms, for an overall response rate of 27 per cent. The participants indicated their sex in all but one case, with 71 reporting that they were male and 91 reporting that they were female. Thus, the response rate was slightly higher among the women business owners than among their male counterparts, at 30 and 24 per cent respectively.

Characteristics of the Sample

Of the participating businesses, 22 per cent were manufacturing firms, 39 per cent were retail/wholesale/general service firms and 39 per cent were professional service firms. The businesses ranged in age from less than one year to 101 years, with an average of almost 22 years. The majority of the business owners (54 per cent) characterized their firms as being in the mature phase of business development, while another 41 per cent characterized their firms as being in the slow or fast-growth phase. Very few indicated that their firms were in the start-up or decline phases. The size of the businesses ranged from zero to 200 employees, in addition to the owner(s), with an average size of approximately 18 employees. Half of the firms were quite small, with 10 employees or less. Average annual gross revenues, reported by 146 of the 163 participants, ranged considerably – from $20000 to $650 million – with a mean of $6908507. One-half of the firms reported gross revenues of less than $1 million per year whereas the other half reported gross revenues of over $1 million per year.

In terms of their socio-demographic characteristics, almost all the owners (89 per cent) were between 30 and 60 years old. Most business owners had high levels of human capital. Less than 10 per cent had only a high school diploma, whereas half had a graduate degree/professional designation or at least some graduate or professional courses. The remainder possessed varying degrees of post-secondary undergraduate education.

With respect to prior experience, business owners exhibited a wide range, possessing on average 7.92 years of prior industry experience, 4.60 years of prior management experience, and 2.17 years of prior business ownership experience.

To explore the representativeness of our sample, we examined whether the male and female business owners and their firms differed in ways apparent in prior research. Table 9.2 contains the results of this comparative analysis. For the most part, these descriptive findings echo those reported in other studies, thereby providing evidence that our sample is representative even though it is geographically restricted in scope. As noted in the upper half of Table 9.2, for instance, the female-headed firms were significantly younger than the male-headed firms, respectively averaging 18.4 versus 25.9 years of age. They were also much smaller in size, comprised of less than half the number of employees, on average, than businesses headed by men. Moreover, the average annual revenues of the female-headed firms amounted to less than one-tenth the average annual revenues of the male-headed firms (although this difference was not statistically significant due to the high variation within each subgroup). The findings presented in the lower half of Table 9.2 provide further evidence of our sample's representativeness. As reported in other research, the female entrepreneurs in our study tended to be younger than their male counterparts and, correspondingly, to possess significantly less industry, management and prior business ownership experience. Significant differences were also evident in their educational backgrounds. Overall, this pattern of findings is similar to that reported in previous studies within the women's entrepreneurship literature – both within North America (Brush et al., 2006a; Jennings and Provorny Cash, 2006) and in other countries around the world (Brush et al., 2006b; Minniti et al., 2005).

Descriptive Statistics for the WFI Strategies

The strategies found in Table 9.1 were operationalized in our survey study of Alberta entrepreneurs. Details on those operationalizations are available from the authors upon request. For this chapter, it is important to note two facts about the measures. First, we used multiple measures (typically three) for each strategy and, in keeping with the sociometric literature on measures, combined these using average, scale or factor analysis. Second, we examined the overall means for the pooled male and female subsamples before testing our specific hypotheses about male–female differences in WFI strategies. Some of the descriptive statistics from this pooled sample are worth discussing in detail.

Table 9.2   Gender-based differentials in the characteristics of the sampled firms and their owner-managers

Sample characteristics	Males	Females	Test statistic
Firms			
Industry sector			
Manufacturing	22.5%	22.2%	
Retail, wholesale or general services	32.4%	38.9%	
Professional services	45.1%	34.1%	$X^2 = 2.62$ (n.s.)[a]
Age and life-cycle stage			
Years in operation	25.90	18.40	$t = 3.03$**
Start-up stage	2.8%	2.2%	
Slow growth stage	32.4%	27.5%	
Fast growth stage	11.3%	11.0%	
Maturity stage	50.7%	58.2%	
Decline stage	2.8%	1.1%	$X^2 = 1.44$ (n.s.)
Size			
Number of employees	27.86	10.76	$t = 4.03$***
Average annual revenues ($m)	13.79	1.08	$t = 1.42$ (n.s.)
Business owners			
Age			
Under 30 years old	0.0%	2.2%	
31 to 40 years old	16.9%	22.0%	
41 to 50 years old	23.9%	38.5%	
51 to 60 years old	45.1%	29.7%	
Over 60 years old	14.1%	7.7%	$X^2 = 8.85$†
Education			
High school	5.9%	10.1%	
Some college or university courses	25.0%	12.4%	
College or university degree	14.7%	31.5%	
Some graduate or professional courses	4.4%	5.6%	
Graduate degree or professional designation	50.0%	40.4%	$X^2 = 9.96$*
Experience			
Industry	9.41	6.80	$t = 1.93$†
Management	5.70	3.80	$t = 1.81$†
Business ownership	3.08	1.52	$t = 2.04$*

Notes:
†$p \leq .10$, *$p \leq .05$, **$p \leq .01$, ***$p \leq .001$.
[a]Industry differences are not significant due to the manner in which the sampling frame was constructed.

Growth-facilitating WFI strategies

Two individual-level, growth-facilitating WFI strategies were considered: (1) segmenting work responsibilities from family obligations while in the business sphere; and (2) making accommodations within the family domain. In our pooled sample, the entrepreneurs did not implement the former strategy to a great degree. Instead, the vast majority (88 per cent) reported that, during the prior year, they were 'never', 'rarely' or only 'sometimes' unable to fulfil family responsibilities (such as caring for a sick child) due to business obligations. The mean score on our three-item measure of segmentation was only 2.42 on a five-point scale. Similarly, our descriptive analyses indicate that the strategy of making accommodations within the family domain was not widely implemented within our sample of entrepreneurs. Behaviourally, the participants reported that they devoted 25 hours per week, on average, to household and family-related responsibilities. Psychologically, the participants also reported that they were highly committed to the family member role (mean = 4.00 on a five-point scale), with very few relaxing their expectations for adequate role performance within the family sphere (mean = 2.88 on a five-point scale).

At the couple level, the growth facilitative WFI strategy of prioritizing the entrepreneur's career was not widely implemented by our study participants. For example, only 12 per cent reported that their spouse/significant other deliberately stayed at home so that the business owner could better fulfil his or her responsibilities as owner-manager. Likewise, only 12 per cent reported that their spouse/significant other worked at 'just a job' instead of pursuing a demanding career of their own. Only 3 per cent reported that their spouse provided unpaid labour to their business. This set of findings suggest that the entrepreneurs in our sample were not just striving to do it all – but that they were attempting to do so, for the most part, without a spouse/significant other who had prioritized the entrepreneur's career over their own.

Nor did participants invoke the second growth-facilitating WFI strategy at the couple level, postponing major transitions within the family sphere. Rather than remaining single, which may have facilitated greater absorption in the business owner role, the vast majority (90 per cent) were married or had a common-law partner. Moreover, rather than forgoing childrearing in order to focus on the business, 65 per cent reported that they had children living with them at the time of our survey.[3] In sum, the preceding findings suggest that the business owners in our sample were not pursuing any of the potentially growth-facilitating WFI strategies derived from Jennings and McDougald (2007) to any great degree – regardless of whether those strategies were enacted primarily at the individual or couple level.

In sum, we found relatively fewer business owners were willing to engage in either individual- or couple-oriented, growth-facilitating WFI strategies than we had anticipated. But respondents seemed keenly aware of the tension between work and family and the existence of these strategies.

Growth-constraining WFI strategies

In terms of individual-level WFI strategies that are likely to interfere with business growth, the first strategy, integrating family responsibilities with work commitments, could not be measured. Instead, we had to construct the opposite measure of integration – the extent to which the entrepreneurs reported that they worked on business-related matters at home instead of spending time with their family members. Although the mean for this indicator was only 2.73 on a five-point scale, almost one-quarter of the participants (22 per cent) admitted that they 'often' or 'almost always' engaged in this form of integration.

The second potentially growth-constraining at the individual level focused upon the behavioural and psychological accommodations that entrepreneurs make within the work domain due to family-role commitments. Behaviourally, the participants reported working long hours in the business domain, averaging 46 hours per week on work-related responsibilities; more specifically, over three-quarters of the entrepreneurs indicated that they spent 40 hours or more per week on their business ownership responsibilities. Psychologically, the participants also reported that they were at least moderately committed to their role as business owner (mean = 3.40 on a five-point scale), with few relaxing their expectations for adequate role performance within the work domain (mean = 2.60 on a five-point scale) and many reporting a high degree of identification with their business (mean = 4.16 on a five-point scale).

At the couple level, one of the main strategies likely to interfere with business growth measured was prioritizing the career of one's spouse (or significant other) over one's career as an entrepreneur. Almost 30 per cent of our participants reported that they performed 'most' or 'all' of family or household tasks. In order to fulfil these obligations, entrepreneurs may intentionally limit – or even reduce – the number of hours that they are willing to work on business-related matters. In our study, 32 per cent admitted that they had frequently set a limit on their hours of work during the prior year. Another 32 per cent reported that they had gone so far as frequently reducing the number of hours spent on business-related responsibilities during the same reporting period.

The second couple-level, growth-constraining WFI strategy that we measured was postponing major transitions within the business sphere. Our study participants rarely enacted this strategy. Only 10 per cent reported that they had frequently made efforts during the prior year to reduce their number of clients or customers. Similarly, only 6 per cent admitted that they had frequently turned down new clients or customers during the same reporting period.

In sum, just as in the case of growth-facilitating WFI strategies, the business owners were less likely to use either individual- or couple-level growth-constraining strategies than we anticipated; yet business owners seemed keenly aware that such strategies existed. Thus, it is an interesting choice as to whether male or female entrepreneurs are likely to draw upon this group of strategies in the face of work–family interface issues. We present the findings pertinent to this question below.

HYPOTHESIS-TESTING RESULTS

Gender Differences in Growth-facilitating WFI Strategies

Table 9.3 summarizes the results from our analysis of the overall usage of male versus female business owners of the various WFI strategies available to them. As foreshadowed by our descriptive results for the pooled sample, we found fewer differences between men and women in the use of growth-facilitating strategies than we expected. At the individual level, no significant differences emerged for our measure of segmentation. The women entrepreneurs in our sample were just as likely as the men to engage in limited segmentation of their work and family roles. Likewise, we found no significant differences between the male and female participants on any of our indicators of making accommodations within the family domain. The female entrepreneurs were just as likely as their male counterparts to spend a high number of hours per week on household and family-related tasks, display a high commitment to the family member role, and engage in little relaxation of their expectations for adequate performance within the family sphere. We thus found no support for our first hypothesis, which had predicted that female business owners would be less likely to enact potentially growth-facilitating WFI strategies at the individual level.

However, as indicated within the lower half of Table 9.3, we did find some support for our second hypothesis, which had predicted that female entrepreneurs would be less likely to engage in potentially growth-facilitating WFI strategies at the couple level. For one, the women were significantly less likely to have a stay-at-home spouse. Almost one-quarter of the men – but only 5 per cent of the women – reported that they were part of a couple with this type of arrangement. Second, the women were marginally less likely to have a spouse who provided unpaid labour to

Table 9.3   Analyses of differences in the growth-facilitating WFI strategies of male and female business owners

Growth-facilitating WFI strategies	Males	Females	Test statistic
Individual level			
Segmentation			
Did not respond to family obligations at work	Mean = 2.33	Mean = 2.50	$t = -1.63$ (n.s.)
Accommodation within family domain			
Weekly hours spent on family tasks	Mean = 23.10	Mean = 26.14	$t = -1.07$ (n.s.)
Family role commitment level	Mean = 3.96	Mean = 4.03	$t = -0.62$ (n.s.)
Relaxed expectations in family sphere	Mean = 2.78	Mean = 2.96	$t = -1.23$ (n.s.)
Couple level			
Prioritization of entrepreneur's career			
Stay-at-home spouse	23.4%	5.2%	$X^2 = 9.98$**
Spouse provides unpaid labour	5.6%	1.1%	$X^2 = 2.74$†
Spouse with 'just a job'	12.2%	17.8%	$X^2 = 0.69$ (n.s.)
Postponement of family transitions			
No spouse/significant other	7.0%	11.0%	$X^2 = 0.74$ (n.s.)
No dependent children/elders	31.0%	37.4%	$X^2 = 0.72$ (n.s.)

Notes: †$p \leq .10$, *$p \leq .05$, **$p \leq .01$, ***$p \leq .001$.

their business. That being said, they were just as unlikely as the men to have a spouse/significant other who was holding down 'just a job' rather than pursuing a demanding career of their own. Moreover, we found no significant gender differences for our two indicators of postponing major family transitions. Although higher proportions of the women had neither a spouse/significant other nor dependent children/elders, these differences were not statistically significant.

Gender Differences in Growth-constraining WFI Strategies

Table 9.4 contains the findings from our investigation into the existence of any gender differences in the extent to which the business owners in our sample engaged in WFI strategies likely to constrain business growth. Once again, we observed very few differences overall. As reported within

Table 9.4 Analyses of differences in the growth-constraining WFI strategies of male and female business owners

Growth-constraining WFI strategies	Males	Females	Test statistic
Individual level			
Integration			
Worked on business-related tasks at home	Mean − 2.65	Mean = 2.79	$t = -0.94$ (n.s.)
Accommodation within work domain			
Weekly hours spent on business tasks	Mean = 45.32	Mean = 46.42	$t = -0.45$ (n.s.)
Business role commitment level	Mean = 3.35	Mean = 3.44	$t = -0.68$ (n.s.)
Relaxed expectations in work sphere	Mean = 2.61	Mean = 2.57	$t = 0.21$ (n.s.)
Identification with business	Mean = 4.14	Mean = 4.18	$t = -0.37$ (n.s.)
Couple level			
Prioritization of spouse's career			
Assumed greater share of household tasks	Mean = 2.37	Mean = 3.37	$t = -7.36$***
Limited the no. of hours spent at work	Mean = 2.83	Mean = 3.03	$t = -1.22$ (n.s.)
Reduced the no. of hours spent at work	Mean = 3.08	Mean = 3.08	$t = 0.04$ (n.s.)
Postponement of business transitions			
Reduced existing client base	Mean = 2.08	Mean = 1.84	$t = 1.48$ (n.s.)
Turned down new clients	Mean = 1.94	Mean = 1.70	$t = 1.55$ (n.s.)

Notes: †$p \le .10$, *$p \le .05$, **$p \le .01$, ***$p \le .001$.

the upper half of this table, no significant gender differences were apparent in any of the individual-level strategies. The female business owners did not integrate work and family role to a greater degree than their male counterparts – nor were they more likely to make behavioural or psychological accommodations within the business sphere in order to fulfil family-role commitments. As such, our third hypothesis received no empirical support.

Our fourth hypothesis predicted that women entrepreneurs would also be more likely to engage in potentially growth-constraining WFI strategies at the couple level of analysis. The findings reported in the lower half of Table 9.4 lend minimal support for this hypothesis. As indicated, no significant gender differences were observable for two of the three indicators of prioritizing the spouse's career over that of the entrepreneur's. Instead, the female participants were just as unlikely as the male participants to report that they had deliberately limited or reduced their working hours in order to fulfil their household and family obligations. Likewise, we found no significant gender differences for our two indicators of postponing major business transitions: that is, reducing the firm's existing number of clients and/or turning down new customers. In fact, the only potentially constraining couple-level strategy that the women engaged in to a greater degree than the men was assuming a disproportionate share of their household's tasks.

Across-context Gender Differences

Given the overall lack of empirical support for the theoretical predictions derived from Jennings and McDougald (2007), we felt obligated to explore potential post hoc explanations. One possibility, consistent with the emerging contingency approach to women's entrepreneurship research (see, for example, Ahl, 2006; Cliff et al., 2005; Justo et al., 2007), is that gender differences in entrepreneurs' WFI strategies may actually be quite pronounced in certain settings yet suppressed in others – and thus masked when examined in the aggregate. We explored this possibility by testing for gender differences within the three distinct industry sectors in which the firms in our sample operated: (1) manufacturing; (2) retail, wholesale and general services; and, (3) professional services. Table 9.5 summarizes the results.

The findings reported in Table 9.5 support this context-dependent explanation. As illustrated in the first column of this table, very few gender differences were apparent among those heading manufacturing firms. In this setting, the WFI strategies of male and female entrepreneurs differed in only two significant ways. For one, almost two-thirds of the female business owners, but less than one-third of the male business owners indicated that they had no dependent children or elders in their households ($X^2 = 4.05$, $p \leq .05$). Second, despite the lack of dependants, the women were much more likely than the men to report that they assumed a disproportionate share of their household's tasks (mean$_F$ = 3.95, mean$_M$ = 2.31; $t = 5.54$, $p \leq .001$).

As noted in the second column of Table 9.5, far more gender differences were evident among those heading retail, wholesale or general service firms. Although the men and women in this setting did not tend to enact different WFI strategies at the individual level that were likely to facilitate business growth, interesting differences were observable at the couple level. In particular, 21 per cent of the male owner-managers of such

Table 9.5   Existence and nature of gender differences in WFI strategies within different contexts

WFI strategies	Manufacturing	Retail/wholesale/ general services	Professional services
Growth-facilitating			
Individual level			
Segmentation	No	No	F>M
Weekly hours spent on family tasks	No	No	No
Family role commitment level	No	No	No
Relaxed expectations in family sphere	No	No	F>M
Couple level			
Stay-at-home spouse	No	F<M	F<M
Spouse provides unpaid labour	No	F<M	No
Spouse with 'just a job'	No	No	No
No spouse/significant other	No	No	No
No dependent children/ elders	F>M	No	No
Growth-constraining			
Individual level			
Integration	No	No	No
Weekly hours spent on business tasks	No	No	No
Business role commitment level	No	F>M	F<M
Relaxed expectations in work sphere	No	No	No
Identification with business	No	F>M	No
Couple level			
Disproportionate share of household tasks	F>M	F>M	F>M
Limited the no. of hours spent at work	No	No	No
Reduced the no. of hours spent at work	No	No	F>M
Reduced existing client base	No	F<M	No
Turned down new clients	No	F<M	No
Total no. gender differences	2	7	6

firms – but none of the females – had a stay-at-home spouse. Moreover, 13 per cent of the men had a spouse who provided unpaid labour to his business whereas none of the women's spouses did so ($X^2 = 5.48, p \le .05$). Further differences were observable amongst the WFI strategies likely to constrain business growth. Here, however, the women reported a significantly higher commitment level to the business owner role (mean$_F$ = 3.62, mean$_M$ = 3.10; $t = 2.55, p \le .01$) and a significantly higher degree of identification with their business (mean$_F$ = 4.36, mean$_M$ = 4.04; $t = 2.20, p \le .05$). Finally, although the female business owners in this setting tended to assume a greater share of their household's tasks (mean$_F$ = 3.25, mean$_M$ = 2.30; $t = 4.44, p \le .001$), they were less likely than their male counterparts to report that they had either reduced their firm's number of customers (mean$_F$ = 1.48, mean$_M$ = 2.35; $t = -3.38, p \le .001$) or turned down new customers (mean$_F$ = 1.41, mean$_M$ = 2.00; $t = -2.35, p \le .01$) during the prior year in order to better fulfil their family-related commitments.

A similar number of gender differences were evident in the professional service firm context as in the retail/wholesale/general services context – but the pattern of differences was not identical within these two settings. It was only in the professional service firm context, for instance, that gender differences were observable in WFI strategies enacted at the individual level that are likely to facilitate business growth. Intriguingly, however, we found that the female professionals were more likely than their male counterparts to report that they had invoked a segmentation strategy (mean$_F$ = 2.63, mean$_M$ = 2.31; $t = 1.98, p \le .05$) and had relaxed their expectations for adequate role performance in the family sphere (mean$_F$ = 3.25, mean$_M$ = 2.84; $t = 2.21, p \le .05$). Like those heading retail, wholesale or general service firms, none of the women heading professional service firms had either a stay-at-home spouse or a partner who provided unpaid labour to their business. Finally, the female professionals were more likely than their male counterparts to engage in WFI strategies likely to constrain business growth, such as reducing their commitment to the business owner role (mean$_F$ = 2.99, mean$_M$ = 3.53; $t = -3.02, p \le .01$), assuming a disproportionate share of household tasks (mean$_F$ = 3.16, mean$_M$ = 2.44; $t = 3.38, p \le .001$), and reducing their hours at work (mean$_F$ = 3.63, mean$_M$ = 2.50; $t = 2.50, p \le .001$).

DISCUSSION

The primary objective of this paper was to offer one of the first empirical tests of the claim that male and female entrepreneurs utilize different strategies to manage the interface between work and family (for example

Brush, 1992; Jennings and McDougald, 2007; Longstreth et al., 1987; Parasuraman et al., 1996). While we may have accomplished that goal, the results were not as we had anticipated. First, the business owners in our sample did not engage in many of the strategies theorized by Jennings and McDougald (2007) to either facilitate or constrain business growth. Second, contrary to the predictions derived from these scholars, we observed very few differences between male and female entrepreneurs overall.

Although, on the surface, these findings may appear to cast doubt on the family embeddedness approach to entrepreneurial phenomena (Aldrich and Cliff, 2003; Dyer, 2003; Firkin et al., 2003; Heck and Trent, 1999), the results of our supplemental across-industry comparison suggest that such a conclusion would be incorrect – or at least premature. True, we found very few differences in the WFI strategies enacted by men and women heading manufacturing firms. Many more gender differences were apparent, however, among those heading retail, wholesale or general services firms. Moreover, among those heading professional service firms, significant gender differences were observable not only for several potentially growth-facilitating and growth-constraining WFI strategies, but also for those enacted at both the individual and couple levels of analysis. These findings imply that family embeddedness considerations may be particularly salient in certain settings, rather than irrelevant.

The preceding inference also provides support for another emergent approach within the entrepreneurship literature: the context-rich perspective (Davidsson, 2004; Sarasvathy, 2004; Zahra, 2007). A central tenet of this approach is that key relationships of interest to entrepreneurship scholars (and practitioners) may differ depending upon the environment in which entrepreneurial processes and outcomes occur. This corresponds with what we observed in this study. Gender differences were limited in certain contexts yet more prevalent in others. Moreover, a distinct pattern of differences was observable within each of the two environments with more pronounced gender-based differentials: that is, the differentials apparent between male and female professional service providers were not identical to those apparent between male and female retailers, wholesalers and general service providers.

In light of the above, we view the research reported in this chapter as offering two main contributions to the entrepreneurship literature. First, our study extends work consistent with the family embeddedness approach more generally, by laying an empirical foundation for continued research on entrepreneurs' WFI strategies more specifically. The limited empirical research conducted on work–family issues to date has tended to focus primarily on entrepreneurs' experienced work–family conflict (for example, Kim and Ling, 2001; Loscocco et al., 1991; Parasuraman et al.,

1996), rather than on their tactics for managing the interface between the two domains. Second, our study provides an illustration of how researchers can respond to the increasingly voiced call for a more heterogeneous and contextualized approach to women's entrepreneurship research (Ahl, 2006; de Bruin et al. 2006, 2007; Hughes, 2005; Jennings and Provorny Cash, 2006; Marlow and Patton, 2005; Rosa and Hamilton, 1994). Instead of merely claiming that context should matter, our work offers a simple empirical demonstration of whether and how it does so.

Further research would strengthen these contributions. On the one hand, the above-noted family embeddedness contribution would be considerably more provocative if longitudinal investigations revealed that business owners' WFI strategies influenced key entrepreneurial outcomes (in either a facilitative or inhibitive manner). Preliminary associational analyses of such relationships, conducted on the cross-sectional survey data described in this chapter, look quite promising in this regard. The above-noted contribution to the context-rich approach, on the other hand, would be much more noteworthy if we had developed theoretically grounded arguments, a priori, to account for the across-context differences that emerged through our post hoc empirical exploration. Why is it, for example, that male and female owners of manufacturing firms tend to manage the work–family interface in similar ways, whereas more notable gender differences are evident among those heading other types of firms? Does this have anything to do with the individuals who are attracted to the different sectors? Or does it have more to do with the nature of the work done within each sector? One can imagine, for example, that certain forms of manufacturing are much more standardized than many forms of professional service work, which may have implications for the scope of WFI strategies that can feasibly be enacted (by either male or female entrepreneurs).

In sum, we hope this chapter encourages researchers to reflect not only upon specific questions such as these – but also upon the nature and impact of family embeddedness considerations more broadly. We also hope that the chapter serves as a gentle reminder to build contextual factors into our investigations. In our view, such efforts will help address the critique that women's entrepreneurship research does not yet capture the diversity inherent amongst female (and male) entrepreneurs.

NOTES

1. We are very grateful for the research assistance provided by Heather Adamski, Jessica Alen, Mel Ashcroft, Amanda Bloom, Megan McDougald and Christina Zschocke – and

for the financial support provided by a SSHRC INE grant (no. 501-2001-0017) awarded to the first author.
2. infoCANADA is the leading online supplier of business and consumer data in Canada, providing regional and industry based directories. It is generally recognized as having high quality data, using external research audits to ensure accuracy. Further information is available at: http://www.infocanada.ca/main_page.aspx.
3. More specifically, 19 per cent of respondents had at least one pre-school child (or children) in their household; 31 per cent had at least one child (or children) of school age; and 15 per cent had an adult child (or children). Another 1 per cent of the study participants reported that a dependent elderly relative lived in their household. The remaining 34 per cent of respondents had no dependants living in their household.

REFERENCES

Ahl, H. (2006), 'Why research on women entrepreneurs needs new directions', *Entrepreneurship Theory and Practice*, **30** (5), 595–621.
Aldrich, H.E. (1989), 'Networking among women entrepreneurs', in O. Hagan, C. Rivchun and D. Sexton (eds), *Women-owned Businesses*, New York: Praeger, pp. 103–22.
Aldrich, H.E. and Cliff, J.E. (2003), 'The pervasive effects of family on entrepreneurship: toward a family embeddedness perspective', *Journal of Business Venturing*, **18** (5), 573–96.
Aldrich, H.E. and Langton, N. (1998), 'Human resource management and organizational life cycles', in P.D. Reynolds, W. Bygrave, N.M. Carter, P. Davidsson, W.B. Gartner, C.M. Mason and P.P. McDougall (eds), *Frontiers of Entrepreneurship Research 1997, Proceedings of the Babson College, Center for Entrepreneurial Studies*, Babson Park, MA: Babson College, pp. 349–57.
Allen, S. and Truman, C. (1992), ' Women, business and self-employment: a conceptual minefield', in S. Arber and N. Gilbert (eds), *Women and Working Lives*, London: Macmillan, pp. 162–74.
Allen, S. and Truman, C. (1993), *Women in Business: Perspectives on Women Entrepreneurs*, London: Routledge.
Anderson, R. and Reeb, D. (2003), 'Founding family ownership and firm performance: evidence from the S&P 500', *Journal of Finance*, **58**, 1301–28.
Becker, P.E. and Moen, P. (1999), 'Scaling back: dual-earner couples' work-family strategies', *Journal of Marriage and the Family*, **61** (4), 995–1007.
Belcourt, M., Burke, R. and Lee-Gosselin, H. (1991), *The Glass Box: Women Business Owners in Canada*, Ottawa: Canadian Advisory Council on the Status of Women.
Boden, R.J. (1999), 'Flexible working hours, family responsibilities, and female self-employment: gender differences in self-employment selection', *The American Journal of Economics and Sociology*, **58** (1), 71–93.
Brush, C.G. (1992), 'Research on women business owners: past trends, a new perspective and future directions', *Entrepreneurship Theory and Practice*, **16** (4), 5–30.
Brush, C.G., Carter, N.M., Gatewood, E.J., Greene, P.G. and Hart, M.M. (2006a), 'Women's entrepreneurship in the United States', in C. Brush, N.M. Carter, E.J. Gatewood, P.G. Greene and M.M. Hart (eds), *Growth-Oriented Women Entrepreneurs and their Businesses: A Global Research Perspective*, Cheltenham, UK and Northampton, MA, USA: Edward Elgar, pp. 184–202.

Brush, C.G., Carter, N.M., Gatewood, E.J., Greene, P.G. and Hart, M.M. (eds) (2006b), *Growth-Oriented Women Entrepreneurs and Their Businesses: A Global Research Perspective*, Cheltenham, UK and Northampton, MA, USA: Edward Elgar.

Buttner, E.H. and Moore, D.P. (1997), 'Women's organizational exodus to entrepreneurship: self-reported motivations and correlates with success', *Journal of Small Business Management*, **35** (1), 34–46.

Carter, N.M., Williams, M. and Reynolds, P.D. (1997), 'Discontinuance among new firms in retail: the influence of initial resources, strategy, and gender', *Journal of Business Venturing*, **12**, 125–45.

Cliff, J.E. (1998), 'Does one size fit all? Exploring the relationship between attitudes between growth, gender and business size', *Journal of Business Venturing*, **13** (6), 523–42.

Cliff, J.E., Langton, N. and Aldrich, H.E. (2005), 'Walking the talk? Gendered rhetoric vs. action in small firms', *Organization Studies*, **26**, 61–89.

Cooper, A.C., Gimeno-Gascon, F.J. and Woo, C.Y. (1994), 'Initial human and financial capital as predictors of new venture performance', *Journal of Business Venturing*, **9**, 371–95.

Cramton, C.D. (1993), 'Is rugged individualism the whole story? Public and private accounts of a firm's founding', *Family Business Review*, **6**, 233–61.

Davidsson, P. (2004), *Researching Entrepreneurship*, Boston, MA: Springer.

Davis, A.B. and Aldrich, H.E. (2000), 'The organizational advantage? Social capital, gender, and small business owners' access to resources', paper presented at the 2000 American Sociological Association meeting, 12–16 August, Washington, DC.

De Bruin, A., Brush, C.G. and Welter, F. (2006), 'Introduction to the special issue: towards building cumulative knowledge on women's entrepreneurship', *Entrepreneurship Theory and Practice*, **30** (5), 585–93.

De Bruin, A., Brush, C.G. and Welter, F. (2007), 'Advancing a framework for coherent research on women's entrepreneurship', *Entrepreneurship Theory and Practice*, **31** (3), 323–39.

Dyer, W.G. (2003), 'The family: the missing variable in organizational research', *Entrepreneurship Theory and Practice*, **27** (4), 401–16.

Edwards, J.R. and Rothbard, N.P. (2000), 'Mechanisms linking work and family: clarifying the relationship between work and family constructs', *Academy of Management Review*, **25** (1), 176–99.

Fabowale, L., Orser, B. and Riding. A. (1995), 'Gender, structural factors, and credit terms between Canadian small businesses and financial institutions', *Entrepreneurship Theory and Practice*, **19** (4), 41–66.

Firkin, P., Dupuis, A. and de Bruin, A. (2003), 'Familial entrepreneurship', in A. de Bruin and A. Dupuis (eds), *Entrepreneurship: New Perspectives in a Global Age*, Aldershot: Ashgate Publishing, pp. 92–108.

Fischer, E., Reuber, R. and Dyke, L. (1993), 'A theoretical overview and extension of research on sex, gender, and entrepreneurship', *Journal of Business Venturing*, **8**, 151–68.

Foley, S. and Powell, G.N. (1997), 'Reconceptualizing work–family conflict for business/marriage partners: a theoretical model', *Journal of Small Business Management*, **35**, 36–47.

Goffee, R. and Scase, R. (1985), *Women in Charge*, London: George Allen and Unwin.

Green, E. and Cohen, L. (1995), 'Women's businesses: are women entrepreneurs breaking new ground or simply balancing the demands of "women's work" in a new way?', *Journal of Gender Studies*, **4** (3), 297–314.

Greenhaus, J. and Parasuraman, S. (1999), 'Research on work, family and gender: current status and future directions', in G.N. Powell (ed.), *Handbook of Gender and Work*, Thousand Oaks, CA: Sage.

Greenhaus, J.H. and Beutell, N.J. (1985), 'Sources of conflict between work and family roles', *Academy of Management Review*, **10**, 76–88.

Haines Jr, G.H., Orser, B.J. and Riding, A.L. (1999), 'An empirical study of banks and the gender of small business clients', *Revue Canadienne des Sciences de l'Administration*, **16** (4), 291–308.

Heck, R.K.Z. and Trent, E.S. (1999), 'The prevalence of family business from a household sample', *Family Business Review*, **12** (3), 209–24.

Hughes, K.D. (2005), *Female Enterprise in the New Economy*, Toronto: University of Toronto Press.

Jennings, J.E. and McDougald, M.S. (2007), 'Work–family interface experiences and strategies: consequences for entrepreneurship research and practice', *Academy of Management Review*, **32**, 747–60.

Jennings, J.E. and Provorny Cash, M. (2006), 'Women's entrepreneurship in Canada: progress, puzzles and priorities', in C.G. Brush, N.M. Carter, E.J. Gatewood, P.G. Greene and M.M. Hart (eds), *Growth-Oriented Women Entrepreneurs and their Businesses: A Global Research Perspective*, Cheltenham, UK and Northampton, MA, USA: Edward Elgar, pp. 53–87.

Jurik, N.C. (1998), 'Getting away and getting by: the experiences of self-employed homeworkers', *Work and Occupations*, **25** (1), 7–35.

Justo, R., Cruz, C. and de Castro, J.O. (2007), 'Perception of success of male and female entrepreneurs: a social identity approach', paper presented at the Diana International Research Conference, 5 June, Madrid.

Kalleberg, A.L. and Leicht, K.T. (1991), 'Gender and organizational performance: determinants of small business survival and success', *Academy of Management Journal*, **34** (1), 136–61.

Kim, J.L.S. and Ling, C.S. (2001), 'Work–family conflict of women entrepreneurs in Singapore', *Women in Management Review*, **16** (5/6), 204–21.

Klein, S.B., Astrachan, J.H. and Smyrnios, K.X. (2005), 'The F-PEC scale of family influence: construction, validation and further implication for theory', *Entrepreneurship Theory and Practice*, **29** (3), 321–40.

Kossek, E.E., Noe, R.A. and DeMarr, B.J. (1999), 'Work-family role synthesis: individual and organizational determinants', *International Journal of Conflict Management*, **10** (2), 102–29.

Lambert, S.J. (1990), 'Processes linking work and family: a critical review and research agenda', *Human Relations*, **43** (3), 239–57.

Longstreth, M., Stafford, K. and Maudin, T. (1987), 'Self-employed women and their families: time use and socioeconomic characteristics', *Journal of Small Business Management*, **25** (3), 30–7.

Loscocco, K.A., Robinson, J., Hall, R.H. and Allen, J.K. (1991), 'Gender and small business success: an inquiry into women's relative disadvantage', *Social Forces*, **70** (1), 65–85.

Marlow, S. and Patton, D. (2005), 'All Credit to Men? Entrepreneurship, finance, and gender', *Entrepreneurship Theory and Practice*, **29** (6), 717–35.

Martins, L.L., Eddleston, K.A. and Veiga, J.F. (2002), 'Moderators of the relationship between work–family conflict and career satisfaction', *Academy of Management Journal*, **45** (2), 399–409.

Milkie, M.A. and Peltola, P. (1999), 'Playing all the roles: gender and the work–family balancing act', *Journal of Marriage and the Family*, **61**, 476–90.

Miller, D. and Le Breton-Miller, I. (2005), *Managing for the Long Run*, Boston, MA: Harvard Business School Press.

Minniti, M., Arenius, P. and Langowitz, N. (2005), *Global Entrepreneurship Monitor: 2004 Report on Women and Entrepreneurship*, Babson Park, MA and London: Babson College and London Business School, available at: www.gem consortium.org (accessed 1 October 2008).

Moen, P. and Wethington, E. (1992), 'The concept of family adaptive strategies', *Annual Review of Sociology*, **18**, 233–51.

Moen, P. and Yu, Y. (2000), 'Effective work/life strategies: working couples, work conditions, gender and life quality', *Social Problems*, **47** (3), 291–326.

Orser, B. and Hogarth-Scott, S. (2002), 'Opting for growth: gender dimensions of choosing enterprise development', *Canadian Journal of Administrative Sciences*, **19** (3), 284–300.

Parasuraman, S., Purohit, Y.S., Godshalk, V.M. and Beutell, N.J. (1996), 'Work and family variables, entrepreneurial career success, and psychological well-being', *Journal of Vocational Behavior*, **48**, 275–300.

Rosa, P. and Hamilton, D. (1994), 'Gender and ownership in U.K. small firms', *Entrepreneurship Theory and Practice*, **18** (3), 11–27.

Rothbard, N.P. (2001), 'Enriching or depleting? The dynamics of engagement in work and family roles', *Administrative Science Quarterly*, **46** (4), 655–84.

Rothbard, N.P. and Edwards, J.E. (2003), 'Investment in work and family roles: a test of identity and utilitarian motives', *Personnel Psychology*, **56** (3), 699–729.

Rothbard, N.P., Phillips, K.W. and Dumas, T.L. (2005), 'Managing multiple roles: work-family policies and individuals' desires for segmentation', *Organization Science*, **16** (3), 243–58.

Ruef, M., Aldrich, H.E. and Carter, N. (2003), 'The structure of founding teams: homophily, strong ties, and isolation among U.S. entrepreneurs', *American Sociological Review*, **68** (2), 195–222.

Sarasvathy, S.D. (2004), 'The questions we ask and the questions we care about: reformulating some problems in entrepreneurship research', *Journal of Business Venturing*, **19**, 707–17.

Sexton, D.L. and Bowman-Upton, N. (1990), 'Female and male entrepreneurs: psychological characteristics and their role in gender-related discrimination', *Journal of Business Venturing*, **5** (1), 29–36.

Smith, C.R. (2000), 'Managing work and family in small "copreneurial" business: an Australian study', *Women in Management Review*, **15**, 283–93.

Stevenson, L. (1986), 'Against all odds: the entrepreneurship of women', *Journal of Small Business Management*, **24** (4), 30–36.

Tenbrunsel, A.E., Brett, J.M., Moaz, E., Stroh, L.K. and Reilly, A.H. (1995), 'Dynamic and static work–family relationships', *Organizational Behavior and Human Decision Processes*, **63** (3), 233–46.

Williams, K. and Alliger, G.M. (1994), 'Role stressors, mood spillover, and perception of work–family conflict in employed parents', *Academy of Management Journal*, **37** (2), 837–68.

Zahra, S.A. (2007), 'Contextualizing theory building in entrepreneurship research', *Journal of Business Venturing*, **22**, 443–52.

10. An integrated view of gender, finance and entrepreneurial capital: theory, practice and policy

Eleanor Shaw, Sara Carter and Wing Lam

INTRODUCTION

Finance has long been recognized as a barrier to women business owners. Prior research reports differences in the financing patterns of businesses owned by men and women (Brush, 1992; Brush et al., 2001; Coleman, 2000) and provides unequivocal evidence that women-owned businesses start with lower levels of capitalization (Carter and Rosa, 1998), lower ratios of debt finance (Haines et al., 1999) and much less likelihood of using private equity or venture capital (Brush et al., 2001; Greene et al., 1999). Explanations for this bimodal funding pattern are far from satisfactory. Early research attributed gender differences to structural (sector, age, size) factors, but studies that have controlled for structural effects persistently report different financing profiles of male-owned and female-owned businesses. Differences in methodological approach, sampling procedures and country context have all contributed to a conflicting base of evidence regarding the relationship between finance and women-owned businesses (Haines et al., 1999). The research field has also been constrained by weak theoretical development and a lack of cumulativeness (Mirchandani, 1999).

Acquiring business finance is a complex process influenced by a range of economic and social variables many of which are not easily identified and are often misunderstood. Drawing upon the theoretical perspectives of Bourdieu (1977, 1990) and network theory (Granovetter, 1973, 1982, 1985; Mitchell, 1969), this chapter seeks to explore the complex relationship between finance, business ownership and gender by considering the impact of non-financial capital on the initial financing of women-owned firms.

BUSINESS OWNERSHIP, FINANCE AND GENDER

Research studies have often presumed that gender-based differences in finance usage are the result of structural dissimilarities between male- and female-owned businesses (Read, 1998). For example, in a large-scale survey analysing bank loan files, Haines et al. (1999) found differences between male and female entrepreneurs (lower sales levels and liabilities, lower levels of salary and drawings), to be a product of business size, age and sector. Fabowale et al. (1995) similarly argued that structural factors accounted for differences in rates of loan rejections between male and female entrepreneurs. Other studies have been less conclusive. Verheul and Thurik (2000) found that most differences in the use of starting capital by male and female entrepreneurs were explained by 'indirect' effects (size, age, sector); however, some 'direct' gender effects survived. More recent studies have controlled for structural factors, comparing matched pairs of male-owned and female-owned businesses in the same sector and at the same time. These studies have reported significant residual funding differences, with women using on average one-third of the start-up capital used by men, but have attributed the cause to an interaction of demand-side and supply-side factors (Carter et al., 2007).

Studies that have specifically considered the impact that gender of business owners may have on bank lending decisions have found little direct evidence of gender discrimination (Buttner and Rosen, 1989; Carter et al., 2007; Fay and Williams, 1993). Collectively these studies, together with those by Orser and Foster (1994) and Coleman (2000) suggest that while gender per se may not influence bank lending decisions, lending criteria including preferred size of business and education, experience, capital, collateral, character and capacity of the business owner may serve to disadvantage women business owners. As Carter et al. (2007: 440) conclude, 'gender remains an important but often hidden variable within bank lending'.

While the weight of research evidence refutes systematic gender discrimination on the part of banks, it unequivocally demonstrates a bimodal funding pattern which can be somewhat, but not entirely, explained by structural dissimilarities between male- and female-owned businesses. The relationship between business ownership, finance and gender is likely to be more complex and nuanced than previously recognized. Critically, the question of why access to and use of external finance continues to pose such challenges for women business owners remains unresolved. Recognizing that business ownership is predicated on the availability of and access to financial and non-financial capital, the study presented in this chapter sought to contribute to continuing debate by exploring the relationship between gender, finance and entrepreneurial capital.

ENTREPRENEURIAL CAPITAL

The concept of capital is not new to the social sciences (cf. Giddens, 2001) yet its application to entrepreneurship is a recent development (Erikson, 2002; Firkin, 2003; Morris, 1998). While most entrepreneurship researchers would cite the origins of capital theory as a development of the resource-based view of the firm (cf. Carter et al., 2001) both Gorton (2000) and Firkin (2003) provide detailed accounts of the value of Bourdieu's (1986) perspective on capital for entrepreneurship. Bourdieu (1986) identified individuals as possessing four types of capital: economic (financial), social, cultural (including human) and symbolic. He reasoned that the social world is comprised of both objective structures – for example, resources and capitals – and also subjective structures created by the subconscious systems of classification which individuals use as symbolic templates for engaging in and interpreting practical activities (Bourdieu, 1977; Bourdieu and Wacquant, 1992). Social phenomena, for example, business owner-ship, emerge from the interplay between these structures, suggesting they are malleable, being socially constructed by the outcomes of interactions between individual agents.

Bourdieu's (1977) perspective on structuralism sheds insight into the relationship between business ownership, entrepreneurial capital and gender. Individual positions within emerging social structures are deter-mined by the amounts and forms of capital possessed and the value placed on capital by others. Thus, it follows that certain types of capital may be more valuable than others. Structures created by human interactions reflect tacitly taken-for-granted assumptions which underpin society's 'natural' attitude toward gender differences. Developing this, Bourdieu (1977) argued that these assumptions create attitudes which connote women with negative qualities (for example, weakness) and men with positive (for example, strength). He suggested that as a consequence of this, emerging social structures are hierarchical and can benefit men, for example by creating opportunities for them to acquire greater economic capital, while disadvantaging women.

Support for this is offered by a number of entrepreneurship scholars who have argued for the benefits of contextualizing studies of gender and entrepreneurship within wider feminist analyses (Ahl, 2002; 2006; Carter et al., 2007; Marlow, 2002). Marlow (2002: 83) argues that a failure to do so has created an impression of women 'as blemished men who must be assisted to become honorary men, and in so doing will then achieve within the existing paradigm of entrepreneurship'. Mirchandani (1999), Bird and Brush (2002) and Ahl (2002, 2006) similarly stress that gender should not be seen simply as a characteristic of individuals, but as a process integral to business ownership. While the view that gender is socially constructed rather than a biological characteristic is a consistent theme within socio-logical analyses (Oakley, 1982), it is rarely observed in entrepreneurship studies (Watson and Newby, 2005). Where the value of applying feminist critique to entrepreneurship has been recognized, discussion suggests that the dominant discourse within entrepreneurship continues to evoke posi-tive images associated with a Western, heroic, white male figure symbol-izing aggression and assertiveness in seeking out new ventures (Ahl, 2006; Ogbor, 2000).

These arguments are important for understanding the dynamic between entrepreneurship, capital and gender. First, within the field of entrepre-neurship, certain types of capital with institutionalized positive meanings might be more sought after than others. Secondly, the 'natural' attitude towards gender differences and assumptions underpinning these suggest that the capital women are able to acquire prior to business ownership may differ in amount and type from that possessed by their male coun-terparts. Significantly, it may be that the capital which women bring to business ownership does not realize the same value as men or is regarded as less legitimate.

Initial research suggests that an entrepreneur's non-financial capital impacts on their experiences of business ownership (Davidsson and Honig, 2003; Firkin, 2003; Morris, 1998). Research indicates a relation-ship between gender, the accumulation of non-financial capital and the financing of entrepreneurial ventures (Boden and Nucci, 2000; Brush et al., 2002; Carter et al., 2003). The concept of entrepreneurial capital sug-gests that in addition to financial (economic) capital, the entrepreneurial process is influenced by human (sometimes referred to as cultural), social and symbolic capital (De Carolis and Saparito, 2006; Casson and Giusta, 2007; Cope et al., 2007; Firkin, 2003; Haber and Reichel, 2007; Shaw, et al., 2008). Boden and Nucci (2000) drew attention to differences in the amount and quality of human capital possessed by new entrepreneurs. Their findings suggest that women's fewer years of work experience, reduced exposure to managerial occupations and different education pro-files – all indicators of human capital as defined by Becker (1964) – provide some explanation of the bimodal funding pattern found between male- and female-owned businesses. Similarly, Carter et al. (2003) examined the influence of social and human capital on entrepreneurs' likely access to various forms of finance. Using Becker's (1964) definition of human capital and Coleman's (1988) definition of social capital to establish the influence of the entrepreneur's social network on their access to venture capital, their study found that only human capital, particularly graduate education, had any significant influence. In contrast, Brush et al. (2002)

found social rather than human capital to be significant in formulating venture capital 'deals' and concluded that even when the entrepreneur and their team had the necessary financial and human capital coupled with goals which meet the requirements of equity investors, the deal is unlikely to progress without the necessary social capital, indicated by relevant network connections. Particular to gender, their finding that women are significantly under-represented in both the demand and supply of venture capital in the US, suggests that women in particular may suffer from such social capital or network disadvantages.

Extant research suggests that human and social capital may be relevant to explaining the complex relationship between entrepreneurship, finance and gender. Such research is however at an early stage and, in common with the dominant discourse within entrepreneurship, has yet to apply a feminist critique to studies of entrepreneurial capital.

METHODOLOGY AND ANALYSIS

The view of gender as a social construction is not new to the field of entrepreneurship, but few studies have systematically used this approach in methodology and analysis. A common weakness is the 'disappearing' of social structure – studies tend to present gender differences and follow this with suggestions for how to 'control' or 'eliminate' these differences. This is incoherent with the view that gender is socially constructed; continuously shaped, reshaped and institutionalized in the social context. In other words, gender differences are both the cause and effect of social structures. Therefore, attempts to 'control' or even to 'eliminate' these differences contradict the ontological and epistemological assumptions of social theory and risk heading towards conforming to a gender-biased social structure. By so doing, this could restrict our understanding of women's entrepreneurship, and risk excluding and undermining the value of their activities. The task of this study was to uncover and question gender differences in order to present the virtually invisible socially constructed reality of women's entrepreneurship. The rationale being that this knowledge is essential to understanding the implications that gender differences have for entrepreneurs, the financing of small firms, government policies and other relevant parties. The findings presented below are drawn from a wider study investigating the relationship between banks and business owners that explores both demand-side and supply-side perspectives. The methodology designed for this larger study involved multiple stages and the negotiation of access to business owners and bank loan officers. The methodology presented here describes the collection of data from business owners (demand side).

In-depth interviews were undertaken with a sample of 30 matched pairs of business owners (30 male, 30 female) who had established a business services venture in central Scotland within the three years prior to the start of data collection, which commenced in 2004. Basic characteristics including age of firm, location and sector were used to guide the selection and precise matching of the sample. Interviews were structured around a detailed questionnaire which replicated questions and scales used in previous studies designed to collect data on entrepreneurs' possession of and access to economic (financial), human and social capital. SPSS was used to statistically analyse numerical data regarding dimensions of entrepreneurs' human capital (age, education, experience), social capital (indicated by the size, diversity, durability, density, contents, intensity and frequency of their networks and network interactions) and financial (economic) capital (amount initially invested). Interpretation of findings was guided by our theoretical framework and also by the findings of previous research, made possible by our use of questions and scales used in previous studies.

FINDINGS AND DISCUSSION

Economic Capital: Start-up Capital and External Sources of Finance

As indicated in Table 10.1 below, entrepreneurs were found to have established their firms with relatively small amounts of capital: 62 per cent reported using less than £5000 of start-up capital, 18 per cent reported that they had set up without any initial capital and a further 8 per cent had invested less than £1000. This pattern is typical for business service sectors characterized as requiring very low levels of initial investment and exhibiting low barriers to entry.

Of all the components of entrepreneurial capital, economic capital has received most research attention (Baum and Silverman, 2004; Brush et al., 2001; Carter and Rosa, 1998; Carter et al., 2003; De Clercq and Sapienza, 2006; Greene et al., 1999; Verheul and Thurik, 2000). In common with that body of work, the findings of this study identified sex of the entrepreneur to be a differentiating factor. Chi-squared analysis revealed male entrepreneurs to have made: higher levels of initial investment (male mean = £18 683.33; female mean = £6433.33); larger personal investment (male mean = £9603.45; female mean = £4733.33) and, despite significantly less of the male sample making use of external financing (14 per cent of men and 43 per cent of women), to have used a greater total amount of external finance. Considered alongside the finding that in the year prior to establishment, both the male and female entrepreneurs reported broadly similar

Table 10.1   Sources and amounts of start-up finance

		Female N = 30 %	Male N = 30 %	Total N = 60 %	Chi-square test
Start up	0	13	23	18	$\chi^2 = 7.279$
investment	1–500	7	0	3	df = 6
	501–1000	10	0	5	Sig. = .296
	1001–2000	7	10	8	
	2001–3000	10	7	8	
	3001–5000	23	17	20	
	Over 5001	30	43	37	
Personal	0	23	30	27	$\chi^2 = 4.230$
investment	1–500	7	3	5	df = 6
	501–1000	7	0	3	Sig. = .646
	1001–2000	7	7	7	
	2001–3000	13	7	10	
	3001–5000	20	17	18	
	Over 5001	23	37	30	
External source	No	57	86	71	$\chi^2 = 6.273$
of finance	Yes	43	14	29	df = 1
					Sig. = .012*

Note: *p < 0.05.

levels of household income (£56900 men, £58803 women), these findings question why, within a small-scale matched-pairs sample that controlled for structural factors, bimodal gender patterns of start-up finance were found. To explore the interplay between gender, non-financial capital and business finance, data relating to the human capital possessed by our match-pairs of entrepreneurs is now considered.

Human Capital

Education, age and experience have been identified as important measures of human capital (Becker, 1964; Boden and Nucci, 2000; Cooper et al., 1988, 1994; Davidsson and Honig, 2003; Manigart et al., 2007). Typical of the business services industry, our results, indicate a highly educated profile of entrepreneurs with 38 per cent holding a postgraduate degree, 32 per cent an undergraduate degree and 22 per cent a professional quali-fication. Previous research has established that the age and experience of the entrepreneur are dimensions of human capital which can impact significantly on the establishment of their firms (Boden and Nucci, 2000;

Carter et al., 2003; Davidsson and Honig, 2003; Stevenson, 1986; Watkins and Watkins, 1984). Of the participants surveyed, 90 per cent were aged between 30 and 59. Chi-square analysis revealed female entrepreneurs to be significantly younger ($\chi^2 = 13.789$, df $= 4$, $p < 0.001$) with 67 per cent of female and only 20 per cent of male owners under the age of 39. While only 10 per cent of female owners were older than 50, the majority of male owners (47 per cent) were aged between 50 and 59. As male owners were significantly older, on average 10 years older than their 'matched' female partner, the men in our sample were found to possess significantly more human capital in terms of their number of years of industry and management experience. This finding echoes prior research which has consistently found women to have fewer years of industry experience (Carter et al., 1997) and less senior management experience (Stevenson, 1986; Watkins and Watkins, 1984). While no other human capital differences were found – most owners (70 per cent) had been in full-time employment immediately prior to setting up their firm and most (75 per cent) had no previous experience of business ownership – the implications of which gender differences in the age and industry profiles of entrepreneurs had for their possession of social capital are considered below.

Social Capital

The social capital possessed by entrepreneurs has, in recent years, attracted a wealth of research attention (Cope et al., 2007; De Carolis and Saparito, 2006; Renzulli et al., 2000). Despite this, research is at an early stage with the mixed and inconclusive results generated so far, suggesting scope for research to consider the impact of social capital on entrepreneurship (Baron and Markman, 2000; Baum and Silverman, 2004; Brush et al., 2002; Carter et al., 2003).

Personal Contact Networks (PCNs): Morphology and Relational Dimensions

An entrepreneur's PCN is typically described as the five people with whom they most regularly discuss their business (Aldrich, 1989; Aldrich et al., 1989; Cromie and Birley, 1992; Renzulli et al. (2000). Having identified these five contacts, established indicators of network morphology and relational dimensions were used to ask owners about their relationship with each of these contacts and about any relationship shared between these contacts. The results are shown in Table 10.2.

Aggregate analysis of the composition of owner networks found a greater presence of male contacts: 53 per cent of female and 62 per cent

Table 10.2   Social capital

Personal contact networks: structure and relational dimensions

		Female N = 30 %	Male N = 30 %	Total N = 60 %	Chi-square test
Gender of business contact	Female contact	47	37	42	$\chi^2 = 2.737$
	Male contact	53	63	58	df = 1 Sig. = .098
Contact same gender as the business owner	No	53	38	46	$\chi^2 = 6.667$
	Yes	47	62	54	df = 1 Sig. = .010**
Prime contact composition by kinship	Friend	30	40	35	$\chi^2 = 12.935$
	Business associate	3	33	18	df = 2
	Family	67	27	47	Sig. = .002**
Aggregate analysis of network composition by kinship	Friend	50	43	47	$\chi^2 = 4.788$
	Business associate	23	35	29	df = 2
	Family	27	22	25	Sig. = .091
Network density – 'To what extent do each of these people also know one another?'	Knows all others well	11	16	14	$\chi^2 = 10.674$
	Knows all others slightly	5	12	8	df = 4
	Knows some, not all others	69	51	60	Sig. = .030*
	Doesn't know others	13	17	15	
	Don't know	3	4	3	

Social interaction content with prime contact – percentage for answering 'yes'

Content	Female N = 30 %	Male N = 30 %	Total N=60 %	χ^2	df	Sig
Finance	87	60	73	5.455	1	.020*
Legal	43	40	42	.069	1	.793
Staff	40	37	38	.071	1	.791
Loan/ investment	33	23	28	.739	1	.390
Premises	43	40	42	.069	1	.793
Marketing	83	73	78	.884	1	.347
Family	77	47	62	5.711	1	.017*

Table 10.2   (continued)

Social interaction content – 'discuss personal matter with contacts?'

	Female mean	Male mean	t-value	df	Sig
Contact 1 (Prime contact)	4.67	3.30	3.665	40.464	.001***
Contact 2	3.93	3.10	1.952	54.056	.056
Contact 3	3.41	2.75	1.592	55	.117
Contact 4	3.29	2.86	1.089	54	.281
Contact 5	3.23	2.96	.626	48	.534
Aggregate	3.73	3.00	3.882	265.614	.000***

Social network durability – length known (year)

	Female mean	Male mean	t-value	df	Sig
Contact 1	12.467	11.510	.432	58	.667
Contact 2	12.002	13.493	−.479	58	.634
Contact 3	6.505	14.351	−2.529	55	.015*
Contact 4	7.518	13.011	−1.944	54	.057
Contact 5	9.654	10.855	−.359	48	.721
Aggregate	9.680	12.691	−2.302	281	.022*

Note: *p<0.05; **p<0.01; ***p<0.001.

of male owner networks contained all male contacts. Concurring with the findings of previous research (Cromie and Birley, 1992), analysis of cross-ties by gender found that all owners identified their prime contact (the first contact they mentioned) to be male. Aggregate analysis of network composition by kinship found relationships with family members to comprise approximately 25 per cent of all networks studied. Cross-tie analysis of these kinship relationships by prime contact established that 67 per cent of female and 27 per cent of male owners ($\chi^2 = 12.935$, df = 2, $p < 0.01$) identified a family member as their prime contact while 33 per cent of men and only 3 per cent of women identified a business associate as their prime contact. Drawing from Renzulli et al.'s (2000) finding that networks comprised of high numbers of kinship ties disadvantages nascent entrepreneurs, it is possible that the female owners in our sample experienced disadvantages as a consequence of the higher presence of kinship ties identified as their prime contact. Aggregate analysis of the length of time each contact had been known (durability) found significant differences with male owners knowing their contacts for an average of 12.69 years and female owners, 9.68 years ($t = 22.302$, df $= 281$, $p < 0.05$). Given the statistically significant differences found across the age and experience profile of our sample, these results might be expected. These findings are also supported by research which has found the network contacts of male entrepreneurs to be both older and to have been known for longer than those of female entrepreneurs (Cromie and Birley, 1992). When asked to describe the networks of each of the five contacts in their PCN (reach), analysis revealed only one statistically significant difference: more women (73 per cent) than men (62 per cent) described the aggregate networks of their contacts as 'large'. From a social capital perspective, it might be argued that as the durability of male owner's networks was significantly higher than that of women; male owners may have particular network advantages including more trusting relationships and greater reciprocity which may impact positively on their business.

To collect data about the contents of their PCNs owners were asked to identify the topics of their conversations with the five key members of their PCN. From the range of options given (finance, legal issues, staffing matters, loans/investments, premises, marketing, family), female owners were significantly more likely to discuss finance ($\chi^2 = 5.455$, df $= 1$, p < 0.05) and family ($\chi^2 = 5.711$, df $= 1$, p < 0.05) with their prime contact. Given that for the majority of women their prime contact was both male and a family member, most likely their domestic male partner, this finding is not surprising. What is questionable however is the extent to which this prime contact possessed the necessary know-how and contacts (social capital) and experience (human capital) to be able to offer useful advice on both family and finance. In view of the bimodal funding profile presented and the higher presence of business associates identified by male owners as their prime contact, these findings might be interpreted to suggest that male owners' prime contact may have been able to offer more useful financial advice.

It has been consistently argued that the 'ideal' network position for an entrepreneur is to be centrally embedded within a network of weak contacts (Aldrich, 1987; Granovetter, 1982). Most recently, Davidsson and Honig (2003) found strength of network tie to be a strong and consistent predictor for nascent entrepreneurs progressing successfully to business start-up. We explored the strength of owners' network ties in a number of different ways. Using a five-point Likert-type scale, statistically significant differences were found in response to whether owners would discuss personal matters within their PCN: more female than male owners stated that they would be more likely to do so, both with their prime contact and at an aggregate level, across their PCN (women mean = 3.73, men mean = 3.00,

$t = 3.882$, $p < 0.001$). Again, as female owners were more likely to identify a family member as their prime contact the former result is unsurprising. However the finding that women entrepreneurs were statistically more likely to discuss personal matters *across* their PCN may have implications for the type of social capital they can acquire from their networks and the value of such capital in supporting and financing their ventures. This is supported by Aldrich et al. (1989) who established that while the networks of male and female owners were similar in several respects, women's networks tended to be organized around spheres of work, family and social life. Significantly, these findings suggest that for many women business owners the context within which they established their businesses differed greatly from that of their male matched partners. Moreover these findings reveal the socially constructed nature of gender, highlighting women entrepreneur's role in the creation of a social structure which benefits men's experiences of entrepreneurship while disadvantaging those of women.

Networking Activity

Networking activity refers to the entrepreneur's frequency of interaction with people in their PCN and with other stakeholders. Research to date has generated mixed results regarding the impact of networking activity on entrepreneurial ventures (Aldrich et al., 1989; Cromie and Birley, 1992; Johannisson, 1988). Analysis of data relating to interactions with other stakeholders revealed two statistically significant differences. First, during the establishment of their firms, female owners were found to have spent more time networking than male owners. Secondly, significantly more female than male owners were found to be members of both mixed-sex business clubs (women 67 per cent, men 30 per cent) and other networking organizations (women 57 per cent, men 30 per cent). Interestingly when asked to identify sources which had helped their business, from the number of options offered (including a variety of business associations and clubs, previous customers, friends/family, bank, lawyer, accountant and others sources) only one statistically significant gender difference was found: despite their higher levels of networking activity and membership of a variety of professional and trade associations, women were significantly more likely to identify friends and family as having helped their business.

Considered collectively, findings regarding owners' social capital appear contradictory. They seem to suggest that women owners identified themselves as 'ideally' embedded within large, loosely connected networks. However, closer analyses of these networks reveals that women were statistically more likely to have more and stronger kinship ties within their network, which have been found to disadvantage nascent entrepreneurs

(Renzulli et al., 2000). Particular to finance, while women were statistically more likely to discuss finance with their prime contact, cross-tie analysis revealed this contact to typically be both male and a family contact, most likely their male, domestic partner. Given the bimodel funding profile found within this matched-pairs study, this questions the financial advice offered to women by their male prime contact. Findings regarding density and durability challenge Granovetter's (1982) strength of weak ties hypotheses suggesting that male owners may have benefited from being embedded within PCNs comprised of durable relationships with mainly friends and business associates.

Findings particular to networking activity add to the confusing profile of women entrepreneurs' social capital found in this study. Despite the time women entrepreneurs invested in networking prior to start-up, they identified friends and family as having helped their business rather than networking organizations. This questions why women entrepreneurs typically joined so many networking organizations. While previous studies have found no statistical differences in the networking activities of male and female owners, they have established that men display a greater propensity to network (Aldrich et al., 1989; Cromie and Birley, 1992; Johannisson, 1988). Our study did not find this. One explanation for this may be the currently large availability of business-owner networks within the UK. However, prior research suggests that men typically would have been more active in these. A more convincing explanation is offered by Bourdieu's (1986) notion of 'symbolic' capital, which has received scant attention within entrepreneurship literature. When asked if they experienced problems being 'taken seriously as a business person', significantly more women (30 per cent) than men (none) expressed that this was something they had encountered. Building on research which has established that within business service industries reputation (a form of symbolic capital) is a key success factor (Baines and Robson, 2001; Silversides, 2001), Bourdieu's (1986) description of perspective on capital suggests that female entrepreneurs recognized that their social capital commanded a lower value than that of male entrepreneurs and that they sought to compensate and legitimize their position as business owners by actively engaging in networks. Put simply, these findings might be interpreted as female business owners seeking to develop network relationships which would convert to valuable symbolic capital thereby legitimizing their activities as entrepreneurs. However, despite these efforts, their activities appear unable to compensate as women owners still identify friends and family as sources of business support and, specific to finance, their firms are established with significantly less finance than those of their matched male partners.

CONCLUSIONS

Bourdieu's (1986) perspective on capital suggests a complex and nuanced relationship between gender, entrepreneurial capital and finance. Applied to this study, this perspective suggests interplay between human and social capital which has implications for entrepreneurship including the possession and acquisition of start-up finance. The finding that male owners were significantly older suggests that age and experience are key components of human capital with implications for social capital. The greater industry experience of male owners suggests they had more time to develop and construct those networks most valuable for assisting the start-up of their firms. Support for this is offered by Bourdieu's (1986) notions of symbolic capital and convertibility of different forms of capital. Bourdieu identifies an interplay between different types of capital and reasons that each type of capital can be converted into other forms of capital. In particular he identifies a strong relationship between social and symbolic capital, suggesting that the more social capital an individual possesses, the more symbolic capital, for example reputation, they are likely to possess. It might be argued that the particular combination of human and social capital possessed by female owners converted to a relatively lesser amount of symbolic capital than their matched male partners and this may have impacted on their experiences of business ownership, including but not restricted to the financing of their firms.

A number of implications for entrepreneurs, future research and government policy can be identified. First, while extant research has sought to explore dimensions of entrepreneurial capital in isolation, it is recommended that entrepreneurs will benefit by recognizing the complex interplay between various forms of entrepreneurial capital. The importance of human capital, especially age and experience is highlighted, emphasizing the benefits to entrepreneurs of setting up in business once they have acquired relevant experience. While this recommendation is unsurprising, the explanation that with more experience, entrepreneurs have time to enhance their industry knowledge and critically, to acquire social and economic capital, provides a deeper insight into the importance of age and experience as key human capital variables for entrepreneurs.

The theoretical and methodological framework developed lays the foundation for further entrepreneurial capital research. In particular it is recommended that future research should seek to better understand the interplay between different types of entrepreneurial capital, gender and business ownership. Moreover, the adoption of a feminist perspective demonstrates the value of considering not *if* but *how* gender impacts on entrepreneurship.

With regard to policy, it is recommended that current UK enterprise policy which has identified women as a key target (HM Treasury/BERR, 2008), acknowledges the interrelationship and implications between social structure and entrepreneurship. This extends to accepting that as meanings of entrepreneurship and entrepreneurs are institutionalized in a historically male-dominated context, gender differences are likely to be interpreted and enacted in ways which benefit men and disadvantage women. For policy-makers the existence of gender differences per se is not problematic. Rather, there is a need to design and deliver enterprise policies which appreciate the differing experiences and contributions of women entrepreneurs. To achieve this, it is essential that policies recognize gender as a consequence of institutionalized social structure which influences the perceptions, attitudes and behaviours of all members of society, including women entrepreneurs. Applied to specific policies, this suggests that efforts, for example, to remove barriers such as childcare and domestic responsibilities, should realize that such duties may be institutionalized and taken for granted by members of society. In other words, it is possible that women entrepreneurs take these responsibilities for granted and, even, that they may not wish to be separated from what they understand to be their 'natural' responsibilities.

Finally, despite the richness of the data collected, limitations of the study include the relatively small sample size and limited industry and geographic coverage. The matching criteria used in this study (age of business, industry subsector, and location) were informed by prior literature on gender and entrepreneurial capital. The results presented demonstrate the importance of also controlling for age of entrepreneur. The differences between male and female entrepreneurs with regard to their network size, density, and industry experience are likely to be influenced by their age as well as their gender. By controlling for age of entrepreneur future studies will be able to more fully explore the nature of the interactions between gender, entrepreneurial capital and finance. Future research should use a larger sample size which can encompass a diversity of firms. Furthermore, it is expected that cross-national comparative studies will have the potential to yield insightful findings to contribute to growing knowledge and interest in entrepreneurial capital and gender.

ACKNOWLEDGEMENT

The research team are grateful for the financial support of the Economic and Social Research Council, UK. Award Reference No RES-000-23-0247.

REFERENCES

Ahl, H. (2002), *The Making of the Female Entrepreneur*, JIBS Dissertation Series No. 015, Jönköping: Jönköping International Business School.
Ahl, H. (2006), 'Why research on women entrepreneurs needs new directions', *Entrepreneurship, Theory and Practice*, **30**, (5), 595–621.
Aldrich, H. (1989), 'Networking among women entrepreneurs', in O. Hagen, C. Rivchum and D. Sexton (eds), *Women Owned Business*, New York: Praeger.
Aldrich, H., Reese, P.R. and Dubini, P. (1989), 'Women on verge of a breakthrough: networking among entrepreneurs in the United States and Italy', *Entrepreneurship and Regional Development*, **1**, 339–56.
Aldrich, H.E. (1987), 'The impact of social networks on business founding and profit: a longitudinal study', *Frontiers of Entrepreneurship Research*, Wellesley, MA: Babson College.
Baines, S. and Robson, L. (2001), 'Being self-employed or being enterprising? The case of creative work for the media industries', *Journal of Small Business and Enterprise Development*, **8** (4), 349–62.
Baron, R.A. and Markman, G.D. (2000), 'Beyond social capital: how social skills can enhance entrepreneurs' success', *Academy of Management Executive*, **14**, 1.
Baum, J.A. and Silverman, B.S. (2004), 'Picking winners or building them? Alliance, intellectual, and human capital as selection criteria in venture financing and performance of biotechnology startups', *Journal of Business Venturing*, **19** (3), 411–36.
Becker, G. (1964), *Human Capital*, Chicago, IL: University of Chicago Press.
Bird, B. and Brush, C. (2002), 'A gendered perspective on organizational creation', *Entrepreneurship Theory and Practice*, **26** (3), 41–65.
Boden, R.J. and Nucci, A.R. (2000) 'On the survival prospects of men's and women's new business ventures', *Journal of Business Venturing*, **15** (4), 347–62.
Bourdieu, P. (1977), *Outline of a Theory of Practice*, trans. R. Nice, Cambridge: Cambridge University Press.
Bourdieu, P. (1986), 'The forms of capital', in J. Richardson (ed.), *The Handbook of Theory and Research for the Sociology of Education*, New York: Greenwood Press.
Bourdieu, P. (1990), *The Logic of Practice*, trans. R. Nice, Cambridge: Polity, and Stanford, CA: Stanford University Press.
Bourdieu, P. and Wacquant, L. (1992), *An Invitation to Reflexive Sociology*, Cambridge: Polity Press.
Brush, C., Carter, N., Greene, P., Gatewood, E. and Hart, M. (2001), 'An investigation of women-led firms and venture capital investment', report prepared for the US Small Business Administration Office of Advocacy and the National Women's Business Council.
Brush, C., Carter, N., Greene, P., Hart, M. and Gatewood, E. (2002), 'The role of social capital and gender in linking financial suppliers and entrepreneurial firms: a framework for future research', *Venture Capital*, **4** (4), 305–23.
Brush, C.G. (1992), 'Research on women business owners: past trends, a new perspective and future directions', *Entrepreneurship Theory and Practice*, **17** (4), 5–30.
Buttner, E.H. and Rosen, B. (1989), 'Funding new business ventures: are decision-

makers biased against women entrepreneurs?', *Journal of Business Venturing*, **4**, 249–61.

Carter, N., Brush, C.B., Greene, P.G., Gatewood, E. and Hart, M. (2003), 'Women entrepreneurs who break through to equity financing: the influence of human, social and financial capital', *Venture Capital*, **5** (1), 1–28.

Carter, N., Williams, M. and Reynolds, P. (1997), 'Discontinuance among new firms in retail: the influence of initial resources, strategy and gender', *Journal of Business Venturing*, **12** (2), 125–45.

Carter, S. and Rosa, P. (1998), 'The financing of male- and female-owned businesses', *Entrepreneurship and Regional Development*, **10**, 225–41.

Carter, S., Anderson, S. and Shaw, E. (2001), 'Women's business ownership: a review of the academic, popular and internet literature', report to the Small Business Service, RR002/01.

Carter, S., Shaw, E., Lam, W. and Wilson, E. (2007), 'Gender, entrepreneurship and bank lending', *Entrepreneurship, Theory and Practice*, May, 427–44.

Casson, M., and Giusta, M.D. (2007), 'Entrepreneurship and social capital: analysing the impact of social networks on entrepreneurial activity from a rational action perspective', *International Small Business Journal*, **25** (3), 220–44.

Coleman, J. (1988), 'Social capital in the creation of human capital', *American Journal of Sociology*, **94**, S95–S121.

Coleman, S. (2000), 'Access to capital and terms of credit: a comparison of men- and women-owned small businesses', *Journal of Small Business Management*, **38** (3), 37–52.

Cooper, A.C., Dunkelberg, W.C. and Woo, C.Y. (1988), 'Survival and failure: a longitudinal study', *Frontiers of Entrepreneurship Research*, Wellesley, MA: Babson College, pp. 225–37.

Cooper, A.C., Gimmeno-Gascon, F.J. and Woo, C.Y. (1994), 'Initial human and financial capital as predictors of new venture performance', *Journal of Business Venturing*, **9**, 371–95.

Cope, J., Jack, S. and Rose, M.B. (2007), 'Social capital and entrepreneurship: an introduction', *International Small Business Journal*, **25** (3), 213–19.

Cromie, S. and Birley, S. (1992), 'Networking by female business owners in Northern Ireland', *Journal of Business Venturing*, **7**, 237–51.

Davidsson, P. and Honig, B. (2003), 'The role of social and human capital among nascent entrepreneurs', *Journal of Business Venturing*, **18**, 301–31.

De Carolis, D.M. and P. Saparito (2006), 'Social capital, cognition, and entrepreneurial opportunities: a theoretical framework', *Entrepreneurship Theory and Practice*, **30** (1), 41–56.

De Clercq, D. and Sapienza, H.J. (2006), 'Effects of relational capital and commitment on venture capitalists', perceptions of portfolio company performance', *Journal of Business Venturing*, **21** (3), 326–47.

Erikson, T. (2002), 'Entrepreneurial capital: the emerging venture's most important asset and competitive advantage', *Journal of Business Venturing*, **17** (3), 275–90.

Fabowale, L., Orser, B. and Riding, A. (1995), 'Gender, structural factors, and credit terms between Canadian small businesses and financial institutions', *Entrepreneurship: Theory and Practice*, Summer, 41–65.

Fay, M. and Williams, L. (1993), 'Gender bias and the availability of business loans', *Journal of Business Venturing*, **8** (4), 363–76.

Firkin, P. (2003), 'Entrepreneurial capital', in A. De Bruin and A.A. Dupuis (eds),

Entrepreneurship: New Perspectives in a Global Age, Aldershot: Ashgate, pp. 57–75.

Giddens, A. (ed.) (2001), *The Global Third Way Debate*, Oxford: Polity.

Gorton, M. (2000), 'Overcoming the structure-agency divide in small business research', *International Journal of Entrepreneurial Behaviour and Research*, **6** (5), 276–92.

Granovetter, M.S. (1973), 'The strength of weak ties', *American Journal of Sociology*, **78** (6), 1361–81.

Granovetter, M.S. (1982), 'The strength of weak ties: a network theory revisited', in P.V. Mardsen and V. Lin (eds), *Social Structure and Network Analysis*, London: Sage, pp. 105–30.

Granovetter, M.S. (1985), 'Economic action and social structure: the problem of embeddedness', *American Journal of Sociology*, November, 55–81.

Greene, P., Brush, C., Hart, M. and Saparito, P. (1999), 'An exploration of the venture capital industry: is gender an issue?', in P.D. Reynolds, W. Bygrave, S. Manigart, C. Mason, G.D. Meyer, H. Sapienza and K.G. Shaver (eds), *Frontiers of Entrepreneurship Research*, Wellesley, MA.: Babson College.

Haber, S. and Reichel, A. (2007), 'The cumulative nature of the entrepreneurial process: the contribution of human capital, planning and environment resources to small venture performance', *Journal of Business Venturing*, **22** (1), 119–45.

Haines, G.H., Orser, B.J. and Riding, A.L. (1999), 'Myths and realities: an empirical study of banks and the gender of small business clients', *Canadian Journal of Administrative Sciences*, **16** (4), 291–307.

HM Treasury/BERR, (2008), *Enterprise: Unlocking the UK's Talent*, London: HMSO.

Johannisson, B. (1988), 'Business formation: a network approach', *Scandinavian Journal of Management*, **4** (3/4), 83–99.

Manigart, S., Collewaert, V., Wright, M., Pruthi, S., Lockett A. and Bruining, C. (2007), 'Human capital and the internationalisation of venture capital firms', *International Entrepreneurship and Management Journal*, **3** (1), 109–25.

Marlow, S. (2002), 'Women and self-employment: a part of or apart from theoretical construct?', *International Journal of Entrepreneurship and Innovation*, **3** (2), 83–91.

Mirchandani, K. (1999), 'Feminist insight on gendered work: new directions in research on women and entrepreneurship', *Gender, Work and Organization*, **6** (4), 224–35.

Mitchell, J.C. (1969), 'The concept and use of social networks', in J.C. Mitchell (ed.), *Social Networks in Urban Situations*, Manchester: University of Manchester Press.

Morris, M. (1998), *Entrepreneurial Intensity: Sustainable Advantages for Individuals, Organisations, and Societies*, Westport, CT: Quorum Books.

Oakley, A. (1982), 'The politics of "sex-differences" research', in M. Evans (ed.), *The Woman Question: Readings on the Subordination of women*, London: Fontana, pp. 91–4.

Ogbor, J.O. (2000), 'Mythicising and reification in entrepreneurial discourse: ideology-critique of entrepreneurial studies', *Journal of Management Studies*, **37** (5), 605–35.

Orser, B.J. and Foster, M.K. (1994), 'Lending practices and Canadian women in micro-based businesses', *Women in Management Review*, **9** (5), 11–19.

Read, L. (1998), *The Financing of Small Business: A Comparative Study of Male and Female Business Owners*, London: Routledge.

Renzulli, L. Aldrich, H. and Moody, J. (2000), 'Family matters: gender, networks, and entrepreneurial outcomes', *Social Forces*, **79** (2), 523–47.

Shaw, E., Lam, W. and Carter, S. (2008), 'The role of entrepreneurial capital in building service reputation', *Service Industries Journal*, **28** (7), 1–19.

Silversides, G. (2001), 'Networking and identity: the role of networking in the public image of professional service firms', *Journal of Small Business and Enterprise Development*, **8** (2), 174–84.

Stevenson, L. (1986), 'Against all odds: the entrepreneurship of women', *Journal of Small Business Management*, **24**, 30–36.

Verheul, I. and Thurik, R. (2000), 'Start-up capital: differences between male and female entrepreneurs. Does gender matter?', *EIM Research Report 9910/E*, Rotterdam: Erasmus University.

Watkins, J. and Watkins, D. (1984), 'The female entrepreneur: background and determinants of business choice – some British data', *International Small Business Journal*, **2** (4), 21–31.

Watson, J. and Newby, R. (2005), 'Biological sex, stereotypical sex-roles, and SME owner characteristics', *International Journal of Entrepreneurial Behaviour and Research*, **11** (2), 129–43.

11. Growing a high-tech business: gender, perceptions and experiences in Northern Ireland

Frances M. Hill, Claire M. Leitch and Richard T. Harrison

INTRODUCTION

Sexton (1997: 407) has observed that 'growth is the very essence of entrepreneurship'; but growth may be more a matter of attitude and preference than of resources and capabilities (Davidsson, 1989) and will not occur unless the owner/manager actually desires it. The relationship between the sex of business owners and the growth of their businesses has been discussed in some detail (Chaganti and Parasuraman, 1996; Ehlers and Main, 1998; Loscocco et al., 1991). However, such discussion has been problematic for a number of reasons, not least because it has tended to treat women, and men, as homogeneous groups, leading to generalized conclusions about their perceptions, attitudes and behaviours. One such 'stylised fact' (Orser et al., 2005) is that women owned/led firms are less likely to seek growth than those owned/led by their male counterparts, which, among other things, has an impact on business size and hence the need for external finance. Yet, women business owners are not a homogeneous group and it is essential that research is designed to capture their heterogeneity as well as their context in terms of time and space (Ahl, 2004; Carter and Brush, 2004; Harrison and Mason, 2007). Moreover, when an attempt is made to control for variables such as the nature of businesses and the individual characteristics of business owners, such generalized conclusions may not be supported (Kalleberg and Leicht, 1991). The persistent preoccupation in the literature that men and women should be different, in terms of entrepreneurial behaviour, precludes discussion of their similarities and of the fact that within-sex variation may be larger than between-sex variation (Ahl, 2004: 172). Indeed, where differences are found in comparative studies of women and men they are usually small (Harrison and Mason, 2007: 464) but the small size differential is often overshadowed in discussion by the fact that the difference exists at all (Epstein, 1988).

The terms 'sex' and 'gender' have been widely conflated in the entrepreneurship literature (Ahl, 2006) and researchers must be careful to draw a distinction between analysis at the level of sex (biological differences between males and females) and analysis at the level of gender, which 'refers to the associations, stereotypes and social patterns that a culture constructs on the basis of actual or perceived differences between men and women' (Nelson, 2008: 456). Within US and European cultures, there is a tendency for certain characteristics to be associated with either masculinity or femininity. Differentiation between sex and gender has informed the design of the research presented in this chapter and the analysis and interpretation of the data. As the aim of the study was to investigate the perceptions and experiences of women and men owner/managers engaged in growing high-technology businesses, we were concerned to 'give voice' to both groups while not privileging one group over the other or attributing particular traits, qualities or characteristics to either. Thus, individuals were assigned to categories on the basis of their physical characteristics and not on the assumption of any specific qualities, traits, purposes and/ or common experiences (Ahl, 2004: 35). Moreover we sought to focus on similarities between the two groups while not ignoring any emergent differences (Ahl, 2004).

This chapter reports on the third phase of an investigation involving a group of women and men owner/managers of high-technology businesses located in Northern Ireland (Hill et al., 2006; Leitch et al., 2006). One aim was to explore their growth aspirations and achievements. Growth is an important issue in the regional context because although many businesses may want to grow, some appear not to be achieving growth or are not growing fast enough to make the contribution to regional productivity levels of which they are capable (Northern Ireland DETI, 2007). Consequently, the research was designed to examine a number of issues relating to business growth, including the characteristics of the businesses and the characteristics of the business owner/managers – especially their growth aspirations and achievements, sex, stocks of human and social capital and their perceptions of the availability and their use of external finance for the purposes of business growth.

METHODOLOGY

Following Ahl (2004), the aim of this research was to compare like with like and to investigate similarities between women and men business owner/managers' growth achievements and aspirations, while acknowledging any differences that might become apparent. A purposive sample (Bryman, 2008; Saunders et al., 2007) of 10 women and 11 men business owner/managers was selected from a database maintained by the regional development agency, Invest Northern Ireland. Women owned/led businesses were defined as those in which one or more of the principal owners or shareholders were women; they had dominant control over the business and participated in its day-to-day operations; and the business was a going concern (Hill et al., 2006). Further, we oriented our sample towards 'gender atypical businesses' (Blake and Hanson, 2005), that is, women owned/led businesses in male-dominated sectors such as construction, engineering and high technology, or with (assumed) male-pattern behaviours such as growth-orientation and exporting. When drawing the sample of men similar criteria were employed, namely, that they were a principal owner or shareholder, had control and actively participated in the day-to-day running of the business. When controls on sample selection are employed, as here, context impacts upon men's and women's businesses to the same extent. Data were collected via semi-structured interviews which, in all but one case, were taped and transcribed.

In Northern Ireland entrepreneurial activity peaks in the 35 to 44 age group (Hart, 2007) which is reflected in the characteristics of our sample (see Table 11.1). Both the women and men in the sample have considerable human and social capital. This derives from their high levels of educational attainment, including professional qualifications, prior employment experience and membership of formal and informal networks.

In this respect the women in the sample are atypical and similar to the 'new modern entrepreneur' (Marlow and Patton, 2005). Therefore, neither their personal profiles nor those of their businesses conform to stereotypes articulated in the literature, for example, that women's ventures tend to be service-oriented and 'cheaper' to finance than those of their male counterparts (Heilbrunn, 2005).

CHARACTERISTICS OF THE BUSINESSES

All the businesses in the sample were selling to other businesses rather than to individual consumers. As can be seen from Table 11.2, the majority were fairly young, that is, less than 15 years old. With regard to the women owned/led businesses, Read (1998) notes that age is an important structural difference between men- and women-owned businesses and that the latter are generally younger, as was the case in this research. This is not surprising in Northern Ireland given the low level of new venture creation

Table 11.1   Characteristics of business owners

Characteristics of business owners	Frequencies	Frequencies
	Women (n = 10)	Men (n = 11)
Role in firm		
MD/CEO	8	6
Founder/partner	0	4
Other	2*	1*
	(*One company secretary and financial director; one general manager)	(*Financial director)
Age		
25–34	0	2
35–44	8	6
45–54	2	3
Highest level of educational attainment		
GCSE	1	1
A-level	1	0
HNC/HND	1	1
Degree	6	5
Postgraduate	0	3
Lack of detail	1	1
Professional qualification		
Yes	5	7
No	4	4
Lack of detail	1	0
Prior employment experience	All of the participants, except one, had had a range of employment experience, mostly at a senior/professional level before becoming a business owner. The exception had had no experience other than working in the family business, founded by her father	All of the participants, except one, had had prior employment experience, though this varied in nature and length. One individual started his business immediately upon leaving university
Ownership of other businesses		
Yes	3	2
No	7	9

among women when compared both to the rest of the UK and international standards (Hart, 2007).

Of the businesses owned/led by women, four were actually owned by husband and wife teams. However, there were no such teams among

Table 11.2   Characteristics of businesses

Characteristics of firms	Frequencies	Frequencies
	Women	Men
Age of firm		
<1 year	1*	0
1–5 years	4	2
6–10 years	1	5
11–15 years	4	2
>15 years	1*	2
	*In one case an old established firm had just been sold, and the owners had started up a new firm, so the participant's experiences relate to both	
Sector		
IT/software	6	6
Construction	2*	0
Media	1	2
Waste management	1	0
Other	1*	3
	*An old established construction firm had just been sold, and the owners had started a new services firm	
Ownership		
Limited company – multiple shareholders	6	10
Limited company – sole shareowner	1	0
Limited partnership	3	0
Partnership	0	1
Number of employees (full- and part-time)		
1–5	3	1
6–10	1	3
11–20	4	2
21–30	2	2
31–40	0	1
41–50	0	0
51–60	0	1
>60	0	1*
		*This company employed approx 180

Table 11.2   (continued)

Turnover		
<£100k	1	0
£100k–£500k	4	2
£501k–£1 million	3	2
>£1–£3 million	1	5
> £3 million	1	1
Not given	0	1

the men. Further, in general, the women tended to have lower owner-ship stakes in their businesses than did the men. Three of the women had been brought into established companies, one as chief executive officer (CEO) and the other two as managing director (MD), specifically for their technical and managerial expertise; two of these individuals had the lowest shareholdings in the sample. One other woman had gone into joint partnership with a male colleague having bought the intellectual property rights of their former employing organization, which had gone into receiv-ership. All but three of the men held at least 50 per cent of their companies' shares. In relation to growth, the extent of an owner/manager's stake in a business may be significant, as the greater their stake, the more they stand to gain from its growth.

FINDINGS AND DISCUSSION

The formation and growth of businesses is directly related to owner/managers' abilities to access an uninterrupted supply of critical resources, including finance, human and social capital (Cowling and Harding, 2005; Davidsson, 1989; Manolova et al., 2006; Uzzi, 1999). Thus, the report of findings and the discussion in the section below are structured around the themes of growth, external finance and network participation, which affords owner/managers access to resources not readily accessible via market mechanisms (Teece et al., 1987).

Growth

In this study we focus on growth as a change in amount, namely increases in numbers employed and turnover (Davidsson et al., 2004), rather than as a process of business development (Penrose, 1959). All the businesses in the sample are small, both in terms of numbers employed and turnover (Table 11.2). Unsurprisingly, the youngest firms were smallest in sales

Table 11.3   Growth – actual and anticipated

Growth – actual and anticipated	Women	Men
Actual growth – employees (over previous 3 years)		
Yes	5	9
Static	0	1
Decline	1	1
N/A	3	0
Not sure	1	0
Actual growth – turnover (over previous 3 years)		
Yes	5	10
Static	0	0
Decline	1	0
N/A	3	1
Not available	1	0
Planning for further growth (next 3 years) – employees		
Yes	10	9
No	0	1
Unsure	0	1
Planning for further growth (next 3 years) – turnover		
Yes	9	10
No	0	0
Unsure	1	1
Exporting*		
Yes	4	5
No	6	6
*Defined as selling outside the UK and the island of Ireland		
Exporting**		
Yes	7	9
No	3*	2
**Selling to Gt Britain and/or Republic of Ireland	*One of these exports outside UK and the island of Ireland	

terms (less than or equal to £500 000), apart from one woman owned/led business which had a turnover of £4.5 million. This business, which develops electronic voting software, had benefited from a recent local election. In general, the older ventures (predominantly men owned/led) had the highest sales levels. Although the growth of all the companies had been slow, in the previous three years the majority of businesses over three years old had reportedly achieved growth in both sales and numbers employed (see Table 11.3).

Further, the vast majority of respondents exhibited an aspiration to grow, forecasting growth in both turnover and numbers employed over the coming three years. However, three of the women respondents stated that they perceived their companies to be at a crossroads in their development and were in the process of having to decide what type of growth strategy to adopt, that is, whether to grow organically or seek external financing for more rapid and significant growth. This crossroads is clearly articulated by two female owners below:

> It depends – the business is at a crossroad.
> 　　　　　　(Female owner and MD of a specialized engineering company)

> This depends on the growth strategy adopted by the company. It is a crucial time for the company. If we adopt a fairly aggressive growth strategy and raise money it will raise the company's profile and we will take on up to ten [staff]. If we go for organic growth, which is more likely at the moment, and do not take finance until the end of 2006 and generate revenue of between £2 and 2.5 million, it is likely we will hire three more sales people and one or two consultants.
> 　　　　　　(Female owner and CEO of a specialized software company)

A fourth woman business owner/manager reported prior experience of a company failure which had led her to desire control over the existing business and to be reluctant to seek finance from banks. Thus, her strategy was to grow the business organically. By way of contrast, another woman stated that, from the outset, she and her partner had been following an aggressive growth strategy and had vigorously pursued external funding. Indeed, she believed that she was the only woman in Northern Ireland to have received funding from venture capitalists. Another respondent indicated that she was currently going through a business merger, which she forecast would enable the company to increase both numbers employed and turnover.

Given the small scale of the local market, firms seeking growth will need to develop markets further afield, especially if they are at the leading edge of technology. Despite this, less than half the sample, including both women and men owned/led businesses, were exporting outside the British Isles, while four were doing business solely in Northern Ireland (see Table 11.3). This has policy implications for the economic development agency, as all but one of these were client companies in receipt of support. Part of its remit is 'to assist new and existing businesses to compete internationally . . . and to achieve sustainable growth in the global marketplace' (Invest Northern Ireland, 2008). Nevertheless, there is a prevailing perception among small companies that selling anywhere outside Northern Ireland (including to the Republic of Ireland and Great Britain) amounts to exporting, a notion which may serve to constrain both aspirations and business growth. On the other hand, Invest NI, while encouraging exporting, needs to resist the temptation to press small companies into doing this before they are ready. 'Local agencies need to be careful not to push SMEs down the exporting road too early – such companies need to get it right at home first' (quote from a female founder and MD of an information and communication technology (ICT)-supported virtual services company). Another respondent cautioned that, while it is easy to export to Great Britain, it is much harder to export worldwide, and believed, moreover, that neither she nor anyone else in her company had the skills to do that yet. This wariness was shared by six other women, all of whom perceived barriers to engaging in export activity, which included lack of language skills, unavailability of accurate and up-to-date market research, cost and a general lack of knowledge and understanding of the process. What this suggests is, that even in the high-technology arena, there is little evidence of a 'born global' mindset (Oviatt and McDougall, 1994, 1995), or even that there is progress beyond the traditional stage models of export development (Johanson and Vahlne, 1977, 1990).

In contrast, the men respondents expressed fewer concerns about exporting and demonstrated an awareness that over-reliance on the Northern Ireland market could limit the development and growth of their businesses. Indeed, seven men had already taken steps to enable their companies to trade outside the region, such as partnering with firms in Great Britain, the Republic of Ireland and Europe, as well as establishing field support in target export countries. One possible explanation for these differences is that the businesses in the sample owned by men were somewhat older than those of the women, and therefore the men may have acquired more knowledge, experience and confidence as business owner/managers than the women. However, it may also reflect 'a tendency for women to focus on the negative. Where a man will look at a job description and say, "I can do most of that", a woman is more likely to focus on the two things she can't do, so she won't apply' (London Times, 2008).

This is reflected in the finding that more of the men respondents, in discussing the performance and achievements of their businesses, expressed confidence about everything they had accomplished and attributed their companies' growth to their own accomplishments and efforts:

> The company has been going for five years and ranks in the top three as a good creative design agency in Northern Ireland.
>
> (Male joint partner of a graphic design company)

The company is good at what it does, the service is excellent value for money
and the company is local.

> (Male MD of a packaging compliance company)

Only two of the women business owners made similar attributions:

> The success of the business since its establishment, it started from nothing.
> (Female founder and MD of an ICT-supported services company)

> Growth from start-up and a leading edge technology product.
> (Female MD of a software company)

External Finance

The majority of the respondents had sought external finance for the start-
up or growth of their businesses, with slightly more women than men
seeking such funding (see Table 11.4).

Given the lack of venture capital and angel finance available in Northern
Ireland at the time the research was carried out (Hill et al, 2006; Leitch et
al., 2006), banks were a popular source of funding; indeed, only two of
the respondents, one woman and one man, had been proactive in gaining
finance from a range of sources. Where men had sought external finance,
they claimed to have received more or less what they needed on fairly
favourable terms and, thus, their perceptions of raising finance tended to
be quite positive:

> The banking needs of entrepreneurs are probably met in Northern Ireland,
> except the banks are inherently conservative – especially at the start-up phase
> of the business, after that it is easier.
> (Male founder and MD of a packaging compliance company)

> The problem isn't actually finance but lack of customers in Northern Ireland.
> Companies need help in developing ideas which is difficult with a small cus-
> tomer base.
> (Male MD of a software company)

> There are loads of opportunities if you have the right business plan.
> (Male co-founder and partner of an e-business solutions company)

On the other hand, while more women than men were dissatisfied with
the amount of funding they received, they were less so with respect to the
terms surrounding the deals negotiated, although the former appears to
have had a negative impact on their perceptions of the availability of business finance in the region:

Table 11.4   External funding

External finance – yes	For start-up	For growth	Other
Women = 9	4	4*	2
		*One individual has sought external finance for start-up and growth	
	Enterprise loan Leasing arrangements Banks* Invest NI* INTERREG* Private US funding*	Business angels* Institutional investors* VCs* Small Firms' Loan Guarantee Scheme* Universities* Invest NI	Leasing company Banks
	*One individual has raised funds from all these sources	*One individual has raised funds from all these sources	
Men = 8	3	3**	3
	Banks VCs Prince's Trust Econ. Development Agency	Private equity* VCs* Bank* Business angels* Small Firms' Loan Guarantee Scheme *One individual has raised funds from all these sources **One individual has sought external finance for start-up and growth	Banks Invest NI

There is not really an entrepreneurial culture in Northern Ireland, there is a public sector focus . . . Some of the banks are too risk averse and need to be more supportive of small businesses.

(Female founder and MD of an ICT-supported virtual services company)

Most people involved in financing are not equipped to do so. They do not understand the volatilities of markets, risk etc.

(Female MD of a software company)

More men than women expressed reservations about seeking external finance and for a number of reasons, including not wanting to release equity, a desire to be self-sufficient, being risk averse and not wanting to incur large amounts of debt, thus the growth of their businesses was being financed through retained earnings, informal sources of funding and/or bootstrapping activities:

> The company could perhaps have grown more quickly by adopting a less cautious approach; however the conservative approach has probably been the best as it is less risky.
>
> (Male founder and financial director of an IT company)

> On reflection, we made the right decision [that is, not seeking external finance]. I know a lot of businesses that have lots of borrowing. However this is very risky, it only takes one or two customers to default and the business goes under.
>
> (Male joint partner of a graphic design company)

Even though external funding might have been available to them, many respondents in the sample have chosen to rely on their own resources. However, one of the downsides of financing a business through retained earnings, informal sources of funding and/or bootstrapping is that growth is likely to be relatively slow, as this study has found.

Informal and Formal Network Participation

The ability to network effectively is a key entrepreneurial competency because, especially for small firms, networks provide access to resources or complementary assets (Teece et al., 1987) not readily accessible via market mechanisms. Limited network access produces multiple disadvantages, including restricted access to knowledge and finance (Ibarra, 1993). 'Social networks are crucial assets for business owners struggling to make a place for themselves in competitive markets. Networking allows them to enlarge their span of action, save time and gain access to resources and opportunities otherwise unavailable' (Aldrich et al., 1997: 2).

Network participation can be an important source of both social and human capital for business owners (Ulrich, 1998). In relation to operating and growing a small business, Snell and Dean (1992) have observed that a business owner/manager's human capital should include skills and knowledge that assist in running the business successfully and impart to him or her the ability to take measures necessary to achieve growth (Wiklund and Shepherd, 2003). In this context specific human capital would comprise skills, knowledge and experience derived, for example, from prior new venture creation, managerial responsibility and/or employment in a rapidly growing organization (Birley and Westhead, 1994; Macrae, 1992; van de Ven et al., 1984).

Social capital emanates from participation in entrepreneurial networks, which assist with goal attainment and are, therefore, potentially the most valuable (Burt, 1992; Greve and Salaff, 2003; Lin, 1999) as they can yield support from knowledgeable others and peer learning (Iles and Preece, 2006). Also, managers with more social capital get higher returns to their human capital as the former can facilitate them in identifying and developing more rewarding opportunities (Burt, 1998).

Hite and Hesterly (2001: 276) observe that as firms progress from start-up, they will need new and additional resources to support continued growth, which should be reflected in changes in business owners' networks from 'identity-based' to more 'calculative' ones. The former they define as 'egocentric networks that have a high proportion of ties where some type of personal or social identification with the other actors motivates or influences economic actions' (ibid.: 278). Calculative networks are those in which an actor's ties are mainly based on expected economic benefits (Williamson, 1993). For business owners seeking growth, such networks should be strategic in nature, that is, large in size and offering greater opportunities for obtaining both intangible information and tangible resources. Large networks also comprise numerous ties, both strong and weak and, thus, business owners are more likely to acquire information that differs from their existing world view and mental models (Butler and Hansen, 2007; Granovetter, 1973). In smaller networks comprising strong ties, members are likely to obtain information that they already possess, thereby confirming their own views and perspectives. Homophily, as McPherson et al. (2001: 415) note, can limit an individual's social world thereby restricting the nature of the information they receive, the attitudes they form and interactions they experience.

Respondents in this study were asked about their participation in both formal and informal networks. The majority participated in formal networks and perceived a variety of benefits deriving from this. However, it is interesting to note that the men reported many more perceived benefits than the women. Those reported by the women included: peer support, business referrals and having access to knowledge and a sounding board. In addition, men mentioned learning, meeting people with similar outlooks as well as those who are different, civic and community responsibility. One of the men explained that, due to the highly specialized nature of the sector in which his business is located (film and media), he was forced to network outside Northern Ireland and largely on an informal basis.

Regarding participation in informal networks, our survey revealed that more men were involved in these than women. For the men the perceived benefits of belonging to informal networks were similar to those emanating from membership of formal ones. However, one of the women made a clear distinction between the two, remarking that,

> formal networking is about getting business and sales. Informal networking is about getting support and both are equally important.
> (Female founder and MD of an ICT-supported virtual services business)

Another woman shared this view but added that,

> all have different benefits. Sector-specific networks are very useful but also working outside the sector provides a different perspective . . . meeting people within the sector and in the business community is very useful.
> (Female owner and MD of a software company)

The majority of both women and men in the sample participated in networks, with most participating in more than one and perceiving this activity as beneficial. However, more men than women belonged to informal networks, which may suggest that the men were willing and/or able to devote more time to networking. One possible reason for this, as noted by Aldrich et al (1989: 339), is that the literature on marriage and the family suggests that women are more likely than men to have domestic responsibilities. If men have more time to devote to networking this might permit them to be more strategic in their networking and be better placed to develop calculative networks (Hite and Hesterly, 2001). As one of the men (owner of an information technology company) noted, although working hard at networking can reap benefits, some time can also be wasted, which again underlines the importance of developing calculative networks. The two women and one man who did not participate in networks cited lack of time and lack of perceived relevance as reasons.

CONCLUSIONS

Ahl (2004: 106) identifies a common thread in the gender and entrepreneurship literature, namely, disquiet that there are fewer than expected systematic gender-based differences emerging from research. Our investigation has confirmed that when one controls for relevant variables, and attempts to compare like with like, more similarities than differences between men and women business owners emerge (Harrison and Mason, 2007).

In relation to their growth aspirations and achievements specifically, there are many similarities between the women and men in the sample. This may be attributed in part to the fact that all the business owner/

managers are atypical for a number of reasons. First, they have high levels of human and social capital; second, their businesses are high-tech in nature and tend to have growth potential; third, they all have growth aspirations and have already achieved varying degrees of business growth. As Davidsson (1989) has noted, in general, a lack of growth and interest in growth applies to most small firms, irrespective of the sex of the owners. One limitation of the study is that we defined growth purely in terms of amount, numbers employed and turnover. If we had included the process of business development as well, more differences between the women and men may have been detected.

A few between-sex differences did emerge from the data. For example, in relation to exporting, more men than women seemed to have been proactive in this respect, with some women expressing a lack of confidence, especially regarding exporting beyond the British Isles. Although the men's exporting proactivity may relate to the fact that their businesses tended to be longer established than those of the women and so they had acquired more knowledge and experience, it may relate also to their confidence in their businesses which in most cases was high, and higher than that expressed by the women. There may be a tendency for women to be less confident about their capabilities and achievements, which in some cases may also act as a constraint on business growth. Such diffidence can, of course, be reduced by participation in relevant networks, important sources of both social and human capital, especially strategic, calculative ones that are large in size and comprise both strong and weak ties. Such networks can yield information and knowledge, exposure to differing perspectives, in some cases access to mentors and both tangible and intangible support. The women in the sample were active networkers, but they identified fewer benefits emanating from this activity and were less likely to belong to informal networks than men, leading one to suspect that perhaps they were not being sufficiently strategic or calculative in their approaches. Networking involves investments in time and other resources and, thus, it is important that business owner/managers receive an adequate return on such investments, especially in periods of economic and financial difficulty.

More men than women expressed reservations about seeking external finance and for a number of reasons, one of which was risk aversion. Furthermore, some conceded that the decision to finance growth from retained earnings, informal sources and/or bootstrapping had meant that the growth achieved was slower than it might otherwise have been. While this attitude to external funding may not be in the best interests of regional economic development, nevertheless it might be appropriate to the individual owner/manager in terms of their personal and family circumstances. Although the women showed a greater propensity to fund growth from external, formal sources, a number were dissatisfied with the amounts of funding they had received which appeared, rightly or wrongly, to have had a negative impact on their perceptions of the availability of business finance in the region. This is undesirable not least because it can lead to what Kon and Storey (2003) refer to as the 'discouraged borrower', that is, a creditworthy individual who does not apply for finance because they believe they will be rejected. While such a perception (or misperception) is quite widespread in the UK (see Allinson et al., 2006: 49), it is not helpful as far as financing business growth is concerned.

While we did not set out to undertake a gendered analysis of men and women business owners' perceptions and experiences of growing their businesses, there are apparent examples of what Ahl (2004) terms 'femaleness' emerging from the women business owners' responses, that is, attitudes and behaviours that reflect socially constructed expectations of women. These include wariness concerning exporting, which may relate to women focusing on what they cannot do rather than on what they can; women not highlighting their accomplishments as much as they should; and women not being sufficiently instrumental in their network participation. This is scarcely surprising given that, as Bruni et al. (2005: 11) note, gender is a social practice enacted by women and men that shapes their actions and their discourse. Moreover, to paraphrase Nelson (2008: 457), there is a prevailing socially constructed assumption that masculine business ownership is associated with masculine superiority and is, therefore, 'good business ownership'; by definition, anything other is inferior (Fine, 1994; Schwalbe et al., 2000), which may have implications for women's perceptions of their own capabilities and achievements. We take the view that such an assumption is inappropriate because business ownership is a multifaceted construct that is enacted in many different contexts and, thus, there can be no 'one best way' of doing it. Instead of dualist analyses, which concentrate on differences rather than similarities, we propose that a more fruitful research strategy would be to adopt inclusive perspectives focusing both on diversity and complementarity.

REFERENCES

Ahl, H. (2004), *The Scientific Reproduction of Gender Inequality*, Copenhagen: Copenhagen Business School.
Ahl, H. (2006), 'Why research on women entrepreneurs needs new directions', *Entrepreneurship Theory and Practice*, **30** (5), 595–621.
Aldrich, H.E., Elam, A.B. and Reece, P.R. (1997), 'Strong ties, weak ties and

strangers: do women owners differ from men in their use of networking to obtain assistance?', in S. Birley and I.C. MacMillan (eds), *Entrepreneurship in a Global Context*, London: Routledge.

Aldrich, H.E., Reese, P.R. and Dubini, P. (1989), 'Women on the verge of a breakthrough: networking among entrepreneurs in the United States and Italy', *Entrepreneurship and Regional Development*, **1**, 339–56.

Allinson, G., Braidford, P., Houston, M. and Stone, I. (2006), 'Myths surrounding growing a business: a focus group based study on behalf of the Small Business Service', Durham Business School Report.

Birley, S. and Westhead, P. (1994), 'A comparison of new businesses established by "novice" and "habitual" founders in Great Britain', *International Small Business Journal*, **12** (1), 38–60.

Blake, M.K. and Hanson, S. (2005), 'Rethinking innovation: context and gender', *Environment and Planning A*, **37**, 681–701.

Bruni, A., Gherardi, S. and Poggio, B. (2005), *Gender and Entrepreneurship: An Ethnographical Approach*, Abingdon: Routledge.

Bryman, A. (2008), *Social Research Methods*, 3rd edn, Oxford: Oxford University Press.

Burt, R.S. (1992), *Structural Holes: The Social Structure of Competition*, Cambridge, MA: Harvard University Press.

Burt, R.S. (1998), 'The gender of social capital', *Rationality and Society*, **10** (1), 5–46.

Butler, J.E. and Hansen, G.S. (2007), 'Network evolution, entrepreneurial success and regional development', *Entrepreneurship and Regional Development*, **3**, 1–16.

Carter, N.M. and Brush, C.G. (2004), 'Gender', in W.B. Gartner, K.G. Shaver, N.M. Carter and P.D. Reynolds (eds), *Handbook of Entrepreneurial Dynamics: The Process of Business Creation*, Thousand Oaks, CA: Sage Publications.

Chaganti, R. and Parasuraman, S. (1996), 'A study of the impact of gender on business performance and management patterns in small businesses', *Entrepreneurship Theory and Practice*, **2** (2), 73–5.

Cowling, M. and Harding, R. (2005) 'Gender and high growth businesses in the UK', paper presented at the second Diana International Research Conference, Stockholm, May.

Davidsson, P. (1989), 'Continued entrepreneurship: ability, need and opportunity as determinants of small business growth', *Journal of Business Venturing*, **6** (6), 405–29.

Davidsson, P., Achtenhagen, L. and Naldi, L. (2004), 'Research on small firm growth: a review', in *Proceedings of European Institute of Small Business*, available at: http://eprints.qut.edu.au/archive/00002072.

Ehlers, T.B. and Main, K. (1998), 'Women and the false promise of microenterprise', *Gender and Society*, **12** (4), 424–40.

Epstein, C.F. (1988), *Deceptive Distinctions: Sex, Gender and the Social Order*, New Haven, CT: Yale University Press.

Fine, M. (1994), 'Working with hyphens: Reinventing self and other in qualitative research', in N. Denzin and Y. Lincoln (eds), *Handbook of Qualitative Research*, Thousand Oaks, CA: Sage.

Granovetter, M. (1973), 'The strength of weak ties', *American Journal of Sociology*, **78**, 1360–80.

Greve, A. and Salaff, J.W. (2003), 'Social networks and entrepreneurship,' *Entrepreneurship Theory and Practice*, Fall, 1–22.

Harrison, R.T. and Mason, C.M. (2007), 'Does gender matter? Women business angels and the supply of entrepreneurial finance', *Entrepreneurship Theory and Practice*, May, 445–72.

Hart, M. (2007), *Northern Ireland – Global Entrepreneurship Monitor*, Belfast, Northern Ireland: Invest Northern Ireland.

Heilbrunn, S. (2005), 'The impact of organizational change on entrepreneurship in community settings', *Journal of Small Business and Enterprise Development*, **12** (3), 422–36.

Hill, F., Leitch, C.M. and Harrison, R.T. (2006), 'Desperately seeking finance? the demand for finance by women owned and led businesses', *Venture Capital: An International Journal of Entrepreneurial Finance*, **8** (2), 159–82.

Hite, J.M. and Hesterly, W.S. (2001), 'The evolution of firm networks: from emergence to early growth of the firm', *Strategic Management Journal*, **22** (3), 275–86.

Ibarra, H. (1993), 'Peripheral networks of women and minorities in management: a conceptual framework', *Academy of Management Review*, **18** (1), 56–87.

Iles, P. and Preece, D. (2006), 'Developing leaders or developing leadership? The Academy of Chief Executives' programmes in the North East of England', *Leadership*, **2** (3), 317–40.

Invest Northern Ireland (2008), http://www.investni.com/index/grow.htm (accessed 11 September 2008).

Johanson, J. and Vahlne, J.-E. (1977), 'The internationalization process of the firm: a model of knowledge development and increasing foreign market commitments', *Journal of International Business Studies*, **8**, 23–32.

Johanson, J. and Vahlne, J.-E. (1990), 'The mechanism of internationalization', *International Marketing Review*, **7** (4), 11–24.

Kalleberg, A.L and Leicht, K.T. (1991), 'Gender and organizational performance: determinants of small business survival and success', *Academy of Management Journal*, **34** (1), 136–61.

Kon, Y. and Storey, D.J. (2003), 'A theory of discouraged borrowers', *Small Business Economics*, **21** (1), 37–49.

Leitch, C.M, Hill, F. and Harrison, R.T. (2006), 'The growth and financing of women-led ventures: The Northern Ireland experience', in C. Brush, N. Carter, E. Gatewood, P. Greene and M. Hart (eds), *Growth Oriented Women Entrepreneurs and Their Businesses: A Global Research Perspective*, Cheltenham, UK and Northampton, MA, USA: Edward Elgar Publishing.

Lin, N. (1999), 'Building a network theory of social capital', *Connections*, **22** (1), 28–51.

London Times (2008), 'Where women want to work: guided path to a higher rank', *The Times*, 8 October, p. 12.

Loscocco, K.A., Robinson, J., Hall, R.H. and Allen, J.K. (1991), 'Gender and small business success: an inquiry into women's relative disadvantage', *Social Forces*, **70** (1), 65–85.

Macrae, D.J.R. (1992), 'Characteristics of high and low growth small and medium sized businesses', *Management Research News*, **15** (2), 11–17.

Manolova, T.S., Manev, I.M., Carter, N.M. and Gyoshev, B.S. (2006), 'Breaking the family and friends' circle: predictors of external financing usage among men and women entrepreneurs in a transitional economy', *Venture Capital: An International Journal of Entrepreneurial Finance*, **8** (2), 109–32.

Marlow, S. and Patton, D. (2005), 'All credit to men? Entrepreneurship, finance, and gender', *Entrepreneurship Theory and Practice*, November, 717–35.

McPherson, M., Smith-Lovin, L. and Cook, J.M. (2001), 'Birds of a feather: homophily in social networks', *Annual Review of Sociology*, **27**, 415–44.

Nelson, J.A. (2008), 'Feminism and economics', in D.E. Hausman (ed.), *The Philosophy of Economics: An Anthology*, 3rd edn, New York: Cambridge University Press, pp. 454–75.

Northern Ireland Department of Enterprise, Trade and Investment (DETI) (2007), *Northern Ireland Economic Bulletin*, available at: http://www.detini.gov.uk.

Orser, B.J., Riding, A.L. and Manley, K. (2005), 'Equity and equity: application and approval for financing women-owned Canadian SMEs', *Proceedings, Administrative Sciences Association of Canada*, Ryerson Polytechnic University, Toronto, 28–31 May.

Oviatt, B.M. and McDougall, P.P. (1994), 'Toward a theory of international new ventures', *Journal of International Business Studies*, **25**, 45–64.

Oviatt, B.M. and McDougall, P.P. (1995), 'Global start-ups: entrepreneurs on a worldwide stage', *The Academy of Management Executive*, **9** (2), 30–43.

Penrose, E. (1959), *The Theory of the Growth of the Firm*, Oxford: Oxford University Press.

Read, L. (1998), *The Financing of Small Business: A Comparative Study of Male and Female Business Owners*, London: Routledge.

Saunders, M., Lewis, P. and Thornhill, A. (2007), *Research Methods for Business Students*, 4th edn, Harlow: FT Prentice Hall.

Schwalbe, M., Godwin, S., Holden, D., Shrock, D., Thompson, S. and Wolkomir, M. (2000), 'Generic processes in the reproduction of inequality', *Social Forces*, **79**, 419–52.

Sexton, D.L. (1997), 'Entrepreneurship research needs and issues', in D.L. Sexton and R.W. Smilor (eds), *Entrepreneurship 2000*, Chicago, IL: Upstart, pp. 401–8.

Snell, S.A. and Dean, J.W. (1992), 'Integrated manufacturing and human resource management: a human capital perspective', *Academy of Management Journal*, **35** (3), 467–504.

Teece, D.J., Pisano, G. and Shuen, A. (1987), 'Dynamic capabilities and strategic management', *Strategic Management Journal*, **18**, 509–33.

Ulrich, D. (1998), 'A new mandate for human resources', *Harvard Business Review*, **76** (1), 128–38.

Uzzi, B. (1999), 'Embeddedness in the making of financial capital: how social relations and networks benefit firms seeking financing', *American Sociological Review*, **64** (August), 481–505.

Van de Ven, A.H., Hudson, R. and Schroeder, D. (1984), 'Designing new business startups: entrepreneurial, organizational, and ecological considerations', *Journal of Management*, **10** (1), 87–107.

Wiklund, J. and Shepherd, D. (2003), 'Aspiring for, and achieving growth: the moderating role of resources and opportunities', *Journal of Management Studies*, **40** (8), 1919–41.

Williamson, O.E. (1993), 'Calculativeness, trust, and economic organisation', *Journal of Law and Economics*, **36**, 453–586.

12. Male and female entrepreneurs' networks at four venture stages

Kim Klyver and Siri Terjesen

INTRODUCTION

Entrepreneurs are embedded in social networks (Aldrich and Zimmer, 1986; Hoang and Antoncic, 2003) which can provide access to valuable resources including information about markets, innovations, capital, investors and other key business inputs (Cromie and Birley, 1992; Low and MacMillan, 1988), as well as emotional support (Brüderl and Preissendörfer, 1998), legitimacy and reputation (Lin, 2001). A growing body of literature demonstrates the dynamic nature of entrepreneurial networks (for example, Greve and Salaff, 2003; Larson and Starr, 1993; Moore and Buttner, 1997). Networks change over time as entrepreneurs activate and configure resources to develop sustainable business opportunities. In this process, entrepreneurs develop networks to support different activities and make decisions (Evald et al., 2006; Larson and Starr, 1993). For example, larger networks may aid entrepreneurs seeking access to non-redundant information about markets, innovations and other key business inputs (Evald et al., 2006; Renzulli et al., 2000). An emerging stream of research investigates the presence of gender differences in entrepreneurs' social networks (for example, McGowan and Hampton, 2007), with mixed results.

Despite the high participation by females in entrepreneurial activities around the world (Allen et al., 2008) and awareness of their role in economic development (OECD, 2000), there is limited academic attention to women's entrepreneurship (Baker et al., 1997; de Bruin et al., 2006). Extant gender research is generally concerned with how female entrepreneurs' practices differ from those of men (for example, Birley, 1989; Fielden and Dawe, 2004), and the impact on various measures of social and economic performance (for example, Collins-Dodd et al., 2004; Kim and Ling, 2001; Orser et al., 2006). It has been suggested that female entrepreneurs are disadvantaged, in part because of a lack of suitable and effective social networks (Fielden et al., 2003; Timberlake, 2005). Research on the social networks of female entrepreneurs is mostly constrained to snapshots at one particular venture stage, such as a new start-up (Menzies et al., 2004) or an existing firm (Cromie and Birley, 1992; Farr-Wharton and Brunetto, 2007), and does not consider the dynamic nature of networks through the entrepreneurship process. Recent reviews call for studies of process differences across individuals' extent of network leverage (Hoang and Antoncic, 2003) and gender (Carter et al., 2001; Godwin et al., 2006).

This study explores differences in the composition of entrepreneurs' social networks at various stages of the venture development. This chapter proceeds as follows. First, we frame a discussion of social network theory in entrepreneurship, focusing on gender. We put forward six hypotheses regarding the composition and use of female and male entrepreneurs' social networks. Next, we examine the theory of network dynamics during the entrepreneurial process and outline three hypotheses related to expected changes in networks by gender and venture stages. Following a description of the data and methodology, the results are presented and discussed. The conclusions highlight the contributions to theory and practice, discuss limitations and suggest directions for future research.

THEORETICAL BACKGROUND

Entrepreneurs' social networks provide access to resources. Without networking activity, many entrepreneurs could not create their new ventures (Aldrich and Zimmer, 1986). An entrepreneur's network consists of many players, including shareholders, financiers, employees, customers, buyers, suppliers, advisors, alliance partners, friends, family members and mentors. Through their social networks, entrepreneurs extract 'social capital' resources including information, access to finance, knowledge, and legitimacy. Entrepreneurs employ different networking activities to help enact their ventures' competitive strategies (Ostgaard and Birley, 1994). (For comprehensive reviews of the social networks of entrepreneurs, see Hoang and Antoncic, 2003 and Kim and Aldrich, 2005). In this study, we explore several characteristics of male and female entrepreneurs' social networks including gender, kin, business relations and emotional support, as well as overall size and density.

GENDER AND SOCIAL NETWORKS

A growing body of research examines how social networks are gendered at work, with a consistent finding that men and women develop different networks (Burke et al., 1995). Among the seminal studies, Ibarra (1992,

1993) describes how women managers' lack of access to informal networks causes them to build different networks from men. In particular, women are more likely to seek other women as friends and supporters, and to seek men for professional advice (Ibarra, 1992). Other studies of gendered management networks report that women have more women in their networks and men have more men in their networks (Burke et al., 1995) and women's exclusion from formal networks limits their ability to advance to the highest echelons in an organization (Bilimoria and Piderit, 1994). In these traditional organizations, individuals cannot readily 'choose' diversity of their work networks (Ragins and Gonzalez, 2003). In contrast, the process of starting a new venture involves the entrepreneur self-selecting individuals to participate in his or her network.

GENDER COMPOSITION

Homophily theory argues that the extent to which individuals communicate with one another is influenced by the degree that they perceive similar demographic, belief, value and activity attributes (Byrne, 1971). Moreover, individuals who share certain characteristics and are attracted to one another are expected to provide positive feedback on abilities and ideas, and thus enhance self-esteem. Individuals are therefore likely to self-select participation in networks which are homogeneous by gender and other characteristics. In fact, gender homogeneous groups have been identified across a wide range of samples, including adolescent groups (Schrum and Creek, 1987), Master of Business Administration (MBA) student projects (Mehra et al., 1998) and volunteer associations (McPherson and Smith-Lovin, 1986).

A growing body of research investigates the presence of gender differences in entrepreneurs' social networks, consistently finding that female entrepreneurs' networks are characterized by higher proportions of females (Aldrich et al., 1989; Cromie and Birley, 1992; Ruef et al., 2003; Smeltzer and Fann, 1989). Based on homophily theory, we contend:

Hypothesis 1:   Compared to male entrepreneurs, female entrepreneurs will have lower proportions of males in their social networks.

KIN COMPOSITION

Brush (1992) describes women's entrepreneurship as an integrated network and focused on relationships. Relational theory (Miller, 1976) is a model of how women's development and sense of self and personal worth is shaped by a sense of connection to others, including family members, and has been identified as salient to the experiences and approaches used by female entrepreneurs (Buttner, 2001). Women spend a large proportion of their lives helping to develop others, and develop important skills such as authenticity, openness, care and compassion. This relational model is in contrast to mainstream male-dominated models, and may emerge from girls' relationships with their mothers, in contrast to boys' desired autonomy (Chodorow, 1978). We expect that relational aspects will be reflected in gender differences in choices about the composition of kin in entrepreneurial networks.

To date, studies on the kin composition of entrepreneurs' networks report mixed results, perhaps due to the lack of a consistent definition of kin or to variations in new venture development stages. Female entrepreneurs are more likely to have kin-homogeneous networks (Renzulli, 1998), and are especially likely to leverage female relationships when taking over an existing firm (Greve and Salaff, 2003). However, other studies identified no differences in the involvement of close family members (Aldrich et al., 1989; Cromie and Birley, 1992; Menzies et al., 2004). Based on the discussion above, we expect the following:

Hypothesis 2:   Compared to male entrepreneurs, female entrepreneurs will have higher proportions of family members in their social networks.

BUSINESS RELATIONS

Entrepreneurs enact activities that provide business value, and must interface with individuals in the business environment. Neergaard's (2005) research on Danish entrepreneurs identifies the following six networking activities undertaken by founding team members: building the new venture team, raising capital, recruitment, finding customers/outlets, obtaining access to relevant advice/knowledge and establishing international contacts. It has been suggested that the interrupted nature of women's careers due to commitments to children, partner's careers and taking care of elderly kin disadvantages women's abilities to build connections in the business world (Metz and Tharenou, 2001). Additionally, social networks atrophy with career absences.

This suggests that entrepreneurs' connections to business relations may be gendered. For example, male business owners are more likely than female business owners to have co-workers in their networks (Renzulli,

1998). Furthermore, men tend to consult other men for assistance with the business, while women consult men to a lesser extent (Aldrich and Elam, 2000). Based on the above, we expect the following:

Hypothesis 3: Compared to male entrepreneurs, female entrepreneurs will have lower proportions of business relations in their social networks.

SIZE

A fourth characteristic of entrepreneurs' networks is size. Entrepreneurs with large networks have better access to information and resources than do entrepreneurs with small networks (Greve, 1995). Previous research on the networks of the overall female and male population indicates no differences in size (Marsden, 1987). Hence, we suspect no significant differences in size between female and male entrepreneurs' networks.

Hypothesis 4: The size of female and male entrepreneurs' social networks will not differ.

DENSITY

Density describes the extent to which individuals in a social network are acquainted with one another. In dense social networks, most people know one another and are likely to form coalitions based on trust and common norms that enhance the collective action capability (Aldrich and Zimmer, 1986; Kim and Aldrich, 2005). Individuals embedded in dense networks are more likely to provide and receive social support from one another, but more likely to obtain redundant information (Marsden, 1987). Kin and neighbours are, due to family and geographic proximity, more likely to know one another than are individuals who are not related to one another or do not live nearby. If, as hypothesized above, female entrepreneurs have more kin and neighbours, then females' networks are likely to be denser. Thus, controlling for proportion of family members, we expect no significant differences in density between female and male entrepreneurs' networks.

Hypothesis 5: Controlling for proportion of family members, the density of social networks will not differ between female and male entrepreneurs.

EMOTIONAL SUPPORT

Social support theory (House, 1987) has been interpreted as comprising four types of support: emotional support, instrumental support, information, and social companionship (Agneesens et al., 2006). Prior research in social support theory indicates that females are more likely to seek and provide emotional support, whereas males are more likely to seek and provide instrumental support (Reevy and Maslach, 2001).

In the entrepreneurship literature, Neergaard et al. (2005) develop a theoretical framework incorporating social support theory in order better to understand women's interactions and role within social networks. This model focuses the discussion on the content, rather than the structure, of entrepreneurial social networks. The few studies that investigate the role of emotional support in the entrepreneurship process do not distinguish between female and male entrepreneurs (for example, Bruderl and Preisendorfer, 1998; Samuelsson, 2004). Meanwhile, Menzies et al. (2004) find no differences between female and male nascent entrepreneurs' social networking practices in terms of received support from family, friends and others. As both female and male entrepreneurs require and access emotional support, we suspect no significant differences in proportion of relations from whom female and male entrepreneurs receive emotional support.

Hypothesis 6:   The proportion of relationships which provide emotional support will not differ between female and male entrepreneurs.

EVOLUTION OF SOCIAL NETWORKS DURING THE ENTREPRENEURIAL PROCESS

Entrepreneurial networks are dynamic (Davidsson and Honig, 2003; Evald et al., 2006; Larson and Starr, 1993). In their quest for new resources at different venture stages, entrepreneurs activate new network ties. To date, the literature on gender and entrepreneurial networks has failed to consider this dynamic nature, instead treating networks as stable.

In this study, we examine different development patterns in entrepreneurs' networks. The extension of these arguments is salient in those cases in which we expect differences between females and males: gender composition, kin composition and business relation composition. Hypotheses 1, 2 and 3 predict gender differences which we articulate in hypotheses 7, 8 and 9 respectively. We now examine each in turn.

GENDER COMPOSITION DYNAMICS

We have described how individuals tend to establish relationships with others with whom they perceive to share similar characteristics and beliefs. We expect that female entrepreneurs will build networks with other females. Literature on gender and social network theory in traditional organizations reveals that, in order to fit in and be promoted in corporate environments, successful women develop social networks similar to those of successful men (Tharenou, 1997). These social networks inevitably include more men, as women reach higher and higher levels in firms. In fact, social capital is more important to women's advancement at higher levels of management than at lower levels of management (Metz and Tharenou, 2001).

Although sparse, the female entrepreneurship literature indicates that women's networks change as they leave corporate environments to start their own firms (Moore and Buttner, 1997; Terjesen, 2005). Godwin et al. (2006: 630) suggest that female entrepreneurs, when faced with hurdles in securing resources and establishing legitimacy, may initiate ties to males in order 'not to fight the system, but to play by its rules'. There may be a bias to 'success' as entrepreneurs proceed through various venture stages, suggesting that entrepreneurs at later venture stages may become more similar. From these arguments, we hypothesize:

Hypothesis 7: The gender composition of female and male entrepreneurs' social networks will not differ at later stages of the venture development process.

KIN COMPOSITION DYNAMICS

Extant research on the social networks of the general population (Moore, 1990) and samples of entrepreneurs (Aldrich et al., 1989) suggests that females have a higher proportion of kin in their networks (see development of hypothesis 2). Females employed in traditional organizations who get promoted tend to develop social networks similar to those of men (Tharenou, 1997). Following this logic, females who progress through venture stages might develop social networks similar to their male counterparts. Hence, we expect to find gender differences in the kin composition between female and male entrepreneurs at early stages of the business. As entrepreneurs move forward in the venture development process, these differences will decrease and may, at some point, totally disappear.

Hypothesis 8:   The kin composition of female and male entrepreneurs' social networks will not differ at later stages of the venture development process.

BUSINESS RELATIONS DYNAMICS

Following the line of reasoning articulated above, we suspect that as entrepreneurs proceed through venture stages, they will need to access more business relations. These network ties are particularly salient to entrepreneurs as business relations provide access to resources which give sustainable competitive advantages. This logic holds for both female and male entrepreneurs.

Hypothesis 9:   The composition of business relations in female and male entrepreneurs' social networks will not differ at later stages of the venture development process.

DATA AND METHODOLOGY

Sample

We use data from a telephone survey of 134 female and 266 male entrepreneurs, conducted in 2003 and 2004. The entrepreneurs are identified through their participation in the Global Entrepreneurship Monitor (GEM) project in Denmark, and asked if they would be willing to be contacted for a future study on social networks. The initial GEM study identifies individuals who are engaged in entrepreneurial activity as nascent entrepreneurs, firm owners or informal investors. The sample is representative of the national population.

For the second telephone interview, upon which this study is based, the overall response rate is 82 per cent in 2003 and 60 per cent in 2004. An analysis of our sample confirms its comparability to the overall GEM sample of entrepreneurs and also the adult population in Denmark.

Variables

Venture stage
The entrepreneurs are classified by their self-reported status as 'intending to start a business' (discovery), 'starting a business' (emergence), 'running a firm for less than 42 months' (young) or 'running a firm for at least 42

months' (established). The telephone interviews are conducted while the entrepreneur was active in the new venture, eliminating biases of hindsight, memory decay and post-hoc rationalization. In total we survey 158, 76, 60 and 106 entrepreneurs at the discovery, emergence, young and established stages, respectively.

Social networks
In this study we employ the name-generator approach (Lin, 2001; Marsden, 1987) to ascertain the composition of entrepreneurs' discussion social networks. This approach has been used extensively for the last three decades, including the General Social Survey (GSS) and focuses on a core discussion network. As previous results indicate that 95 per cent of people report fewer than five persons in the (core discussion) networks (Marsden, 1987), we asked entrepreneurs to 'Identify up to five persons with whom you have discussed your (opportunity; business), and if you have discussed your (opportunity; business) with more than five persons, then the five persons who have influenced you the most'. This results in a size measure, from one to five.

Network node composition
We then ask for characteristics of these individuals, including gender and role-relation. Each entrepreneur's proportion of males, family relations and business relations (for example, colleagues and consultants) are calculated. We also ask each respondent to rate the extent of 'emotional support-related' communication, from 'mostly critical' to 'mostly encouraging'. The share of emotional support relations is calculated as the amount of emotional support relations (those reporting 'mostly encouraging') divided by the network size.

Density
Entrepreneurs are also asked about which contacts in their network were acquainted with each other. Replies are used to calculate a density measure by dividing the amount of relations who knew one another by the maximum number of people who could know each other.

Gender
Entrepreneurs' gender is coded (1 for male; 2 for female).

Control variables
Earlier studies highlight the impact of certain demographic variables on entrepreneurial process outcomes (Greve, 1995; Greve and Salaff, 2003; Jenssen, 1999). Thus, we control age (calculated from year of birth) and

level of education (0 = no vocational or higher education; 1 = vocational education; 2 = higher education less than three years; 3 = higher education between three and four years; 4= higher education more than four years). We also control for the year of survey.

Statistical Analyses

This study incorporates a number of statistical analyses. First, we report descriptive statistics and ANOVAs for the six dependent variables (size, density, and proportion of males, family members, business relations, and emotional support relations) across the four entrepreneurial process stages. We test our first six hypotheses with a series of linear regressions, controlling for age, education level and survey year. To test gender differences in network dynamics, we add an interaction effect and use female entrepreneurs in the discovery stage as the reference.

RESULTS

Descriptive Statistics

Table 12.1 presents means of the six dependent variables across the four stages of the entrepreneurial process as well as a mean for all of four stages taken together.

Table 12.1 reveals no significant gender differences in entrepreneurs' network size, network density, proportion of business relations or proportion of emotional support relations. However, we do find a significant ($p < 0.10$) difference in the composition of family relations: 'established' female entrepreneurs were more likely to have networks with high proportions of kin (40 per cent) compared to male entrepreneurs at the same process stage (28 per cent).

Our multi-stage study also reveals statistical gender differences in the proportion of males ($p < 0.01$) at entrepreneurs' discovery and emergence phases. In the discovery stage, 50 per cent of female entrepreneurs' networks were men, compared with 74 per cent for male entrepreneurs ($p < 0.01$). In the emergence stage, female entrepreneurs' networks are comprised of 55 per cent males, compared to 66 per cent for male entrepreneurs, a difference significant at the .10 level. This dynamic changes at later venture stages, in which both female and male entrepreneurs' networks are comprised of approximately 75 per cent male contacts.

The analyses of means presented in Table 12.1 give support to hypotheses 1, 4, 5 and 6, partial support to hypothesis 2 and no support for

Table 12.1   Network characteristics at four venture process stages:
descriptive statistics and anova results

		Discovery stage	Emergence stage	Young stage	Established stage	Total: all stages
Proportion	Male	0.74	0.66	0.70	0.74	0.72
of males	Female	0.50	0.55	0.74	0.75	0.68
	N	136	75	58	98	367
	Anova	0.00**	0.08*	0.65	0.96	0.00**
Proportion	Male	0.31	0.34	0.32	0.28	0.31
of family	Female	0.32	0.42	0.26	0.40	0.35
relations	N	141	77	58	100	376
	Anova	0.73	0.31	0.54	0.09*	0.19
Proportion	Male	0.27	0.31	0.42	0.44	0.35
of business	Female	0.22	0.27	0.44	0.41	0.30
relations	N	142	76	57	99	374
	Anova	0.41	0.63	0.81	0.71	0.23
Size	Male	3.23	4.41	3.93	3.58	3.66
	Female	3.55	4.44	3.70	3.89	3.82
	N	158	76	60	106	400
	Anova	0.28	0.88	0.58	0.40	0.34
Density	Male	0.70	0.67	0.71	0.70	0.69
	Female	0.69	0.69	0.63	0.78	0.70
	N	124	73	55	89	341
	Anova	0.92	0.78	0.38	0.30	0.85
Proportion	Male	0.79	0.86	0.84	0.77	0.80
of	Female	0.83	0.84	0.84	0.72	0.81
emotional	N	140	74	58	96	368
support	Anova	0.44	0.74	0.96	0.49	0.93
relations						

Note: $* p < 0.10; ** p < 0.01$.

hypothesis 3. Different dynamics of social networks between female and male entrepreneurs were also identified, and further examined using multivariate statistics.

Multivariate Statistics

In order to fully test our hypotheses, we must consider correlations among variables and also whether the correlations remain significant after appropriate control variables are added into the equation. As articulated earlier, certain variables such as age and education may influence network composition, and we include survey year as a control variable. All variables (not including interaction variables) have correlations among them, which are less than 0.8, indicating that there is no multi-collinearity. The correlation between proportion of family relation and proportion of business relations is 0.494 – the highest correlation among the variables. In order to further test for multicollinearity, the variance inflation factors are calculated. They range from 1.056 to 1.500, again indicating that there is no multicollinearity. Table 12.2 shows the results of the six regressions.

Table 12.2 substantiates most of the result from the analyses of means. Female entrepreneurs have significantly larger networks ($p < 0.10$) and significantly lower proportion of males in their networks ($p < 0.01$), however we find no significant differences in other network characteristics. Thus, the linear regressions provide support for hypotheses 1, 5 and 6 on the lower proportion of males in females' networks and similar proportions of density and emotional support. There is no evidence to support hypothesis 3 and 2 regarding the lower proportion of business relations and higher proportions of family members within female networks. From the findings, we can also reject hypothesis 4, since female networks are larger than those of their male counterparts.

Thus far, we have treated social networks as stable. In order to test hypotheses 7, 8 and 9 about the dynamic nature of entrepreneurs' networks, we incorporate an interaction effect of gender by venture stage. Table 12.3 depicts the results.

Our results suggest that, as female entrepreneurs move forward in the entrepreneurial process, they tend to increase their proportion of males in their social networks. The gender differences in entrepreneurial network composition dissipate over time. For example, between the discovery and emergence stages, gender differences are significant on a 0.05 level. This distinction is significant on a 0.01 level between the discovery stage and young business stage and also between discovery stage and established business stage. Our findings support hypothesis 7, but provide no support for hypotheses 8 and 9.

DISCUSSION

Network Composition

This study substantiates major parts of previous knowledge on how social networks differ between female and male entrepreneurs. We find that female entrepreneurs have, on average, a lower proportion of males

Table 12.2 *Entrepreneur networks: linear regression results*

	Size	Density	Proportion of business relations	Proportion of family relations	Proportion of emotional support relations	Proportion of males
Gender	0.218*	0.006	−0.033	−0.003	−0.024	−0.138***
Size	−0.377**	−0.033**	−0.011	−0.023*	−0.017	0.011
Density	−0.138	−0.053	−0.049	0.139***	−0.060	0.018
Proportion of business relations	−0.403*	0.213***	−0.532***	−0.377***	−0.188***	0.025
Proportion of family relations	−0.285	−0.089	−0.255***		−0.086	−0.248***
Proportion of emotional support relations	0.184	0.027	0.034	−0.082	−0.056	−0.055
Proportion of males	−0.011**	−0.002	0.005***	−0.240***	−0.002	0.001
Age	0.17	−0.006	0.010	0.002	0.009	0.000
Education	−0.422***	−0.038	−0.029	−0.014	0.078***	0.075***
Survey year	851307***	76481	58345	0.004	−154387***	−150345***
Constant	324	324	324	−7341	324	324
Number of respondents	0.064	0.064	0.315	324	0.072	0.156
Adjusted R square				0.319		

Note: * p < 0.1; ** p < 0.05; *** p < 0.01.

237

Table 12.3   Entrepreneur network composition: linear regression results

	Proportion of business relations B	Proportion of family relations B	Proportion of males B
Gender	−0.077	−0.086	−0.268***
Size	−0.015	−0.027	0.013
Density	−0.063	0.121	0.006
Proportion of business relations		−0.391	−0.007
Proportion of family relations	−0.559***		−0.267***
Proportion of emotional support relations	−0.228***	−0.068	−0.022
Proportion of males	−0.009	−0.266	
Age	0.004***	0.001	0.001
Education	0.007	−0.017	0.000
Survey year	−0.004	−0.010	0.058**
Stages			
Emergence	−0.086	−0.110	−0.269**
Young	0.056	−0.049	−0.327***
Established	−0.006	−0.143	−0.259**
Interaction effects			
Emergence*gender	0.106	0.146	0.167**
Young*gender	0.054	0.099	0.275***
Established*gender	0.103	0.181	0.252***
Constant	88769	21211	−114802**
N respondent	324	324	324
Adjusted R square	0.331	0.344	0.208
Change in Adjusted R square (compared to Table 12.2)	0.16	0.25	0.52

Note: * $p < 0.1$; ** $p < 0.05$; *** $p < 0.01$.

in their social networks. Our findings regarding the proportion of family relations are consistent with those earlier studies indicating no differences between female and male entrepreneurs. We find that female entrepreneurs report larger social networks than do males. However, we do not find evidence of any significant gender differences regarding entrepreneurial networks' proportion of business relations, proportion of emotional support relations and density.

Network Dynamics

The main contribution of this study is the exploration of gender differences in entrepreneurs' social networks at various venture stages. Compared to male entrepreneurs, female entrepreneurs tend to increase their proportion of males in their social networks as they move forward in the entrepreneurial process. There are vast gender differences in the earliest phases of the venture process, specifically in the discovery stage and the emergence stage, however these differences decline over time. By the established business stage, female and male entrepreneurs report more or less the same proportion of males in their social networks. This result suggests that the difference reported in the extant literature only applies to the earliest stages of the entrepreneurial process.

CONCLUSIONS

We begin our concluding remarks by acknowledging several limitations of our study. First, we take a solo view of the entrepreneur and examine only the social networks of one entrepreneur. Furthermore, we do not control for industry. Although we capture the major characteristics of networks such as family, kin, business discussion and emotional support, there may be other aspects of ties, such as range, frequency, and direction (Aldrich and Zimmer, 1986). Despite these limitations, we believe our study makes a number of key contributions and offers several implications and directions for future research.

Why are the social networks of female and male 'established' entrepreneurs so similar? One explanation is that entrepreneurs face the same *main* challenges, and must make decisions about social networks which enable them to access similar sets of resources to meet these business needs. Major mileposts include obtaining finance, and creating and maintaining business relationships with shareholders such as suppliers and customers.

Meanwhile, although female and male entrepreneurs may face similar challenges and requirements, they may have quite distinct experiences in the new venture process and face different resource requirements. Thus, we are not arguing that females are disadvantaged – we are simply making the case that female and male entrepreneurs must complete certain activities and in order to do so, may need to access similar social networks to obtain key resources. Taken together, these findings may be interpreted to suggest that female and male entrepreneurs may have different pre-venture experiences (for example, labour market) which shape initial networks, but as entrepreneurs work through successive phases and resource requirements in the venture development process, they activate and use similar networks.

Taken together, our findings suggest that just as women in traditional organizations adapt social networks similar to men in order to succeed, their entrepreneurial counterparts build more 'male-oriented' networks as they proceed through venture phases. Longitudinal studies could substantiate these practices, focusing particularly on path dependency and resource flows through the network. Future research on performance and growth could extend our understanding of female entrepreneurs' ventures. Studies incorporating the networks of multiple members of a new venture team, and new measures of relationships may also be helpful in providing a more complete picture of entrepreneurial networks. Finally, as an entrepreneur's social network is one aspect of an integrated entrepreneurial career (Johannisson and Mønsted, 1997), our findings could be extended to research on other types of entrepreneurial participation. For example, individuals with entrepreneurship experience are more likely to act as informal investors (Szerb et al., 2007).

REFERENCES

Agneesens, F., Waege, H. and Lievens, J. (2006), 'Diversity in social support by role relations: a typology', *Social Networks*, **28** (4), 427–41.

Aldrich, H.E. and Elam, A.B. (2000), 'A guide to surfing the social networks', in S. Birley and D. Muzyka (eds), *Mastering Entrepreneurship*, London: Prentice Hall, pp. 143–8.

Aldrich, H.E. and Zimmer, C. (1986), 'Entrepreneurship through social networks', in D. Sexton and R. Smilor (eds), *The Art and Science of Entrepreneurship*, Cambridge, MA: Ballinger, pp. 3–23.

Aldrich, H.E., Reese, P.R. and Dubini, P. (1989), 'Women on the verge of a breakthrough? Networking among entrepreneurs in the US and Italy', *Entrepreneurship and Regional Development*, **1** (4), 339–56.

Allen, E., Elam, A., Langowitz, N. and Dean, M. (2008), *Global Entrepreneurship Monitor: 2007 Report on Women and Entrepreneurship*, Wellesley, MA: Babson College and London: London Business School.

Baker, T., Aldrich, H.E. and Liou, N. (1997), 'Invisible entrepreneurs: the neglect of women business owners by mass media and scholarly journals in the United States', *Entrepreneurship and Regional Development*, **9**, 221–38.

Bilimoria, D. and Piderit, S. (1994), 'Board committee membership: effects of sex-based bias', *Academy of Management Journal*, **37** (6), 1453–77.

Birley, S. (1989), 'Female entrepreneurs: are they really different?', *Journal of Small Business Management*, **27** (1), 32–7.

Brüderl, J. and Preisendörfer, P. (1998), 'Network support and the success of newly founded business organizations', *Small Business Economics*, **10**, 213–25.

Brush, C.G. (1992), 'Research on women business owners: past trends, a new perspective and future directions', *Entrepreneurship Theory and Practice*, **16** (4), 5–30.

Burke, R.J., Rothstein, M.G. and Bristor, J.M. (1995), 'Interpersonal networks of managerial and professional women and men: descriptive characteristics', *Women in Management Review*, **10** (1), 21–7.

Buttner, E.H. (2001), 'Examining female entrepreneurs' management style: an application of a relational frame', *Journal of Business Ethics*, **29** (3), 253–70.

Byrne, D.E. (1971), *The Attraction Paradigm*, New York: Academic Press.

Carter, S., Anderson, S. and Shaw, E. (2001), 'Women's business ownership: review of academic, popular and internet literature', report to the Small Business Service.

Chodorow, N. (1978), *The Reproduction of Mothering*, Berkeley, CA: University of California.

Collins-Dodd, C., Gordon, I.M. and Smart, C. (2004), 'Further evidence on the role of gender in financial performance', *Journal of Small Business Management*, **42** (4), 395–417.

Cromie, S. and Birley, S. (1992), 'Networking by female business owners in northern Ireland', *Journal of Business Venturing*, **7** (3), 237–51.

Davidsson, P. and Honig, B. (2003), 'The role of social and human capital among nascent entrepreneurs', *Journal of Business Venturing*, **18**, 301–31.

De Bruin, A., Brush, C.G. and Welter, F. (2006), 'Introduction to the special issue: towards building cumulative knowledge on women's entrepreneurship', *Entrepreneurship Theory and Practice*, **30** (5), 585–93.

Evald, M.E., Klyver, K. and Svendsen, S.G. (2006), 'The changing importance of the strength of ties throughout the entrepreneurial process', *Journal of Enterprising Culture*, **14** (1), 1–26.

Farr-Wharton, R. and Brunetto, Y. (2007), 'Women entrepreneurs, opportunity recognition and government-sponsored networks', *Women in Management Review*, **22** (3), 187–207.

Fielden, S.L. and Dawe, A. (2004), 'Entrepreneurship and social inclusion', *Women in Management Review*, **19** (3), 139–42.

Fielden, S.L., Davidson, M.J., Dawe, A.J. and Makin, P.J. (2003), 'Factors inhibiting the economic growth of female owned small businesses in North West England', *Journal of Small Business and Enterprise Development*, **10** (2), 152–66.

Godwin, L., Stevens, C. and Brenner, L. (2006), 'Forced to play by the rules: theorizing how mixed-sex founding teams may benefit women entrepreneurs in male dominated contexts', *Entrepreneurship Theory and Practice*, **30** (5), 623–42.

Greve, A. (1995), 'Networks and entrepreneurship – an analysis of social relations, occupational background, and the use of contacts during the establishment process', *Scandinavian Journal of Management*, **11** (1), 1–24.

Greve, A., and Salaff, J.W. (2003), 'Social networks and entrepreneurship', *Entrepreneurship Theory and Practice*, **28** (1), 1–22.

Hoang, H. and Antoncic, B. (2003), 'Network-based research in entrepreneurship: a critical review', *Journal of Business Venturing*, **18** (2), 165–87.

House, J.S. (1987), 'Social support and social structure', *Sociological Forum*, **2** (1), 135–46.

Ibarra, H. (1992), 'Homophily and differential returns: sex differences in network structure and access in an advertising firm', *Administrative Science Quarterly*, **37**, 422–47.

Ibarra, H. (1993), 'Personal networks of women and minorities in management: a conceptual framework', *Academy of Management Review*, **18** (1), 56–87.

Jenssen, J.I. (1999), *Entrepreneurial Networks – A Study of the Impact of Social Networks and Resource Access on Start-up on New Organizations*, Kristiansand: Norwegian School of Economics and Business.

Johannisson, B. and Mønsted, M. (1997), 'Contextualising entrepreneurial networking', *International Studies of Management and Organisation*, **27** (3), 109–36.

Kim, J.L.S. and Ling, C.S. (2001), 'Work–family conflict of women entrepreneurs in Singapore', *Women in Management Review*, **16** (5), 204–21.

Kim, P. and Aldrich, H.E. (2005), 'Social capital and entrepreneurship', *Foundations and Trends in Entrepreneurship*, **1** (2), 1–64.

Larson, A. and Starr, J. (1993), 'A network model of organization formation', *Entrepreneurship Theory and Practice*, **17** (2), 5–16.

Lin, N. (2001), *Social Capital: A Theory of Social Structure and Action*, New York: Cambridge University Press.

Low, M.B. and MacMillan, I.C. (1988), 'Entrepreneurship: past research and future challenges', *Journal of Management*, **14** (2), 139–61.

Marsden, P. (1987), 'Core discussion networks of Americans', *American Sociological Review*, **52** (1), 122–31.

McGowan, P. and Hampton, A. (2007), 'An exploration of the networking practices of female entrepreneurs', in C. Henry, N. Carter, K. Johnston and B. O'Cinneide (eds), *Promoting Female Entrepreneurship: Implications for Education, Training and Policy*, London: Routledge.

McPherson, J.M. and Smith-Lovin, L. (1986), 'Sex segregation in voluntary associations', *American Sociological Review*, **51**, 61–79.

Mehra, A., Kilduff, M. and Brass, D.J. (1998), 'At the margins: a distinctiveness approach to the social identity and social networks of underrepresented groups', *Academy of Management Journal*, **41**, 441–52.

Menzies, T.V., Diochon, M. and Gasse, Y. (2004), 'Examining venture-related myths concerning women entrepreneurs', *Journal of Developmental Entrepreneurship*, **9** (2), 89–107.

Metz, I. and Tharenou, P. (2001), 'Women's career advancement: the relative contribution of human and social capital', *Group & Organization Management*, **26** (3), 312–42.

Miller, J.B. (1976), *Toward a New Psychology of Women*, Boston, MA: Beacon Press.

Moore, D.P. and Buttner, E.H. (1997), *Women Entrepreneurs: Moving Beyond the Glass Ceiling*, London: Sage.

Moore, G. (1990), 'Structural determinants of men's and women's personal networks', *American Sociological Review*, **55** (5), 726–35.

Neergaard, H. (2005), 'Networking activities in technology-based entrepreneurial teams', *International Small Business Journal*, **23** (3), 257–78.

Neergaard, H., Shaw, E. and Carter, S. (2005), 'The impact of gender, social capital and networks on business ownership – a research agenda', *International Journal of Entrepreneurial Behaviour and Research*, **11** (5), 338–57.

Organisation for Economic Co-operation and Development (OECD) (2000), *OECD Small and Medium Enterprise Outlook*, Paris: OECD.

Orser, B.J., Riding, A.L. and Manley, K. (2006), 'Women entrepreneurs and financial capital', *Entrepreneurship Theory and Practice*, **30** (5), 643–65.

Ostgaard, T.A. and Birley, S. (1994), 'Personal networks and firm competitive strategy – a strategic or coincidental match?', *Journal of Business Venturing*, **9**, 281–305.

Ragins, B.R. and Gonzalez, J.A. (2003), 'Organizational diversity: getting a grip on a slippery construct', in J. Greenberg (ed.), *Organizational Behavior: The State of the Science*, Erlbaum, Mahwah, NJ, pp. 125–63.

Reevy, G.M. and Maslach, C. (2001), 'People's use of social support: gender and personality differences', *Sex Roles*, **44**, 437–59.

Renzulli, L. (1998), 'Small business owners, their networks, and the process of resource acquisition', Master's thesis, Department of Sociology, University of North Carolina at Chapel Hill.

Renzulli, L.A., Aldrich, H.E. and Moody, J. (2000), 'Family matters: gender, networks, and entrepreneurial outcomes', *Social Forces*, **79** (2), 523–46.

Ruef, M., Aldrich, H.E. and Carter, N.M. (2003), 'The structure of founding teams: homophily, strong ties and isolation among U.S. entrepreneurs', *American Sociological Review*, **68** (2), 195–222.

Samuelsson, M. (2004), *Creating New Ventures – A Longitudinal Investigation of the Nascent Venturing Process*, JIBS dissertation Series 020, Jönköping.

Schrum, W. and Creek, N.A. Jr (1987), 'Social structure during the school years: onset of the degrouping process', *American Sociological Review*, **52**, 218–23.

Smeltzer L.R. and Fann, G.L. (1989), 'Gender differences in external networks of small business owners/managers', *Journal of Small Business Management*, **27** (2), 25–32.

Szerb, L., Rappai, G., Makra, Z. and Terjesen, S. (2007), 'Informal investments in transition: motivations, characteristics and classifications in Eastern Europe', *Small Business Economics*, **28** (2/3), 257–71.

Terjesen, S. (2005), 'Senior women managers: leveraging embedded career capital in new ventures', *Career Development International*, **10** (3), 246–59.

Tharenou, P. (1997), 'Managerial career advancement', in C. Cooper and I.T. Robertson (eds), *International Review of Industrial and Organizational Psychology*, New York: Wiley, pp. 39–93.

Timberlake, S. (2005), 'Social capital and gender in the workplace', *Journal of Management Development*, **24** (1), 34–44.

13. Gender, opportunity recognition and the role of internal networks

Rodney Farr-Wharton and Yvonne Brunetto

INTRODUCTION

While there has been research examining the differences in management practices for male and female entrepreneurs generally (see Buttner, 2001), there has been less research examining how male and female entrepreneurs use their internal employee networks to search for potential business opportunities. In recent decades there has been significant growth in the influence of female entrepreneurs on economic growth (Greene et al., 2003). Over the past three decades research has demonstrated that female entrepreneurs behave differently to male entrepreneurs in terms of strategic choice, initial resources and the investment process and growth (Greene et al., 2003). However, there is less research on the issue of gender difference in the opportunity identification and development process (Starr and Yudkin, 1996).

There is reasonable evidence to suggest that there is a difference in the way males and females operate their business. For example, Martin (2001) found that female and male entrepreneurs differed in the way they engaged in organizational learning. In particular, she found that women engaged in far greater levels of communication, which is a prerequisite for facilitating organizational innovations. Further, female entrepreneurs tend to operate in a lower risk environment with less focus on pursuing high growth compared with males, suggesting that there is a gender bias in the selection of their market niche (Eddleston and Powell, 2008). Thus it is possible that there is a difference in what opportunities male and female entrepreneurs choose to exploit and therefore a difference in opportunity alertness (Greene et al., 2003; Martin, 2001).

One research approach examining how gender affects entrepreneurship is to analyse entrepreneurs within the context of their existing cultural practices (Berg, 1997; Mirchandani, 1999). This approach assumes that entrepreneurs are a product of the way their histories of past interactions affect their present cultural norms and values, in turn producing entrepreneurial practices that might be different for males and females. One way of capturing an understanding of entrepreneurial values is to examine entrepreneurs' practices in their firms. Hofstede (1998: 18) argues that 'practices – the visible part of culture' represents the 'values – the invisible part' of culture, hence, this chapter examines the similarities and differences in the practices of male and female entrepreneurs seeking business ideas using internal employee networks as a means of gaining insight into their values and norms. The primary research question guiding the study is, *What are the similarities and differences in the management practices of male and female entrepreneurs and how does that affect their behaviour in seeking potential business opportunities using internal employee networks?*

BACKGROUND

Past research suggests that small and medium-sized enterprise (SME) owner/managers display similar entrepreneurial behaviour. Most entrepreneurs believe that they are time poor and that they must focus mostly on operational activities (Garengo et al., 2005) and therefore tend to pursue survival behaviour rather than growth behaviour (Gray, 2002). For this reason, not all entrepreneurs actively engage in identifying potential business ideas. In the case of female entrepreneurs, past research suggests that they tend to be less proactive in searching for new opportunities and are less likely to pursue an aggressive growth strategy because they often are pursuing dual work–family goals. As a consequence, female entrepreneurs are more likely to seek opportunities to further continuity of the business rather than aggressive growth (Verheul and Thurik, 2001). This means that they still have a need to learn about ideas that may potentially become business opportunities; however, their aims may be more about achieving slow steady growth rather than fast expansion of the business.

Networking theory, social capital theory (SCT) and learning organization theory provide the theoretical lens for examining the impact of internal employee relationships on male and female's identification and recognition of potential business opportunities.

NETWORKING THEORY

Within firms, a social network will develop naturally between groups of people with a set of common feelings, positive or negative, providing a structure of constraint or opportunity between members of that particular network (Kilduff and Tsai, 2003). Over time interactions between network members varies from weak to strong depending on the degree to which members rely on one another for help in making major decisions (Kilduff, 1990).

Burt (1992) has suggested that any member positioned centrally within a network may benefit more than others in terms of opportunity identification and availability of strategic information. These centric positions tend to be characterized by the absence of linkages between other members of the network, and the centric position then becomes a 'broker', managing all information flow within the network. The centric position would provide maximum benefit in terms of access to information and the control of that information. It may be that entrepreneurs occupy this centric position in relation to their employees. In Burt's view, entrepreneurs using their employee networks to gain information about potential business opportunities would manoeuvre themselves into brokerage positions by manipulating network ties such that most of the communications are directed towards them. While this may be beneficial for gaining potentially good information about a business idea, it may be so time-consuming that it is counterproductive for achieving day-to-day operations within the enterprise. Moreover, it is unclear whether the central position of entrepreneurs in terms of their employees affects their use of information from them about potential business opportunities. The next section uses the lens provided by social capital theory to explore the behaviour of male and female entrepreneurs in relation to employees.

SOCIAL CAPITAL THEORY (SCT)

The premise of SCT is that the quality of network relationships affects the quality of outcomes because it determines members' access to relevant information, resources, respect and empowerment. The quality of the ties between network members is in turn dependent on whether there are established rules and norms about trust, reciprocity and obligations behaviour (Adler, 2001). These norms are the basis on which relationships are built because they determine what behaviour is acceptable and what is unacceptable (Tsai and Ghoshal, 1998).

While Nahapiet and Ghoshal (1998) have identified three distinct dimensions (structural, relational and cognitive) that can be used to examine outcomes, this study uses only the relational dimension of SCT to examine the importance of internal employee networks for male and female entrepreneurs searching for new business opportunities. The theory argues that there are many potential advantages possible from embedding social capital within a firm for entrepreneurs willing to promote reciprocity of positive behaviours amongst employees (Adler, 2001). Such behaviours become evident in their socializing processes in meetings and conversations (Lin, 2001). The assumption of the theory is that both employees and the owner/manager can benefit from positive workplace relationships (Taylor et al., 2004) because it facilitates greater access to information, resources, respect and empowerment (Lin, 2001), and in turn assists problem-solving in the workplace. In addition, when managers use management strategies aimed at building social capital, the other benefits for employees include: enhanced perceptions of empowerment, increased access to training, incentives (including pay) and flexibility in job design as well as greater employment security. On the other hand, the benefits for entrepreneurs are increased productivity and greater commitment from employees, which all result in improved organizational efficiency and effectiveness of the firm in turn, improving their competitiveness in the marketplace (Bacon and Hoque, 2005).

Similarly, in the case of firms run by female entrepreneurs, Buttner (2001) in her study of 129 female managers found that those who created a workplace based on mutual empowerment were effective. In particular, Buttner (2001) used relational theory (involving analysing female managers' behaviour in terms of four dimensions: preservation, mutual empowerment, achievement and creating teams) as the lens for examining their management practices. She found evidence of 'preserving' in their practices of substituting the roles of absent employees and displaying empathy and having a sense of extra responsibility for employees' welfare. Moreover, she found evidence of 'mutual empowerment' in their predisposition to manage democratically in turn creating an environment of mutual respect. She also found evidence of 'achievement' in their efforts to improve the competence of their employees and evidence of 'creating teams' by sharing their vision and engaging in collaborative decision-making (in turn affecting employees' perception of empowerment).

If entrepreneurs are relational in their management approach, then these same conditions should foster the development of social capital and reciprocity of positive behaviour. This is because over time this same environment is also likely to foster active reciprocity of information sharing, resources and respect. In turn, these are also ideal conditions for sharing information about potential new opportunities. To examine this issue of management approach among male and female entrepreneurs, a secondary research question (SRQ) was proposed to guide the data collection. It is:

Secondary research question 1:   What is the management style used by female and male entrepreneurs?

When SCT is applied to the entrepreneurial context, an ideal management practice is one that promotes reciprocity in information and resource sharing. These same management practices are also ideal for promoting the development of a learning organization because it is promoting an embedded culture of valuing organizational learning. Moreover, if both female and male entrepreneurs are promoting the development of social capital, then the added benefit of such a strategy is that the strategic human resource management (HRM) literature argues that it will also foster a positive learning environment within the firm and lead to business success if the learning can be exploited. This is an important issue because the learning organization literature suggests that the focus on learning within the firm depends on the leader's beliefs and values about learning, which will either result in the development of a learning environment or not. If a learning environment is embedded within the firm then it encourages employees to 'continually expand their capabilities to understand complexity, clarify vision, and improve mental models' (Senge, 1990a: 240). Senge (1990a, 1990b) argues that the role of leaders is pivotal to developing a learning organization mentality.

THE LEARNING ORGANIZATION

The learning organization literature stresses the importance of management practices in facilitating positive learning behaviour within employees (Senge, 1990a; Watkins and Cervero, 2000). For entrepreneurs, this behaviour would appear even more important because their continual existence depends on their ability to identify and recognize a potential business opportunity. Learning is defined by Honig (2001: 21) as any process that 'changes the state of knowledge' held by an individual or firm. A learning organization would have in place systems to learn about new opportunities from mistakes made within the firm (Gibb, 1997). Therefore, effective entrepreneurs are those that use a range of processes (meetings, learning from mistakes) to learn about new opportunities.

Senge (1990a) proposes that to facilitate organizational learning at both the organizational and individual level, the leader must fulfil a number of roles, sometimes being a *designer* (developing the production processes and management and communication mechanisms needed to support production) and/or a *teacher* (selling the vision of the firm and related norms, behaviour and practices to the employees), and sometimes being a *steward* (using the learning from within firms to be innovative within the firm).

This is an important issue because while there is research about the importance of learning for organizational effectiveness (Agashae and Bratton, 2001; Senge, 1990b) there has been far less research examining how female and male entrepreneurs interact with employees as *designers, teachers or stewards* (Agashae and Bratton, 2001). It is also important because the learning practices embedded within a business affects the firms' performance (Cooke and Wills, 1999). Similarly, within the leadership literature, transformational leaders are argued to be able to foster a culture within employees that emulates the norms and values nurtured by the leader (Bass and Avolio, 1993) and this is particularly so when the leader is also the entrepreneur that started the business. This means that transformational leaders would have an effective relational dimension embedded within their firm such that there would be processes in place to capture and reward employees' input (even if it challenged the status quo) and there would also be processes in place to develop employees further. This chapter uses three further research questions to guide data collecting. They are:

Secondary research question 2:   Is there a difference in the way male and female entrepreneurs deal with mistakes made by employees?

Secondary research question 3:   Is there a difference in the way information from meetings is perceived by male and female entrepreneurs?

Secondary research question 4:   Is there a difference in the way male and female entrepreneurs encourage employees to be innovative in the firm?

These secondary research questions are used to guide the data collection process phase.

METHODS

Sampling

The Australian Bureau of Statistics (2001: 1) defines a small business as one that is independently owned, operated and managed and employs less than 20 employees. Interviews were conducted with entrepreneurs that had previously completed questionnaires relating to the role of trust in networking behaviour and employed at least five employees (see Brunetto and Farr-Wharton, 2007; Farr-Wharton and Brunetto, 2008). Firms with at least five employees were chosen because the subject of the chapter is how male and female entrepreneurs manage their employees generally and their employee networks more specifically to learn about potential business opportunities.

A total of 183 of the original 287 entrepreneurs surveyed employed five or more employees. Each of the 183 entrepreneurs with five or more employees was invited to participate in an interview of which 122 entrepreneurs agreed. In total, semi-structured phone or person-to-person interviews were undertaken with 58 female and 64 male entrepreneurs aimed at comparing male and female entrepreneurs' management practices and in turn how they used their internal employee networks to identify potential business opportunities.

Analysis

The qualitative questions sought to solicit information about SME entrepreneurs' management practices in relation to interactions with their employees and how they perceived and used the information as a source of potential business opportunities. In each case, only the first response from each participant was included for analysis in the data and was then transcribed and categorized based on 'commonalities and differences' across emerging themes and then frequencies for each category were determined (Ghauri and Gronhaug, 2002). The systematic patterns that emerged were then used to draw conclusions that can be used to address research questions. In each case, the first response of the entrepreneurs is the only response analysed in this study.

RESULTS

Demographics

Of the sample of 58 female entrepreneurs and 64 male entrepreneurs who employed five or more employees, 11 males and 12 females had a yearly turnover of below \$A500 000, 15 males and 25 females had a turnover between \$A500 000 and \$A1 million and 38 males and 21 females had a turnover above \$A1 million. Table 13.1 indicates that the majority of the sample employed fewer than 20 employees within the manufacturing, processing and building products industries.

To address the first research question on management style, female and male entrepreneurs were asked to describe their management approach. Most gave responses that listed what aspects within the business they focused on. We then asked them to rate their priorities of focus within the business. Because previous research had identified that males tend

Table 13.1   Type of business activity and the number of employees

No of employees	Food and beverage	Tourism	Manufacturing processing, building	Training and public relations	Health services	Total
Male:						
5–20	4	3	20	3	4	34
20–50	4	0	9	2	0	15
> 50	5	2	6	2	0	15
Female:						
5–20	1	0	18	17	3	39
20–50	2	0	3	4	1	10
> 50	1	1	6	2	0	10

to have a greater strategic growth focus and females tend to be relation-ship focused, these findings were expected to be replicated. Two themes emerged from an analysis of the responses. They were that entrepreneurs tended to manage predominantly from either a strategic or a relational perspective. Moreover, the findings replicated previous research in that 58 of the 64 male and 6 of the 58 female entrepreneurs stated that they pursued a strategic goal, whereas 28 of the male and 30 of the female entrepreneurs identified a focus on 'relationship' in their management approach. Examples of the most frequent types of responses are provided below:

Typical male entrepreneurs' responses with a strategic focus:
1. 'Triple bottom line approach with good accounting and appraisal practices as well as equitable relations with employees.'
2. 'I am analytical and bottom-lined focused.'

Typical female entrepreneurs' responses with a strategic focus:
1. 'With a business plan, a marketing plan and good support from technical staff.'
2. 'We adhere to the principle of 1. Company profit, 2. Innovative Product development, 3. Professional Ethics and quality standards, 4. Recognition and reward for employees.'

Typical male entrepreneurs' responses with a relational focus:
1. 'My employees are my greatest assets.'
2. 'I treat my employees more like friends.'

Typical female entrepreneurs' responses with a relational focus:
1. 'Surround yourself with helpful, skilful, happy people.'
2. 'Open communication with employees, seeking involvement and ideas in decision-making.'

The second question asked female and male entrepreneurs to describe how they treated mistakes made by employees. Using the relational dimension of social capital theory and/or relational theory to describe the ideal organizational response to mistake-making, a mistake would be perceived as an opportunity for management and colleagues to support the employee to correct their behaviour by providing information and/or resources and assistance. In contrast, using a learning organization lens to describe the ideal organizational response to a mistake made by employees suggests that the manager would act as *steward* and a *designer* in ensuring that the mistake was used as a learning tool to be innovative and perhaps put in place new systems to ensure that the mistake is not repeated (Senge, 1990b).

Analysis of the responses from this sample suggests that a minority of male and female entrepreneurs used a mixture of these approaches; however, in most cases one approach was dominant. As such, it seems likely that their dominate approach to mistakes was in turn a reflection of the underlying values and beliefs of the entrepreneur. The findings suggest that females used less of a stewardship role (20 out of 58) and more of a relational approach (38 out of 58) to fixing mistakes (support and training approach), while a majority of males' responses (54 out of 64) tended to indicate that mistakes were an opportunity to put in place organizational systems to limit similar mistakes occurring over the longer term, that is, they used the stewardship approach. Only a small number of male entrepreneurs (10 out of 64) used a relational approach to employee mistakes. Therefore, in response to the second research question, it seems likely that there was a difference in the way male and female entrepreneurs responded to mistakes made by employees. Analysis of all scripts suggests that neither males nor females used mistakes as an opportunity for innovation (see Table 13.2).

The third question asked male and female entrepreneurs to describe if they held regular meetings (either formally or informally) and if so how they perceived information given by employees at meetings. In response to the first part of the question, the 39 out of 56 female and 50 out of 64 male entrepreneurs stated that they held formal meetings at scheduled times. In contrast, 19 out of 56 female and 14 out of 64 male entrepreneurs described a history of frequent informal impromptu conversations with employees depending on the needs of the business and employees.

Typical male entrepreneurs' responses about their use of formal meetings:
1. 'Every Monday morning we discuss everything that happened last week and is to happen this week. In addition, we have a six monthly management meeting that includes all staff.'

Table 13.2   Approach to mistakes

Approach	Female	Male	Examples of most frequent emerging themes
Relational	38	10	Female 'Help employees fix the mistake' 'If it is serious we use outside coaching' Male 'Discuss the problem, point out what went wrong and encourage them to try again' 'Work with the employee to resolve the mistake'
Stewardship 'systems failure'	20	54	Female 'Our main goal is to remove the fear; if someone makes a mistake, we automatically look at the system in which they work . . . 85% of mistakes are due to lack of training or poor direction' 'Mistakes are caused by staff not having correct information or procedures to follow – so mistakes are an opportunity to improve procedures' Male 'We review work procedures and attitudes' 'Identify why the mistake happened to see how it can be avoided'

2. 'Yes monthly we discuss financial issues, marketing activities and potential jobs, internal administrative issues, allow employees to make suggestions – all employees have intranet "have a say" facilities.'

Typical female entrepreneurs' responses about their use of formal meetings:

1. 'Our meetings are agenda driven.'
2. 'Daily to discuss days activities and goals.'
3. 'Weekly to discuss how they went with the goals and priorities they set last week and any other issues arising from that, then we set the priorities for this week and then any strategic issue that needs action and finish on "The best thing that happened at work for you last week . . .".'

Typical male entrepreneurs' responses about their use of informal meetings:

1. 'We used to have management meetings. I felt that for a small group many of the issues raised were not important enough to warrant the time commitment and loss of production. I now deal one on one with each employee.'
2. 'There are so few of us, we are constantly discussing everything.'

Typical female entrepreneurs' responses about their use of informal meetings:

1. 'Ask staff for ideas as they are often better than my own.'
2. 'We work as a team and are open about ideas, issues and brainstorming.'

To explore how female and male entrepreneurs used information from these informal and formal meetings, they were asked to describe what type of information was shared during both informal and formal conversations. Using a learning theory lens it was expected that entrepreneurial firms run by both male and females would use their formal and informal internal employee networks to learn about potential business opportunities (*steward role*). However, only a small minority of both males and females used their internal networks for this purpose. Instead, an analysis of the findings using the learning organization theory suggests that both males and females used information relatively similarly – to either improve systems within the firm (*designer role*) or to reiterate the vision and expected practices within the firm (*teacher role*). Hence, in contrast to the aim of a learning organization which is to facilitate organizational learning so as to promote innovative ideas and behaviour (Senge, 1990a), very few male and female entrepreneurs stated that they used formal and informal meetings specifically to learn about new business ideas from their employee networks. However, the responses of a minority of females suggests that they used informal meetings predominantly, to foster and build effective relationships (*relational*), which in turn provided opportunities for entrepreneurs to learn about the ideas of employees (see Table 13.3).

The next question asked female and male entrepreneurs what incentives were in place to encourage employees to generate new ideas that could benefit the business. Five different categories of responses emerged. Past research suggests that offering incentives is a way of building social capital and has been used successfully by managers of SMEs (Bacon and Hoque, 2005). Table 13.4 indicates that almost all female entrepreneurs and all but nine males had a process in place for acknowledging and rewarding good ideas emerging from employees, suggesting that most of these firms did have some management practices in place to build social capital.

Table 13.3   *How information from formal and informal meetings is perceived by male and female entrepreneurs*

Main focus of meetings	Female	Male	Examples of most frequent emerging themes
Build effective relationships	14	2	Female 'Be honest with them and treat them as friends so as they feel special, put their ideas forward, good to brainstorming' 'I believe our relationship to be very good, based on mutually respectful, very open and trusting relations' 'We are a small company and the relationship between myself and my employees is very close both professionally and personally' Male 'We don't have formal meetings but we talk a lot and have a constant exchange of ideas on a daily basis'
Designer organizational learning function (developing production, mgt processes needed to support production)	16	21	Female '[I use meetings to] . . . identify people for training and personal development' 'We are part of the team and work together to fix problems' 'As we work in a service industry the professionalism and skill of our staff is a key driver. [We use meetings to] . . . Ensure staff are well trained and that our systems support us to achieve excellence is critical' Male 'We discuss any changes to staff, processes, customers, work hours etc.' 'We discuss anything that will help to improve internal company communication. We use meetings to thank employees and congratulate others for the best results'
Teacher organizational learning function (selling a vision, and	22	30	Female 'We inform staff of our direction and why, when and how etc. and ways of achieving goals' 'We discuss concerns, directions of business, areas for improvement, pricing

Table 13.3   (continued)

Main focus of meetings	Female	Male	Examples of most frequent emerging themes
related norms and practices)			of services, each person's responsibilities and how we can work together for the common good' Male 'Future direction and plans for the company' 'We discuss short, middle and long-term business issues and strategy'
Steward organizational learning function (using employees to learn about new ideas that might make the firm innovative)	6	11	Female 'We maintain an open door policy and have regular rap sessions with management and employees to get their ideas' 'I am open to their ideas' Male 'Every week we meet to discuss the previous week's activity and new ideas for this week' 'We discuss where we are now, where we are going, what issues and ideas we have'

The majority of males used financial incentives, whereas females used both financial incentives as well as expressions of recognition and praise equally.

The next section examines the findings in totality so as to address the main aim of the study.

DISCUSSION

Using the theoretical frameworks provided by networking theory, relational dimension of social capital and learning organization, this study identifies that male and female entrepreneurs manage similarly – at least at first glance. In this study most males and almost half of the female entrepreneurs managed strategically focusing on achieving stated goals and reviewing actions in the firms accordingly. At one level, this finding contrasts previous research that suggests women use a relational approach to managing (Buttner, 2001) because less than half of the female sample

Table 13.4   How female and male entrepreneurs reward innovative behaviour of employees

	Male	Female	Examples
Recognition and praise	3	20	Female 'We have awards and certificates as part of the recognition programme' 'Verbal appreciation and immediate trialing of the idea and sharing with the team' 'We wouldn't be growing at 80% if they weren't acknowledged – we have that culture – it is everyone's responsibility to follow through to action their ideas' Male 'Yes, positive feedback, status and long-term position'
Salary increase/ bonus	37	20	Female 'Given bonus at end of year – size depends on the impact of the idea on the firm' 'Salary increment and bonuses' Male 'Yes, usually with a cash bonus, but it doesn't happen often' 'Yes, with a salary review'
Small incentive (theatre ticket, dinner)	1	11	Female 'Incentive programme includes dinners and travel' 'Special bottle of wine' Male 'Occasionally with cash, but more often with champagne or a day off'
Large incentive (travel, holiday)	7	3	Female 'We give theatre tickets and overseas trips depending on the idea and contribution to the firm' Male 'Yes, we offer free days in lieu'
Company shares	7	3	Female 'All staff are given shares in the company after being with us for a year' 'Profit sharing' Male

Table 13.4   (continued)

	Male	Female	Examples
No rewards offered – considered part of the job	9	1	'Yes either we offer a share of profits or we issue a few new shares so that he will stay and feel committed to the company' 'Shares would also be considered as there is far too much neglect of rewards for innovation' Female 'Don't know – hasn't happened yet' Male 'We are a team and no individual rewards are given' 'No – it is an inherent part of the business for employees to offer new ideas'

identified a focus on 'relationships' in managing their business, reporting that employees were their first priority within the business.

However, at a deeper level of analysis, the findings from this study do support Buttner's (2001) research because the main difference between the management approaches of females compared with males was that the majority of female entrepreneurs identified multiple foci. In particular, even those females who stated that their first priority was strategy also included a focus on employee relationships as a high priority. This supports the work of Verheul and Thurik (2001) who found in previous studies that female entrepreneurs were more likely to pursue a combination of different goals – both strategic and effective interpersonal relationships, often because they were pursuing multiple work and family goals.

Further evidence of a difference in the management approach of female entrepreneurs emerges when analysing the responses to questions 1, 2 and 5. Their responses provide evidence of female entrepreneurs using a relational approach to managing different aspects of the business. For example, when asked how they responded to mistakes, the findings identified that most entrepreneurs had in place a system to learn from mistakes, which suggests that they were all using management processes that facilitated informal learning (Gibb, 1997). The difference between male and female entrepreneurs was however evident in their approach. For example, in contrast to male entrepreneurs who used a stewardship 'systems failure approach', a majority of females used a relational approach in response to employee mistakes. Approximately two-thirds of the female entrepreneurs perceived themselves as playing a supportive, helpful role in assisting employees. Moreover, a majority of the 20 female entrepreneurs (but no male entrepreneurs) who stated that they used a stewardship approach so as to correct a failure (such as a mistake) in the system also stated that they mostly used a 'training and development' approach (which is a typical relational approach to fixing a problem) as a means of addressing the system failure (mistake).

In addition, proportionally more female than male entrepreneurs had embedded reward systems and processes to remunerate employees who have suggested an idea that will benefit the firm. These findings appear to support research by Buttner (2001) that argued that female entrepreneurs traditionally used a relational approach to managing their businesses and the findings from this research suggests that their management approach contrasts those of male entrepreneurs. Moreover, the findings about the use of incentives and the relational approach in solving work-based problems and correcting mistakes support previous research about best human resource management practices that build social capital within SMEs (Bacon and Hoque, 2005). This means that these female entrepreneurs used management practices that focused more on actively building social capital within their firms by promoting an environment of information sharing and the promotion of mutual trust and empowerment.

Another theme emerging from analysis of the responses suggests that not only do male and female entrepreneurs differ in their management approach, they also differ in the way they use their internal employee networks to gain information about potential business opportunities. In particular, the findings evident in Table 13.3 suggest that approximately a quarter of females used meetings to build effective relationships, another quarter used meetings primarily to develop, review and report progress across every area of the business (*designer organizational learning function*), almost half used meetings for developing and revising strategic direction (*teacher organizational learning function*) and a small minority used meetings as a way of diagnosing problems, brainstorming and findings solutions (*stewardship organizational learning function*). Similarly, only a small percentage of male entrepreneurs acted as *stewards*, with a majority of them using formal meetings mainly as a strategic tool and/or as a means of improving systems in their firms.

In addition, in terms of the learning organization theory, previous research had identified the importance of providing open communication processes as well as the need to embed a culture of recognizing and rewarding those employees whose ideas proved to be business opportunities (Beaver and Prince, 2002). While the findings suggest that a majority of firms engaged in either formal and/or informal communication processes in the form of meetings, much of the communication involved a predominantly one-way flow of information from the entrepreneur to the staff (selling the vision and motivating them). Using the learning organization lens, these findings suggest that few female and male entrepreneurs had the management practices in place to encourage innovative activities. This means that only a small percentage of males and female entrepreneurs acted as stewards to embed the norms and values (explained by Senge, 1990b, 1999) likely to promote workplace learning (as explained by Bandura (1986) and Assanand (2006)).

However, further analysis of the behaviour of a sizeable minority of female entrepreneurs with employees suggested that they focused strongly on building relationships via informal conversations as well as formal meetings and the topic was often about new ideas. This means that these female entrepreneurs were using their established social capital (resulting from their use of a relational approach to managing) to facilitate brainstorming and the flow of new ideas from employees to the entrepreneur. Therefore the findings suggest that a sizeable minority of female entrepreneurs may be using their internal employee networks to learn about potential business opportunities. This new knowledge about the behaviour of some female entrepreneurs appears to significantly contrast the behaviour of male entrepreneurs in the task of gathering information about potential business ideas within the SME context; however, further studies are required to confirm this trend across SMEs in different countries.

This study's findings have a number of limitations. First, the sampling process could have caused bias in the data collection and therefore the generalizability of the findings may be compromised. Moreover, the sample size is limited; hence further research is necessary across numerous countries to improve the generalizability of the study. Moreover, future studies should consider the age of the business and the length of the employment time of employees as variables affecting the quality of the relationship between employees and the entrepreneur.

CONCLUSIONS

Network theory suggests that both internal and external networks assist entrepreneurs search for potential business opportunities (Gargiulo and Benassi, 2000). However, networks are only successful if entrepreneurs are open to receiving that information. Based on networking theory it was expected that both male and female entrepreneurs would exploit the information provided by internal employee networks. Further, based on organizational learning theory, it was expected that entrepreneurs would use the stewardship approach to learning as a means of facilitating innovations in their firms. Instead, the findings suggest that neither male nor female entrepreneurs used their internal employee networks as a means of gaining access to potential business opportunities.

Past research has identified the link between organizational learning and innovative behaviour (Senge, 1990b). However, Agashae and Bratton (2001) argued that there was limited research within the learning organization literature examining how management behaviours affected learning outcomes. The belief in the entrepreneurship literature is that entrepreneurs would seek potential business ideas from their networks – both within and outside their firms. Instead, the findings from this study add new information to the learning organization literature about how entrepreneurs manage (or fail to manage) potential business ideas emanating from their employees. In particular, the findings provide new knowledge about how female and male entrepreneurs learn (or fail to learn) from their employee networks. Specifically, using a learning organization lens, these findings provide further evidence that a majority of entrepreneurs running SMEs do not actively seek new business opportunities from their interactions with employees; instead the focus of many interactions appears more strategic in meetings in that they aim at fixing problems. Hence, irrespective of whether the employees' ideas are good or bad (and, a number of entrepreneurs stated that their employees had better ideas than them) only a small percentage of male and female entrepreneurs used a traditional stewardship approach to identify potential business ideas from their internal employee networks.

Using a social capital lens, this chapter provides further evidence for Martin's (2001) research in that these findings suggest that the quality of social capital is far more important for female entrepreneurs compared with male entrepreneurs. The evidence suggests that female entrepreneurs embed relationship-based management practices that facilitated new ideas from employees being heard (opportunity identification) and acknowledged (opportunity recognition). Female entrepreneurs were more likely to use a relational management approach, which means that they were fostering the development of social capital and reciprocity of positive behaviour such as information sharing, resources and respect. Such behaviour becomes evident in the socializing processes in meetings and conversations (Lin, 2001) promoted by a large minority of female entrepreneurs. These are ideal conditions for entrepreneurs learning about and acknowledging new business opportunities. Hence, one contribution of this research is that it has identified that the management approach of many female entrepreneurs in focusing on relationships may be ideal for building social capital, which in turn, may give them greater access to potential business idea from employees over time. More research is required to confirm these findings across numerous countries for both male and female entrepreneurs, and to differentiate those behaviours evident in entrepreneurs that are interested in engaging in learning about the next business opportunity from internal employee networks.

In summary, the research presented suggests that entrepreneurs in general are lacking in the knowledge of how to use their employee networks. It may be that there is a role for greater entrepreneurship education and government involvement in filling the void of knowledge about the benefits of fostering social capital not just because it fosters mutual reciprocity of information, but because that information may provide knowledge about a potential business opportunity that will benefit the entrepreneur.

REFERENCES

Adler, P. (2001), 'Market, hierarchy, and trust: the knowledge economy and the future of capitalism', *Organization Science*, **12** (2), 215–34.

Agashae, Z. and Bratton, J. (2001), 'Leader–follower dynamics: developing a learning environment', *Journal of Workplace Learning*, **13** (3), 89–103.

Assanand, S. (2006), 'Lecture 15: learning perspective on personality', Department of Psychology, University of British Columbia, available at: http://www.psych.ubc.ca/~assanand/lecture15web.pdf (accessed July 2006).

Australian Bureau of Statistics (ABS) (2001), *Australia Now – a Statistical Profile. Industry Overview: Output and Employment by Industry*, Canberra: Australia Bureau of Statistics.

Bacon, N. and Hoque, K. (2005), 'HRM in the SME sector: valuable employees and coercive networks', *International Journal of Human Resource Management*, **16** (11), 1979–99.

Bandura, A. (1986), *Social Foundations of Thought and Action: A Social Cognitive Theory*, Englewood Cliffs, NJ: Prentice Hall.

Bass, B.M. and Avolio, B.J. (1993), 'Transformational leadership and organizational culture', *Public Administration Quarterly*, **17**, 112–22.

Beaver, G. and Prince, C. (2002), 'Innovation, entrepreneurship and competitive advantage in the entrepreneurial venture', *Journal of Small Business and Enterprise Development*, **9** (1), 28–37.

Berg, N. (1997), 'Gender, place and entrepreneurship', *Entrepreneurship and Regional Development*, **9** (3), 259–68.

Brunetto, Y. and Farr-Wharton R. (2007), 'The moderating role of trust in entrepreneurs' decision-making about collaboration', *Journal of Small Business Management*, **45** (3), 362–88.

Burt, R.S. (1992), *Structural Holes: The Social Structure of Competition*, Cambridge, MA: Harvard University Press.

Buttner, E. (2001), 'Examining female entrepreneurs' management style: an application of a relational frame', *Journal of Business Ethics*, **29** (3), 253–69.

Cooke, P. and Wills, D. (1999), 'Small firms, social capital and the enhancement of business performance through innovation programmes', *Small Business Economics*, **13** (3), 219–34.

Eddleston, K. and Powell, G. (2008), 'The role of gender identity in explaining sex differences in business owners' career satisfier preferences', *Journal of Business Venturing*, **23**, 244–56.

Farr-Wharton, R. and Brunetto, Y. (2008), 'Female entrepreneurs, opportunity recognition and government-sponsored business networks: a social capital perspective', *Females in Management Review*, **22** (3), 187–207.

Garengo, P., Biazzo S. and Bititci, U. (2005), 'Performance measurement systems in SMEs: a review for a research agenda', *International Journal of Management Reviews*, **7** (1), 25–47.

Gargiulo, M. and Benassi, M. (2000), 'Trapped in your own net? Network cohesion, structural holes, and the adaptation of social capital', *Organization Science*, **11** (2), 183–96.

Ghauri, P. and Gronhaug, K. (2002), *Research Methods in Business Studies*, Harlow: Prentice Hall.

Gibb, A.A. (1997), 'Small firms' training and competitiveness: building upon the small business as a learning organisation', *International Small Business Journal*, **15** (3), 13–29.

Gray, C. (2002), 'Entrepreneurship resistance to change and growth in small firms', *Journal of Small Business and Enterprise Development*, **9** (1), 61–72.

Greene, P., Hart, M., Gatewood, E., Brush, C. and Carter, M. (2003), 'Women entrepreneurs: moving front and center: an overview of research and theory' White Paper Series, US Association of Small Business and Entrepreneurship, Boca Raton, FL.

Hofstede, G. (1998), 'Identifying organizational subcultures: an empirical approach', *Journal of Management Studies*, **35** (1), 17–28.

Honig, B. (2001), 'Learning strategies and resources for entrepreneurs and entrepreneurs', *Entrepreneurship: Theory and Practice*, **26** (1), 21–36.

Kilduff, M. (1990), 'The interpersonal structure of decision-making: a social comparison approach to organisational choice', *Organisational Behavior and Human Decision Processes*, **47** (2), 270–88.

Kilduff, M. and Tsai, W. (2003), *Social Networks and Organizations*, London: Sage Publications.

Lin, N. (2001), *Social Capital: A Theory of Social Structure and Action*, Cambridge and New York, Cambridge University Press.

Martin, L. (2001), 'Are women better at organisational learning? An SME Perspective', *Women in Management Review*, **16** (6), 287–97.

Mirchandani, K. (1999), 'Feminist insight on gendered work: new directions in research on women and entrepreneurship', *Gender, Work and Organization*, **6** (4), 224–35.

Nahapiet, J. and Ghoshal, S. (1998), 'Social capital, intellectual capital, and the organizational advantage', *The Academy of Management Review*, **23** (2), 242–66.

Senge, P. (1990a), *The Fifth Discipline*, New York: Doubleday.

Senge, P. (1990b), 'The leader's new work: building learning organisations', *Sloan Management Review*, **32** (1), 7–23.

Senge, P. (1999), 'The gurus speak (panel discussion): complexity and organizations', *Emergence*, **1** (1), 73–91.

Starr, J. and Yudkin, M. (1996), *Female Entrepreneurs: A Review of Current Research*, Wellesley, MA: Wellesley College Centre for Research on Women.

Taylor, D.W., Jones, O. and Boles, K. (2004), 'Building social capital through action learning: an insight into the entrepreneur', *Education and Training*, **46** (5), 226–35.

Tsai, W. and Ghoshal, S. (1998), 'Social capital and value creation: the role of intrafirm networks', *Academy of Management Journal*, **41** (4), 464–76.

Verheul, I. and Thurik, R. (2001), 'Start-up capital: does gender matter?', *Small Business Economics*, **16** (4), 329–33.

Watkins, K. and Cervero, R. (2000), 'Organizations as contexts for learning: a case study in certified accountancy', *Journal of Workplace Learning*, **12** (5), 187–94.

14. 'All by myself': the female high-technology entrepreneur

Maura McAdam and Susan Marlow

INTRODUCTION

Since the 1950s, women have attained increasing visibility within formal waged work such that they now constitute just under half of employees within developed economies overall (OECD, 2003; Women and Equality Unit, 2008). This increasing penetration into the labour market has not yet been echoed within entrepreneurial careers where women constitute, on average, approximately one-quarter of the self-employed and just over one-tenth of business owners across the European Union (OECD, 2003; Global Gender Gap, 2007). Moreover, women-owned businesses tend to be over-represented in locally traded, lower-order services, which constrain growth aspirations and opportunities, as opposed to knowledge-based businesses where there is high growth and export potential (Henry and Johnston, 2003; Carter and Bennett, 2006). Accordingly, women entrepreneurs are heavily under-represented in the science, engineering and technology (SET) sector which, although associated with volatile and high-risk ventures, offers considerable potential for high returns (Smallbone and Wyer, 2006). It might be assumed that this situation is changing; given the increasing numbers of female SET graduates, more women should also be moving into technical entrepreneurship (Mayer, 2006). Female representation in the sciences both at degree and postgraduate level in Ireland is strong, with over 50 per cent of science graduates being female in 2002 compared with a European average of 41 per cent. In the same year the uptake of science, mathematics and computing PhD programmes was 50 per cent female, among the highest in Europe (Forfas, 2003). However, evidence indicates that women are leaving SET careers early (Crump et al., 2007) or are vertically segregated into lower positions. Early career exit has implications for women in general, but for potential entrepreneurs, the exiting trend constrains opportunities to accrue the appropriate levels of entrepreneurial capital and confidence necessary to support successful new start-ups (Wynarczyk and Renner, 2006). This scenario casts some doubt upon the assumption that more women will filter through from SET employment into related entrepreneurial activities.

To explore these arguments further, this chapter considers the particular experiences of a female SET entrepreneur sited within a business incubator unit. Such a location offers an apposite context for discussion as evidence indicates that business incubators are an effective support mechanism for new high-technology based firms offering facilities, advice and ready access to networks (Lee and Osteryoung, 2004; Rice, 2002). This combination of infrastructure and support enhances the confidence of the entrepreneur and the durability of the venture. However, the under-representation of women entrepreneurs within business incubation is rarely recognized or explored. Thus, we investigate the degree to which female entrepreneurs 'fit' within the incubator environment and the extent to which they benefit from such placement. The discussion commences with a critical analysis of entrepreneurship as a gendered activity within a masculine domain; this is followed by a consideration of women's employment and self-employment within the SET sector. The role of the business incubator and its positioning as a masculinized realm is then explored. To illustrate these arguments, case study evidence from a female entrepreneur operating from an incubator unit in the Republic of Ireland is described.

ENTREPRENEURSHIP AS A GENDERED ACTIVITY WITHIN A MASCULINIZED DOMAIN

While there is dissent and considerable critical debate regarding the manner in which female subordination is articulated and experienced (Segal, 1989; Greer, 2000), there is consensus regarding the pervasive and persistent presence of comparative disadvantage. However, using the power of agency to differing extents, women can draw upon various strategies to deal with their particular contextual experiences of subordination. Entrepreneurial activity has been suggested as just one such strategy as it offers women degrees of autonomy and control over their economic activities and the potential to enhance their social status and power. Drawing from discourse theory (Foucault, 1972) for their analysis of the entrepreneurial narrative, however, Smith and Anderson (2004: 137) argue that such autonomy and empowerment may be illusory as, 'the accepted notion of morality in entrepreneurial narratives is patently a "masculine" gendered form'. Ahl (2007: 687) presents convincing evidence for this claim; drawing upon a meta-analysis of published work within the entrepreneurial domain, she concludes that, 'the entrepreneur was consistently described in exactly the same words as those used to describe manhood.

The result of the construction of the entrepreneur as male, is that women as entrepreneurs are rendered invisible'. As such, the female entrepreneur becomes the 'other' (de Beauvoir, 1988) and, so, is seen as an interloper in the field. This analysis suggests that women do not easily 'fit' into the accepted model of entrepreneurship, as that which is associated with the feminine is in opposition to entrepreneurial action and characterization. This argument is usefully illustrated by the fact that, in comparison to their male-owned counterparts, women-owned ventures are both more likely to be pejoratively described as 'underperforming' in terms of growth and profit generation and as 'hobby' businesses (so not a strategic outcome of expertise but a serendipitous one from a leisure interest) (Carter and Shaw, 2005; Carter and Bennett, 2006). The defining theme of such descriptions being that women fail to achieve the normative (male) standards for a successful business – that of a full-time activity with the aim of maximizing economic returns. This argument is now explored in more depth using the example of the SET sector.

FEMININITY, SET CAREERS AND BUSINESS OWNERSHIP

High rates of female entrepreneurial activity within lower-order services have been explained by previous occupational experience, easy access and low capitalization required at start up (Marlow, 2002; Marlow et al., 2008). Axiomatically, women are then over-represented in these traditionally feminized sectors, such as education, health, catering, caring, personal services (Boden and Nucci, 2000; Hundley, 2001), which devalues the business status and lowers returns. Moreover, ease of entry leads to crowding, thus competition is stronger with associated implications for profit generation and sustainability (Meager et al., 2003; Roper and Scott, 2007). In effect, the negative impacts of femininity and female occupational segregation follow women into self-employment, but rather than poorer pay and prospects, the outcome is lower incomes, constrained performance and poor firm viability (Verhcul and Thurik, 2001). The solution to this perceived problem is deemed to be agentic in as much as women themselves need to be assisted and encouraged to gain the necessary financial, human and social capital to act entrepreneurially in sectors that offer better opportunities for normative success (Kepler and Shane, 2007).

Yet, even when women do exercise agency and achieve appropriate qualifications and professional accreditation to enter high-status occupations, traditional masculinized career paths within gendered organizations combine to form so called 'glass ceilings', constraining women's progression (Patterson, 2007; Bolton and Muzio, 2008). This analysis is illustrated within SET careers where progression is based upon long hours and unbroken employment (Blackwell and Glover, 2008) within a culture of competition and aggression (Wajcman, 1991; Crump et al., 2007). Thus, many women are excluded from or, indeed, exclude themselves from such masculinized career-building tactics (Sommerlad and Sanderson, 1998; Wilson, 2004; Bolton and Muzio, 2008). Consequently, even though there are increasing numbers of female SET graduates (Mayer, 2006), they are exiting early from their careers (Wynarczyk and Renner, 2006), largely because as Faulkner et al. (2004: 2) note, there is an exceedingly, 'chilly culture for women in the ICT workforce'. In fact, the SET 'pipeline shrinkage' problem is a well-documented phenomenon where the ratio of women to men falls dramatically from that evident at graduation to that within established careers (Etzkowitz et al., 2000). Drawing from a range of data, Crump et al. (2007) found the industry to be overwhelmingly dominated by men, such that in all but the lowest levels of data-entry work, women constituted less than one-third of the workforce. Reflecting and arising from the masculine culture within the sector, only around one-third of women who interrupt their careers for maternity/caring purposes actually return to the industry; the lack of flexibility is a critical problem, while for those who do return, re-entry is often at a more junior level (Crump et al., 2007; DTI, 2002). Accordingly, the (lack of) flexibility within such careers is instrumental in shaping women's progression and the consequent gender imbalance at senior levels (Blackwell, 2002; Greenfield, 2002; Watts, 2007).

However, self-employment has been seen as a route to surmount gender-related career blocks in hierarchical occupations (Allen and Trueman, 1993; Rouse, 2005). Indeed, 'self employment and enterprise offer women a real alternative means of earning good income and achieving a greater flexibility in their working lives' (Women's Unit, 2000, cited in Perrons, 2003). The business ownership option would, it might be supposed, offer women leaving formal SET careers the opportunity to manage their own routines (Perrons, 2003). Moreover, given the importance of small, innovative firms to the creativity of this sector, entrepreneurial activity is legitimate and credible. Yet, despite the positive perception of entrepreneurship plus the possibilities for greater flexibility and an escape from rigid career structures, women remain heavily underrepresented as SET business owners (Wynarczyk and Renner, 2006). Upon reflection, this is perhaps not that surprising. If women are leaving SET careers at relatively early stages in their careers, they will struggle to accrue the range of tangible and tacit capitals necessary to establish and grow new ventures. Consequently, it has been argued that women require dedicated support and advice mechanisms in order to navigate success-fully through the challenges of beginning new SET ventures (Welter et al., 2003; Godwin et al., 2006).

Although there are convincing arguments for the provision of targeted support for women, this has yet to clearly materialize within the main-stream where small business initiatives remain largely generic (Welter et al., 2003). It is agreed that many of the challenges related to beginning a new venture are common to all who take this path but it is evident that gender-related issues will be an additional element affecting women's entrepreneurial progress. Accordingly, it has been argued that support services should be gender aware in order to recognize and respond to issues that specifically disadvantage women (Prowess, 2007). Thus, in the next section, the role of business incubators as one such example of a generic business support mechanism is examined.

THE BUSINESS INCUBATOR AS A MASCULINE DOMAIN

The National Business Incubation Association (www.nbia.org) defines a business incubator as 'an economic development tool designed to acceler-ate the growth and success of entrepreneurial companies through an array of business support resources and services'. The driving force behind the new venture creation process is the entrepreneur. The incubator seeks to develop this entrepreneurial talent by providing complementary services which support and promote the skills and expertise of the entrepreneur when the firm is most vulnerable to market uncertainty (Lalkaka, 2002; McAdam and Marlow, 2007). Although there are various types of busi-ness incubator with differing priorities reflecting their sources of funding, all share an ambition to support the development and survival of new, entrepreneurial ventures (Hannon and Chaplin, 2003; Wright et al., 2008). Moreover, they may provide low-cost office or laboratory space, admin-istrative services, skilled managerial support and access to a network of professional bodies such as bankers, lawyers and accountants. Such support enables growth as the entrepreneur can concentrate upon product development and marketing strategies rather than practical and admin-istrative matters (Barrow, 2001). Although now dated, Smilor and Gill's comment, 'such an environment should provide an association that should help problems and stimulate the entrepreneur's drive for success' (1986: 20) remains apposite. More contemporary evidence from the National Business Incubation Association (NBIA) indicated that in 2002, 87 per cent of firms that graduated from NBIA were still in business, a survival rate substantially higher than the national two-year (66 per cent) or four-year (50 per cent) rates for small businesses per se (NBIA, 2002).

As well as the provision of practical facilities, incubators create a positive 'clustering' effect in that firms with shared entrepreneurial ambitions, at similar stages of growth and in broadly related sectors, are in close proximity. As De Clercq and Arenius (2006: 343) argue, bringing together those with shared knowledge and expertise 'decreases the ambiguity associated with the entrepreneurial process'. This also encourages and facilitates effective networking and knowledge 'spill over' between the organizations (Acs, 2006). In essence, the incubator firms are sharing resources within the unit and creating new networks between themselves as well as with the external stakeholders necessary to establish sustainability and promote growth (Rothschild and Darr, 2005). It is assumed that business incubators offer a gender-neutral backdrop to support, advise and facilitate the growth of entrepreneurial firms as the focus is upon the commercial potential of the venture, not the personal characteristics of the owner. Yet, there is an absence of women within such units; indeed, fewer than 5 per cent of tenants within Ireland are female, and incubators are very 'male focused' in their marketing and services (Forfas, 2003). As such, it would appear that women are not benefiting from the valuable support that incubation offers to new entrepreneurs and their ventures. It is evident that fewer women start new ventures of the type broadly associated with incubation – fast growth, entrepreneurial firms – to the same extent as men. However, they are not absent from this segment of entrepreneurial activity in sufficient numbers to satisfactorily explain their extremely marginal presence. Rather, there is an assumed 'lack of fit' between women-owned businesses and incubation as the characteristics of stereotypical female entrepreneurs are incongruent with those attributed to successful high-technology entrepreneurs (Heliman, 1983; Watts, 2007). Thus, for women who do wish to benefit from incubation, they must first navigate tacit presumptions regarding their credentials for entry, but then will encounter a masculinized culture unlikely to be conducive to their support and advice needs. Drawing upon this analysis, which links gender, entrepreneurship and incubation, we now explore the female perspective upon how women fit into sectors and environments where traditionally they have been largely absent or excluded.

METHODOLOGY

To investigate this issue further, evidence is presented from an in-depth case study of a female high-technology firm within a business incubator in

Table 14.1   Incubator demographics

Critical success factors	Business incubator
Set up in	1984
Target market	High potential technology start-ups
No. of units	20
Occupancy	85%
Female:male ratio	1:16
On-site business expertise	Advice on business planning, marketing, etc.
Ties to a university: formal/informal	Located within close proximity of the nearby university
Selection process for tenants	High technology start-up criteria
Entrepreneurial education	A three-tiered entrepreneurial programme
Entrepreneurial network	Lawyers, banks, VCs, university, and industry groups
Access to financing and capitalization	VCs and financiers
In-kind financial support	Feasibility grants
Community support	Yes
Concise programme milestones with clear policies and procedures	In-house grants dependent on the achievement of well-defined objectives

the Republic of Ireland. The incubator is located on a science and technology park, linked to a local university. This was Ireland's first digitally networked business incubator offering an effective integrated package of new business development support services, facilities and expertise to assist entrepreneurs to plan, research, develop and build new Irish businesses. The aim of this particular incubator, reflecting the extant literature, is to support new start-ups 'with significant growth potential' (Forfas, 2003: 21). The incubator unit provides an integrated package of business development support services and facilities; it also offers mentoring, training workshops and regular seminars with potential investors. (For incubator demographics see Table 14.1.)

For the purpose of this study, a dense and detailed understanding of the contribution of incubator placement to business development was required, which necessitates an exploration of contextual information using an inductive approach. This single case study approach is deemed appropriate in that the organization is small and the respondent is directly involved and intertwined within the enterprise (Bowman and Ambrosini, 1997). Single case studies have the potential for 'fruitful generalization' (Lijphart, 1971: 693) and as such the unit of analysis can be 'an individual, a community, an organization, a nation-state, an empire, or a civilization' (Lijphart, 1971: 693; Levy, 1988; Sjoberg et al., 1991). As such, this chapter explores one particular female entrepreneur's experience of starting and growing an SET business within an incubator unit.

To complement the single case approach, an oral history was elicited that drew upon the respondent's reflection of her aspirations and emotional experiences of being a woman within the SET sector. The use of oral history in this context is premised upon gaining insight into deeper and different understandings of the role of gender upon growth patterns. For female business owners, this approach is apposite as it sites experiences of entrepreneurship within the wider context of their lives where no written or other form of record exists, so oral history narratives are the vehicle through which they can voice their identities (Haynes, 2004). Although oral history is a well-regarded tool for historians (Thompson, 1988; Vansina, 1985; Yow, 1994), it has rarely been used within the entrepreneurship field. As such, this approach responds to arguments from Ahl (2006, 2007), who calls for more gender-sensitive approaches to researching women's entrepreneurship in order to overcome the inbuilt biases of the standard research methodologies.

The interviewee in this study, Kate, was the first, and to date only, female tenant within the incubator; four meetings were arranged in 2007 where she was encouraged to express her experiences freely without the constraint of a structured format. The conversations were, however, guided around particular key points and critical issues. Both an advantage and disadvantage of this approach is the wealth of data generated. To help address this issue, the interviews were tape-recorded, transcribed and then analysed through the NUD*IST software package.

ENTERING THE FIELD

At the time of the interviews, Kate, a 42-year-old experienced quality engineer, had been in business for eight years; she employed 12 staff and her company provided manufacturing optimization systems. She had attended an exclusively female convent school and had no particular recollection of positive or negative peer pressure regarding her decision to study sciences, rather 'the choice at school was science or domestic science; I remember my Dad saying that "your mother can teach you to bake at home!"' This in itself might be considered somewhat unusual that a father would actively encourage his daughter to challenge normative gender paths in education (but still affording his wife the task of passing on traditional feminine skills). However, Kate's choices were also influenced by positive role models. All her science teachers were both young and lay members of staff, whereas nuns dominated within the humanities. Science subjects were seen both as attractive and 'trendy' and were very popular among Kate's year group. This reflects the work of Culley (1986), who found that girls from single-sex schools were more likely to opt for science subjects in that they were not compromising their femininity in front of male peers. After completing a BSc in Information Technology (IT), Kate was offered a graduate position within an IT company. When asked whether business ownership was considered as a viable career option at this time Kate explained, 'it felt too risky, I thought if I worked for someone else it wouldn't be as risky later on'. So, while she had considered entrepreneurship, Kate felt she had insufficient experience and was, in fact, drawn to the security of full-time employment. After working for a large IT multinational company for 15 years in a variety of roles based on data collection and solutions, she 'realized that there was a need in the market for good many Enterprise Resource Planning (ERP) systems that could help analyse data but would be particularly geared towards SMEs and smaller companies'. Kate's husband also worked within a similar field and supported her business idea, 'so I decided to leave XXX and set up here in the Incubator'. When asked whether entrepreneurial intention ran in her family, Kate referred to her older brother, 'yeah my brother has set up a company; we're both entrepreneurs but I am much more conservative in my growth ambitions than him'.

The launch of the new venture coincided with her husband taking up a position at the local university; this was very important as Kate felt that the security of his job ensured that there was a 'fall back position': 'the mortgage was covered and the kids would be fed'. When prompted further upon the importance of this, Kate remarked, 'to be honest, if my husband had a different job I don't think I would have started the business'. Furthermore, 'we know that whatever risks we take in the business there is a wage coming in and we can live on that, it provides a safety net'. Kate's two school-age children were also recognized as a constraining influence upon business performance: 'having a family has restricted the amount of time that I can dedicate to the business, but I think it is very grounding in one sense, particularly during the start-up stage as you are a lot more disciplined in what you do and tend to focus on the important problems'. In essence, her husband's stable employment had been critical for Kate to feel that domestic and caring duties were being appropriately managed: 'my husband's job is a lot more structured and predictable, so that helps with looking after the kids, I couldn't have done it otherwise'. This last comment is telling. Although Kate accepted that her new enterprise would reduce the time spent with her children, her concern and guilt was somewhat assuaged by the knowledge that her husband would be able to take the 'mothering' role which she would have to forgo. Regarding the balancing of family life with running the business, Kate remarked, 'with holidays looming they say if I'd done teaching I'd have the holidays with them. They're probably tired of hearing "one last summer Mammy working and then I'll take longer holidays".'

BEING A SET ENTREPRENEUR

The discussion then turned to the experience of being a woman in a male-dominated sector: 'No, I haven't met any women in the same position as myself, in a small start-up. I'm not sure whether that has to do with the sector, as there were a lot of female employees in the larger company that I worked for.' After explaining that the identification of a niche market drove her to 'spin out' from a large multinational, Kate began discussing the disadvantages of business ownership, particularly the isolation of being within a male-dominated environment. She felt that men and women need different support networks and a lot of 'lads talk' exacerbated this isolation. 'That's the main thing that I miss about working for the larger company, there were more women there, a lot more socialization so I do miss female company.'

Was Kate the subject of any adverse comments about her position within the firm? For example, was she ever mistaken for the secretary? Kate revealed that 'there have been times when I have answered the phones and they sounded surprised, and they say "can I speak to the person in charge?"' Yet, Kate felt that her gender did not cause her to be treated differently or suffer discrimination. Paradoxically, she then went on to describe how her interpersonal dealings were shaped by gendered assumptions and attitudes. This is not uncommon. For example, Marshall (1984) found in her study of female managers that women were not willing to identify themselves as disadvantaged by discrimination but then referred to many ways in which they had to adjust their behaviour to avoid being devalued as females. In this case, Kate found that customers were more polite when dealing with her, 'particularly if there is an issue, customers are more polite if I'm there and things get resolved more quickly'. Further, 'in negotiations guys are a lot less confrontational, they aren't as competitive and will back down a lot easier. In negotiations, I am treated differently.' While she did not feel overtly patronized because of her femininity, she remarked, 'I do think sometimes, men feel uncomfortable negotiating deals with me, in particular, there was one customer who was considered very tricky and we heard how he had negotiated with other companies, but I think he was more uncomfortable negotiating with a woman, not that I would say I was using any feminine charms but I think he felt uncomfortable trying to be as hard as when he's negotiating with a man.' The disadvantages of the masculine environment are not lost on Kate: 'there is definitely more of a distance between me and them, sometimes when I enter a room the conversation stops because it is boys talk. Sometimes I do feel they're holding themselves back and would other things be said or would they react differently if I wasn't in the room?' These are interesting sentiments, as initially Kate denied that her gender was an issue but then went on to describe, at length, how it intruded into her daily business dealings.

Lehman (1992) identified how discriminatory practices persist in work structures, which might appear to have superficial equality. For example, the exclusion of women from the acquisition of organizational knowledge through the 'old boy network' and the belief that a woman had to behave more like a man to succeed. In order to overcome this isolation, Kate joined a Women in Business Network: 'I do find that I enjoy going to their meetings for female interaction. There is a lot less socialization among business start-ups; I do miss that so I attend the women in business networks mainly for socialization.' This was not confined to her immediate work environment but also that of the incubator; she became more visible at formally organized seminars and events. 'I am always the odd one out, the only female tenant, the other male tenants are always reserved around me, I never get invited to the pub afterwards, that's for sure.' Research (Hoang and Antoncic, 2003) has concluded that there is a great deal of similarity in the networking behaviour of men and women, but the composition of networks varies by sex; this can be detrimental for women (Aldrich, 1989; Cromie and Birley, 1992; Smeltzer and Fann, 1989). In this instance, Kate had found that those in her business networks, 'tend not to be the technology sector but in fashion and, retail'. Thus, Kate found empathy and companionship from her networking but did not benefit from critical information sharing and collaborative problem-solving.

THE FEMALE PRESENCE

Men overwhelmingly outnumber women in the high-technology sector, and so the strong association between masculinity and SET emphasizes women's visibility and difference in this field. Kate was very aware of this: 'I am a bit of a novelty, especially here in the incubator; I get rolled out for the photographs and any press releases, I am a bit of a token.' When the discussion turned to the absence of women both in senior-level SET careers and as SET entrepreneurs, Kate remarked, 'a lot more could be done particularly within schools. I also think we need more relevant role models; science and engineering is not seen as a women's career, it is not glamorous or sexy.'

INCUBATION PRACTICES

Given the absence of women from incubators we were interested to find out how Kate had come to gain entry to the site. It emerged that her brother was highly influential in this decision; he had established and grown his business through the incubator so encouraged Kate to do the same; he was also able to introduce her to the incubator management team and 'put in a good word' for her. Furthermore, it was important to Kate that the incubator was in proximity to where her husband worked, as she drew support and guidance from him, but also he had links with the incubator through the university. In effect, established networks between the university and the incubator managers facilitated the application process. Kate described how the provision of support and office facilities within the incubator meant that her firm was able to organize and commence trading relatively quickly. However, Kate did point out that this provision sometimes did not cater for female business owners with children, particularly during the school holidays: 'A huge debate we had during the first winter we were here, all the heating was on a timer, I asked if I came in early or during holidays could the timers be changed, trying to get changes like that implemented took a while.'

FUTURE GROWTH PLANS

Within the literature one of the main differentiating factors between male and female entrepreneurs is often their growth aspirations in terms of employment and sales (Boden and Nucci, 2000). This is neatly illustrated by Kate who, when asked to articulate her growth strategy for the next five years said, 'the options from here are grow, sell or stay static. The plan is for the first, the second is Plan B, and the third is not really an option.' This discussion then focused on the issue of succession and the handing down of the business to her children: 'If plan A works, the business will be handed on to the children. My 13-year-old son and 8-year-old daughter are interested already, although they see it as a "soft option".' According to the extant literature the success of the self-employed parent is of central importance to a child's perception of entrepreneurship as a viable career

(Davidsson, 1995). In particular, children of successful entrepreneurs are themselves more likely to act entrepreneurially. Another recurrent theme within the literature is the lack of appropriate female role models within the IT industry. When asked if Kate saw herself acting as a mentor to other women either now or during retirement, she commented, 'If I retire I have considered coaching as a next career.' As for her immediate plans, they focused around the sustainability of her venture while ensuring that her children enter third-and second-level education respectively. As for advice to other female SET entrepreneurs, Kate summed up with, 'if I was to do it again and wanted to combine a career and family; I would go for self-employment in my twenties if I had the resources; or wait until my forties when the children are older. But all that is in an ideal world where you meet the ideal life partner at the right time!'

CONCLUSIONS

Successive Irish governments have introduced a range of policy initiatives designed to encourage more people to start new firms. In particular, it is recognized that innovative entrepreneurial ventures within the science, engineering and technology sector have considerable potential to create both wealth and new employment. Accordingly, business incubators offer such ventures ready access to business infrastructure, professional support and advice while enabling tenants to develop and share networks and gain credibility with potential stakeholders. Hence, access to and acceptance within an incubator is a considerable fillip to a new business and enhances durability and growth potential. However, a notable feature of business incubators, regardless of location or affiliation, is an absence of female entrepreneurs. The purpose of this chapter has been to explore the reasons underlying women's exclusion from business incubators. Ostensibly, it might be argued that because of traditional gendered divisions, which spill over from employment into self-employment, women are less likely to begin new ventures within sectors particularly suitable for incubation. Therefore, while incubators are gender-neutral sites of operation, women are structurally excluded as their enterprises do not 'fit'. As such, the problem does not lie with the incubator model itself.

In fact, Kate certainly agreed that her business had benefited from incubation. In terms of how being a woman in this environment shaped her experiences in the incubator, this prompted expressions of gender bias from Kate; within our discussions she frequently referred to herself as a strong character, well qualified and able to hold her own ground. By drawing upon such imagery, the entrepreneurial characterization was presented as being more powerful than the female characterization. In effect, Kate was attempting to 'undo' gender (Butler, 2004) at what Pullen and Knights (2007: 505) describe as 'levels of identity, self, text and practice'. In so doing, Kate was anxious to construct her identity as a business owner rather than a woman yet she was keenly aware that her gender singled her out as 'different' within the context of the incubator. To some extent, she put a positive 'spin' on this, finding advantages within more consensual negotiation styles and customer attitudes but was aware of being excluded from conversations, information exchanges and networking. In fact, incubator culture was exposed as highly gendered. For instance, the homo-sociability evident amongst her male colleagues effectively excluded Kate from her peer group so to compensate for her 'lack of fit' and a sense of alienation from the 'boys talk', Kate deliberately sought alternative networking opportunities with other female entrepreneurs. Yet, although Kate referred to the benefits of such networks in terms of finding empathy and shared business values, there were no other SET business owners present with whom to share specific sectoral information and ideas. To some degree, networking with those outside of her realm of expertise contributed to Kate's isolation in as much as she made few attempts to access the networks within the incubator but was not able to share sector specific issues with members of her women's network. It is clearly difficult to construct supportive and productive business networks when the potential membership is so scarce, as is the case for the high-technology female entrepreneur.

Current programmes and initiatives to encourage women to engage with business ownership may eventually increase female entrepreneurial activity. This may not necessarily spill over into high growth, successful enterprises unless greater attention is afforded to the tensions between the demands of starting and growing new ventures and the reality of women's lives. Finally, for many women and indeed men, their definition of a successful business may not necessarily reflect the normative model of economic attainment if the enterprise satisfies their own ambitions. Yet, in broader terms these ventures are not afforded the status and reverence of those which demonstrate normative success, so for women to be recognized as participants in the contemporary entrepreneurial project, they must achieve upon such normative terms.

Rather, greater consideration of post-structural feminist arguments, which critically analyse the sexist construction of career and the hegemonic assumption underpinning the narratives that shape our understanding of activities, need to be more closely debated. Within this study, the fact that Kate had to fight for a petty concession such as getting heating provided to suit her working day is a useful example. The importance of challenging structures and their exclusionary impetus can only be articulated through critical feminist debate that challenges masculine dominance and consistently presents women as outsiders to the norm. Business incubation has been used in this chapter to illustrate this point. It is assumed that business incubators support and facilitate the growth of entrepreneurial firms but the extent to which women can benefit from what is, in essence, a masculinized environment is rarely recognized or explored. Consequently, women are largely invisible within an important support mechanism for growth-oriented firms. Business incubators offer women training and assistance to become honorary men without ever challenging the fundamental values that underpin the barriers faced by female business owners in SET sectors or recognizing the constraining influence of culture. Such initiatives assist women to accommodate their specific disadvantages while not addressing their source. Moreover, the lack of appropriate role models and mentors within incubators are particularly evident where 'success stories' continue to be overwhelmingly male. It is not suggested that such supportive programmes should be abandoned but, greater recognition and value should be afforded to women's business performance and operating preferences.

REFERENCES

Acs, Z. (2006), 'Innovation and the small business', in D. Jones-Evans and S. Carter (eds), *Enterprise and Small Business*, London: Prentice Hall.

Ahl, H. (2006), 'Why research on women entrepreneurs needs new directions', *Entrepreneurship Theory and Practice*, **30** (5), 595–621.

Ahl, H. (2007), 'Sex business in the toy store: a narrative analysis of a teaching case', *Journal of Business Venturing*, **22**, 673–93.

Aldrich, H.E (1989), 'I heard it through the grapevine: networking among women entrepreneurs', in O. Hagen, C. Raychem and d. sexton (eds), *Women Owned Businesses*, New York: Praeger.

Allen, S. and Truman, C. (1993), *Women in Business: Perspectives on Women Entrepreneurs*, London: Routledge.

Barrow, C. (2001), *Incubators: A Realist's Guide to the World's Business Accelerators*, Chichester: Wiley.

Blackwell, L. (2002), 'Women's scientific lives on new research on women, science and higher education', proceedings of the conference, London, Athena Project 21 September.

Blackwell, L. and Glover, J. (2008), 'Women's scientific employment and family formation: a longitudinal perspective', *Gender Work and Organization*, **15** (6), 579–99.

Boden, R. and Nucci, A. (2000), 'On the survival prospects of men's and women's new ventures', *Journal of Business Venturing*, **15**, 347–62.

Bolton, S. and Muzio, D. (2008), 'The paradoxical processes of feminism in the professions: the case of established, aspiring and semi-professions', *Work, Employment and Society*, **22**, 281–99.

Bowman, C. and Ambrosini, V. (1997), 'Using single respondent in strategy research', *British Journal of Management*, **8**, 119–31.

Butler, J. (2004), *Undoing Gender*, Oxford: Routledge.

Carter, S. and Bennett, D. (2006), 'Gender and entrepreneurship', in S. Carter and D. Jones-Evans (eds), *Enterprise and Small Business*, London: Prentice Hall.

Carter, S. and Shaw, E. (2005), *Women's Business Ownership: Recent Research and Policy Developments*, DTI Small Business Service Research Report, London: DTI.

Cromie, S. and Birley, S. (1992), 'Networking by female business owners in Northern Ireland', *Journal of Business Venturing*, **7**, 237–51.

Crump, B.J., Logan, K. and McIlroy, A. (2007), 'Does gender still matter? A study of the views of women in the ICT industry in New Zealand', *Gender, Work and Organisation*, **14** (4), 349–70.

Culley, L. (1986), *Gender Differences and Computing in Secondary Schools*, Loughborough: Loughborough Department of Education.

Davidsson, P. (1995), 'Determinants of entrepreneurial intentions', paper presented at the Rent IX Conference, Piacenza, Italy, November.

De Beauvoir, S. (1988), *The Second Sex*, London: Pan. First published 1949.

De Clercq, D. and Arenius, P. (2006), 'The role of knowledge in business start-up activity', *International Small Business Journal*, **24** (4), 339–58.

Department of Trade and Industry (DTI) (2002), *Maximising Returns to Science, Engineering and Technology Careers*, Report URN 02/514, London: DTI.

Etzkowitz, H., Kemelgor, C. and Uzzi, B. (2000), *Athena Unbound: The Advancement of Women in Science and Technology*, Cambridge: Cambridge University Press.

Faulkner, W., Sorenson, K., Gansmo, H. and Rommes, E. (2004), 'Gender inclusion with the ICT workforce', http://www.sigis-sit.org (accessed June 2008).

Foucault, P. (1972), *The Archaeology of Knowledge and the Discourse on Language*, New York: Pantheon Books.

Forfas (2003), *A Report on Women and Science: A review of the situation in Ireland*, Dublin: Forfas.

Global Gender Gap (2007), 'Global gender gap report 2007', available at: http://www.globalgendergapindex.org (accessed June 2008).

Godwin, L.N., Stevens, C.E. and Brenner, N.L. (2006), 'Forced to play by the rules? Theorizing how mixed sex founding teams benefit women entrepreneurs in male dominated texts', *Entrepreneurship Theory and Practice*, **30**, 621–42.

Greenfield, S. (2002), *SET Fair: A Report on Women in Science, Engineering and Technology*, London: Department for Trade and Industry.

Greer, G. (2000), *The Whole Woman*, New York: Anchor Books.

Hannon, P.D. and Chaplin, P. (2003), 'Are incubators good for business? Understanding incubation practice – the challenges for policy', *Environment and Planning C*, **21**, 861–81.

Haynes, K. (2004), 'Transforming identities: accounting professionals and the transition to motherhood', Working Paper No. 6, Department of Management Studies, University of York.

Heliman, M.E. (1983), 'Sex bias in work settings: the lack of fit model', *Research in Organisational Behaviour*, **5**, 269–98.

Henry, C. and Johnston, K. (2003), *State of the Art of Women's Entrepreneurship in Ireland: Access to Financing and Financing Strategies*, Dundalk: Centre for Entrepreneurship Research, Dundalk Institute of Technology.

Hoang, H. and Antoncic, B. (2003), 'Network based research in entrepreneurship: a critical review', *Journal of Business Venturing*, **18** (2), 165–87.

Hundley, G. (2001), 'Why women earn less than men in self employment', *Journal of Labour Research*, **12** (4), 817–29.

Kepler, E. and Shane, S. (2007), 'Are male and female entrepreneurs really that different?', Washington, DC, U.S. Small Business Administration, Office of Advocacy, available at: http://www.sba.gov (accessed 12 October 2008).

Lalkaka, R. (2002), 'Technology business incubators to help build an innovation based economy', *Journal of Change Management*, **3** (2), 167–76.

Lee, S.S. and Osteryoung, S.J. (2004), 'A comparison of critical success factors for effective operations of university business incubators in the United States and Korea', *Journal of Small Business Management*, **42** (4), 418–26.

Lehman, C.R. (1992), 'Herstory in accounting: the first eighty years', *Accounting Organisations and Society*, **17** (3–4), 261–85.

Levy, S. (1988), 'Information technologies in universities: an institutional case study', unpublished doctoral dissertation, Northern Arizona University, Flagstaff.

Lijphart, A. (1971), 'Comparative politics and comparative method', *American Political Science Review*, **65**, 682–93.

Marlow, S. (2002), 'Self-employed women: a part of or apart from feminist theory?', *Entrepreneurship and Innovation*, **2** (2), 23–37.

Marlow, S., Carter, S. and Shaw, E. (2008), 'Constructing female entrepreneurship policy in the UK: is the US a relevant benchmark?', *Environment and Planning C: Government and Policy*, **26** (2), 335–51.

Marshall, J. (1984), *Women Managers: Travellers in a Male World*, Chichester: John Wiley and Sons.

Mayer, H. (2006), 'Economic trends and location patterns of women high-tech entrepreneurs', in A. Zacharakis, S. Alvarez, P. Davidsson, J. Fiet, G. George, D.F. Kuratko, C. Mason, M. Maula, M. Minniti, S. Sarasvathy, D.A. Shepherd, P. Westhead, J. Wiklund, M. Wright and S.A. Zahra (eds), *Frontiers of Entrepreneurship Research*, Wellesley, MA: Babson College.

McAdam, M. and Marlow, S. (2007), 'Building futures or stealing secrets? Entrepreneurial cooperation and conflict within business incubators' *International Journal of Small Business*, **25** (4), 359–77.

Meager, N., Bates, P. and Cowling, M. (2003), *Business Start-up Support for Young People Delivered by The Prince's Trust*, report to the Department of Work and Pensions, London: HMSO.

National Business Incubation Association (NBIA) (2002), *The State of the Business Incubation Industry*, Athens, OH: NBIA.

Organisation for Economic Co-operation and Development (OECD) (2003), *Women's Entrepreneurship: Issues and Policies*, working party on small and medium-sized enterprises and entrepreneurship, Paris: OECD.

Patterson, N. (2007), 'Women entrepreneurs: jumping corporate ship or gaining new wings?', paper presented to the thirtieth ISBE Conference, Glasgow, November.

Perrons D. (2003), 'The new economy and the work–life balance: conceptual explorations and a case study of new media', *Gender Work and Organizations*, **10** (1), 65–93.

Prowess (2007), *Women-Friendly Incubators and Managed Workspaces for Science, Engineering and Technology (SET) Business*, ed. A. Westall, Norwich, UK: Prowess Ltd.

Pullen, A. and Knights, D. (2007), 'Editorial: undoing gender: organising and dis-organising performance', *Gender, Work and Organisation*, 14 (6), 505–11.

Rice, M.P. (2002), 'Co-production of business assistance in business incubators: an exploratory study', *Journal of Business Venturing*, 17 (2), 163–87.

Roper, S. and Scott, J. (2007), 'Gender differences in start-up finance – an econo-metric analysis of GE data', paper presented to the twenty-seventh Institute of Small Business and Entrepreneurship Conference, Glasgow, November.

Rothschild, L. and Darr, A. (2005), 'Technological incubators and the social con-struction of innovation networks: an Israeli case study', *Technovation*, 25 (1), 59–69.

Rouse J, (2005), 'Pregnancy and maternity in self-employment: individualised social reproduction?', paper presented at the twenty-eighth Institute for Small Business Entrepreneurship National Conference, Blackpool, November.

Segal, M.W. (1989), 'The nature of work and family linkages: a theoretical per-spective', in G.L. Bowen and D.K. Orthner (eds), *The Organization Family: Work and Family Linkages in the U.S. Military*, New York: Praeger.

Sjoberg, G., Williams, N., Vaughan, T. and Sjoberg, A. (1991), 'The case study approach in social research', in J. Feagin, A. Orum and G. Sjoberg (eds), *A Case for Case Study*, Chapel Hill, NC: University of North Carolina Press, pp. 27–79.

Smallbone, D. and Wyer, P. (2006), 'Growth and development in the small busi-ness', in S. Carter and D. Jones-Evans (eds), *Enterprise and the Small Business*, London: Prentice Hall.

Smeltzer, L.R. and Fann, G.L. (1989), 'Gender differences in external networks of small business owners/managers', *Journal of Small Business Management*, 27 (2), 25–32.

Smilor, R.W. and Gill, M.D. (1986), *The New Business Incubator – Linking Talent, Technology, Capital and Know-how*, Lexington, MA and Toronto: Lexington Books.

Smith, R. and Anderson, A.R. (2004), 'The devil is in the e-tail: forms and struc-tures in the entrepreneurial narratives', in D. Hjorth and C. Steyaert (eds), *Narrative and Discursive Approaches in Entrepreneurship*, Cheltenham, UK and Northampton, MA, USA: Edward Elgar, pp. 125–43.

Sommerlad, H. and Sanderson, P. (1998), *Gender, Choice, and Commitment: Women Solicitors in England and Wales and the Struggle for Equal Status (Socio-Legal Studies)*, Aldershot: Ashgate.

Thompson, P. (1988), *The Voice of the Past: Oral History*, Oxford: Oxford University Press.

Vansina, J. (1985), *Oral Tradition as History*, Madison, WI: University of Wisconsin Press.

Verheul, I. and Thurik, R. (2001), 'Start-up capital: does gender matter?', *Small Business Economics*, 16 (4), 329–45.

Wajcman, J. (1991), *Feminism Confronts Technology*, Cambridge: Polity Press.

Watts, J.H. (2007), 'Porn, pride and pessimism: experiences of women working in professional construction roles', *Work, Employment and Society*, 21 (2), 299–316.

Welter, F., Smallbone, D., Aculai, E, Isakova, N. and Schakirova, N. (2003),

'Female entrepreneurship in post Soviet countries', in J. Butler (ed.), *New Perspectives on Women Entrepreneurs*, Greenwich, CT: Information Age Publishing, pp. 77–100.

Wilson, F. (2004), 'Women in Management in the UK', in M.J. Davidson and R.J. Burke (eds), *Women in Management Worldwide: Facts, Figures and Analysis*, Aldershot, UK: Ashgate.

Women and Equality Unit (2008), 'Working and living', available at: http://www. womenandequalityunit.gov.uk/work_life/index.htm (accessed 26 September 2008).

Wright, M., Lui, X., Black, T. and Filatotchev, I. (2008), 'Returnee entrepreneurs, science park location choice and performance: an analysis of high-technology SMEs in China', *Entrepreneurship Theory and Practice*, **32** (1) 131–5.

Wynarczyk, P. and Renner, C. (2006), 'The "gender gap" in the scientific; labour market: the case of science, engineering and technology-based SMEs in the UK', *Equal Opportunities International*, **25** (8), 660–73.

Yow, V.R. (1994), *Recording Oral History*, London: Sage.

15. Physician as feminist entrepreneur: the gendered nature of venture creation and the Shirley E. Greenberg Women's Health Centre

Barbara Orser and Joanne Leck

INTRODUCTION

This study explores the gendered nature of the venture creation process through the evolution of a 'for women and by women', public health care centre (The Ottawa Hospital Shirley E. Greenberg Women's Health Centre – SEGWHC). The work seeks to understand ways in which gender is embedded in opportunity recognition, resource acquisition and organizational form. Building on the literature, the study presents a gender-based typology of new venture organizations and the construct of feminist entrepreneur. Theory is then tested through action-based, participant-observation and in doing so, the study contributes to the literature in several ways.

First, to the best of our knowledge, no study has sought to examine how gender is enacted in the venture creation process. Second, the majority of entrepreneurship studies in the health care sector are predicated on 'for-profit' (primarily American) models of economic exchange. Scholars have described efficient revenue models (Hadley and Zuckerman, 2005), attributes of successful entrepreneurial physicians (Bottles, 2000), legal and ethical issues (Herndon Puryear, 1994; Kluge, 1993). Such observations may not be applicable to countries that afford universal publicly funded women's health care. The study explores social entrepreneurship in a public health care setting. Third, only one study explicitly examined women's entrepreneurship in the health care context. Nadin (2007) draws on a sample of female owner/operators of private health care facilities to describe the ways in which sector culture serves to 'silence' female entrepreneurial identity while embracing stereotypical male behaviour. She argues that women's entrepreneurship in health care is overlooked and that the impact of bureaucratic and political structural arrangements upon their experience is ignored. A lack of research, 'serves, ultimately, to sustain the status quo and its associated patriarchal biases, with gender differences then seen as reflecting the natural order of things' (Nadin, 2007: 456). This study responds by examining women's entrepreneurship and innovation in the Canadian health care sector.

To establish the study context, the literature review focuses on entrepreneurship and feminist theories. These perspectives inform construction of a gender-based typology of new venture organizations. Building on a theoretical foundation, the study documents how Dr Elaine Elizabeth Jolly, OC, MD, FRCS(C) legitimized and, ultimately operationalized a vision to enhance women's health care. The study's methodology is described and observations are presented. The chapter closes with a discussion of findings, including the implications for health care and research. A chronology of key events is available upon request. So, how did one individual build a multidisciplinary and integrated women's health centre in the face of facility rationalization and budget cuts?

REVIEW OF LITERATURE

Shane and Eckhardt (2003) describe venture creation as sequential and assume that opportunities (innovative ideas about women's health care) respond to changes in supply (medical standards, materials and diagnostics) and/or demand (changing patient expectations). However, opportunity alone (a vision for enhanced health care) does not create value. Entrepreneurs must acquire human, financial, social (network) and often political capital to overcome 'inertial forces' and barriers to start-up, barriers that may include: preference for the status quo, competing resource priorities and hospital hierarchy. In a more complex model of venture creation, Ardichvili et al. (2003: 118) suggest that the 'core process' of opportunity development only begins when the entrepreneur has an *above-threshold level of knowledge* or entrepreneurial alertness, including the ability to spot suboptimal deployment of resources.

It is useful to recall that the 'venture' examined is situated in the public sector. Hence, a process model that is sensitive to social outcomes is also warranted. While neoclassical entrepreneurship theory has focused on profit maximization, social entrepreneurship focuses on social outcomes and the leveraging of social capital. Social capital is described as a network attribute or public good (Coleman, 1988; Guclu et al., 2002), and as a resource accrued to an individual or to groups through relationships of mutual acquaintance and recognition (Westlund and Bolton, 2003). Among social entrepreneurs, social networks create norms of reciprocity and trust and facilitate cooperation for mutual benefit (Putnam, 2000). And like above-threshold levels of entrepreneurial alertness described above, different types of social capital are important, to varying degrees, at different stages of venture growth (Mosek et al., 2008).

The for-profit and social entrepreneurship models of venture creation are complementary. Both recognize that knowledge and experience are critical components of entrepreneurial alertness and that entrepreneurs must build reputation and trust in order to bridge social networks and attract financial capital. The models differ with respect to inputs (capital, labour, social capital) and outcomes (profit versus social need, assets and impact).

In contrast to the models described above, Sarasvathy (2001) presents the theory of effectuation and entrepreneurial contingency – a theory that challenges the relevance of linear or sequential venture creation processes. Sarasvathy defines an 'effect' as the operationalization of an abstract human aspiration (for example, enhanced health care for women). She asserts that the concept of effectuation is particularly useful in the context of nascent or non-existent markets (for example innovative and integrated medical models or processes). Furthermore, rather than assume a market exists (and hence, the need for the entrepreneur to segment, target and position a product or service to particular customers), effectuation theory assumes that the original idea (or set of causes) does not create one single effect or 'one single strategic universe for the firm' (Sarasvathy, 2001: 247). She suggests that ventures are created through alliances and cooperative strategies, acts that require listening to customers (patients), building networks and strategic partnerships (professional associations, women's health advocates) and the ability to respond to serendipitous events thereby (and only then) identifying the 'workable' segment profiles. Sarasvathy (2001) concludes that early entrants in a new industry are more likely to have used effectuation processes than causation processes. Given the infancy of medical models predicated on social determinants of health (the vision for the women's health care program), effectuation theory seems potentially relevant. Hence, several models (neoclassical, social and effectuation theory) provide the theoretical foundation from which to observe the venture creation process being studied here. However, all three are mute with respect to gender or 'the feminine voice' in the venture creation process. The next section therefore summarizes feminist criticism of the literature.

LIMITATIONS OF ENTREPRENEURSHIP THEORY

Feminist scholars have argued that entrepreneurship theory is predicated on male norms, behaviours and processes, and that it is important to look beyond entrepreneurship theory to inform discussion about women's entrepreneurship (Ahl, 2004, 2006; Bruni et al., 2004; Brush, 1992; de Bruin et al., 2006). Arguments about gender differences in social interaction, relationship structure and power are also linked to observations about women entrepreneurs' experiences in the health care sector (Nadin, 2007). It is important therefore to examine how culture and institutional decision-making discourage innovative ideas to improve women's quality of life and well-being. Two relevant perspectives to inform discussion are liberal and social feminist theory (Fischer et al., 1993).

Liberal feminism holds that men and women are essentially equal. Gender differences are the consequence of structural barriers or discrimination. In the health care context, structural barriers are reflected in: limited access to medical specialists, availability of women-friendly diagnostics and equipment, and an absence of women in clinical trials, funding committees and hospital boards. Hence, gender differences in health care are the outcome of women's secondary positions in health care decision-making structures.

Social feminism focuses on the unique needs, experiences, competencies and values of women, as women (Black, 1989; Gordon, 1976). Gender is not distinct or separate from decision-making. Social feminism implies that researchers must employ analytical frameworks that explicitly consider the 'ways in which structures support, perpetuate and even create gender differences, rather than merely reflecting on the orientations of those within them' (Mirchandani, 1999: 227). Hence, health care must respond to unique gender differences in the determinants of health.

The two feminist theories reflect different assumptions about gender in the health care context. For some, gender equity means equivalent access to health care resources. For others, biology and women's unique experiences are an integral aspect of 'need identification' and resource provision across all areas of service infrastructure and delivery systems. These different perspectives point to the importance of researchers and health care providers being alert to entrepreneurs' 'gendered' assumptions about need and hence, opportunity recognition. However, this is not straightforward. There are many different perspectives regarding how gender influences inputs and outcomes. Consequently, there are no received definitions or validated measures to capture 'gendered' perspectives. To further explore intersects between feminist and entrepreneurship theory, the following section considers how gender may be enacted within the venture creation process.

THEORY-BUILDING ABOUT THE GENDERED NATURE OF VENTURE CREATION

Only one study identified explicitly discussed gender in the context of venture creation.[1] Bird and Brush (2002: 46–7) describe five dimensions (concept of reality, time, action/interaction, power and ethics) that differentiate the creation process of masculine and feminine entrepreneurial ventures. In summary, concept of reality is associated with entrepreneurial vision. A feminine reality is described as reflective, diffuse, vague and ambivalent. Ideas may initially appear to lack clear direction. In contrast, a traditional (masculine) vision is described as analytical and futuristic wherein agents seek to control. Orientation of time describes the evolution of start-up process. Within feminine ventures, promising ideas are described as non-linear and lacking direction. As a result, multiple concept iterations are common. Time orientation is contrasted to the masculine start-up processes that are characterized as linear, fast-paced and futuristic. Actions and interactions among stakeholders reflect the 'idiosyncrasies of the founder'. Feminine actions and interactions are viewed as emotional, cooperative, harmonizing and empathetic. Masculine actions are described as rational, strategic, competitive, aggressive, violent and distant. Power is identified as a differentiating motive for start-up of a business. Owners of feminine organizations are thought to be motivated by the desire to seek self-mastery or contribute to the social good. Traditional or masculine motives are reflective of behaviour that seeks mastery over others as power is centralized and used for self-benefit or gain. Feminine ethic is described as responsive to others. Owners are open to negotiation and conciliation with apparent aggressors. They are less likely to apply the rule of law. Conflict is mediated. Management of masculine organizations is characterized as restrained, aggressive, and controlling.

While Ahl (2006) does not examine the venture creation *process*, she examines stereotypical (masculine/feminine) entrepreneurial (and opposite) attributes. She reminds scholars that gender differs in time (such as, potentially throughout the venture creation process), place (such as, within public/private spheres) and context (such as, private versus public health care). These masculine/feminine nomenclatures provide a useful schema with which to construct a gendered typology of new venture organizations.

The constructs described as a 'feminine' reality of time, actions and interactions and entrepreneurial attributes are similar to the model of venture creation, as described by effectuation theory (Sarasvathy, 2001). Authors vision the entrepreneurial process to be non-linear or sequential and the outcome of cooperation and alliance-building. Outcomes are also associated with the ability of individuals to respond to serendipitous events. From the literature, we conclude that gender is observed in entrepreneurial (owner and firm) attributes and acted upon within the venture creation process. Gender is theorized to be embedded in opportunity recognition vis-à-vis owner/founder motives, subsequent organizational form, structure, governance and other decision-making processes.

Building upon the above models of venture creation, feminine/ masculine nomenclature advanced by Bem (1981) and described by Ahl (2004) and Bird and Brush (2002), a two-by-two grid of gendered attributes of new venture creation is presented in Table 15.1. Briefly, the horizontal axis depicts a continuum of feminine and masculine 'entrepreneurial' attributes. At one end of the continuum are individuals/organizations that exemplify masculine stereotypes and at the other, feminine stereotypes. The vertical axis depicts a continuum of economic to social and humanitarian outcomes. Given page limitations, the stereotype profile of each quadrant is briefly described.

- *Neoclassical entrepreneurs* are typified as individuals who operate growth-oriented enterprises in the for-profit (primarily private) sector. Stereotypical traits include being self-reliant, assertive, forceful, dominant, willing to take risks and makes decisions easily in addition to being able to take a stand (Ahl, 2004: 57).
- *Contemporary entrepreneurs* operate for-profit (primarily private) sector firms. Individuals are typified as characteristically feminine (affectionate, loyal, sympathetic, warm tender, gentle, sensitive to the needs of others, understanding, compassionate; Ahl, 2004: 58).
- *Social entrepreneurs* are community innovators. Most operate in the not-for-profit and non-governmental sectors and within community facilities, service groups and/or associations. Motives are a blend of social and business principles as individuals seek to limit dependency on donations and government funding (Dorado, 2006). Entrepreneurial traits are associated with social capital defined as a network attribute and a public good (Coleman, 1988; Mort et al., 2003), a resource accrued to an individual or to groups through relationships of mutual acquaintance and recognition (Westlund and Bolton, 2003). Outcomes of social enterprise are focused on community development through self-sufficiency.
- Finally, the lower right quadrant presents *communal entrepreneurs*, individuals who are motivated by humanitarian outcomes (such as to improve the quality of life and well-being of others). They operate primarily (but not exclusively) in the public sector. Owner attributes are stereotypically feminine (Ahl, 2004). A subset of communal

Table 15.1 Gendered attributes of new venture organizations*

Theoretical context		Masculine attributes (high) / Feminine attributes (low)	Feminine attributes (high) / Masculine attributes (low)
Economic/financial (low/high)	Neoclassical entrepreneurship (private enterprise)	*Neoclassical entrepreneurs* Motives: growth, profit maximization Attributes: self-reliant, assertive, strong personality, forceful, has leadership abilities, willing to take risks, self-sufficient, dominant, (Ahl, 2004: 57) Outcomes: financial gain Governance: private shareholders Structure: formal, centralized, clear boundaries, hierarchy	*Contemporary entrepreneurs* Motive: self-determination, autonomy, value driven Attributes: affectionate, loyal, sympathetic, sensitive to others, understanding, compassionate, warm, gentle (Ahl, 2004: 58) Outcomes: balanced financial and non-financial Governance: shared leadership, relational Structure: informal, boundaries are fuzzy, participative
outcomes ········· Social (high/low)	Social entrepreneurship (not-for-profit, NGOs, community and industry associations, other social enterprises)	*Social entrepreneurs* (Dorado, 2006; Mort et al., 2003) Motives: social mission, responsive to social/community needs, limit dependence on donations and government Attributes: social, conscientious, ambitious, visionary Outcomes: community development Governance: volunteers Motives: social good, self-sufficiency Outcomes: community well-being Governance: community leaders and volunteers Structure: responsive to social/community need and internal social assets	*Communal (feminist) entrepreneurs* Motive: to improve quality of life and well-being of others Attributes: affectionate, loyal, sympathetic, sensitive, understanding, compassionate, gentle (Ahl, 2004: 58) Outcomes: collective benefit, group empowerment Motives: to act as change agents Opportunity: a perceived inequality Governance: community, relational, process focused *Feminist entrepreneurs* create enterprises to help address women's subordination to men (for example, for women and by women enterprises)

Note: *Feminine/masculine attributes advanced by Bem (1981) and described by Bird and Brush (2002) and Ahl (2004, 2006).

entrepreneurs is *feminist entrepreneurs*, defined as individuals who found and operate enterprises with the explicit purpose of improving women's quality of life and to redress women's subordination to men. Motives for start-ups are also explicitly (although not exclusively) to enhance women's life conditions. A stereotypical venture can be described as a 'by women, for women enterprise'.

This typology provides a gender-based model of venture creation process. To examine empirically the ways in which gender may be enacted in the venture creation process, the following section outlines the methodologies used to explore entrepreneurial action, as observed in the evolution of an innovative public women's health care centre.

METHODOLOGY

The study employed participant-observation and content analysis of key informant interviews and documents to examine how gender is enacted within the entrepreneurial process. Data collection included: access to SEGWHC documents (internal memos, financial reports, briefings and press releases); attendance at industry and public briefings; one author was an initial member of the Ottawa Community Women's Health Council (hereafter, referred to as Council); periodic unstructured discussions with the Centre founder (Dr Jolly); and unstructured interviews with the focal entrepreneur (now, Director of Medicine of the SEGWHC), the Executive Director of the Council, the Chair of the Council, as well as Council members. Analysis focused primarily on opportunity recognition, resource acquisition strategy, the operating model and social impact of the creation process (as described by Guclu et al., 2002). Potential gendering of actions and interactions are considered.

Rationale

Observational data enabled the researchers to scrutinize strategies and chronicle key events associated with the start-up process. Participant-observation enhanced understanding of behaviour (Yin, 1994). The Ottawa Hospital SEGWHC was chosen as the study's focus for several reasons. The Centre's founder (Dr Jolly) epitomizes attributes of a feminist entrepreneur. The SEGWHC mandate also exemplifies the tenets of liberal and social feminist thought (for example, to respond to the unique needs of women and to improve the welfare of women). Finally, a member of the research team was acquainted with Dr Jolly as a patient and former advisory council member. These relationships facilitated access to key informants and study documents.

Study Observations

Dr Jolly's initial interest in women's health arose from her being one of very few women among her class of medical students. During her early years of medical practice, she was the sole female staff physician at The Ottawa Hospital. Opportunity recognition or the vision for integrated women's health care was the product of her medical specializations (obstetrics and endocrinology) and the breadth and depth of clinical experience. Like serial entrepreneurs, Dr Jolly had previously established a number of medical programs (adolescent genecology, male infertility, mature women's health program). The establishment of these programs during the 1980s and 1990s paralleled a growing awareness about the women's health care movement and social determinants of women's health (for example, different women served or not served because of who they are, where they come from). Her growing interest in holistic care was also a response to observations about an increasing of medical sub-specializations and calls for improved women's health care aligned with patient-centred, collaborative care. Reflecting on the influences that motivated her vision for a women's health centre, Dr Jolly recalled:

> So what is happening at the same time in 1995? The Beijing conference,[2] the women's health movement, the issues related to women's health, looking at five [federally supported] women's health centres of excellence . . . This is a good thing I'm thinking, But pretty much heresy health, because women's health centres of excellence had social mores. They weren't looking at the health of women the way I knew it, because I was the physician.

Drawing from over twenty years of clinical practice, Dr Jolly's vision for integrated women's health care emerged. Her vision focused on the need for comprehensive, multidisciplinary medical services with better utilization of nurses; comprehensive screening; early diagnosis and treatment; training of physicians in integrated gender-specific medicine; patient and public education; and expansion of medical and sociocultural research about and for women. These observations are consistent with the concept of an above-threshold level of entrepreneurial alertness (Ardichvili et al., 2003) about women's health care (Mitchinson, 1988; Munch, 2006).

Actions associated with Dr Jolly formalizing the entrepreneurial vision followed two critical events: unanticipated open heart surgery and, on the *same* day, being awarded Officer of the Order of Canada.[3] Hence, while the vision emerged slowly, documentation of the concept occurred in a very brief post-surgery period (for example, overnight brainstorming session with her daughter). With document in hand, the physician/founder was equipped to formally present her vision to peers, supervisor, the hospital executive and provincial political and bureaucratic decision makers. The next section presents summary observations about the process of *actualizing* a promising idea.

Venture Formation and Resource Acquisition

Initial support came almost exclusively from outside the medical community. This observation is consistent with the findings of Nadin (2007) who has reported about the silencing of women's entrepreneurship within the (American) health care sector. Most colleagues encouraged Dr Jolly to 'stick to what you are doing' particularly given all departments had been asked to rationalize budgets.

> Everybody said, this is crazy, because there are no resources. Everything is falling apart. We don't even know where we are going to be. It sounds very nice in theory, but stick to what you are doing now. You are very good at hormones and menopause and do your lectures and talk about heart health. This was very, very hard.

Dr Jolly's requests to present her vision were declined by her immediate manager. She was therefore forced to by-pass her supervisor and communicate directly with hospital executives. In 2000, Dr Jolly presented her vision to a senior provincial health care committee seeking consultation on program rationalization. An executive briefing was arranged as a result of encouragement from a female Ottawa Hospital Board member. A sympathetic senior physician who had previously established and now managed an Ottawa Hospital Centre also encouraged Dr Jolly to secure support outside the hospital establishment. While moral support was forthcoming from the hospital executive and one member of the provincial committee, funding and administrative support was not. Securing resources to ensure the concept became a reality was solely the responsibility of Dr Jolly.

Ultimately, it was a small group of influential female patients of the physician/entrepreneur who supported her vision. Informal discussions led to introductions to other influential women who were knowledgeable about health care bureaucracy and politics at the provincial and national levels. These series of introductions are described as 'the first breakthrough'. Discussions also led to the establishment of the Ottawa Community Women's Health Council in January 2001.

And it was not an unimpressive group, it was women who had backgrounds in a whole cross-section of areas and professions and political formations and so that was a very crucial first meeting because we all knew each other and saw each other in a new context. It was a very specific, defined, and achievable project. . . . We all agreed that the millions that were needed were certainly achievable. We needed to have a start with at least one, and from that we could build, and we would use our various political, professional, personal networks to do both, to do a variety of things at the same time, which included not just fundraising obviously, but awareness within the political, private and public sector, of the need for such a centre, what it would do, how it could be achieved and why it was necessary now, and what we would do to make sure it was achieved.

Council members donated critical seed funding (approximately CDN $20 000) that enabled a start-up team to establish dedicated office space, legitimized the vision and demonstrated financial commitment by Council members. Two volunteers, including one full-time member, worked closely with Dr Jolly to spearhead the start-up process. A number of respondents indicated that without the volunteer Council, the Centre would not have been built.

Not surprisingly, financing posed a significant challenge. Several members of the Council were engaged in fundraising on a near full-time basis. Grassroots fundraising, while important, was not sufficient to secure executive and political support. While some Council members were active in community-based fundraising, others worked to identify a major donor. In July 2001, a major financial donation was secured. This was the second breakthrough as the prominent donor provided additional project legitimacy. For example, a social event recognizing the donor was attended by senior provincial bureaucrats, The Ottawa Hospital executive and members of The Ottawa Hospital Board of Trustees. Several respondents noted that without the support of one lead donor, the hospital administration would not have supported the establishment of the Centre.

A related challenge identified by a Council member was the need for a full-time person(s) with specialized training to ascertain funding options and to prepare the proposals. This never happened. To ensure that almost 100 per cent of monies raised went to the Women's Health Centre (atypical in fundraising circles), fundraising was undertaken entirely by volunteers. The Centre is the outcome of extraordinary efforts by, primarily female, volunteers over a protracted (five-year) period.

In Canada, health care is provincially funded. The Centre broke ground in June, 2004 without having secured the full commitment by the provincial government: the province still has not yet provided the promised operational funding. By fall 2008, the provincial Ministry of Health had provided approximately CDN $250 000 of the CDN $2 million for the purchase of vital equipment that was originally requested by the Council. As a result, Centre staff is now faced with ongoing fundraising.

Observations about the Council's Operating Model

The Council's mandate was to build an integrated women's health care program. The Council also contributed ideas and questions about established administrative practices. Through Council deliberations, the initial proposal for an integrated health care program evolved into a stand-alone (brick and mortar) facility or centre. The revised objective, to build a Centre, helped to further legitimize the health care concept and presented an attainable target for Council.

Exemplifying the importance of reputation and expert knowledge about due process within health bureaucracy, the Council was composed of influential women from a cross-section of professional and political backgrounds. Some had worked together on feminist projects such as Canada's Charter of Rights. Council operated outside the hospital administration and medical community, both figuratively and physically. While Council members briefed hospital administrators about their operational plans, there continued to be little demonstrated interest by most of Dr Jolly's immediate colleagues. It is interesting to observe that there was little discussion about alternative medical or health care delivery models.[4] The single focus (to build a Centre) may have served to avoid Council dissention. A Council member explains the subtleties of that situation:

> We almost were sidelined at one point because of some differences about definitions of women's health, but (XX) was quite clear that this was about building a medical facility which would provide at its core medical service but which would have an educational networking component as well, an outreach which maybe in another report you may look at whether that was achieved, but the idea was that this was a medical facility, part of The Ottawa Hospital, it would provide medical services, and in addition to that, we would all lend our various expertises, as guest lecturers, or whatever, but the idea was that, initially, that it was a medical place.

Council structure was hierarchical with articulated expectations about member roles and responsibilities. The seed funding provided from Council members reflected a membership populated by well-established, relatively affluent members. As such, Council members were aware that the early Council did not reflect the profile of the anticipated Centre's client base. Council member's long-term (five-year) and substantial voluntary commitment appears to be the product of respect for Dr Jolly as well as her reputation. Council members also expressed trust and respect for the founder's motives. For example, 'For 5 years there was true commitment to the idea and to the concept and to the building of this centre that hadn't existed before. I think there was a mentality of we are a team; it will only happen if we work together on these things'.

Observations about Social Impact

The Centre was positioned as a business case for consolidating medical services. The Centre would therefore enhance rather than replace existing services. In addition to sub-specialized diagnostics and treatment regimes, the vision called for care predicated on the social determinants of women's health. To build community support and secure funding, public communication focused on knowledge sharing about topics associated with women's health and, only then, on the fundraising. Communications were targeted to women's groups. Monitoring was undertaken to ensure messaging was accurate. For example, in 2002, information was received that the project was perceived as providing services for *mature* women's health rather than a place specializing in women's health. Adjustments were made such as ensuring youth representatives were among the steering committee. The broad base of the Centre's programs, Dr Jolly feels, worked for the Centre's benefit:

> I think more of the political issue that it was a good news story for [the] government. And that's how we sold it; we said 'What a perfect model.' We have a community, we are not developing a program out of the blue that the clinical team thinks is important and the community doesn't support. . . . this could be a demonstration project for other programs to develop with the same kind of model, and indeed that is what happened with other models that had community support.

Currently, the SEGWHC is an amalgamated Centre within The Ottawa Hospital. Citing observations that the Centre was the outcome of *external* lobbying and fundraising, respondents expressed concern that the Centre is now vulnerable to conflicting hospital priorities. Respondents also voiced concern about the lack of advocacy and/or benchmarking performance of the Centre's long-term vision (for example, ensuring policies and programs concerning health promotion, disease prevention and treatment address the economic and socio-political realities of women's lives; placing a high priority on involving women in decision-making about their health; developing innovative strategies that foster the pursuit of quality and efficiency; strengthening partnerships and links with universities, community colleges, professional associations, health services and community agencies).

DISCUSSION

The physician's entrepreneurial alertness was an outcome of being a woman within a medical education and hospital system. Formulation required a social network (female patients) and cooperative alliances (joint events with DIVA Foundation Canada, a women's health advocacy organization, Women-in-Law, executive women's network, University of Ottawa Faculty of Engineering). Social ties among Council members were strong. Trust and respect for Dr Jolly and a single focus (build a centre) fostered Council cohesiveness. Respondents were consistent in their view that without Council support, strategic lobbying and a lead donation, the Centre concept would not have received hospital or provincial support.

These observations align with effectuation theory and the role played by highly regarded individuals that endorse the start-up concept (Hoang and Antoncic, 2003). Council served as a 'process-orientated network' (Starr and MacMillan, 1990), one that enabled the physician/entrepreneur to access hospital executives, politicians, senior provincial bureaucrats and investors (a key donor). The network also provided reputation capital and signalled project legitimacy.

Consistent with the construct of feminist entrepreneur, the physician/entrepreneur exemplifies stereotypical social outcomes such as the desire to enhance women's quality of life and well-being. However, observations hint that while 'promising ideas' may reflect feminine attributes, actions and interactions required to operationalize ideas (for example, resource strategy) typified feminine *and* masculine stereotypical behaviours. The venture formation process is only partially consistent with the 'feminine reality', as described by Bird and Brush (2002). Knowledge sharing was directly associated with the act of caring. However, the venture creation process was also analytical antecedents of stereotypical masculine behaviour described by Bird and Brush (2002). With respect to *concept of reality*, the Centre's mandate typifies a feminine organization (for example, empowering women to make informed choices, integration of services). The *orientation of time* was long term, with multiple concept iterations as well as futurist vision. Actions and interactions were rational, strategic, and aggressive. While Council discussion was collaborative, there was little emotion in the governance and operational process. Again, these behaviours are consistent stereotypical masculine behaviour described by Bird and Brush (2002). With respect to *power* and *ethics*, the physician/entrepreneur and Council member motives were consistent with 'feminine organizations', where intentions are characterized by a desire to contribute to the social good.

CONCLUSIONS

This study's objective was to examine how one physician/entrepreneur successfully built a women's health centre in the face of rationalization and budget cuts. The question provided context to examine the gendered nature of creation venture (Ahl, 2004; Bird and Brush, 2002). The literature found that no single theory adequately captures the gendering of venture creation. In response, a two-by-two grid that describes gendered attributes of new venture organizations was developed. The construct of *feminist entrepreneur* was also defined. The study then provided insights about the attributes of feminist entrepreneurs. Observations illustrate the ways in which gender is enacted within opportunity recognition and enterprise start-up.

Opportunity recognition was the product of the physician/entrepreneur's unique medical and clinical knowledge – including awareness about the need for holistic care to counterbalance medical sub-specializations, insights gained from the women's health movement and calls for political engagement. The Centre was positioned as an innovative solution to improve health care efficiencies and at the political level, to garner votes. Lynchpins in project success were: the physician's entrepreneurial drive; establishment of an external and prominent advisory council; social networks comprised of family members, patients and other experienced and knowledgeable women; discrete and strategic political and bureaucratic lobbying by Council members; outreach that resulted in a large lead donation; and targeted knowledge sharing.

While the physician/entrepreneur was motivated to contribute to women's well-being (a feminine attribute), acquiring resources to formulate her vision reflected masculine/feminine behaviour. One explanation for the hybrid process is that while opportunity recognition (social need) reflected a female experience, the political, bureaucratic and financial resources required to operationalize the opportunity (vision) are controlled primarily by men. This explanation is consistent with concerns identified in the women's health care movement.

Implications for Health Care

The study provides insight about the challenges facing those who seek to champion innovative, multidisciplinary women's health programs. For example, the women's health care movement has called for patient-centred, gender-specific medical practices and accreditation standards (DIVA Foundation of Canada; Ehrenreich and English, 1978; Mitchinson, 1988; Spirit of Women).[5] The SEGWHC embodies many such attributes. Respondents also noted that the lessons learned from the SEGWHC provide insight for administrators of other hospitals' systems about medical models predicated on the social determinants of health, particularly with respect to women's health care.

The study found that the physician/entrepreneur was encouraged to maintain the status quo. Requests to present the health care concept were declined. At the executive level, indifference (for example, moral but no financial support) stymied efforts to effect change. Trust, respect, administrative assistance and capital acquired through an influential and predominately female advisory council ultimately led to hospital and provincial support.

Service integration is a relationship process rather than a medical practice. Given that the SEGWHC is one of several centres at The Ottawa Hospital, given that scarcity of resources is ongoing, and given the concerns voiced by study respondents, the long-term vision of the SEGWHC may be threatened. Integration of women's health care across The Ottawa Hospital and larger community requires clear performance targets that are established at the executive and provincial levels. Political leadership is also required given (American) research that indicates women's health outcomes are directly influenced by regional health care policies (Wisdom et al., 2005). This study may facilitate discussion among practitioners, hospital administrators, policy makers and women heath advocates about strategies to overcome systemic barriers to innovative, women-centred health care.

With respect to future health care research, work should include development of a gender-sensitive service delivery scorecard predicated on the social determinants of health. Such a scorecard would complement existing patient-focused women's health indices (for example, The Women's College Women's Health Index). Documenting lessons learned from (American) women's health advocacy accreditation programs (for example, The Spirit of Health) and estimating the incremental impact and cost efficiencies of integrated health care are additional next steps.

Implications for Entrepreneurship Research

The study illustrates the need to differentiate stereotypical feminine/masculine attributes inherent in opportunity recognition (vision) from other processes within new venture formation (resource acquisition). One potential reason for this observation is that while opportunity recognition may reflect stereotypical female (feminine) experiences, the political, bureaucratic and financial resources required to operationalize the 'opportunity' are controlled primarily by men. This explanation is consistent with concerns identified in the 'women's health care movement'. Alternatively, perhaps venture formation is androgynous. This study motives further examination about how gender is enacted in venture formation. For example, research is required to explore further the attributes of feminine and feminist entrepreneurs and the association of opportunity recognition (feminist vision) to venture formulation and performance. The study also lends further support for development of 'feminist entrepreneurship theory', theory that seeks to not only explain gender in the venture creation process but to 'do something about it'.

ACKNOWLEDGEMENTS

The research team would like to acknowledge the important contributions of Dr Elaine Jolly (Medical Director of The Ottawa Hospital SEGWHC), Maureen McTeer, Linda Schumacher and other members of the (former) Ottawa Women's Health Council. Your insights and recollections about the history of the SEGWHC were invaluable in preparing this report. Thanks also to Amanda Grant-Orser who acted as a Research Assistant in the early stage of report writing. Editorial assistance was kindly provided by Lynn Fraser, Pam Midgley, Allan Riding and Susan Redmond.

NOTES

1. DeTienne and Chandler (2007) compare sequential decision processes of male and female students and entrepreneurs. Application of results in the current study context is limited.
2. The 1995 Beijing World Conference on Women mission statement calls for women's full and equal share in economic, social, cultural and political decision-making, shared power and responsibility, and equality (United Nations, 2008).
3. The Order of Canada is 'the centrepiece of Canada's honours system and recognizes a lifetime of outstanding achievement, dedication to the community and service to the nation'.
4. Medical advisers did, however, seek to identify a 'handful' of pilot research projects in women's health that needed attention and to use such projects to determine how (and if) the medical teams could work together (for example, nurse practitioners, using telemedicine, wireless communication technologies to provide education in area). As such, Council activities were primarily focused on 'what we have to offer and what we are willing to do' to build a Centre (OCWHC, meeting minutes of 27 January 2001).
5. The DIVA Foundation is a Canadian not-for-profit organization dedicated to advancing, rewarding, and celebrating achievements that improve the health and well-being of women (see: http://www.DIVAfoundation.org/awardsgala.html). Spirit of Women (Hospital Network) is a coalition of accredited American hospitals and health care providers that meet standards of excellence in women's health, education, and community outreach (see: http://www.spiritofwomen.org/spirithospitals.html).

REFERENCES

Ahl, H. (2004), *The Scientific Reproduction of Gender Inequality*, Copenhagen: CBS Press.
Ahl, H. (2006), 'Why research on women entrepreneurs needs new directions', *Entrepreneurship Theory and Practice*, **30** (5), 595–621.
Ardichvili, A., Cardozo, R. and Ray, S. (2003), 'A theory of entrepreneurial opportunity identification and development', *Journal of Business Venturing*, **18** (1), 105–23.
Bcm, S.L. (1981), 'Gender schema theory: a cognitive account of sex typing', *Psychological Review*, **88**, 354–64.
Bird, B. and Brush, C. (2002), 'A gendered perspective on organizational creation', *Entrepreneurship Theory and Practice*, **26** (3), 41–65.
Black, N. (1989), *Social Feminism*, New York: Cornell University Press.
Bottles, K. (2000), 'The ideal physician entrepreneur', *The Physician Executive*, **26** (6), 55–8.
Bruni, A, Gherardi, S. and Poggio, B. (2004), 'Entrepreneur mentality, gender and the study of women entrepreneurs', *Journal of Organizational Change Management*, **17** (3), 256–68.
Brush, C.G. (1992), 'Research on women business owners: past trends, a new perspective and future directions', *Entrepreneurship, Theory and Practice*, **16** (4), 5–30.
Coleman, J.S. (1988), 'Free riders and zealots: the role of social networks', *Sociological Theory*, **6** (1), 52–7.
De Bruin, A., Brush, C. and Welter, F. (2006), 'Advancing a framework for coherent research on women's entrepreneurship', *Entrepreneurship Theory and Practice*, **31** (3), 323–39.
DeTienne, D. and Chandler, G. (2007), 'The role of gender in opportunity identification', *Entrepreneurship Theory and Practice*, **31** (3), 365–86.
Dorado, S. (2006), 'Social entrepreneurial ventures: different values so different process of creation, no?', *Journal of Developmental Entrepreneurship*, **11** (4), 319–43.
Ehrenreich, B. and English, D. (1978), *For Her Own Good: 150 Years of the Expert's Advice to Women*, Garden City, NY: Anchor Books.
Fischer, E., Reuber, R. and Dyke, L. (1993), 'A theoretical overview and extension of research on sex, gender, and entrepreneurship', *Journal of Business Venturing*, **8** (2), 151–68.
Gordon, L. (1976), *Women's Body, Woman's Right: A Social History of Birth Control in America*, New York: Grossman.
Guclu, A., Dees, J.G. and Anderson, B.B. (2002), 'The process of social entrepreneurship: creating opportunities worthy of serious pursuit', Center for the Advancement of Social Entrepreneurship: Duke – The Fuqua School of Business, available at: http://www.caseatduke.org/faculty/publications.html (accessed 1 September 2008).
Hadley, J. and Zuckerman, S. (2005), 'Physician-owned specialty hospitals: a market signal for medicare payment revisions', *Health Affairs*, **24**, 491–3.
Herndon Puryear, J. (1994), 'The physician as entrepreneur. The state and federal restrictions on physicians joint ventures', *North Carolina Law Review*, **73** (1), 293–328.

Hoang, H. and Antoncic, B. (2003), 'Network-based research in entrepreneurship. A critical review', *Journal of Business Venturing*, **18** (2), 165–87.

Kluge, E.H. (1993), 'The physician as entrepreneur', *Canadian Medical Association Journal*, **149** (2), 204–5.

Mirchandani, K. (1999), 'Feminist insight on gendered work: new directions in research on women and entrepreneurship', *Gender, Work and Organization, 6* (4), 224–35.

Mitchinson, W. (1988), 'The medical treatment of women', in S. Burt, L. Code and L. Dorney (eds), *Changing Patterns: Women in Canada*, Toronto: McClelland and Stewart, pp. 237–60.

Mort, G., Weerawardena, J. and Carnegie, K. (2003), 'Social entrepreneurship: towards conceptualization', *International Journal of Non-profit and Voluntary Sector Marketing*, **8** (1), 76–88.

Mosek, L., Gillin, M. and Katzenstein, L. (2008), 'Evaluating the tension within a not-for-profit organization, when developing a business model for the maintenance of a sustainable profitable business venture', *Australia Graduate School in Entrepreneurship Conference Proceedings*, Melbourne: Australia Graduate School in Entrepreneurship, pp. 501–16.

Munch, S. (2006), 'The women's health movement: making policy, 1970–95', *Social Work in Health Care*, **43** (1), 17–32.

Nadin, S. (2007), 'Entrepreneurial identity in the care sector: navigating the contradictions', *Women in Management Review*, **22** (6), 456–67.

Putnam, R. (2000), *Bowling Alone. The Collapse and Revival of American Community*, New York: Simon and Schuster.

Sarasvathy, S.D. (2001), 'Causation and effectuation: toward a theoretical whift from economic inevitability to entrepreneurial contingency', *Academy of Management Review*, **26** (2), 243–63.

Shane, S. and Eckhardt, J. (2003), 'The individual-opportunity nexus', in Z. Acs and D. Audretsch (eds), *Handbook of Entrepreneurship Research*, Boston, MA: Kluwer, pp. 55–80.

Starr, J.A. and MacMillan, I.C. (1990), 'Resource cooptation via social contracting: resource acquisition strategies for new ventures', *Journal of Strategic Management*, **11**, 79–92.

United Nations (2008), 'Fourth World Conference on Women', available at: http://www.un.org/womenwatch/daw/beijing/beijingdeclaration.html (accessed 15 September 2008).

Westlund, H. and Bolton, R. (2003), 'Local social capital and entrepreneurship', *Small Business Economics*, **21** (2), 77–12.

Wisdom, J.P., Berlin, M. and Lapidus, A. (2005), 'Relating health policy to women's health outcomes', *Social Science & Medicine*, **61** (8), 1776–84.

Yin, R.K. (1994), *Case Study Research, Design and Methods*, 2nd edn, Newbury Park, CA: Sage Publications.

16. Mentoring women entrepreneurs in the Russian emerging market

Jill Kickul, Mark D. Griffiths, Lisa K. Gundry and Tatiana Iakovleva

INTRODUCTION

The presence of women leading small and entrepreneurial organizations has had a tremendous impact on employment and global business environments (Diana Project, 2005; Minniti et al., 2005). The size and growth of this phenomenon has attracted considerable attention from academics, practitioners and policymakers. Many studies identifying the success factors of small and medium-sized enterprises (SMEs) have been carried out in advanced countries (Anna et al., 2000; Chaganti and Parasuraman, 1997; Lerner and Almor, 2002). Economic research on entrepreneurship in transitioning economies is less developed with respect to the use of rigorous scientific approaches (Tkachev and Kolvereid, 1999). In emerging economies, the expanding network of entrepreneurial firms is at the forefront of economic development (Neace, 1999), and factors that influence the growth of these enterprises are of particular research interest. In particular, *how do entrepreneurs in emerging markets obtain the knowledge and information needed to enhance business development and success?* How exactly does the growing network of enterprises described by Neace (1999) help entrepreneurs? For example, *does it provide the opportunity for social learning?* The study presented in this chapter focuses on a large group of Russian women entrepreneurs and the role mentoring plays in facilitating entrepreneurial self-efficacy, decision-making, and firm performance.

Research has shown that entrepreneurial learning is crucial to the survival and growth of entrepreneurial businesses and, as Sullivan (2000) argues, mentors provide value-added interventions that contribute to the long-term success of these businesses. Mentors may provide the support entrepreneurs need when it matters most. Mentoring has been studied principally in the context of the large corporation and within the framework of career development, training and performance. Very little research has been conducted on the role of mentors in the development and growth of entrepreneurial businesses, particularly in the context of transitioning economies. Studies have often looked at mentoring and networking together, although these processes may be distinct from one another in the degree of formality, and the frequency and type of interactions that distinguish mentors and protégés from activities that involve participation in professional networks.

In the entrepreneurial context, such social sources of information that are related, for example, to opportunities, are gaining greater research attention (Ozgen and Baron, 2007). As shown, mentors help protégés acquire useful information, skills and knowledge, and help them avoid or cope with the problems and challenges confronting them (Clutterbuck and Ragins, 2002). While acknowledging that much of the research on mentoring has been focused on larger organizations, it is increasingly becoming apparent that entrepreneurs can also reap benefits from mentors. Ozgen and Baron (2007) suggested that mentors help entrepreneurs by offering them frameworks for interpreting complex information, such as the process of opportunity recognition.

While contemporary research has shown that women entrepreneurs recognize the precursors of growth and the importance of activities such as information seeking and planning to their strategic leadership role (Cliff, 1998; Gundry and Welsch, 2001; Kickul et al., 2007), our study seeks to extend previous research by investigating the influence of mentors on perceptions of entrepreneurial self-efficacy and its relation to the performance of women-led firms. Thus, we are investigating both the direct and indirect role of mentors in helping women entrepreneurs in emerging markets achieve superior performance.

With their need for knowledge and information about business development and growth, mentors may be attractive resources to these women. We know that entrepreneurs learn from a variety of incidents and experiences. Of particular interest is whether entrepreneurs who are new entrants in a developing market economy can benefit from the presence of mentors and gain the confidence they need to make appropriate and effective decisions. Research has suggested that transitioning economies present a promising context in which to investigate linkages between individual perceptions and strategic behavior of firms (Peng and Luo, 2000).[1]

ENTREPRENEURSHIP IN RUSSIA: BUSINESS CREATION WITHIN A TRANSITIONING ECONOMY

Entrepreneurship in a transitioning economy is distinctive, and the transformation to a market-based economy is fraught with challenges and obstacles. Characteristics of such economies include unpredictable and often hostile external environments and resource (especially financial) scarcity (Smallbone and Welter, 2001). The study of entrepreneurship in transition economies over the last 10–15 years has included research on start-ups in Poland (Erutku & Vallée, 1997), venture capital in Hungary, Poland and Slovakia (Karsai et al., 1998), as well as studies on the growth of women-owned firms in Turkey (Esim, 2000; Hisrich and Ozturk, 1999) and India (Mitra, 2002).

Perhaps the largest transitioning economy, other than India or China, is Russia where the development of the entrepreneurship and small business sector has been slower than in some other transition economies. Further, Russian entrepreneurial activity is relatively low in terms of international comparison (Verkhovskaya et al., 2007). As we discuss below, this is partly explained by the unfriendly operating environment for entrepreneurs and small businesses which is characterized by extensive bureaucracy, corruption and weakly developed financial markets and state support mechanisms for beginning entrepreneurs (Karhunen et al., 2008; Verkhovskaya et al., 2007). But also, the Russian entrepreneurial culture is young, and entrepreneurial attitudes of many older Russians are still influenced by the Soviet past, where private enterprise activity was considered as immoral and even criminal activity.

The characteristics of Russian entrepreneurs working in small-value trade marketplaces are different from the entrepreneurship population in general: they are mostly women (70 per cent), and a disproportionate number of them are either pensioners or students (Babaeva, 1998). Previous research has also found that most entrepreneurs perceive the external environment as unfriendly. High taxes, an inconsistent legislation system, high dependence of economic life upon political turbulence, and inflation were mentioned as factors prohibiting business in Russia (Iakovleva, 2001, Ylinenpää and Chechurina, 2000).[2] Lack of start-up capital in the face of the prevailing business laws and the tax system are particularly challenging for women's entrepreneurship in Russia. Other barriers limiting entrepreneurship development mentioned by Russian female entrepreneurs in the Ylinenpää and Chechurina study included: high taxes (90 per cent of respondents), inconsistency of laws (81 per cent), availability of capital (67 per cent), banks' instability (66 per cent), inflation (66 per cent), corruption (55 per cent), and criminality (39 per cent).[3] While earlier studies of female Russian entrepreneurs depicted a stark contrast between them and their US counterparts with respect to their major issues of concern (Babaeva, 1998), more recent studies suggest that the goals and concerns of women entrepreneurs across cultures may be more alike than dissimilar. For example, the Wells et al. (2003) study of over 500 Russian women business owners, who reported that growth and expansion were their most important business goals, indicated they were pursuing innovative strategic practices and import/export initiatives at a rate that exceeded their American counterparts.

Among the common characteristics of transitioning economies, including Eastern Europe and the former Soviet republics, is the lack of institutions that support market activities (Khanna and Palepu, 1997). Thus, entrepreneurs need basic activities such as collecting market information and interpreting policies and regulations (Khanna and Palepu, 1997). Further, interpersonal ties developed by managers, and in this case, entrepreneurs, are likely to have a significant influence on firm performance (Peng and Luo, 2000).

Russian women generally have a high level of education (80 per cent), and many possess more than one degree from institutions of higher education. This factor, combined with their responsibility, their patience in running their businesses and their ability to establish relationships, leads to steadier levels of employment and higher income generation in women-owned companies (Gorbulina, 2006). While the profile of Russian entrepreneurs as well as their motivation to start their businesses was explored in studies over the past decade, this study takes an additional step and proposes a theoretically driven model explaining the important role of mentoring for fostering stronger firm performance of women SMEs in Russia.

That said, when the gender-related characteristics of the attitude toward entrepreneurship are examined, there is an absence of substantial differences between men and women in rating most of the factors described. The only exception is the score for the knowledge, qualifications and abilities for starting a business where men are twice as self-confident and think they possess sufficient knowledge to set up their own business. Men are more predisposed to risk, as one in three experiences no fear before creating a new business. At the same time, only one in every four women believes herself capable of entrepreneurial activity (Verkhovskaya et al., 2007). This difference was a prime motivator in our desire to examine the role of mentoring among women entrepreneurs in Russia.

FACTORS AFFECTING VENTURE PERFORMANCE: A ROLE FOR MENTORING?

While the performance of new ventures has been widely studied (see for example, Chandler and Hanks, 1994; Kolvereid and Shane, 1995; Westhead et al., 2005), there is no consensus regarding the basic constructs that affect a new venture performance. The personality of the entrepreneur is often perceived by practitioners as one of the most fascinating topics in the field of entrepreneurship (Delmar, 2000). Some believe that a successful entrepreneur is a result of the special set of personal abilities and characteristics, rather than other factors. Often the human capital characteristics of the entrepreneur or of the members of the founding team provide personal abilities that facilitate small firm growth and performance (Bird, 1993; Chandler and Jansen, 1992; Davidsson, 1989).

Human capital theorists argue that the breadth of human capital resources will be associated with higher levels of productivity (Becker, 1993). Specific human capital is most valuable when the contributing individuals have characteristics closely related to the new venture's needs. Business similarity, prior start-ups, years of previous entrepreneurial experience and role models including mentoring were shown to have positive effects on performance (Brown, 1990; Graham and O'Neill, 1997). Thus, the specific role of mentoring in a transitioning market context is worthy of exploration.

THE INFLUENCE OF ROLE MODELS AND MENTORS: A SOCIAL LEARNING THEORY PERSPECTIVE

Social learning theory (SLT) proposes that one way learning occurs vicariously, through the observation of others seen as role models (Bandura, 1977, cited in Scherer et al., 1989). Adapting the principles of SLT to entrepreneurial role models in the form of mentors would suggest that individuals having greater exposure to other entrepreneurs are more likely to engage in entrepreneurial ventures and activities (Shaver and Scott, 1991). Further, scholars have noted that networking activities are one predictor of survival under uncertain conditions for ventures existing in formally controlled economies (Lyles et al., 2004). Mentoring in the context of support to novice entrepreneurs has been defined as a protected relationship between a veteran and a newcomer in which learning and experimentation can take place, guidance is provided, and new skills can be developed in the pursuit of personal goals and business success (Brown, 1990; Graham & O'Neill, 1997). In addition to experienced entrepreneurs, entrepreneurial mentors also appear in the form of other family members, employers, teachers, or anyone whom the individual has had an opportunity to observe (Sexton and Smilor, 1986). Private sector partnerships for mentoring have been described as one of the determinants of success in new venture creation (Lalkaka, 2003). However, Cope and Watts (2000) caution against the assumption that mentoring is the most important form of learning, since experiential learning in which entrepreneurs learn from their own mistakes as well as successes is very powerful (Bechard and Toulouse, 1991; Cope and Watts, 2000).

Mentors typically support entrepreneurs as they start and grow their businesses by providing expert help and assistance in problem solving, influencing behavioral and attitudinal change (Sullivan, 2000). A mentor's role can be strategic and developmental by calling attention to specific events or critical incidents that have occurred in the history of the business and relating them to the present circumstances. For women, the role of mentors as role models may be particularly significant. There is a substantial body of research on the role of mentoring in organizations (for example, Lankau and Skandura, 2002; Murrell et al., 2008). The importance of a role model – someone who has achieved goals to which they may be aspiring and is a source of strategies for both success and survival – is crucial to the career development of women. Previous research in this area has identified (for example, Ozgen and Baron, 2007) the need for knowledge and information on how to identify opportunities and grow their businesses. Our study seeks to explore the role of mentoring on firm performance of women-led entrepreneurial businesses in a transitioning economy.

Hypothesis 1:   Mentoring is positively associated with firm performance of women entrepreneurs in the transitioning Russian economy.

ENTREPRENEURIAL SELF-EFFICACY AND VENTURE PERFORMANCE

Cognitive models offer the most sophisticated theoretical frame of reference to explain both entrepreneurial intentions and performance, which incorporates the complexity of entrepreneurial behavior, and enables the actual test of the model (Delmar, 2000). The cognitive behavioral models explain both highly complex behavior and differences in choices and performance through entrepreneurial competencies. Often, the competencies of founders are found to be crucial to venture performance (Brush and Hisrich, 1991; Lerner et al., 1997). These competencies, in turn, depend upon both general and specific human capital characteristics. Self-assessed competencies are the core of an individual's self-efficacy beliefs about their personal 'capabilities to mobilize the motivation, cognitive resources, and courses of action needed to exercise control over events in their lives' (Wood and Bandura, 1989: 364). It was found that entrepreneurs with higher perceived self-efficacy achieve higher performance (Westerberg, 1998). Recently, a global study of women's entrepreneurial activity has shown the importance of self-efficacy as a factor in determining actual entrepreneurial participation. The perception of having the needed skills was shown to be a dominant variable that had an effect independent of other contextual variables (Minniti et al., 2005).

One of the core entrepreneurial competencies (and self-efficacy issues) is opportunity competence – the ability to recognize and develop market opportunities through various means. Since this competency is deemed especially important for new ventures in emerging economies, it is of research interest to assess the influence of the entrepreneurial self-efficacy of the respondents on the performance of their firms. Individuals with strong entrepreneurial characteristics, in particular with high self-efficacy operationalized as opportunity competence, are hypothesized to be more likely to have successful and higher performing ventures than entrepreneurs who do not have these characteristics (Covin and Miles, 1999; Stewart et al., 1998). Thus, the following hypothesis:

Hypothesis 2: Entrepreneurial self-efficacy of Russian women entrepreneurs is positively related to firm performance.

DETERMINANTS OF ENTREPRENEURIAL SELF-EFFICACY: THE 'ROLE' OF MENTORS

If, as has been shown, self-efficacy has a significant impact on the choice of career path and firm performance, then it is of interest to explore possible antecedents to self-efficacy. Boyd and Vozikis (1994) proposed that self-efficacy can be enhanced by some human capital variable, such as previous work experience, entrepreneurial experience and role models. Bandura (1992) posits that our confidence in our ability to perform certain tasks is developed in four ways: 'mastery experiences', 'modeling', 'social persuasion' and 'judgments of our own physiological states'. Research by Scherer et al. (1990) suggests that lower self-efficacy among women, and their lower intentions for entrepreneurship, stem in part from a paucity of personal or related experiences which are associated (at least by them) with being successful as an entrepreneur. In addition, to the extent that mentors are role models, this result may be due in part to the importance of 'modeling' as a way of developing self-efficacy (Bandura, 1992). That is, in addition to the 'mastery experiences' described above, self-efficacy can be enhanced through social persuasion, or the positive encouragement and feedback that individuals are given by role models (Cox et al., 2002).

Additionally, many of the functions of the mentor relationship may increase entrepreneurial self-efficacy, such as sponsorship, coaching, access to challenging work assignments, and access to important informal social networks through which information and new opportunities are exchanged (Kram, 1983). These aspects of mentoring have the important effect of providing a road map to women as they navigate their careers. As women undertake business creation in an emerging market context, they may rely on mentors to provide the crucial information and learning needed to develop their businesses.

Finally, social support theory proposes that the support received from interpersonal relationships has a positive effect on how one copes with stress or life change. Individuals rely on relationships to provide emotional reassurance, needed information and instrumental aid (Fisher, 1985). Mentoring has been shown to be a crucial source of social support. The relationship has been connected to greater feelings of confidence, competence and credibility (Thomas, 2001). Based on the research, the following propositions are provided:

Hypothesis 3: The greater the degree of mentoring, the higher the entrepreneurial self-efficacy of Russian women entrepreneurs.

Hypothesis 4: The greater the degree of entrepreneurial self-efficacy stemming from mentoring, the higher the firm performance. That is, self-efficacy will serve as a critical link in the relationship between mentoring and firm performance for Russian women entrepreneurs.

METHODOLOGY

Participants

The sample consisted of 555 Russian women entrepreneurs associated with the Russian Women's Microfinance Network (RWMN). Currently, RWMN operates in six regions in Russia: Kostroma, Tver, Kaluga, Belgorod, Vidnoe and Tula, with the head office in Moscow. A preliminary questionnaire was designed in English and evaluated by the research team during 2004. As a standard test of translation accuracy, the questionnaire was then translated into Russian and translated back into English. After the questionnaire was constructed and pre-tested, it was sent electronically to the RWMN that was responsible for printing and distributing the instrument to its divisions.

A face-to-face data collection process was then used to gather responses from a large number of respondents who would be encouraged to answer most questions. One coordinator was assigned for each of the six RWMN regions, reporting data to the managing coordinator in Moscow. A total

Table 16.1   Sample characteristics

Variables	Number	Percentage
Respondents		
Respondent status		
Founders and/or owners (shareholders)	525	95
Directors and/or managers (employees)	30	5
Average respondent age (years)	40	
Entrepreneurial experience of parents		
Yes	76	14
No	469	86
Enterprises		
Subsidiary of another business		
Yes	24	5
No	525	95
Family business		
Yes	310	56
No	242	44
Average firm age	8	
Average number of employees	4	
Limited liability companies	33	6
Closed joint-stock companies	3	0.5
Open joint-stock companies	2	0.4
Sole proprietorships	514	93
Manufacturing	28	5
Trade	442	80
Service	81	15

of 555 questionnaires were adequately completed and received (see Table 16.1 for descriptive statistics).

Dependent Variable: Firm Performance

It is suggested that studies should include the multiple dimensions of performance and use multiple measures of those dimensions (Murphy et al., 1996). Thus, performance is measured by both the importance and satisfaction questions (see Table 16.2). Respondents were asked to indicate the degree of importance their enterprise attached to the following items over the previous three years: sales level, sales growth, turnover, profitability, net profit, gross profit and the ability to fund enterprise growth from profits. They were then asked how satisfied they were with these same indicators. A slightly modified version of the questions used by Iakovleva

Table 16.2   PCA for composite performance

Variables	Factor loadings	Commonality
Composite performance		
Sales level satisfaction × importance	0.87	0.76
Sales growth satisfaction × importance	0.89	0.80
Turnover satisfaction × importance	0.87	0.75
Profitability satisfaction × importance	0.90	0.81
Net profit satisfaction × importance	0.88	0.78
Gross profit satisfaction × importance	0.88	0.78
Ability to fund business from the profit satisfaction × importance	0.80	0.64
Eigenvalue	5.31	
Percentage variance explained	75.85	
Cronbach's alpha	0.95	

Notes:
Factor loadings 0.3 or smaller are suppressed.
KMO = 0.925, Bartletts's test of Sphericity App. χ^2 = 3392.079; df = 21, Sig. 000.

(2005, 2007) was employed. Importance questions were re-scaled from a seven-point Likert scale to range between −3 and 3, and then satisfaction and importance scores were multiplied. Next, principal component analysis was performed resulting in one factor that we labelled 'performance' (α = 0.95).

Independent Variables

Mentoring
Mentoring roles and functions was measured with a six-item scale that was adapted from Scandura and Hamilton (2002). Table 16.3 includes the items and functions based on factor analysis results.

Entrepreneurial self-efficacy
Entrepreneurial self-efficacy was measured using the De Noble et al. (1999) six-item self-efficacy measure that focuses on innovation and product development skills. Cronbach's alpha was .83 (see Table 16.4).

RESULTS

Multiple regression analysis was used to test hypotheses (1) and (2). Mediated regression approach recommended by Baron and Kenny (1986)

Table 16.3   PCA for mentoring

Variables	Factor loadings	Commonality
Mentoring		
I exchange confidences with my mentor	0.781	0.611
My mentor gives me special coaching as an entrepreneur	0.763	0.582
I admire my mentor's ability to motivate others	0.752	0.566
My mentor has devoted special time and consideration to my entrepreneurial career	0.743	0.552
My mentor has taken a personal interest in my entrepreneurial career	0.707	0.500
I try to model my behaviour after my mentor's	0.684	0.468
Eigenvalue	3.278	
Percentage variance explained	54.639	
Cronbach's alpha	0.82	

Notes:
Factor loadings 0.3 or smaller are suppressed.
KMO = 0.835, Bartletts's test of Sphericity App. χ^2 = 498.425; df = 15, Sig. 000.

was used to test hypotheses (3) and (4). In conducting our analyses, we found support for hypothesis (1). That is, mentoring (role models) was positively associated with firm performance (see Table 16.5). In addition, we also found support for hypothesis 2, in that self-efficacy was also positively related to the firm performance (see Table 16.6). Moreover, results also revealed support for hypothesis 3 in that the greater the degree of mentoring, the higher the entrepreneurial self-efficacy (see Table 16.7). However, in our final set of mediated analyses, we found only partial support for hypothesis 2. More specifically, self-efficacy partially mediated the relationship between the mentoring and firm performance (see Table 16.8).

DISCUSSION AND CONCLUSIONS

The study presented in this chapter investigated the role of mentoring and self-efficacy on the performance of women-led entrepreneurial firms in the Russian transition economy. Results from our study suggest that mentoring is an important developmental relationship for entrepreneurial women, especially for those in emerging and developing markets. By understanding how mentors and role models support women in

Table 16.4   PCA for self-efficacy

Variables	Factor loadings	Commonality
Self-efficacy		
Design products or services that solve current problems	0.869	0.755
Identify new areas for potential growth	0.861	0.741
Bring a product concept to a market in a timely manner	0.787	0.619
Discover new ways to improve existing products/services	0.779	0.607
See new market opportunities for new products/services	0.774	0.600
Create product/services that fulfil customer unmet needs	0.739	0.546
Eigenvalue	3.86	
Percentage variance explained	64.466	
Cronbach's alpha	0.83	

Notes:
Factor loadings 0.3 or smaller are suppressed.
KMO = 0.858, Bartletts's test of Sphericity App. χ^2 = 1782.433; df = 15, Sig. 000.

Table 16.5   Result of MRA of mentoring on performance (test of hypothesis 1)

	Base model St. Beta, listwise	Model 1 St. Beta, listwise	Tolerance for model 1
Trade	−.060	.005	.332
Service	−.058	−.023	.337
Firm age	.128	.116	.988
Munificence	.356***	.312***	.946
Mentoring		.233***	.926
F	9.875	11.108	
Adjusted R^2	0.137***	0.184***	
Number of cases		225	

Note: † < 0.1;* < 0.05; ** < 0.01; *** < 0.001.

these tenuous environments, we may be better able to create the support systems needed to nurture and support women's entrepreneurial performance efforts and self-efficacy in sustaining and building their businesses to the next level of growth. That is, a challenge for many business

Table 16.6   Result of MRA of self-efficacy on performance (test of hypothesis 2)

	Base model St. Beta, listwise	Model 1 St. Beta, listwise	Tolerance for model 1
Trade	−.091	−.068	.322
Service	−.081	−.086	.319
Firm age	−.001	−.019	.976
Munificence	.348***	.255***	.870
Self-efficacy		.272***	.872
F	18.447	24.006	
Adjusted R^2	0.12***	0.183***	
Number of cases		513	

Note: † < 0.1;* < 0.05; ** < 0.01; *** < 0.001.

Table 16.7   Result of MRA of mentoring on self-efficacy (test of hypothesis 3)

	Base model St. Beta, listwise	Model 1 St. Beta, listwise	Tolerance for model 1
Trade	−.257	−.191	.308
Service	−.129	−.090	.314
Firm age	.006	.001	.983
Munificence	.275***	.241***	.960
Mentoring		.224***	.939
F	7.023	8.436	
Adjusted R^2	0.094***	0.139***	
Number of cases		213	

Note: † < 0.1;* < 0.05; ** < 0.01; *** < 0.001.

owners lies in obtaining the appropriate guidance, assistance and information needed to take the business to the next level of growth (Gundry et al., 2002).

Entrepreneurs in transitioning economies tend to have relatively low levels of managerial skills (Lyles et al., 2004). Particularly for women in emerging markets such as Russia, access to information and knowledge is necessary and desired since most were raised and educated within a centralized, planned economy. As highlighted earlier, entrepreneurial mentors can assist their protégés in obtaining useful information, skills and knowledge, and further aid them in confronting new and reoccuring

Table 16.8   Results of hierarchical MRA on performance (test of hypothesis 4)

	Base model St. Beta, listwise	Model 1 St. Beta, listwise	Tolerance for model 2
Trade	.011	.049	.326
Service	−.021	−.002	.336
Firm age	.113	.106	.986
Munificence	.316***	.264***	.876
Mentoring	.239***	.206**	.896
Self-efficacy		.191**	.845
F	11.425	11.335	
Adjusted R²	.189***	.218***	
Number of cases		224	

Note: † < 0.1;* < 0.05; ** < 0.01; *** < 0.001.

firm problems and challenges (Clutterbuck and Ragins, 2002). While most of the research on mentoring has been conducted on more established firms, the latest work by Ozgen and Baron (2007) advocates that mentors can help entrepreneurs by giving them the confidence and frameworks for interpreting complex information and identifing opportunities to aid in firm performance and sustainability. While not the aim of this particular study, additional research should examine how women entrepreneurs *across* other cultures access and leverage mentoring resources, including information seeking and specifically training and education, to develop and grow their businesses. Comparisons can then be made to evaluate some of the common best practices and approaches across cultures and institutional and governmental regimes.

The results hold implications for public policy initiatives, such as entrepreneurial assistance programs supporting the development of mentoring programs for women entrepreneurs. Building on previous work, the results of our study offer information pertinent to supporting the overall mission of programs that assist women entrepreneurs. Experienced mentors can be beneficial to nascent entrepreneurs, and programs that encourage mentors to enter such relationships with women entrepreneurs would be helpful. Such programs may be industry based, or focus on the specific skills and knowledge most useful to nascent entrepreneurs, such as opportunity recognition, creating market awareness, or financing of new ventures.

Scholars have noted that in transitional economies, close personal ties are very important to business survival and growth. Without deep network relations, entrepreneurs may find their path to be especially challenging (Peng, 2001). Mentorship programs provide women entrepreneurs with the opportunity to take what they learn, apply it to their business strategy and get feedback from women who have been through the arduous, but highly rewarding, process of starting their own businesses. These relationships give women an outlet to test concepts and ideas and learn from valuable past experiences of successful female entrepreneurs. Mentors can provide entrepreneurs a first-hand insight into the complexities of launching and managing a new venture. This might include advice about the unique challenges faced by women entrepreneurs such as raising capital, building credibility and forming strategic partnerships. Some businesswomen may even offer the opportunity to intern or job shadow for an extended period of time – providing a woman entrepreneur with the unique opportunity of gaining first-hand experience with a venture in progress and harnessing additional knowledge about the role of a female business owner.

While this study included a large group of women operating in a transitioning economy, there are some limitations and suggestions for future research. First, the sample was obtained in connection with a women's business association, and it may differ from other samples obtained from the population of Russian women entrepreneurs. Further, future research can build on our study by focusing on differential roles of 'expert' capital versus general social capital in the context of gendered entrepreneurship, including how general social capital is instrumental to developing networks of expert capital (or vice versa).

The understanding of how mentors and role models support women entrepreneurs may facilitate the creation of support systems needed to nurture and propel women's entrepreneurial self-efficacy and efforts. While there are stark differences between men and women in their perceptions of entrepreneurial self-efficacy and intentions (women have lower levels of self-efficacy and intentions; see Wilson et al., 2007), mentoring may reduce these gender differences for those women with entrepreneurial aspirations and aid them further in the development and growth of their own firms. In this way, mentoring (and the creation of such support programs) can be positioned as an equalizer, possibly reducing the limiting effects of low self-efficacy and ultimately increasing the chances for venture creation and firm success. More importantly, and as shown with our study with Russian women entrepreneurs, mentoring may be immensely useful for women in emerging and transitioning economies as they seek out, define and leverage their own networks towards the sustainability of their businesses as well as the creation of wealth for themselves and their broader local and regional communities.

NOTES

1. We use the terms emerging markets and trasitioning economies interchangeably.
2. The World Bank Group ranked the Russian Federation 120th out of 181 countries in terms of the 'Ease of doing business' (http://www.doingbusiness.org/economyrankings/).
3. Transparency International (TI) ranked the Russian Federation 147th out of 180 countries with a score of 2.1 in their Corruption Perception Index for 2008 (see http://www.transparency.org/policy_research).

REFERENCES

Anna, A.L., Chandler, G.N., Jansen, E. and Mero, N.P. (2000), 'Women business owners in traditional and non-traditional industries', *Journal of Business Venturing*, **15**, 279–303.

Babaeva, L. (1998), 'Russian and American female entrepreneurs', ('Российские м Американские женщины-предприниматели'), *Sociological Review*, (Социологические исследования), **8**, 134–5.

Bandura, A. (1992), 'Exercise of personal agency through the self-efficacy mechanism', in R. Schwarzer (ed.), *Self efficacy: Thought Control of Action*, Washington, DC: Hemisphere.

Bandura, A. (1997), *Self-efficacy: The Exercise of Control*, New York: Freeman Press.

Baron, R.G. and Kenny, D.A. (1986), 'The moderator-mediator variable distinction in social psychological research: conceptual, strategic, and statistical considerations', *Journal of Personality and Social Psychology*, **51** (6), 1173–82.

Bechard, J. and Toulouse, J. (1991), 'Entrepreneurship and education: viewpoint from Education', *Journal of Small Business and Education*, **9** (1), 3–13.

Becker, G.S. (1993), *Human Capital: A theoretical and Empirical Analysis with Special Reference to Education*, 3rd edn, Chicago, IL: University of Chicago Press.

Bird, B. (1993), 'Demographic approaches to entrepreneurship: the role of experience and background', in J.A. Katz and R.H. Brockhause (eds), *Advances in Entrepreneurship, Firm Emergence and Growth*, vol. 1, Greenwich: JAI Press, pp. 11–48.

Boyd, N. and Vozikis, G. (1994), 'The influence of self-efficacy on the development of entrepreneurial intentions and actions', *Entrepreneurship Theory and Practice*, **18** (4), 63–77.

Brown, T.L. (1990), 'Match up with a mentor', *Industry Week*, **239** (October), 18.

Brush, C.G. and Hisrich, R.D. (1991), 'Antecedent influences on women-owned businesses', *Journal of Managerial Psychology*, **6** (2), 9–16.

Chaganti, R. and Parasuraman, S. (1997), 'A study of the impacts of gender on business performance and management patterns in small businesses', *Entrepreneurship Theory and Practice*, **21** (2), 73–6.

Chandler, G. and Hanks, S. (1994), 'Founder competence, the environment, and venture performance', *Entrepreneurship Theory and Practice*, **18** (3), 223–37.

Chandler, G. and Jansen, E. (1992), 'Founder's self assessed competence and venture performance', *Journal of Business Venturing*, **7** (3), 223–36.

Cliff, J.E. (1998), 'Does one size fit all? Exploring the relationship between attitudes towards growth, gender, and business size', *Journal of Business Venturing*, **13** (6), 523–42.

Clutterbuck, D., and Ragins, B.R. (2002), *Mentoring and Diversity: An International Perspective*, Burlington, MA: Butterworth-Heineman.

Cope, J. and Watts, G. (2000), 'Learning by doing: an exploration of experience, critical incidents and reflection in entrepreneurial learning', *International Journal of Entrepreneurial Behavior and Research*, **6** (3), 104.

Covin, J.G. and Miles, M. (1999), 'Corporate entrepreneurship and the pursuit of competitive advantage', *Entrepreneurship Theory and Practice*, **23**, 47–63.

Cox, L.W., Mueller, S.L and Moss, S.E. (2002), 'The impact of entrepreneurship education on entrepreneurial self-efficacy', *International Journal of Entrepreneurship Education*, **1** (2), 229–45.

Davidsson, P. (1989), *Continued Entrepreneurship and Small Firm Growth*, Stockholm: Stockholm School of Economics.

De Noble, A.F., Jung, D. and Ehrlich, S.B. (1999), 'Entrepreneurial self-efficacy: the development of a measure and its relationship to entrepreneurial action', in R.D. Reynolds, W.D. Bygrave, S. Manigart, C.M. Mason, G.D. Meyer, H.J. Sapienza and K.G. Shaver (eds), *Frontiers of Entrepreneurship Research*, Waltham, MA: P&R Publications, pp. 73–87.

Delmar, F. (2000), 'The psychology of the entrepreneur', in S. Carter and D. Jones-Evans (eds), *Enterprise and Small Business: Principles, Practice and Policy*, Harlow: Financial Times.

Diana Project (2005), *The Diana International Project: Research on Growth Oriented Women Entrepreneurs and Their Businesses*, Stockholm: ESBRI. See http://www.esbri.se/diana.asp (accessed 30 September 2006).

Erutku, C. and Vallée, L. (1997), 'Business start-ups in today's Poland: who and how?', *Entrepreneurship and Regional Development*, **9** (2), 113–26.

Esim, S. (2000), 'Solidarity in isolation: urban informal sector women's economic organizations in Turkey', *Middle Eastern Studies*, **1**, 140–52.

Fisher, C. (1985), 'Social support and adjustment to work: a longitudinal study', *Journal of Management*, **11** (3), 39–53.

Gorbulina, I. (2006), 'Women's small and medium enterprises – path to overcome poverty', paper presented at the Women Leaders Network Meeting, Vietnam, 12 December 2008, available at: http://www.apecwln.org/main/images/WLN%202006/Irina%20Gorbulina%20-%20Women's%20Small%20and%20Medium%20Enterprises%20-%20Path%20to%20Overcome%20Poverty.pdf

Graham, L. and O'Neill, E. (1997), 'Sherpa or shepherd? The adviser relationship in small firms – mentor and/or consultant?', paper presented to the International Small Business Association Small Firms Policy and Research Conference, November. Belfast.

Gundry, L.K. and Welsch, H.P. (2001), 'The ambitious entrepreneur: High-growth strategies of women-owned enterprises', *Journal of Business Venturing*, **16** (5), 453–70.

Gundry, L.K., Ben-Yoseph, M. and Posig, M. (2002), 'The status of women's entrepreneurship: pathways to future entrepreneurship development and education', *New England Journal of Entrepreneurship*, **5** (1), 39–50.

Hisrich, R. and Ozturk, S.A. (1999), 'Women entrepreneurs in a developing economy', *The Journal of Management Development*, **18** (2), 114–25.

Iakovleva, T. (2001), *Entrepreneurship Framework Conditions in Russia and in Norway: Implications for the Entrepreneurs in the Agrarian Sector*, Hovedfagsoppgaven, Norway: Bode Graduate School of Business.

Iakovleva, T. (2005), 'Entrepreneurial orientation of Russian SME', in G.T. Ving and R.C.W. Van der Voort (eds), *The Emergence of Entrepreneurial Economics*, Oxford: Elsevier, pp. 83–98.

Iakovleva, T. (2007), *Factors Associated with New Venture Performance: The Context of St-Petersburg*, Høgskolen i Bodø, PhD serie No. 12-2007.

Karhunen, P., Kettunen, E. Sivonen, T. and Miettinen, V. (2008), *Determinants of knowledge-intensive entrepreneurship in Southeast Finland and Northwest Russia*, Helsinki School of Economics, Mikkeli Business Campus Publications N-77.

Karsai, J., Wright, M., Dudzinski, Z. and Morovic, J. (1998), 'Screening and valuing venture capital investments: evidence from Hungary, Poland and Slovakia', *Entrepreneurship and Regional Development*, **10** (3), 189–202.

Kickul, J. R., Gundry, L.K. and Sampson, S.D. (2007), 'Women entrepreneurs preparing for growth: the influence of social capital and training on resource acquisition', *Journal of Small Business & Entrepreneurship*, **20** (2), 169–82.

Khanna, T. and Palepu, K. (1997), 'Why focused strategies may be wrong for emerging markets', *Harvard Business Review*, **75** (4), 41–51.

Kolvereid, L. and Shane, S. (1995), 'National environment, product strategy and performance: a three country study', *Journal of Small Business Management*, **33** (2), 37–50.

Kram, K.E. (1983), 'Phases of the mentor relationship', *Academy of Management Journal*, **26** (4), 608–25.

Lalkaka, R. (2003), 'Business incubators in developing countries: characteristics and performance', *International Journal of Entrepreneurship & Innovation Management*, **3** (2), 31–55.

Lankau, M.J. and Skandura, T.A. (2002), 'An investigation of personal learning in mentoring relationships: content, antecedents, and consequences', *Academy of Management Journal*, **45**, 779–90.

Lerner, M. and Almor, T. (2002), 'Relationships among strategic capabilities and the performance of women-owned small ventures', *Journal of Small Business Management*, **40** (2), 109–25.

Lerner, M., Brush, C. and Histich, R. (1997), 'Israel women entrepreneurs: An examination of factors affecting performance', *Journal of Business Venturing*, **12**, 315–39.

Lyles, M.A., Saxton, T. and Watson, K. (2004), 'Venture survival in a transitional economy', *Journal of Management*, **30** (3), 351–75.

Minniti, M., Arenius, P. and Langowitz, N. (2005), '2004 report on women and entrepreneurship', *Global Entrepreneurship Monitor*, Wellesley, MA: Center for Women's Leadership at Babson College.

Mitra, R. (2002), 'The growth pattern of women-run enterprises: an empirical study in India', *Journal of Developmental Entrepreneurship*, **7** (2), 212–37.

Murphy, G.B., Trailer, J.W. and Hill, R.C. (1996), 'Measuring performance in entrepreneurship research', *Journal of Business Research*, **36** (1), 15–23.

Murrell, A.J., Blake-Beard, S., Porter, D.M. and Perkins-Williamson, A. (2008), 'Interorganizational formal mentoring: breaking the concrete ceiling sometimes requires support from the outside', *Human Resource Management*, **47** (2), 275–94.

Neace, M.B. (1999), 'Entrepreneurs in emerging economies: creating trust, social capital, and civil society', *The ANNALS of the American Academy of Political and Social Science*, **565** (1), 148–61.

Ozgen, E. and Baron, R.A. (2007), 'Social sources of information in opportunity recognition: effects of mentors, industry networks, and professional forums', *Journal of Business Venturing* **22**, 174–92.

Peng, M.W. (2001), 'How entrepreneurs create wealth in transitional economies', *Academy of Management Executive*, **15** (1), 95–108.

Peng, M.W. and Luo, Y. (2000), 'Managerial ties and firm performance in a transition economy: the nature of a micro-macro link', *Academy of Management Journal*, **43** (3), 486–501.

Scandura, T.A. and Hamilton, B.A. (2002), 'Enhancing performance through mentoring', in, S. Sonnentag (ed.), *The Psychological Management of Individual Performance. A Handbook in the Psychology of Management in Organizations*, Chichester: Wiley, pp. 293–308.

Scherer, R.F., Adams, J.S., Carley, S.S. and Wiebe, F.A. (1989), 'Role model performance effects on development of entrepreneurial career preference', *Entrepreneurship: Theory and Practice*, **13** (3), 53–71.

Scherer, R.F., Brodzinski, J.D. and Wiebe, F.A. (1990), 'Entrepreneur career selection and gender: a socialization approach', *Journal of Small Business Management*, **28** (2), 37–44.

Sexton, D.L. and Smilor, R.W. (1986), *The Art and Science of Entrepreneurship*, Cambridge, MA: Ballinger.

Shaver K.G. and Scott, L.R. (1991), 'Person, process, choice: the psychology of New venture creation', *Entrepreneurship: Theory and Practice*, **16** (2), 23–45.

Smallbone, D. and Welter, F. (2001), 'The distinctiveness of entrepreneurship in transition economies', *Small Business Economics*, **16**, 249–62.

Stewart, W.H., Watson, W.E., Carland, J.C. and Carland, J.W. (1998), 'A proclivity for entrepreneurship: a comparison of entrepreneurs, small business owners, and corporate managers', *Journal of Business Venturing*, **14**, 189–214.

Sullivan, R. (2000), 'Entrepreneurial learning and mentoring', *International Journal of Entrepreneurial Behaviour and Research*, **6** (3), 160–78.

Thomas, D.A. (2001), 'The Truth about mentoring minorities: race matters', *Harvard Business Review*, **79** (4), 98–107.

Tkachev, A. and Kolvereid, L. (1999), 'Self-employment intentions among Russian students', *Entrepreneurship and Regional Development*, **11** (3), 269–80.

Verkhovskaya, O.R., Dermanov, V.K. Dorohina, M.V. and Katkalo, V.S. (2007), *Globalnyi monitoring predprinimatelstva* (*Global Entrepreneurship Monitoring*), *Country Report on Russia 2006*, St Petersburg State University, Higher School of Management (in Russian).

Wells, B.L., Pfantz, T.J. and Bryne, J.L. (2003), 'Russian women business owners: evidence of entrepreneurship in a transition economy', *Journal of Developmental Entrepreneurship*, **8** (1), 59–71.

Westerberg, M. (1998), 'Managing in turbulence: an empirical study of small firms operating in a turbulent environment', doctoral thesis, DT 1998: 43, Luleå University of Technology.

Westhead, P., Ucbasaran, D. and Wright, M. (2005), 'Decisions, actions and performance: do novice, serial and portfolio entrepreneurs differ?', *Journal of Small Business Management*, **43** (4), 393–417.

Wilson, F., Kickul, J. and Marlino, D. (2007), 'Gender, entrepreneurial self-efficacy, and entrepreneurial career intentions: implications for entrepreneurship education', *Entrepreneurship Theory and Practice*, **31** (3), 387–406.

Wood, R. and Bandura, A. (1989), 'Social cognitive theory of organizational management', *Academy of Management Review*, **14** (3), 361–84.

Ylinenpåå, H. and Chechurina, M. (2000), 'Perceptions of female entrepreneurs in Russia', in D. Deschoolmester (ed.), in seminar proceedings *Entrepreneurship under difficult circumstances*, Best Paper in thirtieth European Small Business Seminar, Ghent, Belgium.

17. Gender differences in the growth aspirations and technology orientation of Slovenian entrepreneurs

Karin Širec, Polona Tominc and Miroslav Rebernik

INTRODUCTION

Firm growth is critical to economic development and the creation of wealth and employment. According to the Global Entrepreneurship Monitor (Rebernik et al., 2008) and the Slovenian Entrepreneurship Observatory (Rebernik and Širec, 2009), entrepreneurial potential in Slovenia is not fully utilized. Indeed, small-firm growth, the focal point of this chapter, is neither a self-evident phenomenon nor a matter of chance. Rather, it is the result of an owner's/entrepreneur's clear, positively motivated business intentions and actions, driven by the belief that (s)he can produce the desired outcomes (Gray, 2000; Maki and Pukkinen, 2000). Consequently, exploring issues and challenges facing particular entrepreneurs, such as female entrepreneurs, may offer valuable insights into promoting firm growth.

Female entrepreneurs are a diverse and complex group, with varied backgrounds, circumstances, and worldviews. The majority of research has found that female entrepreneurs generally underperform male entrepreneurs on a variety of measures, including revenues, profit, growth and discontinuance rates (Du Rietz and Henrekson, 2000). Moreover, an extensive literature review of studies on gender issues from the past 25 years demonstrated that many questions still remain unanswered (Greene et al., 2003), particularly in three primary areas: human capital, strategic choice and structural barriers. Interestingly, in discussing inhibiting factors, Brush (1997) applied a broader perspective to studying the barriers and challenges that inhibit growth, finding that opportunities for female entrepreneurs actually improved with the use of technology, and that this aspect could also be a positive contributor to growth.

Previous research has revealed that small and medium-sized enterprises (SMEs) can overcome the disadvantage of their small size by using technology to reach new customers and operate more efficiently (Cavusgil and Knight, 1997; Dutta and Evrard, 1999). One of the causes of business stagnation is risk avoidance (Ward, 1997), which, among entrepreneurs, may frustrate the adoption of new technology and the allocation of resources to foster growth. Prior research has shown that female entrepreneurs (on average) may be more risk averse than male entrepreneurs (Anna et al., 1999; Cooper, 1993; Širec, 2007). Thus, gender may affect the use of technology in Slovenian companies and, consequently, their growth aspirations.

This chapter stemmed from the desire to explore the perceived difference in growth aspirations among female and male Slovenian entrepreneurs, as well as the perception that not all elements of technological change in a company positively affect them. The research concentrates on the relationship among various dimensions of entrepreneurship (that is, entrepreneurs' attributes, gender and company attributes, technological orientation) and one possible operational measure of entrepreneurial performance (that is, growth). Different studies have demonstrated that growth intentions and likely eventual growth impact are not evenly distributed across the population of entrepreneurial firms. For example, the Global Entrepreneurship Monitor (GEM) research on high-expectation entrepreneurship (Autio, 2005) indicated that high-aspiration entrepreneurs, who represented, on average, less than 10 per cent of the population of nascent and new entrepreneurs in GEM countries, were responsible for up to 80 per cent of total expected job creation by all entrepreneurs. In the UK, Storey (1994) found that a mere 4 per cent of new firms established in any given year accounted for 50 per cent of all the jobs created by the surviving firms within the cohort after 10 years had elapsed. Thus, it appears that the capability of an economy to grow and employ is significantly dependent on the capability of that economy to create gazelles. Autio (2005) reported that, in the US, gazelles represented only about 3 per cent of the firm population but accounted for more than 70 per cent of employment growth between 1992 and 1996. Similarly, in Finland, approximately 1 per cent of top growing firms created about 40 per cent of the aggregate impact over four years, in terms of both sales and employment growth. Slovenia's 500 fastest growing firms in 2003 created 7940 new jobs between 1998 and 2002. In 1998, the average gazelle employed 24 workers; by the year 2002, this number had risen to 40. Meanwhile, sales increased four times on average, while exports increased 5.5 times in four years. Slovenian gazelles employed 2160 more workers at the end of 2006 than they did three years previous, resulting in an average of 72 new employees per company per year.

Although not all expectations materialize, growth aspirations have been shown to be a good predictor of eventual growth (Liao and Welsch, 2003). At least part of the explanation for this phenomenon may be found in the characteristics of entrepreneurs' firms, especially with regard to the extent of their technology orientation. This chapter proceeds as follows. After discussing some basic statistical data and theoretical background concerning gender in Slovenia, a theoretical framework is established for the study based on the review of prior research in the area. The research methodology is then outlined and the findings of the research are presented. Finally, conclusions are drawn and some policy implications are outlined.

COUNTRY CONTEXT

Data for the second half of 2006 (*Statistical Yearbook of the Republic of Slovenia*, 2007) suggest that women represented 45.3 per cent of active paid employment in Slovenia. While the highest percentage of active working women occurred among civil servants (65 per cent), saleswomen and those employed in other services (63 per cent), and professionals (59.5 per cent), the lowest occupation groups were in the non-industrial sectors (8.2 per cent). In addition, more than half of the registered unemployed were women (54.4 per cent), and this rate continues to increase. The unemployment rate for men was 5.6 per cent in the fourth quarter of 2006, as compared to 6.9 per cent for women. Four per cent of unemployed women found new work in less than one month, but 30 per cent had to wait more than two years before finding a new job. Furthermore, women are generally somewhat more educated than men. This is especially true for the age 25 to 44 years age group, where twice as many women have a higher level of postgraduate education than men. Despite this, women earn around 93 per cent of the average man's gross monthly salary.

The gender gap described above is also evident in the 'Gender Gap Index 2008', which ranks Slovenia fifty-first among 130 countries (Global Gender Gap Report, 2008). The index is based on the average of four main sub-indexes that measure economic participation and opportunity, educational attainment, health and survival, and political empowerment. The most negative impact on ranking is the field of political empowerment, which values women in parliament and ministerial positions. Here, the inequality situation among genders ranked Slovenia eighty-fifth.

Meanwhile, the *Global Competitiveness Report 2007–2008* includes, among other things, the Technology Readiness Index, on which Slovenia ranked twenty-ninth (above its average ranking of 39). However, a closer look at the pillars shows that foreign direct investment (FDI) and technology transfer (122), firm-level technology absorption (62) and availability of the latest technologies (50) present rankings significantly lower than the overall ranking. The relatively good overall score stems from Internet users (13), personal computers (25), laws relating to information and communication technology (ICT) (30), broadband Internet subscribers (31) and mobile telephone subscribers (31). Such findings present further reasons to investigate the research questions outlined herein.

The GEM's examination of entrepreneurial behaviour around the globe (Allen et al., 2008) yielded a clearly defined gender gap in venture creation and ownership activity. Overall, with the exception of Japan, Thailand, Peru and Brazil, men are more likely to be involved in entrepreneurial activity than women. The largest gender divide occurs among high-income countries (the gross domestic product per capita for this group, which includes Slovenia, averages close to US$35 000), where men are almost twice as likely as women to be active in early-stage entrepreneurial activities. In Slovenia, an average of 7.81 per cent of men and 3.33 per cent of women were involved in established entrepreneurial activities in 2008, while the total entrepreneurial activity (early-stage and established) included on average 16.25 per cent of the men and 7.34 per cent of the women (Rebernik et al., 2008).

This entrepreneurial gender gap exhibits varying dimensions and characteristics, but research results indicate that, for the expected growth potential of business based upon the use of technology, level of competition and novelty of products or services offered, similar patterns are evident among both female and male entrepreneurs for all countries participating in the GEM in 2007. Yet other researchers have claimed that gender is an influential factor that affects a company's actual growth. Being female is supposed to have a negative effect on growth, and female entrepreneurs rarely become 'growth entrepreneurs' (Kjeldsen and Nielsen, 2004). However, additional circumstances should be taken into account. For example, Slovenia, as a Central and Eastern European country, is facing a transition process that is not yet complete, despite its relatively recent (May 2004) entry into the European Union.

Transitional countries share many common features with regard to female participation in the labour force, including, for example, the average level of education, the gender wage gap, and so on. The transition process has affected both men and women, creating a loss in job security and employment costs. However, women seem to have taken over a larger share of the adjustment costs (Ruminska-Zimny, 2003). Moreover, transition changes have also had important and often negative effects on women's position in society (Stoyanovska, 2001), whereas under the communist regime, men and women were supposedly equal in all aspects of society. According to Gal and Kligman (2000), state socialism only officially supported equality between men and women through women's full participation in the labour force; the state significantly intruded on women's reproductive lives in a direct manner, although this latter debate is beyond the scope of the current paper. With the fall of the communist regime, structural inequalities between men and women became evident (Tominc, 2002), as did the challenge inherent in learning the inner workings of the market economy (Ogloblin, 1999).

Furthermore, the economic, political and social processes of transition affected women differently in different countries. For instance, during the communist period in Hungary, full-time employment and the employment of women were definitive elements of the prevailing ideology (IHF, 2000). Although the level of employment decreased significantly after the transition, it remained socially acceptable for women to have professional careers, despite household activities and childcare responsibilities continuing to be perceived as women's tasks. Slovenian women enjoyed a similar social status (IHF, 2000). Meanwhile, Leinert-Novosel (2000) claims that, in Croatia, the politics of the past 10 to 15 years, which highlighted the role of the church and decreed that women's place was primarily in the home, has considerably worsened the status of women and discouraged them in their attempts to improve their status in society through work and career advancement.

A common characteristic of labour market developments during the transition process is gender asymmetry, as seen in employment, sectoral changes of employment, income and wages, access to jobs in the private sector, and so on. Smallbone and Welter (2001) pointed out that the distinctive features of entrepreneurial behaviour reflect the unstable and hostile nature of the external environment as well as the scarcity of various key resources. In such circumstances, informal networks often play a key role in helping entrepreneurs mobilize resources, win orders, and cope with the constraints at different levels of the economic system as well society as a whole. These findings concur with the research results related to women entrepreneurship in Slovenia (Drnovšek and Glas, 2006), which indicated that women entrepreneurs lack networking components and social capital assets as they have to contract these resources through their strong ties with family members.

In this context, the OECD report (2004) on female entrepreneurship highlighted a fundamental feature of the market that is significant for the research presented in this chapter, namely, the portioning of knowledge among individuals. Such knowledge is idiosyncratic because it is acquired through each individual's personal experiences and from areas such as individual occupations, on-the-job routines, social relationships, and daily life (Acs, 2002). Women differ from men in their experience because they hold different occupations (often less appropriate for self-employment and entrepreneurship) and have different on-the-job routines, social relationships and daily life activities. Moreover, women identify business opportunities differently and try to exploit them differently. Evidence suggests that women are less involved in networks than men, and that their types of network differ. The strong and personal networks in which women traditionally engage are those linked mainly to family-related tasks (Lin, 1999). In transitional countries, such gender differences appear to be even more pronounced (Drnovšek and Glas, 2006; Smallbone and Welter, 2001).

THEORETICAL FOUNDATION AND PROPOSED HYPOTHESES

Entrepreneurship is a complex phenomenon involving individuals, firms, and the environment in which it occurs (Begley, 1995, in Solymossy, 1998: 5). Although such complexity is easy to recognize, the nature of the relationship among these three elements is not yet understood (Solymossy, 1998: 5). In this chapter, only the narrow segment of companies' technological orientation and its impact on companies' growth aspirations are examined. The relevant literature includes two main streams (Tominc and Rebernik, 2006): research demonstrating that the actual growth and research designs are longitudinal (Gundry and Welsch, 2001; Liao and Welsch, 2003) and research focusing on the growth expectations of those entering into entrepreneurship, where growth expectations can be divided into those subjectively expected by the entrepreneur and those objectively possible (for example, type of business, expected export levels, competition) (Bager and Schott, 2004; Delmar and Davidsson, 1999; Tominc and Rebernik, 2007a). This chapter deals with the second of these research streams.

Empirical growth studies researching factors of growth frequently address issues of specific interest to the researcher in a way that makes comparability with other studies difficult. However, studies of gender differences related to the topic at hand have yielded contradictory findings (Kolvereid, 1992; Orser et al., 1998). Indeed, researchers have not clearly established whether the growth aspirations of male and female entrepreneurs are statistically different. Previous studies related to differences in growth aspirations among female and male entrepreneurs in Slovenia revealed that, although women are on average less likely to be involved in entrepreneurship than men, their growth aspirations do not differ significantly from those of men (Tominc and Rebernik, 2006, 2007b). For example, results on employment-related growth aspirations, which is found among early-stage entrepreneurs who intend to increase the number of jobs by six or more in the next five years, showed that such growth aspirations existed in an average of 42.45 per cent of males and 37.25 per cent of females in the early-stage of entrepreneurship in Slovenia – a statistically significant difference. One caveat to these results is that women tend to be less likely to start an entrepreneurial career but, once started, tend to have growth aspirations as high as those of men.

Cooper and Kleinschmidt (1995, in de Jong et al., 2001: 14) stated that the availability and mastering of techniques and technologies present preconditions for innovativeness for both production- and service-intensive industries. A positive impact exists between the achieved level of techniques and technologies used and the improvement of a company's innovation potential: the better equipped the company is and the more knowledge it possesses, the easier new knowledge and ideas will be accepted and successfully developed (de Jong and Brouwer, 1999). Consequently, company growth might occur. Here, the emphasis is on ICT, which enables the flow of data and information while promoting the gathering of ideas from different sources (Business-To-Business (B2B), Business-To-Consumer (B2C), Consumer-To-Consumer (C2C)) (Sundbo, 1998: 151). Thus, the first research question in this study is whether the intensity of applied new technologies and types of applied novelties relate to growth aspirations. As women seem to be less comfortable taking risks than men (Arch, 1993), they may find the level of technology, with which they tend to be less familiar than men, more important for the future growth of their businesses than men. To determine the gender differences regarding this research question, the following hypothesis was tested:

Hypothesis 1: The intensity of applied new technologies relates to growth aspirations and differs among genders.

Without modern technologies, new products that address the needs of sophisticated users cannot be developed. Due to the increase in the complexity of the competitive business world, developing the necessary products oneself is often too risky, too slow and too expensive, which is why companies (especially small ones) often buy new products along with technologies for their usage. Such handling stimulates innovative ideas and novelties on the side of the product as well as on the side of the processes, organization, and leadership methods in working procedures (*sc.* 'reinventing' according to Rogers, 1995: 392). Business process modifications are crucial for long-term company's success, but present a risky and difficult endeavour. In general, entrepreneurship is often perceived as a male domain (DiMaggio, 1997). Entrepreneurship is expected to involve risk-taking with leadership, a sense of adventure, and aggressiveness – all activities assumed to be masculine, as men seem to be more comfortable taking risks than women (Arch, 1993). Males are 'more likely to see a challenge that calls for participation' in a risky situation, whereas females more commonly perceive such activities as threatening and try to avoid them. As male entrepreneurs have higher growth anticipations than females, they likely expect higher outcomes from their entrepreneurial activity, whereas females tend to prefer more certainty in their entrepreneurial activities, and thus expect lower but less risky outcomes. Based on this understanding, the following hypothesis was developed:

Hypothesis 2: Business process modifications are related to growth aspirations and differ among genders.

The role of gender in a company's growth is vague. Liao and Welsch (2003) reported on a study of Norwegian entrepreneurs conducted by Kolvereid (1992), which found no significant relationship between entrepreneurs' growth aspirations and their experience, gender, location or size of their business. As previously stated, other researchers have claimed that gender is an influential feature for a company's growth; being female is supposed to have a negative effect on growth, and female entrepreneurs rarely become 'growth entrepreneurs' (Kjeldsen and Nielsen, 2004). Previous research (for example, Bager and Schott, 2004) also indicated that entrepreneurial aspirations seem to be higher in nascent/new (in this study, younger) entrepreneurs than among established entrepreneurs. As it has not been clearly established whether growth aspirations of male and female entrepreneurs are statistically different, the next hypothesis is proposed in order to enhance understanding of this topic in Slovenia. The companies studied were on average 13.4 years old; the average age of female-owned companies was 10 months younger than male-owned companies. The following hypothesis seeks to explore the relationship between a company's age and the aspired growth of investigated categories:

Hypothesis 3:   The younger the company, the higher the growth aspiration; this relationship differs among genders.

Following up on technological advancement occurs not only with purchase and development, but also with precisely planned information gathering and learning. The global trends of technological development at home and abroad need to be known and taken into consideration, especially in the narrow industry environment of the company. Important sources of information include suppliers, customers, competitors, and research and development (R&D) institutions. Our study sought to determine the most common ways of obtaining modern equipment and technologies (for example, purchasing new equipment and technology, acquiring licenses and own development). Statistical data show that, despite the fact that a high proportion of women have higher professional, university, specialist, graduate, and doctoral-level educations in Slovenia, women still occupy different fields than men, especially fields that are less technology oriented. In 2006, 64 per cent of higher education graduates in Slovenia were women, but less than 8 per cent of female upper-level students graduated in science, mathematics, computing, engineering, manufacturing, or construction; meanwhile, almost 30 per cent of males graduated in these fields (*Statistical Yearbook of the Republic of Slovenia*, 2007). According to the demographic data, we assume that statistically significant differences exist in the ways in which modern equipment and technologies are acquired by Slovenian entrepreneurs. Thus, hypothesis 4 states:

Hypothesis 4: Ways to obtain modern equipment and technology differ among genders.

The developed framework conceptualized entrepreneurship by incorporating measures relating to technology orientation. This involves refinement of previously proposed, but inadequately tested, theoretical constructs into an empirically testable framework. Indeed, one of the objectives of our study was to develop and test a valid and reliable survey instrument that lends itself to establishing this framework for future research, enabling international comparison of a multidimensional conceptualization of entrepreneurship phenomena. The frame for this analysis is presented in Figure 17.1.

METHODOLOGY

Variables

Our survey investigated established companies, in which entrepreneurs are identified as individuals who are the owners or co-owners of the company and also help manage it. This part of the survey provided insights into the technological orientation of Slovenian SMEs through five questions in accordance with certain previously conducted surveys (Krošlin, 2004; Ruzzier, 2004). Respondent companies also indicated whether they had performed any kind of technical or technological development activities

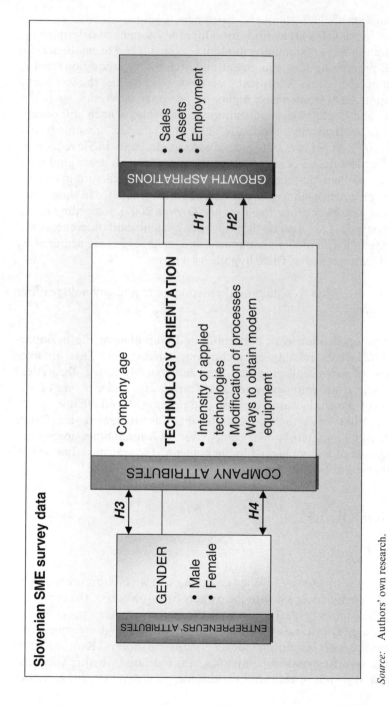

Source: Authors' own research.

Figure 17.1   Testing for gender differences in technology orientation

in the past two years, estimating the number of newly applied technologies, types of applied novelties (products/services that were new for the company, products/services that were new in a market and improvement of existing products/services), and the frequency as well as the various kinds of business process modifications in the past two years. Finally, respondents assessed the importance of different ways of obtaining modern equipment and technology (purchase of new equipment and technology, license acquisition, internal development, cooperation with suppliers or customers regarding development, and cooperation with faculties or research institutes regarding development). The respondents assessed the described items on a Likert-type scale ranging from 1 = 'completely unimportant' to 5 = 'extremely important'.

Respondents also assessed the dependent variables with regard to their growth aspirations for the upcoming three years in terms of the increase in sales revenue, company assets and employment. The scale for each of the items was based on a five-point Likert-type scale ranging from 1 = 'well above industry average' to 5 = 'well below industry average'. Entrepreneurs' gender was included as a binary (female = 1, male = 2). In addition, the age of the company was taken into account.

Data

The data were derived from research conducted on the statistical population of Slovenian small and medium-sized companies (joint-stock companies, limited liability companies, and non-limited liability companies) in all Standard Industry Classification (SIC) categories. In accordance with quota sampling, the selection of units from each segment was based on company size, regional representation, SIC representation, and appropriate share of males and females in the sample (70:30).

The sample size comprised 201 respondents. Questionnaires were used to gather data. A core difficulty facing research seeking to accumulate primary data about companies' activities is ensuring a satisfactory response rate. In our study, the preparation and realization of the survey were subordinated to the need of ensuring the highest possible response rate. The response rate was 11.4 per cent. Interviews were conducted using the Computer Assisted Telephone Interviewing (CATI) method.

The methodology included an extensive review of the literature as well as empirical research to determine the current stage of knowledge regarding the determinants of companies' technology orientation. To measure the associations or correlation among variables, the Pearson correlation for data was used in the form of measurements on quantitative variables. An independent sample *t*-test was used with quantitative variables to compare averages between different groups. The general criterion for accepting the hypothesis was that the difference is statistically significant at the 5 per cent level (two-tailed test). For data reduction, a factor analysis was performed.

FINDINGS

Almost 50 per cent of respondents claimed that they had performed technical or technological development activities in the past two years in order to discover new knowledge or possibilities for use, either on their own or in cooperation with partners. Most (36 per cent) stated they used two to three such types of new technologies. However, 30 per cent did not start using any new technologies, although, the authors acknowledge that these results may be dubious due to the ambiguity of the definition of 'new technology'. Furthermore, on average, almost 50 per cent of the companies interviewed did not change their business processes within a one-year time frame. Approximately 20 per cent said they did change them once a year, focusing most frequently on production/service processes.

An exploratory factor analysis was used to test hypotheses 1 and 2. After the reduction in variables, two factors were defined. Table 17.1 presents the results of the first-step factor analysis, which helped define the measurement for identifying the intensity of applied new technologies and the novelty of products and services, as well as the frequencies of business process modifications.

After defining factors for measuring the intensity of applied new technologies and frequencies of business processes modification, correlation analyses were performed with growth aspiration measurements (increases

Table 17.1   First-step factor analysis regarding technology orientation

Variable	Communalities	Rotated factors	Defined factors	Reliability tests
X_1	0.646	0.719	Factor 1:	Kaiser Meyer-
X_2	0.665	0.815	Intensity of applied	Olkin: 0.78
X_3	0.579	0.757	new technologies	Bartlett's test of
X_4	0.585	0.744	(Chronbach α: 0.77)	sphericity:
X_5	0.642	0.786	Factor 2:	$\chi^2_{(21)} = 348\,959$
X_6	0.627	0.791	Modification of	$p = 0.000$
X_7	0.537	0.701	business processes	Variance
			(Chronbach α: 0.67)	explained:
				61%

in sales revenue, company assets, and employment). The first part of hypothesis testing for hypotheses 1 and 2 related to the entire sample, while the second part was gender specific. Table 17.2 presents the correlation coefficients.

The results indicate that a positive and statistically significant relationship exists between the intensity of applied new technologies and Slovenian SMEs' growth aspirations with regard to sales revenue and company assets, but not with regard to employment. According to the results, the first part of hypothesis 1 is partially confirmed. In addition, certain differences can be distinguished between genders. The correlation coefficients show that male entrepreneurs, who have demonstrated an extreme focus on applying new technologies, aspire to increase their company's sales revenue in the upcoming three years. Meanwhile, although female entrepreneurs aspire to grow the company's assets, none of them aspires to enhance employment growth. It is also interesting that females who intensively applied new technologies aspire to decrease the number

Table 17.2   Results of testing hypotheses 1 and 2 for both genders

Entire sample		Growth aspiration		
		Sales revenue	Company assets	Employment
Factor 1	Pearson correlation	**0.219****	**0.204****	0.022
	Sig. (2-tailed)	**0.002**	**0.004**	0.760
Factor 2	Pearson correlation	**0.148***	0.134	0.077
	Sig. (2-tailed)	**0.040**	0.063	0.285
Male				
Factor 1	Pearson correlation	**0.250****	0.155	0.130
	Sig. (2-tailed)	**0.004**	0.075	0.138
Factor 2	Pearson correlation	**0.221***	0.160	0.159
	Sig. (2-tailed)	**0.011**	0.066	0.068
Female				
Factor 1	Pearson correlation	0.149	**0.324***	−0.161
	Sig. (2-tailed)	0.252	**0.011**	0.208
Factor 2	Pearson correlation	−0.005	0.082	−0.053
	Sig. (2-tailed)	0.969	0.529	0.680

Table 17.3   Results of testing hypothesis 3 for both genders

Entire sample		Growth Aspiration		
		Sales revenue	Company assets	Employment
Company age	Pearson correlation	**0.142***	**0.254****	0.069
	Sig. (2-tailed)	**0.049**	**0.001**	0.342
Male				
Company age	Pearson correlation	**0.181***	**0.269****	**0.182***
	Sig. (2-tailed)	**0.039**	**0.002**	**0.037**
Female				
Company age	Pearson correlation	0.004	0.165	−0.222
	Sig. (2-tailed)	0.978	0.203	0.080

of their company's employees (however, this correlation is not statistically significant). This finding is consistent with Kjeldsen and Nielsen's (2004) research, which claimed that females are supposed to have a negative effect on growth and that female entrepreneurs rarely become 'growth entrepreneurs'. Thus, hypothesis 1 is partially confirmed.

According to hypothesis 2, a weaker relationship between the types and frequency of business processes modification and growth aspirations has been identified. A statistically significant relationship was confirmed only with regard to an aspired increase in sales revenue, although differences between genders again emerged. Those who aspire to the described increase are primarily men, not women. Therefore, hypothesis 2 can also be confirmed only partially.

Table 17.3 reports the results on companies' age regarding growth aspirations (hypothesis 3). The findings for the entire sample as well as for both genders are presented. Notably, the data point to the fact that males (owning younger companies) have higher growth aspirations than females, thereby confirming hypothesis 3, which states that younger companies have higher growth aspirations. These results point to similar findings, as previously indicated, in terms of employment growth, that is, the differences for the entire sample are not statistically significant, with females also showing negative in terms of employment. Furthermore, males expressed statistically significant growth aspirations, whereas females did not. These results are consistent with previous findings (for example, Bager and Schott, 2004), indicating that entrepreneurial aspirations seem to be higher in nascent/new entrepreneurs than among established entrepreneurs. These results are also consistent with previous findings claiming that being female is supposed to have a negative effect on growth (although in the current case, it is not negative, only statistically insignificant). Various explanations can be found in the literature regarding why entrepreneurial aspirations in nascent/new entrepreneurs are, as a rule, higher than the aspirations of established entrepreneurs (Brown and Kirschoff, 1997; Carter et al., 1997). Two possible explanations for this can be found in the survival of ventures and learning. A large number of new ventures do not survive, and it is likely that those that do not survive have the highest and most unrealistic expectations. It is also very likely that nascent/new entrepreneurs acquire specific knowledge and skills about enterprises and the entrepreneurial environment, subsequently lowering their expectations.

Hypothesis 4 sought to prove that ways by which modern equipment is obtained differ among Slovenian entrepreneurs according to gender. Our study revealed that the most common way of adapting to new equipment and technologies is to buy them (45 per cent), followed by own development in cooperation with suppliers and customers. The least common way (only 11 per cent of cases in this study) is through cooperation with faculties and research institutions.

Female entrepreneurs acquire licenses and purchase new equipment and technologies more frequently than men, whereas men more frequently use the remaining methods of acquisition. The only statistically significant difference between genders and their ways to obtain modern equipment and technologies was cooperation with suppliers or customers with regard to development. Men assessed such cooperation as being more important than women ($p = 0.036$). Thus, hypothesis 4 can be partially confirmed, as most answers do not show statistically significant differences.

No statistically significant correlations were found among technology orientation measurements and their employment growth aspirations. One explanation for this can be the sample size structure; 87 per cent of the sampled companies are micro companies, employing fewer than 10 employees, and thus do not meet the criteria to be categorized as high growth potential companies. The second part of the explanation lies in anticipation – namely, that technology orientation is not necessarily related to increasing the number of new jobs. On the other hand, significant correlations were found among technology orientation measurements and aspired growth in sales revenue and growth of assets, suggesting that modern technologies contribute to companies' efficient use of their resources (which may result in decreasing the number of employees while generating more sophisticated, value-added products/services), and applied new equipment increases the value of companies' assets.

CONCLUSIONS

Technology orientation and firm growth – the focus of this research – are complex, multidimensional issues in both scope and character. Thus, increasing our understanding of the described phenomena is of utmost importance for different target groups. From a theoretical perspective, such knowledge can strengthen the empirical micro-level basis of theories of entrepreneurship and theories of innovation. From a societal perspective, more knowledge about the factors that promote or impede entrepreneurship and innovativeness in SMEs can benefit owners, consumers and communities. With regard to policy implications, supportive measures should not be targeted at entrepreneurship in general, but be more focused and selective towards those individuals and companies that are motivated towards growth and have high growth aspirations.

Overall, our analysis of the specific characteristics of businesses related to technological orientation revealed that the current growth potential among entrepreneurs in Slovenia differs according to gender. In addition, a positive and significant relationship between the intensity of applied new technologies and growth aspirations among Slovenian SMEs has been confirmed. Our study further identified certain gender differences regarding growth aspirations. Males aspire to increase sales revenue, whereas women aspire to grow their company assets. However, none aspires to promote employment growth.

The results herein (although not statistically significant) go even further. Females who intensively applied new technologies aspired to decrease the number of company employees, which is consistent with previous research findings (Kjeldsen and Nielsen, 2004) claiming that being female has a negative effect on growth and that female entrepreneurs rarely become 'growth entrepreneurs'. Regarding the types and frequency of business processes' modification and growth aspirations, the significant aspiration of sales revenue growth was present only in the sample of male entrepreneurs. Furthermore, males owning younger companies expressed higher growth aspirations than women. These findings are also consistent with previous findings (for example Bager and Schott, 2004), demonstrating that entrepreneurial aspirations seem to be higher in nascent/new entrepreneurs than among established entrepreneurs. Various explanations of these phenomena exist in the literature. For example, a large number of new ventures do not survive, most probably those that have the highest and yet most unreal expectations. Entrepreneurs' growth aspirations are their own anticipations; as they are self-estimated, they are not necessarily objectively possible. In other words, entrepreneurs in the early stages of entrepreneurship are likely subjectively projecting higher potential growth than those who have been entrepreneurs for a longer period. According to previous research, some early-stage entrepreneurs estimate their business to have high growth potential for the wrong reasons (for example incompetence, over-optimism), while others are more modest. Morcover, the first group are more likely to abandon their start-up business (Davidsson, 2006) than the latter. Nascent/new entrepreneurs may seek to acquire specific knowledge and skills about enterprises and the entrepreneurial environment, subsequently lowering their expectations. As such, a special need exists for a well-developed entrepreneurial environment that stimulates potential entrepreneurs to follow and exploit opportunities. Finally, ways to obtain modern equipment differs among Slovenian entrepreneurs. This result was expected given the demographic data, which indicate that less than 8 per cent of females graduated in science, mathematics, computing, engineering, manufacturing, or construction, whereas almost 30 per cent of males graduated in these fields (*Statistical Yearbook of the Republic of Slovenia*, 2007).

The findings herein are consistent with social feminist theory (Fischer et al., 1993), which posits that men and women indeed differ due to differences in the socialization processes they experience. Males and females are perceived as two separate groups, each with equally effective and valid, but distinct, ways of thinking and rationalizing (Johnsen and McMahon, 2005: 118). Social feminist theory expects findings on men and women to differ in terms of motivation to start and run a business, business skills, level of education, measurements of success, level of self-confidence, personal attributes and prioritization of business tasks (Moore and Buttner, 1997). The current investigation confirmed many of the issues described herein; however, further investigation is still warranted. Policymakers need to bear in mind that, in certain fields (especially in high-growth, ambitious, technology-oriented companies), differences among genders do exist. Therefore, the 'high-growth entrepreneurship policy' presents an imperative as firms that want to grow have many specific needs that must be addressed with flexibility and agility.

In addition to the quantity of entrepreneurial activity, the quality of entrepreneurship is even more influential. In this context, the importance of technology adoption and its development is evident in many aspects of today's global competitive environment. Europe's 500 listing, for example, proves that dynamic, entrepreneurial, growth-focused companies can exist in any business sector. In fact, it is not the sector, but the commitment to growth that facilitates companies' rapid growth. A closer look into classification clearly demonstrates that the most dominant sector is 'IT Services, Information, and Communication Technologies' (with 90 companies), followed by the 'Construction and Real Estate' sector (42 companies) (Europe's 500, 2007).

As the results of this study and the literature reviewed herein have demonstrated, growth is crucially based on the mindset of the entrepreneur. The entrepreneur must first accept the decision to grow and then understand (and complete) the array of activities that must be undertaken to succeed in this endeavour. Policymakers should recognize that mindsets differ and various cultural, economic and social factors influence their formation.

Ultimately, each entrepreneur is different; they express different aspirations and, as such, need to be treated separately. Based on the results presented in this study, it is clear that policymakers must focus on encouraging entrepreneurship among well-educated individuals who might have the potential to establish pro-growth, technologically oriented companies. Activating the entrepreneurial potential of these individuals requires the promotion of technological and growth-oriented entrepreneurship. Establishing effective and meaningful incentives while promoting role models is also crucial. Meanwhile, further research will help distinguish effective policy instruments for promoting growth-oriented entrepreneurship.

REFERENCES

Acs, Z.J. (2002), *Innovation and the Growth of Cities*, Cheltenham, UK and Northampton, MA, USA: Edward Elgar.

Allen, I.E., Elam, A., Langowitz N. and Dean, M. (2008), *Global Entrepreneurship Monitor: 2007 Report on Women and Entrepreneurship*, Wellesley, MA: Global Entrepreneurship Research Association (GERA).

Anna, A.L., Chandler, G.N., Jansen, E. and Mero, N.P. (1999), 'Women business owners in traditional and non-traditional industries', *Journal of Business Venturing*, **15** (3), 279–303.

Arch, E.C. (1993), 'Risk-taking: a motivational basis for sex differences', *Psychological Reports*, **73**, 3–11.

Autio, E. (2005), *Global Entrepreneurship Report 2005*, *Report on High-Expectation Entrepreneurship*, Babson Park, MA: Babson College and London: London Business School.

Bager, T. and Schott, T. (2004). 'Growth expectations by entrepreneurs in nascent firms, baby businesses and mature firms: analysis of the Global Entrepreneurship Monitor surveys in Denmark 2000–2003', paper presented at the first GEM Research Conference, Berlin, 1–3 April.

Begley T. (1995), 'Using founder status, age of firm, and company growth rate as the basis for distinguishing entrepreneurs from managers of smaller businesses', *Journal of Business Venturing*, **10**, 249–63.

Brown, T.E. and Kirschoff, B.A. (1997), 'The effects of resource availability and entrepreneurial orientation on firm growth', *Frontiers of Entrepreneurship Research*, Wellesley, MA: Babson College, pp. 32–46.

Brush, C.G. (1997), 'Women-owned businesses: obstacles and opportunities', *Journal of Developmental Entrepreneurship*, **2** (1), 1–24.

Carter, N., Gartner, W.B. and Reynolds, P.D. (1997), 'Exploring start-up sequences', *Journal of Business Venturing*, **11**, 151–66.

Cavusgil, T. and Knight, G. (1997), 'Explaining an emerging phenomena for international marketing: global orientation and the born global firm', working paper, Michigan State CIBER.

Cooper, A.C. (1993), 'Challenges in predicting new firm performance', *Journal of Business Venturing*, **8** (3), 241–53.

Cooper, R.G. and Kleinschmidt, E.J. (1995), 'Performance typologies of new product projects', *Industrial Marketing Management*, **24**, 439–56.

Davidsson, P. (2006), 'Nascent entrepreneurs: empirical studies and developments', *Foundations and Trends in Entrepreneurship*, **1** (2), 1–70.

De Jong, J.P.J. and Brouwer, E. (1999), *Determinants of Innovative Ability of SMEs*, Zoetermeer: EIM, Small Business Research and Consultancy.

De Jong, J.P.J., Kemp, R. and Snel, C. (2001), *Determinants of Innovative Ability*, Zoetermeer: EIM, Small Business Research and Consultancy.

Delmar, F. and Davidsson, P. (1999), 'Firm size expectations of nascent entrepreneurs', *Frontiers of Entrepreneurship Research 1999*, Wellesley, MA: Babson College, pp. 90–104.

DiMaggio, P. (1997), 'Culture and cognition', *Annual Review of Sociology*, **23**, 263–87.

Drnovšek, M. and Glas, M. (2006),'Women entrepreneurs in Slovenia: by fits and starts', in F. Welter, D. Smallbone and B.N. Isakova (eds), *Enterprising Women in Transition Economies*, Aldershot: Ashgate.

Du Rietz, A. and Henrekson, M. (2000), 'Testing the female underperformance hypothesis', *Small Business Economics*, **14**, 1–10.

Dutta, S. and Evrard, P. (1999), 'Information technology and organisation within European small enterprises', *European Management Journal*, **17** (3), 239–51.

Europe's 500 (2007), available at: http://www.europes500.com/results.html (accessed January 2009).

Fischer, E.M., Reuber, R.A. and Dyke, L.S. (1993), 'A theoretical overview and extension of research on sex, gender, and entrepreneurship', *Journal of Business Venturing*, **8** (2), 151–68.

Gal, S. and Kligman, G. (2000), *The Politics of Gender after Socialism: A Comparative-Historical Essay*, Princeton, NJ: Princeton University Press.

Global Competitiveness Report 2007–2008, available at: http://www.weforum.org/en/initiatives/gcp/Global%20Competitiveness%20Report/index.htm (accessed September 2008).

Global Gender Gap Report (2008), available at: http://www.weforum.org/en/Communities/Women%20Leaders%20and%20Gender%20Parity/GenderGapNetwork/index.htm (accessed January 2009).

Gray, C. (2000), 'Formality, intentionality, and planning: features of successful entrepreneurial SMEs in the future?', paper presented at the ICSB World Conference 2000, Brisbane, June.

Greene, P.G., Hart, M.M., Gatewood, E.J., Brush, C.G. and Carter, N.M. (2003), 'Women entrepreneurs: moving front and center: an overview of research and theory', *Coleman White Paper Series*, **3**, 1–47, available at: http://www.usasbe. org (accessed September 2008).

Gundry, L.K. and H.P. Welsch (2001), 'The ambitious entrepreneur: high growth strategies of women-owned businesses', *Journal of Business Venturing*, **16**, 453–70.

International Helsinki Federation for Human Rights (IHF) (2000), 'Women 2000: an investigation into the status of women's rights in Central and South-Eastern Europe and the Newly Independent States', Vienna, available at: http://www. onlinwwomenpolitics.org/beijing12/Women_2000.pdf (accessed January 2009).

Johnsen, G.J. and McMahon, R.G.P. (2005), 'Owner-manager gender, financial performance and business growth amongst SMEs from Australia's Business Longitudinal Survey', *International Small Business Journal*, **23** (2), 115–42.

Kjeldsen, J. and Nielsen, K. (2004), 'Growth creating entrepreneurs: what are their characteristics and impact, and can they be created?', in M. Hancock and T. Bager (eds), *Global Entrepreneurship Monitor Denmark 2003*, Copenhagen: Borsens Forlag.

Kolvereid, L. (1992), 'Growth aspirations among Norwegian entrepreneurs', *Journal of Business Venturing*, **5**, 209–22.

Krošlin, T. (2004), 'Vpliv dejavnikov invencijsko-inovacijskega potenciala na uspešnost podjetij' ('The impact of the determinants of inventive-innovative potential on the firm performance'), master's thesis, Faculty of Economics and Business, University of Maribor.

Leinert-Novosel, S. (2000), *Žena na pragu 21. stoljeća: između majčinstva i profesije* (*Women at the Beginning of the 21st Century:Between Motherhood and Profession*), Zagreb: Women's Group TOD.

Liao, J. and Welsch, H. (2003), 'Social capital and entrepreneurial growth aspiration: a comparison of technology- and non-technology-based nascent entrepreneurs', *Journal of High Technology Management Research*, **14**, 149–70.

Lin, N. (1999), 'Social networks and status attainment', *Annual Review of Sociology*, **25**, 467–87.

Maki, K. and Pukkinen, T. (2000), 'Barriers to growth and employment in Finnish small enterprises', paper presented at the ICSB World Conference 2000, Brisbane, June.

Moore, D. and Buttner, H. (1997), *Women Entrepreneurs Moving Beyond the Glass Ceiling*, Thousand Oaks, CA: Sage.

Ogloblin, G.C. (1999), 'The gender earnings differential in the Russian transition economy', *Industrial and Labor Relations Review*, **52** (4), 602–27.

Organisation for Economic Co-operation and Development (OECD) (2004), *Women's Entrepreneurship: Issues and Policies*, Paris: OECD.

Orser, B.J., Hogarth-Scott, S. and Wright, P. (1998), 'On the growth of small enterprises: the role of intentions, gender and experience', *Frontier of Entrepreneurship Research*, Wellesley, MA: Babson College, pp. 366–80.

Rebernik, M. and Širec, K. (2009), *Dynamics of Slovenian Entrepreneurship: Slovenian Entrepreneurship Observatory 2008*, Maribor: Faculty of Economics and Business, University of Maribor.

Rebernik, M., Tominc, P. and Pušnik, K. (2008), *Premalo razvojno usmerjenih*

podjetij: GEM Slovenija 2007 (*Too Few Growth-Oriented Enterprises: GEM Slovenia 2007*), Slovenian Entrepreneurship Observatory, Maribor: Faculty of Economics and Business, University of Maribor.
Rogers, M.E. (1995), *Diffusion of Innovations*, 5th edn, New York: Free Press.
Ruminska-Zimny, E. (2003), 'Women's entrepreneurship and labour market trends in transition countries', in *Women's Entrepreneurship in Eastern Europe and CIS Countries*, Geneva: United Nations, pp. 1–16.
Ruzzier, M. (2004), 'The internationalization of small and medium enterprises: the influence of the entrepreneur's human and social capital on the degree of internationalization', dissertation, Faculty of Economics, University of Ljubljana.
Širec, K. (2007), 'Vpliv poslovnih priložnosti, sposobnosti podjetja in osebnih lastnosti podjetnika na rast malih in srednjevelikih podjetij' ('The impact of entrepreneurial opportunities, firm abilities and entrepreneurs' personal characteristics and SMEs' growth'), dissertation, Faculty of Economics and Business, University of Maribor.
Smallbone, D. and Welter, F. (2001), 'The distinctiveness of entrepreneurship in transition countries', *Small Business Economics*, **16** (4), 249–62.
Solymossy, E. (1998), 'Entrepreneurial dimensions: the relationship of individual, venture, and environmental factors to success', dissertation, Department of Marketing and Policy, Weatherhead School of Management, Case Western Reserve University.
Statistical Yearbook of the Republic of Slovenia (2007), Ljubljana: Statistical Office of the Republic of Slovenia.
Storey, D. (1994), *Understanding the Small Business Sector*, London and New York: Routledge.
Stoyanovska, A. (2001), *Jobs, Gender and Small Enterprises in Bulgaria*, Geneva: ILO.
Sundbo, J. (1998), *The Theory of Innovation: Entrepreneurs, Technology and Strategy*, Cheltenham, UK and Lyme, NH, USA: Edward Elgar.
Tominc, P. (2002), 'Some aspects of the gender wage gap in Slovenia', *Društvena istraživanja*, **11** (6), 879–96.
Tominc, P. and Rebernik, M. (2006), 'Female entrepreneurial growth aspirations in Slovenia: an unexploited resource', in C.G. Brush, N.M. Carter, E. Gatewood, P.G. Greene and M.M. Hart (eds), *Growth-oriented Women Entrepreneurs and their Businesses: A Global Research Perspective*, Cheltenham, UK and Northampton, MA, USA: Edward Elgar, pp. 330–47.
Tominc, P. and Rebernik, M. (2007a), 'Growth aspirations and cultural support for entrepreneurship: a comparison of post-socialist countries', *Small Business Economics*, **28** (2/3), 239–55.
Tominc, P. and Rebernik, M. (2007b), 'Gender differences in early-stage entrepreneurship in three European post-socialist countries', *Društvena istraživanja* (Zagreb), **16** (3), 589–611.
Ward, J.L. (1997), 'Growing the family business: special challenges and best practices', *Family Business Review*, **10** (4), 323–37.

Index